Ludwig Pastor

The History of the Popes

from the close of the middle ages - drawn from the secret Archives of the Vatican and other original sources - from the German - Vol. 27: Gregory XV. and Urban VIII.

(1621 - 1644)

Ludwig Pastor

The History of the Popes
from the close of the middle ages - drawn from the secret Archives of the Vatican and other original sources - from the German - Vol. 27: Gregory XV. and Urban VIII. (1621 - 1644)

ISBN/EAN: 9783337247553

Printed in Europe, USA, Canada, Australia, Japan

Cover: Foto ©Lupo / pixelio.de

More available books at **www.hansebooks.com**

HISTORY OF THE POPES
VOL. XXVII.

PASTOR'S HISTORY OF THE POPES

THE HISTORY OF THE POPES. Translated from the German of LUDWIG, FREIHERR VON PASTOR. Edited, as to Vols. I.–VI. by the late FREDERICK IGNATIUS ANTROBUS, and, as to Vols. VII.–XXIV. by RALPH FRANCIS KERR, of the London Oratory, and Vols. XXV.–XXIX. by DOM ERNEST GRAF, of Buckfast Abbey. In 29 Volumes.

Vols. I. and II.	A.D. 1305–1458
Vols. III. and IV.	A.D. 1458–1483
Vols. V. and VI.	A.D. 1484–1513
Vols. VII. and VIII.	A.D. 1513–1521
Vols. IX. and X.	A.D. 1522–1534
Vols. XI. and XII.	A.D. 1534–1549
Vols. XIII. and XIV.	A.D. 1550–1559
Vols. XV. and XVI.	A.D. 1559–1565
Vols. XVII. and XVIII.	A.D. 1566–1572
Vols. XIX. and XX.	A.D. 1572–1585
Vols. XXI. and XXII.	A.D. 1585–1591
Vols. XXIII. and XXIV.	A.D. 1592–1604
Vols. XXV. and XXVI.	A.D. 1605–1621
Vols. XXVII. to XXIX.	A.D. 1621–1644

The original German text of the *History of the Popes* is published by Herder & Co., Freiburg (Baden).

THE
HISTORY OF THE POPES

FROM THE CLOSE OF THE MIDDLE AGES

DRAWN FROM THE SECRET ARCHIVES OF THE VATICAN AND OTHER ORIGINAL SOURCES

FROM THE GERMAN OF

LUDWIG, FREIHERR VON PASTOR

TRANSLATED BY

DOM ERNEST GRAF, O.S.B.

MONK OF BUCKFAST

VOLUME XXVII.
GREGORY XV. AND URBAN VIII. (1621–1644)

LONDON
KEGAN PAUL, TRENCH, TRUBNER & CO., LTD.
BROADWAY HOUSE: 68-74 CARTER LANE, E.C.
1938

Alia ratio est rerum saecularium, alia divinarum, nec praeter illam petram, quam Dominus in fundamento posuit, stabilis erit ulla constructio.

LEO M., *Epistola 104 ad Marcianum Augustum* c. 3.
(MIGNE, *Patr. Lat.* LIV 995.)

Imprimi potest

Sublaci, ex Proto-Coenobio Stae Scholasticae,
die 29 Decembris 1937.

D. Emmanuel Caronti, O.S.B., Abbas Generalis.

CONTENTS OF VOLUME XXVII.

	PAGE
Collections of Archives and Manuscripts referred to in Volumes XXVII., XXVIII. and XXIX	vi
Complete Titles of Books quoted in Volumes XXVII., XXVIII. and XXIX	viii
Table of Contents	xxxv
List of Unpublished Documents in Appendix	xxxix
Gregory XV. 1621-3—Introduction	1
Election, Antecedents, and Character of Gregory XV. the Ludovisi	29
Gregory XV.'s Activity within the Church—Creations of Cardinals—Bull on Papal Election—Canonization—Furthering of the Orders	86
Foundation of Propaganda and State of the Missions—Position of Catholics in Holland and England	129
Progress of the Catholic Reformation and Restoration in France, Switzerland and the German Empire	197
Appendix of Unpublished Documents	297
Index of Names	331

COLLECTIONS OF ARCHIVES AND MANUSCRIPTS REFERRED TO IN VOLUMES XXVII., XXVIII. AND XXIX.

AMBERG—Library.
ANCONA—Communal Library.
AQUILA—Dragonetti Archives.
AREZZO—Library of the Fraternità di S. Maria.
ARICCIA—Archives of Prince Chigi.

BERLIN—State Library.
BOLOGNA—Communal Library.
———— University Library.
BREGENZ—Capuchin Archives.
BRESCIA—Quirini Library.
BRUSSELS—Archives.

COLMAR—City Library.
CUNEO—Communal Library.

DRESDEN—Library.

EGGENBERG—Herberstein Archives.

FERRARA—Library.
FLORENCE—State Archives.
———— Marucelliana Library.
———— National Library.
FOLIGNO—Communal Library.
———— Faloci Pulignani Library.
FORLÌ—Library.
FRANKFORT A. MAIN—City Library.

GENOA—Civic Library.
GUBBIO—Lucarelli Library.

INNSBRUCK—Pastor Library.
———— Library of the Servites.

LEMBERG—Ossoliniana Library
LONDON—British Museum.
LUCCA—Library.
LUCERNE—Library of the Capuchins on the Wesemlin.
LYONS—City Library.

MILAN—Brera Library.
———— National Library.
MANTUA—Gonzaga Archives.
METZ—City Library.
MODENA—State Archives.
MUNICH—State Archives.
———— State Library.

NAPLES—National Library.
———— Library of the *Società di storia patria*.

ORVIETO—Communal Archives.

PARIS—Archives for foreign affairs.
———— State Archives.
———— Bibliothèque des Arsenals.
———— National Library.
———— Library of St. Geneviève.
PARMA—Library.
PERUGIA—State Library.
PISA—University Library.
PISTOIA—Fabroniana Library.

RIMINI—Biblioteca Comunale.
ROME—
    Archives:
        Barberini, Private Archives of Prince.

ROME (cont.)—
  Archives:
    Boncompagni.
    Compagnia di S. Girolamo della Carità.
    Fabbrica di S. Pietro.
    Gaetani, Archives of.
    S. Pantaleone, Archives of.
    Papal Secret Archives.
    Fabbrica di S. Pietro, Archives of.
    Propaganda, Archives of.
    Roman Seminary, Archives of.
    Rospigliosi, Archives
    Spanish Embassy, Archives of.
    State Archives.
    Theatines, Archives of.
    University, Archives of.

  Libraries:
    Altieri.
    Angelica.
    Anima.
    Barberini (Vatican).
    Campo Santo.
    Casanatense.
    Chigi (Vatican).
    Corsini.
    Corvisieri.
    S. Croce in Gerusalemme.
    Ferraioli.
    Ottoboniana.
    S. Pietro in Vincoli.
    Vallicelliana.
    Vatican.
    Vittorio Emanuele.

ROVIGO—Library of the Accademia dei Concordi.

SALZBURG—Library.
  ———— Studienbibliothek.
SIENA—Bichi-Ruspoli Archives.
  ———— Library.
SIMANCAS—State Archives.
SPOLETO—Episcopal Archives.
  ———— Campello Archives.
STOCKHOLM—Library.
SUBIACO—Abbey Library.

TRENT—City Library.
TURIN—State Archives.

UPSALA—Library.

VENICE—State Archives.
  ———— Library of S. Marco.
VIENNA—Archives of the Count of Harrach.
  ———— Liechtenstein Library.
  ———— State Archives.
  ———— State Library.

COMPLETE TITLES OF BOOKS QUOTED IN VOLUMES XXVII., XXVIII. AND XXIX.

Abschiede, Die Eidgenössischen. Der amtlichen Abschiedsammlung, Vol. 5, 2, Basel, 1875.
Acta Sanctorum quotquot tote orbe coluntur. . . . Collegit etc. Ioannes Bollandus. Antverpiae, 1643 seqq.
Ademollo, A., Francesco de Noailles, in the Riv. Europea VIII. (1877), 193 seqq.
Ademollo, A., Giacinto Gigli e i suoi Diarii del sec. XVII. Firenze, 1877.
Ademollo, A., La questione dell'independenza Portughese in Roma, 1640-1670. Firenze, 1878.
Ademollo, A., La bell'Adriana ed altre virtuose del suo tempo alla corte di Mantova. Città di Castello, 1889.
Ademollo, A., I Teatri di Roma nel secolo decimosettimo. Roma, 1889.
Adlzreitter, Ioh., Annalium Boicae gentis Partes III. usque ad annum 1651. Francofurti a. M., 1710.
Agata dei Goti, S., = C. Huelsen, C. Cecchelli, G. Giovannoni, Monneret de Villard, A. Muñoz, S. Agata dei Goti. Roma, 1925.
Allatii, L., Apes Urbanae, sive de viris illustribus, qui ab anno 1630 per totum 1632 Romae adfuerunt. Romae, 1633.
Amabile, L., Fra Tommaso Campanella e la sua congiura, i suoi processi e la sua pazzia. 3 Vols., Napoli, 1883.
Amabile, L., Il S. Officio della Inquisizione in Napoli. 2 Vols., Città di Castello, 1892.
Amayden, Teodoro, La storia delle famiglie Romane. Con note di C. A. Bertini. 2 Vols., Roma, 1910 and 1914.
Ambros, Aug. Wilh., Geschichte der Musik. Vol. 4., 2nd ed., Leipzig, 1881.
Analecta Bollandiana. 1882 seqq.
Analecta Iuris Pontificii. Dissertations sur divers sujets de droit canonique, liturgie et théologie. Rome, 1855 seqq.
Angeli, D., Le chiese di Roma. Roma (undated).
Annovazzi, V., Storia di Civitavecchia. Roma, 1853.
Anthieny, Johann, Der päpstliche Nuntius Carlo Carafa. (Programm) Berlin, 1869.
Anzeigen, Göttingische Gelehrte. Göttingen, 1802 seqq.
Archiv für Frankfurts Geschichte und Kunst. Frankfort, 1839 seqq.
Archiv für katholisches Kirchenrecht. Innsbruck, 1857 seqq.
Archiv für oesterreichische Geschichte. Vienna, 1865 seqq.
Archiv für schweizer Geschichte. 1843 seqq.
Archivio della R. Società Romana di storia patria. Vol. 1 seqq. Roma, 1878 seqq.

Archivio storico dell'arte, pubbl. per Gnoli. Vol. 1 *seqq.* Rome, 1888 *seqq.*
Archivio storico italiano. 5 Series, Florence, 1842 *seqq.*
Archivio storico Lombardo. Vol. 1 *seqq.* Milan, 1874 *seqq.*
Archivio storico per le provincie Napolitane. Vol. 1 *seqq.* Naples, 1876 *seqq.*
Arens, B., Handbuch der katholischen Missionen. Freiburg i. Breisgau, 1920.
Aretin, C. M. v., Bayerns Auswärtige Verhältnisse seit dem Anfang des 16 Jahrh. Passau, 1839.
Aretin, C. M. v., Geschichte des bayrischen Herzogs und Kurfürsten Maximilian des Ersten. First (only) Vol. Passau, 1842.
Arezio, L., La politica della S. Sede rispetto alla Valtellina dal concordato d'Avignone alla morte di Gregorio XV. (12 Novembre 1622-8, Luglio, 1623) Cagliari, 1899.
Argentré, Carolus du Plessis d', Collectio iudiciorum. Parisiis, 1724.
Armanni, Berichte über Rossettis Sendung nach England, in Archivio stor. ital. 4 Series, Vol. 12-18.
Armellini, M., Le chiese di Roma dalle loro origine sino al secolo XVI. 8 Vols., Rome, 1887. 2nd ed., 1891.
Arnauld, Antoine, Oeuvres complettes. 43 Vols., édit. Hautefage, 1783.
Arte, L', Continuation of " Archivio storico dell'arte ". Roma, 1898 *seqq.*
Astráin, A., S. J., Historia della Compañia de Jesus en la Asistencia de España. Vols. 1-5, Madrid, 1902 *seqq.*
Aumale, Duc d', Histoire des princes de Condé. 8 Vols., Paris, 1869-1895.
Avenel, D', Lettres, instructions et papiers d'Etat de Richelieu. 8 Vols., Paris, 1853-1874.
Avenel, D', Richelieu et la monarchie absolue. 4 Vols., Paris, 1884-1890.

Bachelet, see *Le Bachelet*.
Baglione, Giov., Le nove chiese di Roma. Roma, 1639.
Baglione, Giov., Le vite de' pittori, scultori et architetti dal pontificato di Gregorio XIII. del 1572 in fine a'tempi di Papa Urbano VIII. nel 1642. Napoli, 1733.
Balan, P., Delle relazioni fra la chiesa cattolica e gli Slavi della Bulgaria, Bosnia, Serbia, Erzegovina. Roma, 1880.
Balan, P., Storia d'Italia. Vol. 6, Modena, 1882.
Baldinucci, F., Die " Vita " des Giov. Lorenzo Bernini, mit Übersetzung und Kommentar vom A. Riegl, hersg. von A. Burda und O. Pollak. Wien, 1912.
Bangen, J. H., Die römische Kurie, ihre gegenwärtige Zusammensetzung und ihr Geschäftsgang. Münster, 1850.
Barbier de Montault, X., Oeuvres complètes. 6 Vols., Poitiers et Paris, 1889-1890.
Barozzi, N., et Berchet, G., Le relazioni degli stati Europei lette al senato dagli ambasciatori Veneziani nel sec. 17. Series 1 :

Spagna, 2 Vols., Venezia, 1856-1862; Series 2: Francia, 3 Vols., *ibid.*, 1857-1863; Series 3: Italia, Vol. 1: Torino, *ibid.*, 1862: relazioni di Roma, 2 Vols., Venezia, 1877 and 1879; Series 4: Inghilterra, 1 Vol., *ibid.*, 1863; Turchia: 1 Vol., *ibid.*, 1871-2.

Bartoli, S., Dell'Inghilterra. (Opere Vols. 3-4), Torino, 1825.

Bartoli, D., Dell'istoria della Compagnia di Gesù. L'Italia, prima parte dell'Europa. Libro primo e secondo. (Opere, Vol. 5.) Torino, 1825.

Bartoli, D., Della vita di Roberto cardinal Bellarmino, arcivescovo di Capua, della Comp. di Gesù, in " Delle opere del Padre Daniello Bartoli della Comp. di Gesù ". Vol. 22, Torino, 1836.

Battistella, A., Il S. Offizio e la Riforma religiosa in Bologna. Bologna, 1905.

Batiffol, P., Histoire du Bréviaire Romain. 2ᵉ édit. Paris, 1894.

Batterel, Louis, Mémoires domestiques pour servir à l'histoire. Publiés par A.-M.-P. Ingold. 4 vols. Paris, 1902 *seq.*

Bäumer, S., Geschichte des Breviers. Freiburg, 1895.

Baumgartner, A., Geschichte der Weltliteratur. Vol. 5: Die französische Literatur. Vol. 6: Die italienische Literatur. Freiburg, 1905 and 1911.

Baur, Jos., Philipp von Sötern, geistlicher Kurfürst von Trier, und seine Politik während des Dreissigjährigen Krieges. Speier, 1897.

Bazin, Histoire de la France sous Louis XIII. et sous le ministère de Mazarin. 2 Vols., Paris, 1846.

Bazzoni, A., Un Nunzio straordinario alla corte di Francia nel sec. 17. Firenze, 1882.

Bellesheim, A., Geschichte der katholischen Kirche in Schottland von der Einführung des Christentums bis auf die Gegenwart. Vol. 2, 1560-1878. Mainz, 1883. [English translation by Hunter-Blair, William Blackwood, Edinburgh.]

Bellesheim, A., Geschichte der katholischen Kirche in Irland von der Einführung des Christentums bis auf die Gegenwart. Vol. 2, 1509-1690. Mainz, 1890.

Belloni, A., Il Seicento, in Storia letteraria d'Italia (n.d. or place).

Bellori, G. P., Le vite dei pittori, scultori ed architetti moderni. Roma, 1672. (Quotations from the Pisa, 1821 ed.)

Beltrani, G. B., Felice Contelori e i suoi studi negli archivi del Vaticano, in Arch. di Soc. Rom. di stor. patria. II (1879), 165 *seqq.*, 257 *seqq.*, III (1880), 1 *seqq.*

Benigni, U., Die Getreidepolitik der Päpste. Ins Deutsche übertragen von R. Birner, hrsg. von G. Ruhland. Berlin, 1898.

Benkard, Ernst., Giovanni Lorenzo Bernini. Frankfurt a. M., 1926.

Bentivoglio, G. (Cardinale), Memorie ovvero Diario. Amsterdam, 1648.

Bergner, H., Das barocke Rom. Leipzig, 1914.

Berliner, A., Geschichte der Juden vom den ältesten Zeiten bis zur Gegenwart. 2 Vols., Frankfurt a. M., 1893.
Berteaux, E., Rome de l'avènement de Jules II. à nos jours. Paris, 1905.
Bertolotti, A., Agostino Tassi, suoi scolari e compagni pittori in Roma, in " Giornale di erudiz. artistica ", V., Perugia, 1876, 193 *seqq.*
Bertolotti, A., Artisti subalpini in Roma nei sec. 15, 16 e 17. Torino, 1877 (Mantova, 1884).
Bertolotti, A., Artisti Belgi e Olandesi in Roma nei secoli 16 e 17. Firenze, 1880.
Bertolotti, A., Artisti Lombardi in Roma nei sec. 15, 16 e 17. Studi e ricerche negli archivi Romani. 2 Vols., Milano, 1881.
Bertolotti, A., Artisti Veneti in Roma nei sec. 15, 16 e 17. Venezia, 1884.
Bertolotti, A., Artisti Bolognesi in Roma, *in the* " Atti d. Deput. di storia patria d. Romagna ". 1886.
Bertolotti, A., Artisti Francesi in Roma nei secoli 15, 16 e 17. Mantova, 1886.
Bertolotti, A., Martiri del libero pensiero e vittime della S. Inquisizione nei sec. 16, 17 e 18. Roma, 1891.
Bertolotti, A., Artisti Suizzeri in Roma. Bellinzona, 1886.
Bertrand, Jos., La mission de Maduré d'après des documents inédits. 3 Vols., Paris, 1847–1854.
Biaudet, Henri, Les Nonciatures apostoliques permanentes jusqu'en 1648. (Annales Academiae scientiarum Fennicae, Ser. B., Vol. II, 1), Helsinki, 1910.
Blok, P. J., Geschichte der Niederlande. Vols. 3–4, Gotha, 1907 *seqq.*
Blok, P. J., Relazioni Veneziane. Venetiaansche berichten over de Vereenigde Nederlanden (1600–1795). Haag, 1909.
Blume, Fr., Iter Italicum. 4 Vols., Halle, 1824 *seqq.*
Boglino, L., La Sicilia e i suoi cardinali. Palermo, 1884.
Böhn, M. v., Guido Reni. Bielefeld u. Leipzig, 1910.
Böhn, M. v., Lorenzo Bernini. Seine Zeit, sein Leben, sein Werk. Bielefeld, 1912.
Bonanni, Ph., Numismata Pontificum Romanorum quae a tempore Martini V. ad annum 1699 vel authoritate publica vel privato genio in lucem prodiere. Vol. 2, Romae, 1699.
Bonanni, Ph., Numismata templi Vaticani historiam illustrantia. Ed. 2, Romae, 1700.
Bonelli, Notizie istorico-critiche della chiesa di Trento. 3 Vols., Trento, 1761.
Borzelli, B., Il cavalier Giovan Battista Marino (1569–1625). Napoli, 1898.
Bossi, La Pasquinata. Roma, 1889.
Bougaud, E., Die hl. Johanna Franziska von Chantal und der Ursprung des Ordens von der Heimsuchung. Deutsch bearbeitet. 2 Vols., 2nd ed., Freiburg, 1910.
Boverius, Zach., Annales seu sacrae historiae ordinis Minorum

S. Francisci qui Capucini nuncupantur. Vol. 1, Lugduni, 1632 ; Vol. 2, *ibid.*, 1639.
Braun, J., Die Kirchenbauten der deutschen Jesuiten. 2 Parts, Freiburg, 1908 and 1909.
Bremond, Histoire du sentiment religieux en France. Vols. 1-5, Paris, 1916-1920.
Breuer, K., Der Kurfürstentag zu Mühlhausen 18 Okt, bis 12 Nov. 1627. Bonn, 1904.
Briefe und Akten zur Geschichte des Dreissigjährigen Krieges in den Zeiten des vorwaltenden Einflusses der Wittelsbacher. New series, Part II, Vol. 1, see Goetz.
Briggs, M. S., Barockarchitektur. Berlin, 1914.
Brinckmann, A. E., Barockskulptur. 2 Vols., Berlin-Neubabelsberg, 1919.
Brinckmann, A. E., Die Baukunst des 17 und 18 Jahrh. in den romanischen Ländern. Berlin-Neubabelsberg, 1919.
Brom, G., Archivalia in Italië. Vol. 1, 's Gravenhage, 1908.
Brosch, M., Geschichte des Kirchenstaates. Vol. 1, Gotha, 1880.
Brosch, M., Cromwell und die puritanische Revolution. Frankfurt, 1886.
Brosch, M., Geschichte Englands. Vols. 6 and 7, Gotha, 1890 *seqq.*
Bühring, Joh., Venedig, Gustav Adolph und Rohan. Halle, 1885.
Bullarium ordinis Fratrum Minorum S. Francisci Capucinorum sive Collectio bullarum, brevium etc., quae a Sede Apost. pro ordine Capucinorum emanarunt. Vols. 1-7, Romae, 1740 *seqq.*
Bullarium Carmelitanum, ed. a Iosepho Alberto Ximenez. 4 Vols., Romae, 1715-1768.
Bullarium Casinense, ed. Cornel. Margarinus (O.S.B.). Vol. 1, Venetiis, 1650 ; Vol. 2, Tuderti, 1670.
Bullarium Diplomatum et Privilegiorum Summorum Romanorum Pontificum. Taurinensis editio. Vol. 6, Augustae Taurinorum, 1860 ; Vol. 7 *seqq.*, Neapoli, 1882 *seqq.*
Bullarium ordinis Praedicatorum, ed. *Ripoll-Bremond*. Vol. 4 *seqq.*, Romae, 1733.
Bullarium Congregationis de Propaganda Fide. 7 Vols., Romae, 1839 *seqq.*
Bullarium Vaticanum, *v.* Collectio.
Burckhardt, Jakob, Geschichte der Renaissance in Italien. Mit Illustrationen. Stuttgart, 1868. 3rd ed., von Heinrich Holtzinger, Stuttgart, 1891.
Burckhardt, J., Beiträge zur Kunstgeschichte von Italien. Basel, 1898.
Burckhardt, J., Erinnerungen aus Rubens. 2nd ed., Basel, 1898.
Burckhardt, J., Cicerone. Anleitung zum Genuss der Kunstwerke Italiens. 8th ed., 1901.
Burckhardt, J., Vorträge, ed. by Dürr. 2nd ed., Basel, 1918.
Burgus, Petrus Bapt. Genuensis, De bello Suecico commentarius. Leodii, 1633.
Buss, F. J. v., Die Gesellschaft Jesu. 2 Vols., Mainz, 1853.

Calisse, Carlo, Storia di Civitavecchia. Firenze, 1898.
Callewaert et Nols, Jansénius. Ses derniers moments, sa soumission au St. Siège. Louvain, 1893.
Cambridge Modern History, The, planned by the late Lord Acton, edited by A. W. Ward, G. W. Prothero, and Stanley Leathes. Cambridge, 1903 seqq. IV: The Thirty Years' War, 1907.
Campeggi, R., Racconto degli eretici iconomiasti giudiziati. Bologna, 1623.
Campello della Spina, P., Il castello di Campello. Roma, 1889.
Cancellieri, Fr., De secretariis basilicae Vaticanae veteris ac novae libri II. Romae, 1786.
Cancellieri, Fr., Storia dei solenni possessi dei Sommi Pontefici detti anticamente processi o processioni dopo la loro coronazione dalla basilica Vaticana alla Lateranense. Roma, 1802.
Cancellieri, Fr., Il Mercato, il lago dell'Acque Vergine ed il Palazzo Panfiliano nel Circo Agonale detto volgarmente Piazza Navona descritti. Roma, 1811.
Cancellieri, Fr., Lettera di F.C. al Ch. Sig. Dott. Koreff sopra il tarantismo, l'aria di Roma e della sua campagna ed i palazzi pontifici dentro e fuori di Roma, con notizie di Castel Gandolfo e de'paesi circonvicini. Roma, 1817.
Canonizzazione, La, dei SS. Ignazio di Loiola e Francesco Saverio. Ricordi del terzo centenario. Roma, 1923.
Capriata, P. G., Dell'historia libri dodeci, nei quali si contengono tutti i movimenti d'arme successi in Italia dal 1613 al 1634. Genova, 1638.
Carabelli, G., Dei Farnese e del ducato di Castro e di Ronciglione. Firenze, 1865.
Carafa, C., Commentaria de Germania sacra restaurata. Coloniae, 1637; ad a. 1641 continuata, Francofurti, 1641.
Carafa, C., Relatione del stato dell'impero e ecclesia in Germania, ed. by J. G. Müller im Archiv für österr. Geschichte XXIII., Wien, 1860, 105-449.
Cardella, L., Memorie storiche de' cardinali della s. Romana Chiesa. Vols. 5 and 6, Roma, 1793.
Carini, Isid., La Biblioteca Vaticana, proprietà della Sede Apostolica. Roma, 1893.
Carte Strozziane, Le. Inventario. 1 Serie, 2 Vols., Firenze, 1884.
Caruso, G. B., Discorso istorico-apologetico della Monarchia di Sicilia, composto d'ordine di Vittorio Amadeo, per la prima volta pubbl. ed annotato per G. M. Mira. Palermo, 1863.
Carutti, D., Storia della diplomazia della corte di Savoia. 4 Vols., Torino, 1875-1880.
Castellucci, Il risveglio dell'attività missionaria e le prime origini della s. congregazione de Prop. Fide. Roma, 1924.
Castro, G. de, Fulvio Testi. Milano, 1875.
Cauchie, A., Sources MSS. à Rome. Bruxelles, 1892.

Cauchie, A., et Maere, R., Recueil des Instructions générales aux Nonces de Flandre (1596-1635). Bruxelles, 1904.
Cecchelli, C., Il Vaticano. Roma, 1928.
Celli, A., Storia della malaria nell'Agro Romano. Opera postuma, con illustr. del Dr. P. Ambrogetti. Città di Castello, 1925.
Cerboni, Giano Nicio Eritreo. Città di Castello, 1909.
Cerrati, M., Tiberii Alpharani de basilicae Vaticanae antiquissima et nova structura liber, p. p. M.C. Romae, 1914.
Challoner, K., Memoirs of Missionary Priests, Burns Oates and Washbourne, London.
Charavay, Et., Inventaire des autographes et documents historiques réunis par M. Benjamin Fillon, décrits par Et. Ch. 3 Vols., Paris, 1879-1881.
Chattard, Giov. Pietro, Nuova descrizione del Vaticano. Vols. 1-3, Roma, 1762-7.
Chledowski, C. v., Rom. Die Menschen der Renaissance. Übers. aus dem Polnischen von R. Schapira. München, 1913.
Ciaconius, Alph., Vitae et res gestae Pontificum Romanorum et S. R. E. Cardinalium . . . ab August. Oldoino, S.J., recognitae. Vols. 3 and 4, Romae, 1677.
Ciampi, S., Bibliografia critica delle corrispondenze dell'Italia colla Russia, colla Polonia, etc. 3 Vols., Firenze, 1834-1842.
Colasanti, G., Le Fontane d'Italia. Milano, 1926.
Collectanea S. Congregationis de Propaganda Fide, seu decreta, instructiones, rescripta pro apostolicis missionibus. Vol. 1, Ann. 1622-1866. Romae, 1907.
Collectio bullarum, brevium aliorumque diplomatum sacrosanctae basilicae Vaticanae. T. II, ab Urbano V. ad Paulum III. productus. Romae, 1750.
Conclavi de' Pontefici Romani. Nuova ediz. I. Colonia, 1691.
Contarini, Pietro, Relazione di Roma 1623-1627, in Barozzi-Berchet, Relazioni, etc. Serie III, Roma, 1 (Venezia, 1877), 199-220.
Contarini, Angelo, Relazione di Roma, 1627-1629, *ibid.*, 257-312.
Contarini, Alvise, Relazione di Roma, 1632-1635, *ibid.*, 353-405
Coppi, A., Memorie Colonnesi compilate. Roma, 1855.
Cordara, I., Historiae Soc. Iesu Pars VI. Romae, 1750.
Coste, Pierre, Saint Vincent de Paul. Correspondence, Entretiens, Documents. 14 Vols., Paris, 1920 *seqq.*
Couderc, J.-B., Le vénérable cardinal Bellarmin. 2 Vols., Paris, 1893.
Cousin, V., La jeunesse de Mazarin. Paris, 1865.
Coville, H., Etude sur Mazarin et ses démêlés avec le Pape Innocent X. Paris, 1914.
Crétineau-Joly, J., Histoire de la Compagnie de Jésus. 6 Vols., 3rd ed., Paris, 1851.
Cristofori, Fr., Storia dei Cardinali di s. Romana Chiesa. Roma, 1888.
Cronholm, A., Gustav Adolph in Deutschland. Übersetzt von H. Helms. Leipzig, 1857 *seqq.*
Cuevas, M. (S.J.), Historia de la Iglesia en Mexico. Tom. III., 1600-1699. Tlalpam (Mexiko), 1924.

Cupis, C. de, Le vicende dell'agricoltura e della pastorizia nell'Agro Romano e l'Annona di Roma. Roma, 1911.
Dahmen, P., Robert de'Nobili. Münster, 1924.
Dami, L., Il giardino italiano. Milano, 1924.
Dändliker, K., Geschichte der Schweiz. 2 Vols., 3 Aufl. Zürich, 1900–1904.
Decreta, diplomata, privilegia aliqua ex multis, quae in favorem religionis catholicae et catholicorum in Germania emanarunt ab a. 1620 usque ad a. 1629 ex cancellaria aulica imperii. No date or place of publication. (Appendix to Carafa, Commentaria.)
Degert, A., Histoire des Séminaires français jusqu'à la Révolution. 2 Vols., Paris, 1912.
Delplace, L. (S.J.). Le catholicisme au Japon, St. François Xavier et ses premiers successeurs, 1540–1660. Bruxelles, 1909.
Demaria, G., La guerra di Castro e la spedizione de'presidi 1639–1649, in Miscellanea di storia italiana XXXV. Torino, 1898, 191–256.
Denis, P., Nouvelles de Rome, précédées de listes de tous les fonctionnaries de la cour de Rome. I : 1601–1661. Paris, 1913.
Denis, P., Le card. Richelieu et la réforme des monastères bénédictins. Paris, 1913.
Desjardins, A., Négociations diplomatiques de la France avec la Toscane. Documents recueillis par Giuseppe Canestrini. Vol. 1, seqq., Paris, 1859 seqq.
Diana, Ant., Coordinatus seu omnes resolutiones morales. Vol. 4, Lugduni, 1680.
Dictionnaire de Théologie catholique, by *Vacant-Mangenot.* Vol. 1 seqq., Paris, 1903 seqq.
Dierauer, Joh., Geschichte der Schweizerischen Eidgenossenschaft. Vol. 3, 1516–1648. (Geschichte der europäischen Staaten, ed. *A. H. L. Heeren, F. A. Uckert, W. v. Giesebrecht,* und *K. Lamprecht,* Vol. 26.) Gotha, 1907.
Döberl, M., Geschichte Bayerns. Vol. 1, München, 1906, 3rd ed., 1916.
Dolfi, P. Sc., Cronologia delle familie nobili di Bologna. Bologna, 1670.
Döllinger, J. J. V., Geschichte der Moralstreitigkeiten in der römisch-katholischen Kirche seit dem 16 Jahrh, ed. Reusch. Nördlingen, 1889.
Döllinger, J., und *Reusch, H.,* Die Selbstbiographie des Kardinals Bellarmin. Lateinisch und deutsch, mit geschichtlichen Erläuterungen. Bonn, 1887.
Donatus, Al., Roma vetus ac recens. Romae, 1638.
Droysen, J. G., Geschichte der preussischen Politik. 14 Vols., 1855–1886.
Duhr, B., S.J., Jesuitenfabeln. 3rd ed., Freiburg, 1892.
Duhr, B., S.J., Geschichte der Jesuiten in den Ländern deutscher Zunge im 16 Jahrh. Vol 1, Freiburg, 1907 ; Vol. 2, Parts 1 and 2, Freiburg, 1913.

Du Mont de Carels-Croon, Corps universel diplomatique. Vol. 1 Amsterdam, 1728.
Dupin, Louis Ellies, Histoire ecclésiastique du dix-septième siècle. 4 Vols., Paris, 1713 seqq.
Durm, J., Die Baukunst der Renaissance in Italien. (Handbuch der Architektur, 2nd Part, Vol. 5.) Stuttgart, 1903, 2nd ed., 1914.

Ebe, G., Die Spät-Renaissance. 2 Vols., Berlin, 1886.
Egger, H., Kritisches Verzeichnis der Sammlung architektonischer Handzeichnungen der K. K. Hofbibliothek. Wien, 1903.
Ehrle, Fr., La grande veduta Maggi-Mascardi (1615) del Tempio e del Palazzo Vaticano, stampata con rami originali, con introduzione di Fr. E., S.J. Roma, 1914.
Ehrle, Fr., Roma al tempo di Urbano VIII. La pianta di Roma Maggi-Maupin-Losi del 1625, riprodotta da uno dei due esemplari completi finora conosciuti, a cura della Biblioteca Vaticana, con introduzione di Fr. Ehrle, S.J. Roma, 1915.
Ehrle, Fr., Dalle carte e dai disegni di Virgilio Spada, in Memorie della Pontif. Accademia Rom. di Archeol. Roma, 1927.
Eichmann, E., Der recursus ab abusu nach deutschem Recht. Breslau, 1903.
Eisler, Alex., Das Veto der katholischen Staaten bei der Papstwahl. Wien, 1907.
Escher, Konrad, Barock und Klassizismus. Studien zur Geschichte der Architektur Roms. Leipzig, 1910.
Estrées, D', Mémoires du maréchal d'Estrées sur la régence de Marie de Médicis (1610–1616) et sur celle d'Anne d'Autriche publiés par P. Bonnefon. Paris, 1910.

Fabisza, P. W., Wiadomość o Legatach i Nunzyuszach Apostolskich w dawnej Polsce 1076–1865. Ostrow, 1866.
Fagniez, G., Le père Joseph et Richelieu, 1577–1638. 2 Vols., Paris, 1894.
Faloci Pulignani, M., Notizie del ven. G. B. Vitelli da Foligno e del suo carteggio. Foligno, 1894.
Favaro, A., Opere di Galileo Galilei. Ediz. naz. 19 Vols., Firenze, 1890–1913.
Fea, C. D., Considerazioni storiche, fisiche, geologiche. Roma, 1827.
Fea, C. D., Storia dell'Acque in Roma e dei condotti. Roma, 1832.
Federn, K., Richelieu. Wien, 1927.
Ferrari, Giulio, La tomba nell'arte italiana dal periodo preromano all'odierno. Milano.
Fiedler, Jos., Die Relationen der Botschafter Venedigs über Deutschland und Österreich im 17 Jahrh. (Fontes rerum austriacarum 2 Abt., Vol. 26), Wien, 1867.
Fillon, see *Charvay*.
Fish, M. C. Russell, Guide to the Materials of American History. Washington, 1911.

Flassan, Gaétan de Raxis, Histoire de la diplomatie française. 6 Vols., Paris, 1808.
Foley, H. (S.J.), Records of the English Province of the Society of Jesus. 7 Vols., London, 1877 seqq.
[*Fontaine, Jacques de la*], SS. D. N. Clementis Papae XI. Constitutio, Unigenitus theologice propugnata. Romae, 1717–1724.
Forcella, V., Iscrizioni delle chiese e d'altri edifici di Roma dal secolo XI. fino ai giorni nostri. 14 Vols., Roma, 1869–1885.
Fouqueray, H., S.J., Histoire de la Compagnie de Jésus en France, des origines à la suppression (1528–1762). Vol. 4 : Sous le ministère de Richelieu, 1re Partie ; Vol. 5 : 2e Partie. Paris, 1925.
Fraknói, V., P. Pázmány. 3 Vols., Pest, 1867–1872.
France chrétienne, La, dans l'histoire. Paris, 1896.
Fraschetti, St., Il Bernini. Milano, 1900.
Frey, D., Bramante-Studien. Wien, 1915.
Frey, D., Beiträge zur römischen Barockarchitektur, im Jahrbuch für Kunstgeschichte, 1924.
Friedberg, E., Die Grenzen zwischen Staat und Kirche und die Garantien gegen deren Verletzung. Historisch-dogmatische Studie. Tübingen, 1872.
Fromentin, Eug., Les Maîtres d'autrefois. Belgique-Hollande. Paris, 1918.
Fumi, L., L'Inquisizione e lo stato di Milano. Milano, 1910.

Gabrieli, G., Il carteggio scientifico ed accademico fra i primi Lincei 1603–1630. Roma, 1925.
Galante, A., Il diritto di placitazione e l'economato dei benefici vacanti in Lombardia. Milano, 1884.
Galluzzi, R., Istoria del granducato di Toscana sotto governo della casa Medici. Cambiagi, 1781.
Gams, P. B., Series episcoporum ecclesiae catholicae quotquot innotuerunt a beato Petro apostolo. Ratisbonae, 1873.
Garampi, G., Saggi di osservazioni sul valore delle antiche monete pontificie. Con appendice di documenti. Undated. Roma, 1766.
Gardiner, Samuel R., History of England from the accession of James I. to the outbreak of the Civil War, 1603–1642. 10 Vols., London, 1883 seqq.
Gardiner, Samuel R., The Thirty Years War. 6th ed., London, 1884.
Gardiner, Samuel R., History of the great Civil War, 1642–1649. 4 Vols., London, 1893.
Gasquet, A., History of the venerable English College at Rome. London, 1920.
Gatticus, I. B., Acta caeremonialia s. Romanae Ecclesiae ex miss. codicibus. Vol. 1. Romae, 1753.
Gaudentius, P., Beiträge zur Kirchengeschichte des 16. und

17 Jahrh. Bedeutung und Verdienste des Franziskanerordens im Kampfe gegen den Protestantismus. Vol 1, Bozen, 1880.

Gazette des Beaux-Arts. Paris, 1859 seqq.

Gazier, A., Histoire générale du mouvement janséniste depuis ses origines jusqu'à nos jours. 2 Vols., Paris, 1924.

Geijer, E. G., Geschichte Schwedens. Deutsche Übersetzung. 3 Vols., Hamburg, 1832–6.

Gerberon, G., Histoire générale du Jansénisme. 3 Vols., Amsterdam, 1700.

Gfrörer, A. F., Gustav Adolph. 4th ed., von Onno Klopp. Stuttgart, 1863.

Gindely, A., Zur Geschichte der Einwirkung Spaniens auf die Papstwahlen, namentlich bei Gelegenheit der Wahl Leos XI. im Jahre 1605, in den Sitzungsberichten der Akad. der Wissensch. zu Wien, Phil.-hist. Kl., Vol. 28, Wien, 1858.

Gindely, A., Geschichte des 30 jährigen Krieges. Vol. 1–4, Prag, 1869–1880.

Gindely, A., Waldstein während seines ersten Generalats im Lichte der gleichzeitigen Quellen, 1625–1630. 2 Vols., Prag, 1885 seqq.

Gindely, A., Geschichte der Gegenreformation in Böhmen, ed. Th. Tupetz. Leipzig, 1894.

Ginzel, I. A., Legatio apostolica Petri Aloysii Carafae, Episc. Tricariensis. Würzburg, 1840.

Gioda, C., La vita e le opere di Giovanni Botero. 3 Vols., Milano, 1895.

Giornale storico della letteratura italiana, diretto e redatto da A. Graf, F. Novati, R. Renier. Vol. 1 seqq. Roma-Torino-Firenze, 1883 seqq.

Goldast, M., Monarchia Romani imperii. 3 Parts, Hann.-Francof, 1611–13.

Goll, J., Die französische Heirat, Frankreich und England 1624 und 1625. Prag, 1876.

Golzio, V., Il Palazzo Barberini, Roma [1925].

Gori, F., Archivio storico, artistico, archeologico e letterario della città e provincia di Roma. Vols. 1–4, Roma e Spoleto, 1875–1883.

Gothein, M. L., Geschichte der Gartenkunst. Vol. 1, Jena, 1914.

Goetz, W., Die Politik Maximilians I. und seiner Verbündeten. Vol. 1, 1623–4, Leipzig, 1908 ; Vol. 2, 1625, ibid., 1918. (Briefe und Akten II.)

Goyau, G., Histoire religieuse. Vol. 6 by Hanotaux : Histoire de la Nation française. Paris [1922].

Gregorovius, F., Urban VIII. im Widerspruch zu Spanien und dem Kaiser. Stuttgart, 1879.

Grisar, H., Galileistudien. Historisch-theologische Untersuchungen über die Urteile im Galilei-Prozess. Regensburg, 1882.

Gröne, V., Die Papstgeschichte. Vol. 2., 2nd ed., Regensburg, 1875.

Grossi-Gondi, F., Le Ville Tusculane nell'epoca classica e dopo il Rinascimento. La Villa dei Quintili e la Villa di Mondragone. Roma, 1901.
Grottanelli, L., Il Ducato di Castro. I Farnesi ed i Barberini. Firenze, 1891.
Grottanelli, L., Claudia de'Medici e i suoi tempi. Firenze, 1986.
Grottanelli, L., La Riforma e la guerra de' Trent 'Anni. Ricordi studiati sulla corrispondenza degli ambasciatori Toscani. Firenze, 1899.
Grünhagen, C., Geschichte Schlesiens. 2 Vols., Gotha, 1884 u. 1886.
Guglielmotti, Alb., Storia delle fortificazioni nella spiaggia Romana. Roma, 1880.
Guglielmotti, Alb., La squadra permanente della marina Romana. Storia dal 1573 al 1644. Roma, 1882.
Guhl, E., Künstlerbriefe, übersetzt und erläutert. 2 Vols., Berlin, 1853 seqq.
Guidi, M., Le Fontane barocche di Roma. Zurigo, 1917.
Günter, H., Das Restitutionsedikt von 1629 und die katholische Restauration Altwirtembergs. Stuttgart, 1901.
Günter, H., Die Habsburger Liga 1625-1655. Briefe und Akten aus dem Generalarchiv zu Simancas. Berlin, 1908.
Gurlitt, Cornelius, Geschichte des Barockstiles in Italien. Stuttgart, 1887.

Haeser, Heinrich, Lehrbuch der Geschichte der Medizin und der epidemischen Krankheiten. Vol. 1 u. 3, Dritte Bearbeitung. Jena, 1875-1882.
Haffter, E., Georg Jenatsch. Ein Beitrag zur Geschichte der Bündner Wirren. Davos, 1894.
Hammer-Purgstall, J. Frh. v., Geschichte des osmanischen Reiches. 4 Vols., 2nd ed., Pest, 1834-6.
Hammer-Purgstall, J. Frh. v., Klesls des Kardinals, Direktors des geh. Kabinetts Kaiser Matthias', Leben. 4 Vols., Wien, 1847-1851.
Hanotaux, G., Histoire du cardinal Richelieu. 2 Vols., Paris, 1893-4, 2nd ed., 1896.
Hanuy, Petri, Cardinalis Pázmány epistolae. 2 Vols., Budapest, 1910 seq.
Hase, K. A., Kirchengeschichte auf Grundlage akademischer Vorlesungen. 3 Vols., Leipzig, 1885-1892.
Hebeisen, G., Die Bedeutung der ersten Fürsten von Hohenzollern und des Kardinals Eitel Friedrich von Hohenzollern für die katholische Bewegung Deutschlands ihrer Zeit. Hechingen, 1923.
Heimbucher, M., Die Orden und Kongregationen der katholischen Kirche. 3 Vols., 2nd ed., Paderborn, 1907-8.
Helbig, W., Führer durch die öffentlichen Sammlungen klassischer Altertümer in Rom. 2 Vols., 2nd ed., Leipzig, 1899, 3rd ed., 1912.
Hempel, E., Francesco Borromini. Wien, 1924.

Hergenröther, J., Katholische Kirche und christlicher Staat in ihrer geschichtlichen Entwicklung und in Beziehung auf die Fragen der Gegenwart. Historisch-theologische Essays und zugleich ein Anti-Ianus vindicatus. 2nd Part, Freiburg, 1872.
Hergenröther, J., Handbuch der allgemeinen Kirchengeschichte. Neu bearbeitet von J. P. Kirsch. 4 Vols., 6th ed., Freiburg, 1924-5.
Hermant, G., Mémoires sur l'histoire ecclésiastique du XVIIe. siècle (1630-1663), ed. Gazier. 6 Vols., Paris, 1905-1910.
Herzog, see Real-Enzyklopädie.
Heyne, O., Der Kurfürstentag zu Regensburg von 1630. Berlin, 1866.
Hilgers, J., S.J., Der Index der verbotenen Bücher. Freiburg, 1904.
Hinschius, P., System des katholischen Kirchenrechts. 6 Vols., Berlin, 1869 seqq.
Histoire des conclaves depuis Clément V. jusqu'à présent. Cologne, 1703.
Historisch-politische Blätter für das katholische Deutschland. Vols. 1-171, München, 1838-1923.
Hjärne, Sigismund svenska resor. Upsala, 1884.
Högl, M., Die Bekehrung der Oberpfalz durch Kurfürst Maximilian I. Regensburg, 1903.
Holl, K., Fürstbischof Jakob Fugger von Konstanz (1604-1626) und die katholische Reform der Diözese im ersten Viertel des 17 Jahrh. Freiburg, 1898.
Holzapfel, Heribert, Handbuch der Geschichte des Franziskanerordens. Freiburg, 1909.
Houssaye, M., M. de Bérulle et les Carmélites de France. Paris, 1872.
Houssaye, M., Le cardinal de Bérulle et Richelieu. 2 Vols., Paris, 1876.
Huber, A., Geschichte Österreichs. Vols. 4 and 5, Gotha, 1892 seq.
Hubert, E., Les Pays-Bas Espagnols et la Républiques des Provinces Unies. La question religieuse et les relations diplomatiques, in Mémoires de l'Academie Royale de Belgique, 2 Serie, Vol. 2, Bruxelles, 1907.
Hughes, Thom., History of the Society of Jesus in North America colonial and federal. Text, 2 Vols., London, 1907-1917; Documents, 2 Vols., 1907, 1910.
Huelsen, Chr., Saggio di bibliografia ragionata delle piante iconografiche e prospettive di Roma dal 1551 al 1758. Roma, 1915.
Huelsen, Chr., Römische Antikengärten des 16 Jahrhunderts. Heidelberg, 1917.
Huonder, A., S.J., Der einheimische Klerus in den Heidenländern. Freiburg, 1909.
Huonder, A., Der chinesische Ritenstreit. Aachen, 1921.
Hürbin, J., Handbuch der Schweizergeschichte. 2 Vols., Stans, 1901-9.

Hurter, Fr., Geschichte Kaiser Ferdinands II. und seiner Eltern bis zu dessen Krönung in Frankfurt. 11 Vols., Schaffhausen, 1850-1864.
Hurter, Fr., Friedensbestrebungen Kaiser Ferdinands II. Wien, 1862.
Hurter, H., Nomenclator literarius theologiae catholicae. 5 Vols., 3rd ed., Oeniponte, 1903 seqq.

Ilg, Geist des hl. Franziskus Seraphikus, dargestellt in Lebensbildern aus der Geschichte des Kapuzinerordens. 2 Vols., Ausburg, 1876 u. 1879.
Imago primi saeculi Societatis Jesu. Antverpiae, 1640.
Inventario dei monumenti di Roma. Vol. 1., Roma, 1908-1912.
Irmer, G., Hans Georg von Arnim. Leipzig, 1894.

Jahrbuch, Historisches, der Görres-Gesellschaft. Vols. 1-48., Münster and München, 1880-1928.
Jahrbuch der preussischen Kunstsammlungen. Berlin, 1880 seqq.
Jann, A. O., Die katholischen Missionen in Indien, China und Japan. Ihre Organization und das portugiesische Patronat vom 15 bis ins 18 Jahrh. Paderborn, 1915.
Janssen, J., Geschichte des deuschen Volkes seit dem Ausgang des Mittelalters. Vols. 1-5, 19 u. 20 editions besorgt von L. v. Pastor. Freiburg, 1913-17.
Jessen, K. F. W., Die Botanik der Gegenwart und Vorzeit in kulturhistorischer Entwicklung. Leipzig, 1864.
Jorga, N., Geschichte des rumänischen Volkes. 2 Vols. (Allg. Staatengesch., 1 ed. : Geschichte der europäischen Staaten, 34 Werk.) Gotha, 1905.
Jorga, N., Geschichte des osmanischen Reiches nach den Quellen dargestellt. Vol. 3, Gotha, 1910.
Justi, K., Velasquez und seine Zeit. 2 Vols., 3rd ed., München, 1922.
Jus Pontificium = Juris Pontificii de Propaganda Fide Pars I. Vols. 1-6, Romae, 1886 seqq. (In quotations Part I. is understood.)

Katholik, Der. Zeitschrift für katholische Wissenschaft und kirchliches Leben. Jahrg. 1 seqq. Strassburg und Mainz, 1820 seqq.
Keller, L., Die Gegenreformation in Westfalen und am Niederrhein. Aktenstücke und Erläuterungen. 3 Parts. (Publikationen aus den K. Preussischen Staatsarchiven 9, 33 u. 62.) Leipzig, 1881-1895.
Kerschbaumer, A., Kardinal Klesel. Wien, 1865.
Keyssler, J. G., Neueste Reise durch Deutschland, Böhmen, Ungarn, die Schweiz, Italien und Lothringen. 3 Vols., Hannover, 1740.
Khevenhüller, F. Ch., Annales Ferdinandei, 1578-1626. 9 Vols., Regensburg u. Wien, 1640-46.

Kiewning, H., Nuntiaturberichte aus Deutschland. Nuntiatur des Pallotto 1626-1630, ed. by H. K. 2 Vols., Berlin, 1895 u. 1897.
Kink, R., Geschichte der kaiserlichen Universität zu Wien. 2 Vols., Wien, 1854.
Kirchenlexikon oder Enzyklopädie der kathol. Theologie und ihrer Hilfswissenschaften. Ed. by H. J. Wetzer und B. Welte. 12 Vols., Freiburg, 1847-1856, 2nd ed., begonnen von Joseph Kard. Hergenröther, fortgesetzt von Fr. Kaulen. 12 Vols., Freiburg, 1882-1901.
Klopp, Onno, Der Dreissigjährige Krieg bis zum Eingreifen Gustav Adolphs. 3 Vols., Paderborn, 1891-6.
Knieb, Joh., Geschichte der Reformation und Gegenreformation auf dem Eichsfelde. Nach archivalischen und andern Quellen bearbeitet. Heiligenstadt (Eichsfeld), 1900.
Knuttel, W., De toestand der katholieken onder der Republick I. Haag, 1892.
Koch, M., Geschichte des deutschen Reiches unter der Regierung Ferdinands III. 2 Vols., Wien, 1865 *seq.*
Kollmann, I., Acta sacrae congregationis de Propaganda Fide res gestas Bohemicas illustrantia. Tom. I., Pars 1 (1622-1623). Pragae, 1923.
Komp, G. J., Fürstabt Joh. Bernhard Schenk zu Schweinsberg, der zweite Restaurator des Katholizismus im Hochstift Fulda, 1623-1632. Fulda, 1878.
Krasinski, V. A., Geschichte der Reformation in Polen. Deutsch von M. A. Lindau. Leipzig, 1841.
Kraus, Fr. X., Geschichte der christlichen Kunst. 2 Vols., 2 Abt., 2 Hälfte, fortgesetzt und ed. by *J. Sauer.* Freiburg, 1908.
Kretschmayr, H., Geschichte von Venedig. 1 *seq.* Gotha., 1905 *seq.*
Kretzschmar, J., Gustav Adolphs Pläne und Ziele in Deutschland. Hannover, 1905.
Kristeller, P., Kupferstich und Holzschnitt in vier Jahrhunderten. Berlin, 1905.
Krones, F., Handbuch der Geschichte Österreichs. 5 Vols., Berlin, 1876-9.
Kropf, Fr. X., Historia provinciae Soc. Jesu Germaniae superioris. Pars IV. (1611 bis 1630). Monaci, 1746.
Kröss, A., Geschichte der böhmischen Provinz der Gesellschaft Jesu. Vol. 2, ed. 1, Wien, 1927.
Kuhn, Alb., Allgemeine Kunstgeschichte. Einsiedeln, 1891 *seqq.*
Kunstmann, Fr., Die gemischten Ehen unter den christlichen Konfessionen Deutschlands geschichtlich dargestellt. Regensburg, 1839.

Lämmer, H., Analecta Romana. Kirchengeschichtliche Forschungen in römischen Bibliotheken und Archiven. Eine Denkschrift. Schaffhausen, 1861.

Lämmer, H., Zur Kirchengeschichte des 16 und 17 Jahrh. Freiburg. 1863.
Lämmer, H., Zur Kodifikation des kanonischen Rechts. Denkschrift. Freiburg, 1899.
Laemmer, H., Meletematum Romanorum mantissa. Ratisbonae, 1875.
Lancelot., Cl., Mémoires touchant la vie de M. de St.-Cyran. Cologne, 1638.
Lanciani, R., Storia degli scavi di Roma. Roma, 1902 seqq.
Lauer, Ph., Le Palais du Latran. Paris, 1911.
Laugel, Fragments d'histoire . . . Gustave Adolphe et Richelieu. Paris, 1886.
Lavisse, E., Histoire de France. Vol. 1 seqq, Paris, 1901 seqq.
Le Bachelet, X. M., Auctarium Bellarminianum. Supplément aux Œuvres du cardinal Bellarmin. Paris, 1913.
Legrand, E., Bibliographie hellénique ou description raisonée des ouvrages publiés en grec par des Grecs au 17e siècle. 4 Vols., Paris, 1894-6.
Leman, A., Recueil des instructions générales aux Nonces ordinaires de France, de 1624 à 1634. Lille-Paris, 1919.
Leman, A., Urbain VIII. et la rivalité de la France et de la maison d'Autriche de 1631 à 1635. Lille-Paris, 1919.
Lemmens, B., Acta s. congregationis de Propaganda Fide pro Terra Sancta. Quaracchi, 1921-2.
Leo, H., Geschichte der italienischen Staaten. 5 Vos., 1829-1832.
Letarouilly, P., Edifices de Rome moderne. Paris, 1825-1857.
Letarouilly-Simil, Le Vatican et la basilique de St. Pierre de Rome. 2 Vols., Paris, 1882.
Likowski, E., Die ruthenisch-römische Kirchenvereinigung, gen. Union zu Brest. Deutsch von P. Jedzink. Freiburg, 1904.
Lingard, John, A History of England from the first Invasion by the Romans. Vols. 7-9, London, 1838 seq.
Litta, P., Famiglie celebri italiane. Disp. 1-183. Milano e Torino, 1819-1881.
Lodge, R., Richelieu. London, 1896.
Looshorn, Geschichte des Bistums Bamberg. 6 Vols., Bamberg, 1886-1903.
Loserth, J., Briefe und Korrespondenzen zur Geschichte der Gegenreformation in Innerösterreich unter Ferdinand II. 2 Vols., Wien, 1906 u. 1907.
Lubowski, E., G. L. Bernini als Architekt und Dekorator unter Papst Urban VIII. Tübingen, 1919.
Lundorp, M. C., Acta publica. Frankfurt, 1621-5.
Lungo, Isidoro del, Dino Compagni. 3 Vols., Firenze, 1879 seqq.
Lünig, I. Chr., Codex Italiae diplomaticus, 1725-1735.
Luxio, A., e Torelli, P., L'Archivio Gonzaga di Mantova. 2 Vols., Verona, 1920-2.

Magni, G., Il barocco nell'architettura a Roma. Torino, 1911.
Mailáth, J., Geschichte des österreichischen Kaiserstaates. 5 Vols., Hamburg, 1834-1850.

Malvasia, C. C., Felsina pittrice. Vite de' pittori Bolognesi. 2 Vols., Bologna, 1841.
Manilli, Jacomo, Villa Borghese fuori di Porta Pinciana descritta da J. M. Roma, 1650.
Manni, D. M., Istoria degli Anni Santi. Firenze, 1750.
Marcellino da Civezza (O.F.M.), Storia delle missioni francescane. Vol. 2, 1 Part. Prato, 1883.
Mariéjol, Histoire de France. (Histoire de France by Lavisse, Vol. 6), Paris, 1904.
Marini, G., Memorie istoriche degli archivi della Santa Sede, ed. A. Mai. Romae, 1825.
Marsand, A., I Manoscritti italiani della regia biblioteca Parigina. 2 Vols., Paris, 1906.
Martin, V., Le Gallicanisme et la Réforme catholique. Essai hist. sur l'introduction en France des décrets du concile de Trente, 1563-1615. Paris, 1919.
Martinelli, F., Roma ricercata nel suo sito e nella scuola di tutti gli antiquarii. Roma, 1644.
Martini, E. M., L'assedio di Benevento nel 1633 e le peripezie di Don Fabrizio Carafa. Benevento, 1915.
Martinori, E., Annali della Zecca di Roma. Gregorio XV. e Urbano VIII. Roma, 1919.
Marx, J., Geschichte des Erzstiftes Trier. 5 Vols., 1858-1864.
Mayer, Joh. Georg, Das Konzil von Trient und die Gegenreformation in der Schweiz. 2 Vols., Stans, 1901 u. 1903.
Mayer, Joh. Georg, Geschichte des Bistums Chur. 2 Vols., Stans, 1908-1910.
Maynard, Saint Vincent de Paul, Sa vie, son temps, ses œuvres, son influence. 4 Vols., Paris, 1860.
Mazzuchelli, G. M., Gli scrittori d'Italia. 2 Vols., Brescia, 1753 seq.
Meaux, De, Les luttes religieuses en France au XVIe. siècle. Paris, 1879.
Meaux, De, La Réforme et la politique française en Europe, jusqu'à la paix de Westphalie. 2 Vols., Paris, 1889.
Mejer, O., Die Propaganda, ihre Provinzen und ihr Recht. 2 Vols., Göttingen, 1852.
Mélanges d'archéologie et d'histoire. (École française de Rome.) Vol. 1 seqq., Paris, 1881 seqq.
Memmoli, D., Vita del cardinale Giov. Garzia Millino Romano. Roma, 1644.
Mémoires pour servir à l'histoire de Port-Royal et à la vie de la Rev. Mère Marie Angélique Arnauld. 3 Vols., Utrecht, 1742.
Menzel, K. A., Neuere Geschichte der Deutschen von der Reformation bis zum Bundesakt. 12 Vols., Berlin, 1826-1848.
Mergentheim, Leo, Die Quinquennalfakultaten pro foro externo. 2 Vols., Stuttgart, 1908.
Metzler, J., Die Apostolischen Vikariate des Nordens. Paderborn, 1919.
Meyer, Albert de, Les premières controverses jansénistes en France (1640-1649). Louvain, 1917.

Michaelis, A., Die archäologischen Entdeckungen des 19 Jahrh. Leipzig, 1906.
Mignanti, F. M., Istoria della sacrosanta patriarcale basilica Vaticana. Roma, 1867.
Migne, Dictionnaire des Cardinaux. Paris, 1857.
Miller de Brassó, J. F., Epistolae cardinalis Petri Pázmány ad pontifices, imperatores, reges, principes, etc. 2 Vols., Budae, 1822.
Miscellaneae Ceriani. Milano, 1910.
Missirini, M., Memorie per servire alla storia della Romana Accademia di S. Luca, fino alla morte di Ant. Canova. Roma, 1823.
Mitteilungen des Justituts für österreichische Geschichtsforschung. Vol. 1 seqq., Innsbruck, 1880 seqq.
Mommsen, W., Richelieus politisches Testament und kleinere Schriften. Übersetzt von F. Schmidt, eingeleitet von W. M. Berlin, 1926.
Montor, Artaud de, Histoire des souverains Pontifes Romains. Vols. 7–9, Paris, 1847.
Morf, H., Frankreich zur Zeit Richelieus und Mazarins, in der Internat. Wochenschrift V. 165 seqq., 199 seqq.
Moroni, G., Dizionario di erudizione storico-ecclesiastica da S. Pietro sino ai nostri giorni. 109 Vols., Venezia, 1840–1879.
Mortier, Histoire des Maîtres généraux de l'ordre des Frères prêcheurs. Paris, 1903 seqq.
[*Morus*], Biblioteca Picena, o sia notizie istoriche delle opere e degli scrittori Piceni. Osimo, 1790.
Mourret, F., Histoire générale de l'Eglise. L'ancien Régime. Paris, 1912.
Müllbauer, Max., Geschichte der katholischen Missionen in Ostindien von Vasco di Gama bis zur Mitte des 18 Jahrhunderts. München, 1851.
Müller, A., Galileo Galilei und das kopernikanische Weltsystem. Freiburg, 1909.
Müller, A., Nikolaus Kopernikus, der Altmeister der neueren Astronomie. Ein Lebens-und Kulturbild. Freiburg, 1898.
Müller, J., Das Friedenswerk der Kirche in den letzten drei Jahrhunderten. Berlin, 1926.
Muñoz, Ant., Roma barocca. Milano-Roma, 1919.
Muratori, L. A., Annali d'Italia dal principio dell'era volgare sino all'anno, 1749. 12 Vols., Milano, 1742–9.
Muratori, Il, Raccolta di documenti storici inediti o rari. Roma, 1892 seqq.
Muther, R., Geschichte der Malerei. 3 Vols., Leipzig, 1909.
Mutinelli, Storia arcana d'Italia. Vol. 1, Venezia, 1855.

Nani, G., Relazione di Roma, 1640, in Barozzi-Berchet, Roma, II. 9–42.
Narducci, H., Catalogus codicum manuscriptorum in Bibliotheca Angelica. Romae, 1893.

Navenne, F. de, Rome, le Palais Farnèse et les Farnèse. Paris [1913].
Negri, P., Urbano VIII. e l'Italia, in the *Nuova Rivista stor. VI.* (1922).
Negri, P., La guerra per la successione di Mantova. Prato, 1924.
Nibby, A., Le mura di Roma. Roma, 1820.
Nicii Erythraei, Iani, Pinacotheca imaginum illustrium. Coloniae, 1632.
Nicolai, Memorie, leggi ed osservazioni sulle campagne e sull'Annona di Roma. Roma, 1803.
Nols, v. Callewaert.
Novaes, G. de, Storia de'pontefici. Vols. 8 u. 9, Siena, 1805.

Opel, J. O., Der niedersächsisch-dänische Krieg. 3 Vols., Magdeburg, 1874-1894.
Orbaan, J. A. F., Bescheiden in Italië omtrent nederlandsch Kunstenaars. 's Gravenhage, 1911.
Orbaan, J. A. F., Der Abbruch von Alt-St-Peter, in Jahrbuch der preuss, Kunstsammlungen, Appendix to Vol. 39, Berlin, 1919, S. 1 seqq.
Orbaan, J. A. F., Documenti sul barocco. Roma, 1920.

Pagès, Histoire de la religion chrétienne au Japon. Paris, 1869-1870.
Pagliucchi, P., I castellani del Castel S. Angelo. 2 Vols., Roma, 1928.
Pallavicino, Sforza, Della vita di Alessandro VII. Prato, 1840.
Pappus, L., Epitome rerum germanicarum ab anno 1617 ad annum 1648, ed. L. Arndts. 2 Vols., Wien, 1856-8.
Parent, P., L'architecture des Pays-Bas méridionaux au 16e-18e siècles. Paris, 1926.
Pascal-Wendrock = Litterae provinciales Lud. Montaltii a Will. Wendrockio [Nicole] translatae. Coloniae, 1658.
Pascoli, L., Vite de 'pittori, scultori ed architetti moderni. 2 Vols., Roma, 1730-1742.
Passeri, G. B., Vite de' pittori, scultori ed architetti che hanno lavorato in Roma, morti dal 1641 fino al 1673. Roma, 1772.
Passerini, Alcune lettere del card. Ippolito Aldobrandini a Carlo Emanuele, Duca di Savoia. Roma, 1881.
Pastor, L. v., Die Stadt Rom zu Ende der Renaissance. 4-6th edition. Freiburg, 1925.
Pasture, A., La restauration religieuse aux Pays-Bas catholiques sous les archiducs Albert et Isabelle (1596-1633). Louvain, 1925.
[*Patouillet, Louis*], Dictionnaire des livres jansénistes. 4 Vols., Anvers, 1752.
Paulus, N., Hexenwahn und Hexenprozess vornehmlich im 16 Jahrh. Freiburg, 1910.
Perraud, A., L'Oratoire de France. 2nd edition. Paris, 1866.
Perrens, F., Les mariages espagnoles sous Henri IV. Paris, 1869.

Perrens, F., L'Eglise et l'Etat en France sous Henri IV. 2 Vols., Paris, 1872.
Pesaro, G., Relazione di Roma 1630-1632, in Barozzi-Berchet, 3 Serie : Roma I., 317-348.
Petit de Julleville, L., Histoire de la langue et de la littérature française des origines à 1900. 8 Vols., Paris, 1896 seqq.
Petrucelli della Gattina, F., Histoire diplomatique des conclaves. Vol. 2 seqq, Paris, 1864 seqq.
Pflugh-Harttung, J. v., Weltgeschichte. Neuzeit. Berlin, 1908.
Pfotenhauer, Die Missionen der Jesuiten in Paraguay. 3 Vols., Gütersloh, 1891-3.
Philippi, A., Die Kunst der Nachblüte in Italien. Leipzig, 1900.
Phillips, G. J., Das Regalienrecht in Frankreich. Halle, 1873.
Phillips, G. J., Kirchenrecht. Vols. 1-7, Regensburg, 1845-1872 ; Vol. 8, Part 1, by F. H. Bering, *ibid.*, 1889.
Piccolomini, P., Carteggio di Fabio Chigi poi Papa Alessandro VII. Siena, 1908.
Pichler, A., Geschichte der kirchlichen Trennung zwischen dem Orient und Okzident von den ersten Anfängen bis zur jüngsten Gegenwart. 2 Vols., München, 1864-5.
Picot, Essai historique sur l'influence de la réligion en France pendant le XVIIe. siècle. Vol. 1, Louvain, 1824.
Pieper, A., Die Propaganda-Kongregation und die Nordischen Missionen im 17 Jahrh. Köln, 1886.
Pierling, P., Rome et Démétrius. Paris, 1878.
Pierling, P., La Russie et le Saint-Siège. Vol. 1 seqq, Paris, 1896 seqq.
Piolet, J.-B., Les Missions catholiques françaises. 6 Vols., Paris, 1902-3.
Pirenne, H., Geschichte Belgiens. Vol. 4, Gotha, 1909.
Pistolesi, E., Il Vaticano descritto ed illustrato. 8 Vols., Roma, 1829-1838.
Platner-Bunsen, Beschreibung der Stadt Rom, von Ernst Platner, Karl Bunsen, Eduard Gerhard und Wilhelm Rostell. 3 Vols. Stuttgart und Tübingen, 1829-1842.
Pollak, Fr., Lorenzo Bernini. Eine Studie. Stuttgart, 1909.
Pollak, O., Alessandro Algardi (1602-1654) als Architekt, in Zeitschrift für Geschichte der Architektur Dez. 1910, Jan., 1911.
Pollak, O., Künstlerbriefe. (Beiheft zum Jahrbuch der preuss. Kunstsammlungen Vol. 34.) Berlin, 1913.
Pollak, O., Die Kunsttätigkeit unter Urban VIII. Aus dem Nachlass hrsg. by D. Frey, unter Mitwirkung von Fr. Juraschek. Wien-Augsburg-Köln [1927].
Poncelet, Alfred, La Compagnie de Jésus en Belgique. Without date or place of publication.
Portrait Index, ed. by W. Coolidge Lane and Nina E. Browne. Washington, 1906.
Posse, H., Das Deckenfresko des Pietro da Cortona im Palazzo Barberini und die Deckenmalerei in Rom, in Jahrbuch der preuss. Kunstsammlungen XL. (1919), 91 seqq.

Posse, H., Der römische Maler Andrea Sacchi. Leipzig, 1925.
Prat Jan Marie, Recherches historiques et critiques sur la Compagnie de Jésus en France du temps du P. Coton, 1564-1626. 5 Vols., Lyon, 1876-8.
Premoli, O., Storia dei Barnabiti nel Seicento. Roma, 1913.
Presenzini, A., Vita ed opere del pittore A. Camessei. Assisi, 1880.
Prinzivalli, Gli Anni Santi. Appunti storici con molte note inedite. Roma, 1899.
Prunel, L., La réforme catholique en France au 17e siècle. Paris, 1921.
Puyol, Edmund Richer, Etude sur la rénovation du gallicanisme au commencement du XVIIe. siècle. 2 Vols., Paris, 1876.

Quartalschrift, Römische, für christliche Altertumskunde und für Kirchengeschichte. Ed. by A. de Waal, H. Finke und St. Ehses. Jahrg, 1 *seqq.*, Rom, 1887 *seqq.*
Quartalschrift, Tübinger Theologische. Jahrg, 1 *seqq.*, Tübingen, 1819 *seqq.*
Quazza, R., Politica Europea nella questione Valtellinica. La Lega Franco-Veneto-Savoiarda e la Pace di Monçon. Venezia, 1921.
Quazza, R., La guerra per la successione di Mantova e del Monferrato (1628-1631). Mantova, 1926.
Quellen zur Schweizer Geschichte. Ed. by the Allg. Geschichtsforschenden Gesellschaft der Schweiz, 1 *seq.*, Basel, 1877 *seq.*
Quellen und Forschungen aus italienischen Bibliotheken und Archiven. Ed. by the Preuss. Hist. Institut. Vol. 1 *seqq.*

Ranke, L. v., Französische Geschichte vornehmlich im 16 und 17 Jahrh. 1-2 Vols., 2nd ed., Stuttgart, 1856 (1st ed., 1854).
Ranke, L. v., Englische Geschichte. Vol. 1 *seq.*, Berlin, 1859 *seq.*
Ranke, L. v., Zur deutschen Geschichte vom Religionsfrieden bis zum 30 Jährigen Kriege. Leipzig, 1868.
Ranke, L. v., Die Osmanen und die spanische Monarchie im 16 u. 17 Jahrh. 4th ed. of the work entitled : Fürsten und Völker von Südeuropa im 16, und 17 Jahrh. Leipzig, 1877.
Ranke, L. v., Die römischen Päpste in den letzten vier Jahrhunderten, 1 u. 3. Vols. 6-7 Ed. Leipzig, 1885.
Rapin, R., Histoire du Jansénisme, ed. by Domenech. Paris, 1861.
Räss, A., Die Konvertiten seit der Reformation nach ihrem Leben und aus ihren Schriften dargestellt. 13 Vols., Freiburg, 1866-1880.
Raumer, Briefe aus Paris zur Erläuterung der Geschichte des 16 und 17 Jahrhunderts. Leipzig, 1831.
Raupach, B., Das evangelische Österreich oder historische Nachricht von den vornehmsten Schicksalen der evangelisch-lutherischen Kirche im Erzherzogtum Österreich. Hamburg, 1732-1744.

Real-Enzyklopädie für protest. Theologie und Kirche begründet und herausg. von J. J. Herzog. 23 Vols., 3rd ed., von A. Hauck. Leipzig, 1896-1909.
Reiffenberg, Fr., Historia Societatis Iesu ad Rhenum inferiorem ab a 1540 ad 1626. Coloniae, 1764.
Reinhardt, H., Die Korrespondenz von Alfonso und Girolamo Casati, spanischen Gesandten in der Schweizerischen Eidgenoßenschaft, mit Erzherzog Leopold V. von Österreich 1620 bis 1623. Fribourg, in Switzerland, 1894.
Rela ye Nuncyus ów Apostolskich i innych osób o Polsce od roku 1548 do 1690, ed. E. Rykaczewski. Vol. 1, Berlin-Poznań, 1864.
Renazzi, F. M., Storia dell'università degli studi di Roma, detta la Sapienza. 2 Vols., Roma, 1803 *seqq*.
Reumont, A. v., Beiträge zur italienischen Geschichte. 6 Vols., Berlin, 1853-1857.
Reumont, A., Bibliografia dei lavori pubblicati in Germania sulla storia d'Italia. Berlino, 1863.
Reumont, A. v., Geschichte der Stadt Rom. Vol. 3, Berlin, 1870.
Reumont, A. v., Geschichte Toskanas. 1 Part, Gotha, 1876.
Reusch, H., Der Index der verbotenen Bücher. 2 Vols., Bonn, 1883-5.
Reusch, Bellarmins Selbstbiographie, ed. by Reusch and Döllinger. Bonn, 1887.
Revue historique. Vol. 1 *seqq*. Paris, 1876 *seqq*.
Revue des questions historiques. Livraison 1 *seqq*. Paris, 1866 *seqq*.
Reymond, U., Le Bernin. Paris, 1910.
Rezek, A., Geschichte Böhmens und Mährens unter Ferdinand III. bis zum Ende des Dreissigjährigen Krieges. 2 Vols., Prag, 1890 (in Czech.).
Ricci, C., Baukunst und dekorative Skulptur der Barockzeit in Italien. Stuttgart, 1912.
Riccius, Ios., De bellis Germanicis. Venetiis, 1644.
Richter, Wilh., Geschichte der Paderborner Jesuiten. 1 Part, Paderhorn, 1882.
Ricotti, Erc., Storia della monarchia Piemontese. 6 Vols., Firenze, 1861 *seqq*.
Rieger, P., und H. Vogelstein, Geschichte der Juden in Rom. 2 Vols., Berlin, 1895 *seqq*.
Riegl, A., Die Entstehung der Barockkunst in Rom. Wien, 1908.
Riezler, S., Geschichte Bayerns. Vols. 4-6, Gotha, 1899 *seq*.
Ripoll, see Bullarium ord. Praed.
Ritter, M., Deutsche Geschichte im Zeitalter der Gegenreformation und des Dreissigjährigen Krieges (1555-1648). 3 Vols., Stuttgart, 1889-1908.
Ritter, M., Über den Ursprung des Restitutionsediktes, in der Histor. Zeitschrift LXXVI. (1896), 62-102.
Rivista storica italiana. Vol. 1 *seqq*. Torino, 1884 *seqq*.
Roca, E., Le grand siècle intime. Le régne de Richelieu 1617-1642 d'après des documents originaux. Paris, 1906.

Rocco da Cesinale, Storia delle missioni dei Cappuccini. 3 Vols., Parigi, 1867.
Rodocanachi, E., Le St. Siège et les Juifs. Le Ghetto à Rome. Paris, 1891.
Rodocanachi, E., Le Capitole Romain antique et moderne. Paris, 1904.
Rodocanachi, E., Le château Saint-Ange. Paris, 1909.
Rodocanachi, E., Les monuments de Rome après la chute de l'Empire. Paris, 1914.
Rodocanachi, E., La Réforme en Italie. 2 Vols., Paris, 1920-1.
Roma. Rivista di studi o di vita romana, diretta da Carlo Galassi Paluzzi. Roma, 1922 *seqq.*
Romanin, S., Storia documentata di Venezia. 10 Vols., Venezia, 1853-1861.
Rose, H., Spätbarock. München, 1922.
Rott, E., Histoire de la représentation diplomatique de la France auprès des cantons Suisses. Vol. 3, L'affaire de la Valtelline, 1610-1626. Berne, 1907.
Rühs, Chr. Fr., Geschichte Schwedens. 1-5 (Allg. Hallische Weltgeschichte. Vols. 63-6). Halle, 1905.
Rule, History of the Inquisition. 2 Vols. (2nd ed.), London, 1874.
Russo, R., La politica del Vaticano nella dieta di 1630, in Arch. stor. ital. 7. Serie V., Firenze, 1926, 25-88, 233-286.

Sägmüller, Joh. Bapt., Die Papstwahlbullen und das staatliche Recht der Exklusive. Tübingen, 1892.
Sainte-Beuve, C. A., Port-Royal. 4th ed., Paris, 1878.
Salvatori, Ph. M., Vita della s. madre Angela Merici. Roma, 1807.
Scala, Ferd. della, Fidelis von Sigmaringen, ein Lebens- und Zeitbild. Mainz, 1896.
Schaeffer, E., Van Dyck. Des Meisters Gemälde in 537 Abbildungen, ed. by E. Sch. Stuttgart, 1909.
Schäfer, H., Geschichte von Portugal. 5 Vols., Hamburg, 1836 *seqq.*
Schlosser, Julius v., Materialien zur Quellenkunde der Kunstgeschichte. Wien (Sitzungsberichte der Akademie), 1914 *seqq.*
Schlosser, Julius, Die Kunstliteratur. Wien, 1924.
Schmerber, Hugo, Betrachtungen über die italienische Malerei im 17 Jahrh. Strassburg, 1906.
Schmidl, I., Historiae Societatis Jesu provinciae Bohmiae Pars I.-IV. Pragae, 1747-1759.
Schmidlin, J., Geschichte der deutschen Nationalkirche in Rom, S. Maria dell'Anima. Freiburg, 1906.
Schmidlin, J., Die Restaurationstätigkeit der Breslauer Fürstbischöfe nach ihren frühesten Statusberichten an den römischen Stuhl. Rom, 1907.
Schmidlin, J., Katholische Missionsgeschichte. Steyl, 1925.

Schmidt, J., Die katholische Restauration in den ehemaligen Kurmainzer Herrschaften Königstein und Rieneck. (Erl. und Erg. zu Janssens Geschichte des deutschen Volkes, ed. by L. Pastor.) Freiburg, 1902.
Schnitzer, J., Zur Politik des Heiligen Stuhles in der ersten Hälfte des Dreiszigjährigen Krieges, in der Röm. Quartalschrift XII. (1899).
Schreiber, Th., Die antiken Bildwerke der Villa Ludovisi in Rom. Leipzig, 1880.
Schudt, L., Giulio Mancini. Viaggio per Roma per vedere le pitture. Leipzig, 1923.
Schulte, Joh. Friedr. v., Die Geschichte der Quellen und Literatur des kanonischen Rechts von der Mitte des 16 Jahrh. bis zur Gegenwart. 3 Vols. (2nd Part), Stuttgart, 1880.
Schwager, Die Heidenmission der Gegenwart. 2 Vols., Steyl, 1907 u. 1909.
Schwicker, J. H., P. Pázmány und seine Zeit. Köln, 1 88.
Scriptores rerum Polonicarum. Vol. 14 : Historici diarii domus professae Societatis Iesu Cracoviensis. Cracoviae, 1889.
Segesser, A. Ph. v., Rechtsgeschichte der Stadt und Republik Luzern. 4 Vols., Luzern, 1851–1888.
Seminario Pontificio Romano. Roma, 1914.
Sentis, F. J., Die *Monarchia Sicula*. Eine his orisch-kanonistische Untersuchung. Freiburg, 1869.
Sentis, F., Clementis Papae VIII. Decretales quae vulgo nuncupantur Liber septimus Decretalium Clementis VIII., primum edidit, annotatione critica et historica instruxit, constitutionibus recentioribus sub titulis competentibus insertis auxit F. S. Friburgi Br., 1870.
Serafini, C., Le monete e le bolle plumb e pontificie del Medagliere Vaticano. 4 Vols., Roma, 1910 seqq.
Serbat, L., Les assemblées du clergé de France. Paris, 1906.
Serra, L., Domenichino. Roma, 1909.
Severano, G., Memorie sacre delle sette chiese di Roma. Roma, 1630.
Sinnacher, F. A., Beiträge zur Geschichte der bischöflichen Kirche Säben und Brixen in Tirol. Vols. 7 and 8. Brixen, 1830 u. 1832.
Siri, V., Memorie recondite dall'anno 1601 all'anno 1641. 2 Vols., Ronco-Paris-Lyon, 1677–9.
Smolka, Stanislaus v., Die Reussiche Welt. Historisch- politische Studien. Vergangenheit und Gegenwart. Wien, 1916.
Sobotka, G., Die Bildhauerei der Barockzeit, ed. by Teitze. Wien, 1927.
Soden, Fr. v., Gustav Adolph und sein Heer in Süddeutschland. 3 Vols., Erlangen, 1865 seqq.
Solerti, Aug., Vita di Torquato Tasso. 3 Vols., Torino, 1895.
Sommervogel, C., S. J., Bibliothèque de la Compagnie de Jésus, p.p. de Backer. Nouv. éd., 9 Vols., Bruxelles-Paris, 1890-1900.
Spicilegio Vaticano di documenti inediti e rari estratti dagli archivi e dalla bibl. della Sede Apost. Vol. 1, Roma, 1890.

Spicilegium Ossoriense, being a collection of original Letters and Papers illustrative of the History of the Irish Church from the Reformation to the year 1800, by P. F. Moran. 2 Vols., Dublin, 1877 u. 1878.

Spillmann, Joseph, S.J., Geschichte der Katholikenverfolgung in England 1535-1681. 4 Parts: Die Blutzeugen unter Jakob I., Karl I. und dem Commonwealth 1603 bis 1654. Freiburg, 1905.

Steinberger, L., Die Jesuiten und die Friedensfrage in der Zeit vom Prager Frieden bis zum Nürnberger Friedensexekutionshauptrezess 1635-1650. Freiburg, 1907.

Steinhuber, Andr., Geschichte des Kollegium Germanikum Hungarikum in Rom. Vol. 1, 2nd ed., Freiburg, 1906.

Steinmann, E., Die Sixtinische Kapelle. 2 Vols., München, 1901-1905.

Stimmen aus Maria-Laach. Vol. 1 *seqq.* Freiburg, 1871 *seqq.*

Streit, R., Bibliotheca Missionum. Monasterii, 1916.

Strong, E., La Chiesa Nuova (S. Maria in Vallicella). Roma, 1923.

Studi e documenti di storia e diritto. Pubblicazione periodica dell'Accademia di conferenze storico-giuridiche. 1st year, *seqq.* Roma, 1880 *seqq.*

Stuve, C., Geschichte der Stadt Osnabrück. 2 Vols., Jena, 1816-1820.

Stuve, C., Geschichte des Hochstifts Osnabrück. 3 Vols., Jena, 1853-1882.

Synopsis Actorum S. Sedis in causa Societatis Iesu, 1605-1773. Lovanii, 1895. In MS. and for private circulation only: quotations refer to Synopsis II.

Tacchi Venturi, P., Storia della Compagnia di Gesù in Italia. Vol. 1, Roma, 1909.

Tacchi Venturi, P., Opere storiche di M. Ricci. 2 Vols., Macerata, 1911-13.

Taja, Agostino, Descrizione del Palazzo Apostolico Vaticano. Opera postuma . . . revista ed accresciuta. Roma, 1750.

Tetius, Hier., Aedes Barberinae ad Quirinalem descriptae. Romae, 1642.

Theiner, Aug., Codex diplomaticus dominii temporalis S. Sedis. Recueil de documents pour servir à l'histoire du gouvernement temporel des états du Saint-Siège, extraits des Archives du Vatican. Vol. 3, 1389-1793. Rome, 1862.

Theiner, Aug., Vetera monumenta Poloniae et Lithuaniae gentiumque finitimarum historiam illustrantia ad maximam partem nondum edita, ex tabulariis Vaticanis deprompta, collecta ac serie chronologica disposita ab A. Th. Vol. 3: A Sixto PP. V. usque ad Innocentium PP. XII., 1585-1696. Romae, 1863.

Thieme, U., und Becker, F., Allgemeines Lexikon der Bildenden Künstler von der Antike bis zur Gegenwart. Vol. 1 *seqq.* Leipzig, 1907 *seqq.*

Thomas, A., Histoire de la mission de Pékin. Paris, 1923.
Thuanus, I. A., Historiae sui temporis. Paris-Orléans, 1604–1620.
Tiraboschi, G., Storia della letteratura italiana. 10 Vols., Modena, 1772 seqq.
Titi, F., Descrizione delle pitture, sculture e architetture esposte al pubblico in Roma. Roma, 1763.
Tomassetti, Giuseppe, La Campagna Romana antica, medioevale e moderna. Vols. 1–4, Roma, 1910 seq.
Tomba, Ph. N., Arcivescovi di Bologna. Bologna, 1787.
Tomek, W. W., Geschichte Böhmens. Prag, 1864.
Totti, L., Ritratto di Roma moderna. Roma, 1639.
Tupetz, Th., Der Streit um die geistlichen Güter und das Restitutionsedikt 1629. Wien, 1883.
Turgenevius (Turgenjew), A. I., Historica Russiae monumenta. Vol. 2, Petropoli, 1842.

Ughelli, F., Italia sacra, sive de episcopis Italiae et insularum adiacentium rebusque ab iis gestis opus. Editio 2, ed. N. Coletus. 10 Vols., Venetiis, 1717 bis 1722.
Ugolini, F., Storia dei Conti e Duchi d'Urbino. Firenze, 1859.

Vacant, see *Dictionnaire*.
Vandenpeereboom, A., Cornelius Jansénius, septième évêque d'Ypres, sa mort, son testament, ses épitaphes. Bruges, 1882.
Venanzio da Lago Santo, Apostolo e diplomatico: Il P. Giacinto dei Conti Natta da Casale Monferrato Cappuccino. Milano, 1886.
Venuti, R., Numismata Rom. Pontificum praestantiora a Martino V. ad Benedictum XIV. Romae, 1744.
Villa-Urritia, De, El Palacio Barberini. Madrid, 1925.
Voll, Karl, Malerei des 17 Jahrh. Leipzig, 1917.
Voss, H., Die Malerei der Spät-Renaissance in Rom und Florenz. 2 Vols., Berlin, 1920.
Voss, H., Die Barock-Malerei in Rom. Berlin, 1925.

Waal, A. de., Der Campo Santo der Deutschen zu Rom. Geschichte der Nationalen Stiftung. Freiburg, 1896.
Wahrmund, L., Das Ausschliessungsrecht (ius exclusivae) bei den Papstwahlen. Wien, 1889.
Weech, F. v., Badi che Geschichte. Karlsruhe, 1890.
Weisbach, W., Der Barock als Kunst der Gegenreformation. Berlin, 1921.
Wenzelburger, K. Th., Geschichte der Niederlande. 2 Vols., Gotha, 1886.
Werner, K., Geschichte der apologetischen und polemischen Literatur der christlichen Theologie. 4 Vols., Schaffhausen, 1865.

Wessels, C., Early Jesuit Travellers in Central Asia. The Hague, 1924.
Widmann, H., Geschichte Salzburgs. 3 Vols., Gotha, 1907.
Wiedemann, Th., Geschichte der Reformation und Gegenreformation im Lande unter der Enns. Vols. 1–5, Prag, 1879 seqq.
Wiens, E., Fancan und die französische Politik 1624–1627. Heidelberg, 1908.
Wilpert, J., Die Römischen Mosaiken und Malereien der kirchlichen Bauten vom 4 bis 13 Jahrh. 4 Vols., Freiburg, 1916; 2nd ed. ibid., 1917.
Winter, G., Geschichte des Dreissigjährigen Krieges. Berlin, 1893.
Wirz, K., Bullen und Breven aus italienischen Archiven. (Quellen zur Schweizer Geschichte XXI.) Basel, 1902.
Wittich, K., Magdeburg, Gustav Adolph und Tilly. Berlin, 1874.
Wohlwill, Emil, Galileo Galilei und sein Kampf für die kopernikanische Lehre. 2 Vols., Hamburg-Leipzig, 1909, 1926.
Wölfflin, H., Renaissance und Barock. 4th ed. by Rose. München, 1926.
Woltmann, Alfred, Geschichte der Malerei. 3 Vols., Leipzig, 1879–1882.

Zaleski, K. St., Jesuici w Polsce. Vols. 1–4, Lwow, 1900 seqq.
Zeitschrift, Historische, ed. by H. v. Sybel. Vol. 1 seqq. München-Leipzig, 1859 seqq.
Zeitschrift für katholische Theologie. Vol. 1 seqq. Innsbruck, 1877 seqq.
Zeitschrift für Kirchengeschichte, ed. by Brieger. Vol. 1 seqq. Gotha, 1877 seqq.
Zeitschrift für Missionswissenschaft, ed. by J. Schmidlin. Vol. 1 seqq. Munster i. W., 1911 seqq.
Zeller, B., Etudes critiques sur le règne de Louis XIII. Le connétable de Luynes, Montauban et la Valtelline. Paris, 1879.
Zeller, B., Richelieu et les ministres de Louis XIII. de 1621 à 1624. Paris, 1880.
Zeno, Renier, Relazione di Roma 1621–1623, in Barozzi-Berchet, Roma, I., 139–193.
Zinkeisen, J. M., Geschichte des osmanischen Reiches in Europa. 4 Parts, Gotha, 1840 seqq.
Zwiedineck-Südenhorst, H. v., Die Politik Benedigs während des Dreissigjährigen Krieges. 2 Vols., Stuttgart, 1882–1885.

TABLE OF CONTENTS OF VOLUME XXVII.

INTRODUCTION.

A.D.		PAGE
	Era of Paul III.	1
	Movements of reform	2
	Pontificates of Pius IV.	4
	Pius V.	5
	Gregory XIII. and	7
	Sixtus V.	8
	Solution of French problems	9
	Clement VIII.	10
	Paul V.	12
	Baroque Art	13
	European position	15
	Gregory XV.	16
	Urban VIII.	18
	Cardinal Richelieu	19
	Protestantism threatened	20
	The Thirty Years' War	21
	Policy of Richelieu and of	24
	Urban VIII.	25

CHAPTER I.

ELECTION, ANTECEDENTS AND CHARACTER OF GREGORY XV.—THE LUDOVISI.

1621	Cardinals concerned in the election of Gregory XV.	29
	Discussions in the Conclave	32
	Conflict of parties	34
	Agreement on Ludovisi	39
	Election of Gregory XV.	41
	Character of the new Pope	42
	His previous career as	43
	Referendary of the Segnatura and	44
	Archbishop of Bologna	45
	His personal characteristics	47
	Cardinal Ludovisi—	51
	His tact and ability	54
	Nepotism of Gregory XV.	55
	The Nephew's Villas	57
	Cardinal Ludovisi as patron of Art	60
	His charities	64
	The relatives of the Pope	65

A.D.		PAGE
	Foundation of the *Accademia dei virtuosi*	69
	Giovan Battista Agucchi	70
	Attacks on the Pope and the Nephews	72
	Gregory XV.'s admonitions to Ludovisi	74

CHAPTER II.

GREGORY XV.'S ACTIVITY WITHIN THE CHURCH—CREATIONS OF CARDINALS—BULL ON PAPAL ELECTIONS—CANONIZATIONS—FURTHERING OF THE ORDER.

A.D.		PAGE
1621	Creation of Cardinals	86
	Their names and characteristics	87
	Further creations	88
	The Pope's relations with his Cardinals	91
	The death of Bellarmine	92
	Papal efforts for the release of Klesl	93
	Which was obtained	95
	Imprisonment of Lerma	96
	Remonstrances of the Pope	97
	Situation in Spain	98
	Antagonism of Venice	101
	Instruction to Venetian Nunzio	103
	Action of the Inquisition	105
	Reconciliation of de Dominis	106
	Extension of the Inquisition's powers	107
	Reform of Papal Elections	108
	The Bull promulgating new regulations	115
	A second Bull	118
	Devotion of Gregory XV. to the Saints	119
	Canonizations	120
	Observance of festivals	123
	Foundation of Religious Institutes	125
	Cardinal Ludovisi's esteem for Jesuits and Capuchins	127

CHAPTER III.

FOUNDATION OF PROPAGANDA AND STATE OF THE MISSIONS—POSITION OF CATHOLICS IN HOLLAND AND ENGLAND.

A.D.		PAGE
1622	Foundation and Origin of Propaganda	129
	Its scope and	133
	Finance	134
	The division of its work and	135
	Its ministry	137
	Canonical visitations	138
	The Jesuits in the East and	142

TABLE OF CONTENTS.

A.D.		PAGE
	In Africa	145
	The Franciscans in India	146
	Jesuit missions there and	147
	In China	149
	Mission work in Japan	150
	In America and	151
	In Northern Europe	153
	Oppression in Holland	154
	Difficulties in England	156
1621	Suggested Spanish marriage	159
	Anti-Catholic excitement in Parliament	161
	Violent speeches	164
	Dissolution of Parliament	166
	The Spanish marriage again	167
	More exacting conditions imposed by Rome	168
	Character of the Infanta Maria	171
	Her reluctance to the match	173
	Further negotiations	174
1623	Prince Charles in Madrid	176
	The efforts of Olivares	179
	Are defeated	180
	The Pope's anxiety for the match	181
	To bring amelioration to English Catholics	182
	Thus the Dispensation was granted	183
	Further difficulties and delays	187
	Gregory's letter to Prince Charles	189
	Its reception with "utmost reverence"	190
	Further letter to King James	191
	James I.'s difficulties	193
	Antagonism in England	195
	Marriage treaty signed in vain	196

CHAPTER IV.

PROGRESS OF THE CATHOLIC REFORMATION AND RESTORATION IN FRANCE, SWITZERLAND AND THE GERMAN EMPIRE—DEATH OF GREGORY XV.

1621	The struggle for Catholic Restoration	196
	The Valtellina dispute	197
1621	The Mission of Corona in Turin	206
	And in Paris—	207
	Its failure—	209
	The Articles of Milan	211
1622	The Murder of St. Fidelis of Sigmaringen	212
	Subjugation of the Grisons	213
1623	The League of Lyons	215
1623	Papal troops enter the Valtellina	218
	Final settlement still under discussion	219

A.D.		PAGE
	When Gregory XV.'s death supervened	220
	Instruction to French Nunzio	221
	Stressing reform of Clergy and	222
	Supervision of literary publications	223
	Conversion of the Duke de Lesdiguières	225
	Church reform in France and Netherlands	227
	Briefs sent to German Princes	228
	Instruction to the Nunzio Carafa	231
	Papal subsidies to the Emperor	235
	Methods of raising the necessary money	237
	Activities of Maximilian of Bavaria	238
	Further Papal subsidies	241
	Capitulations in the Rhine Palatinate	243
	The Palatine Library is	244
1622	Presented to the Holy See	245
	Transport of the Library	247
	Controversy over the Electorate	249
	Papal support of Maximilian	251
	Secret transfer of the Electorate	255
	Brief of December, 1621, to the Emperor	257
	Giacinto da Casale's failure at Madrid	259
	Carafa more successful in Vienna	260
	Opposition of Elector of Mayence	261
1623	Maximilian becomes an Elector	263
	Satisfaction of the Holy See	265
	Papal congratulations—	266
	Action of Gregory XV. in Bohemia	267
	Lamormaini's Report on that country	269
	Suggestions for Catholic Restoration therein	273
	Carafa's policy as Nuncio	275
	The great work of the Jesuits	282
	Fifteen Missions founded by them	283
	Their devotion to works of charity and education	285
	Catholic Restoration in the Palatinate	287
	Ill-health of Gregory XV.	288
	His death on July 8th, 1623	289
	Criticism of his Government	290
	Significance of his Pontificate	292
	Revival of Religious sentiment	293

LIST OF UNPUBLISHED DOCUMENTS IN APPENDIX.

		PAGE
1	On the Policy of Urban VIII. during the Thirty Years' War	300
2	The Papabili before the Opening of the Conclave of 1621	316
3	Programme for the Reform of the Church in Germany presented to Gregory XV. by the Nuncio of Cologne, Ant. Albergati	317
4	Giunti's Life of Cardinal Ludovisi	320
5	Jacopo Accarisi's Biography of Gregory XV	326
6	Antonio Possevino to the Duke of Mantua. July 16th, 1621	327
7	Antonio Possevino to the Duke of Mantua. August 14th, 1621	327

GREGORY XV. 1621-1623.

INTRODUCTION.

THE two niches which flank the altar of the apse of St. Peter's, are filled by the magnificent monuments of Paul III. and Urban VIII. whose unusually long pontificates are like milestones in the story of the Popes.[1] The monument of the Farnese Pope, the work of Guglielmo della Porta, is a valuable creation of the late renaissance, whereas that of Urban VIII., a masterpiece from the chisel of Bernini, belongs to the baroque period. The century between the election of Paul III. and the death of Urban VIII. (1534-1644), is one of the most important and most brilliant epochs in the history of the papacy, the Catholic reformation and restoration forming its outstanding characteristics.

The era which opened with Paul III. was one of internal renewal as well as of resistance to Protestantism which was then raising its head in threatening fashion in every European country, Italy not excepted. In view of the ever increasing apostasy of the Germanic peoples, a like action was to be feared on the part of the Romance and Slavonic nations. A peculiar light is thrown upon the situation by the inscription which John Oldecop, a genuinely Catholic chronicler, had affixed to his house at Hildesheim in the year 1549: "Virtue perishes, the Church is shaken, the clergy err, the devil rules, simony prevails, God's word endures for ever."[2] As a matter of fact, once again the promise was verified which was made to the first Pope, and which sparkles in letters of gold from the dome of St. Peter's. By the wondrous leading of Providence

---

[1] The length of Paul III.'s reign was 15 years, that of Urban VIII. 20 years and 11 months. Of all the successors of Peter until now, only nine have lived longer than the Barberini Pope; see v. LOBKOWITZ, *Statistik der Päpste*, Freiburg, 1905, 69.

[2] See JANSSEN-PASTOR, VIII. [13-14], 427.

this fresh and heavy trial proved, in the end, of great benefit to the Church. Though bleeding from a thousand wounds and bewailing the loss of some of her noblest members, the Church not only withstood the storm of the religious revolution, she also found the way to an internal renewal. The heavy struggle renewed her strength, and her adversaries could not but be astonished at her wonderful spiritual vigour and incomparable powers of recuperation.

The regeneration of the Church came from within. As so often happens when great changes occur, here also the beginnings were most humble. The movement of reform, at first wholly unconnected with the perils that threatened from without by reason of the rise of Protestantism, had begun in most unobtrusive fashion with the "Oratories of divine love" at Vicenza, Genoa and Rome. The first impulse came, not from the Holy See, but from men animated by the Spirit of God, who, tenacious of the treasure of the ancient faith and inspired by obedience to lawfully constituted ecclesiastical authority, first sought their own personal sanctification and only then thought of the amendment of their contemporaries. The occupants of Peter's chair approved and confirmed the aims of Carafa, Giberti and Ignatius and thus made it possible for the efforts of these men to gain strength and efficacy within the Church. In the end the Popes took the lead in the movement, so much so that the history of the reform almost coincides with that of the Holy See. By degrees the Catholic reform, which had displaced the renaissance, also permeated the social, literary, scientific and artistic life.

By a special dispensation of Providence, at a time when Peter's barque was battered by tempestuous seas, the helm was entrusted to men of such excellent character as no other princely throne could boast.[1] Though they differed greatly as regards birth, age, temperament and character, every one of them devoted himself wholeheartedly and intelligently to the solution of the fresh problems raised by the new age.

[1] This is the opinion of L. v. Ranke in a letter to his brother Henry on February 2, 1827; see DOVE, *Zur eigenen Lebensgeschichte von L. v. Ranke*, ed. by Dove, Leipzig, 1890, 164.

Paul III., whose reign of fifteen years (1534-1549) marks the transition from the renaissance to the Catholic reform, remained to a large extent the child of the worldly period in which he had grown up, especially as regards nepotism; but for all that, he discharged his ecclesiastical duties in a way that differed greatly from that of the Medici Popes. The opening of the General Council for which the whole of Christendom longed so ardently and prayed so insistently, the suppression of numerous abuses, the elevation of many excellent men to the College of Cardinals, the checking of apostasy from the faith, chiefly in Italy, by the creation of the Roman Inquisition, the fostering of foreign missions and the new Orders, such as the Theatines, the Barnabites, the Somaschans, the Ursulines, the Capuchins and the Jesuits—all this was due to him. If to some extent, as a consequence of his worldly tendencies, he was not the right man to secure decisive results, nevertheless, under his pontificate certain useful preparatory tasks were realized without which there could not have been any improvement of conditions within the Church.

The election, on April 9th, 1555, of Cardinal Cervini, meant a considerable triumph for the party which aimed at a strict reform within the Church, but a cruel fate seemed to have shown Marcellus II. to the world, only to withdraw him immediately in the same way as, at one time, Adrian VI. In the person of the seventy-nine year old Cardinal Carafa, the joint founder of the Theatines, a Pope took up the reins who was, in the fullest sense of the word, a man of the Catholic reform. Paul IV., a man of burning zeal, pursued, as head of the Church (1555-9), the same purpose to which he had up till then devoted his whole mind and energy. With iron determination, regardless of persons, and with the utmost vigour, he was resolved to labour for the restoration of the honour and power, the purity and dignity of the Church at that time so hard pressed by its enemies both within and without. In his idealism he sought to impose the authority of the Holy See even on the Christian princes, as had been possible during the great centuries of the Middle Ages. In this respect he failed to take note of the fact that times had changed. The Pope's policy led to disastrous conflicts, the sharpest being with Philip II. In his inexperience of the world, and from motives both ecclesiastical and national, Paul IV. risked a struggle with the Spanish world power which ended in his utter discomfiture. When he saw his political plans shattered, the Carafa Pope once more devoted all his energy to the reform within the Church and to the uprooting of heresy. If in this action he proceeded with unmeasured severity, and if his conduct bore all the marks of an inexorable repression, which caused him often enough to exceed all bounds, it is nevertheless his merit to have furthered and quickened into life the reform initiated by Paul III. and the enforcement of strict ecclesiastical principles. Thus successive Popes of the age of restoration were able to build successfully on foundations so solidly laid down.

The pontificate of Pius IV. (1559–1565), who was personally of a more worldly bent, but who had by his side an incomparable counsellor in the person of his nephew, Charles Borromeo, was one of decisive importance by reason of the reopening of the Council of Trent, notwithstanding every imaginable opposition, as well as its happy termination. Though the Council proved unable to realize the unity of the faith for the re-establishment of which it had been originally convened, it nevertheless brought into the religious situation a clarification which had long been sadly wanting. Henceforth there could be no doubt as to what was and what was not Catholic. In addition to giving to the Church a comprehensive and systematic statement of Catholic dogma, by its reform decrees the Council likewise laid down a solid foundation for the spiritual regeneration of her children.

The founder of the Jesuits once expressed himself to the effect that it was his belief that a Pope who would reform himself, the Roman Court, and the city of Rome, would also reform the world.[1] Pius V. (1566–1572) was such a man.

[1] " que tres cousas pareciam necessarias e sufficientes para qualquer papa reformar o mundo, scilicet : a reformaçao de sua mesma pessoa, a reformaçao de sua casa e a reformaçao da corte e cidade de Roma " (*Memoriale P. Consalvii*, n. 94 : *Mon. Ignat. Ser.*, 4, vol. I, p. 199, *cf.* n. 343, p. 316).

He concludes the first, and marks the transition to the second line of great Popes who carried the Catholic reform and restoration to victory. Venerated by his very contemporaries as a Saint, this son of St. Dominic, by the asceticism of his life, atoned for all the shortcomings of the Popes of the renaissance. A kindred spirit to Paul IV., but without the latter's weaknesses and mistakes, this man of steel in all matters of principle, withstood the omnipotence of the Spanish State with the same undaunted courage with which he fought the still rising flood of the religious revolt. But before all else he was determined to carry through in their totality the decrees of the Council, and to exterminate abuses which had struck deep roots during the period of the renaissance.

In the person of Pius V. the Holy See became the leader and protagonist of the Catholic reform, of which the Pope himself was the purest embodiment. Only now did the new movement gain the necessary strength in the countries which had remained true to the ancient faith. It is wonderful to see how wide-spread was the holy Pontiff's solicitude. He reformed the Roman Court, the Dataria, the Penitentiaria, the College of Cardinals and the clergy of Rome. In every Catholic country he likewise pressed for the execution of the decrees of Trent which he still further supplemented and completed. Clerical seminaries, synods, visitations, enforcement of the duty of residence, were to be the means of creating a blameless secular clergy and of counteracting every form of simony. The Orders also were subjected to a reform in strict conformity with the decrees of the Council. Thus was life breathed into the dead letter of these ordinances and the countenance of the Church rejuvenated. In his efforts for the preservation of the religious, hence also of the national unity of Italy, Pius V. was wholly successful, but his attempt to overthrow that irreconcilable enemy of the Catholic faith, Elizabeth of England, by means of a Bull of excommunication, miscarried and led to a fierce persecution of English Catholics, of whom there remained a great number. In France, in Germany, in Switzerland and in Poland, the Pope also saw the Catholic faith most grievously threatened, whilst there were not wanting most hopeful beginnings of a reawakening of religious vitality. At the close of his reign, after protracted and wearisome negotiations, Pius V. had the satisfaction of entering into a league with Venice and Spain, whose joint armed forces destroyed the Turkish fleet at the battle of Lepanto, October 7th, 1571. Though the mutual jealousy of Venice and Spain frustrated an exploitation of so great a victory, that day nevertheless marked the beginning of the decline of the Turks' sea power, southern Europe was freed from the danger of being swept by an Islamic flood, and the legend of Ottoman invincibility shattered. It is easy to understand the wave of indescribable joy which swept over the whole of Christendom under the first impression of such an event. With this glorious triumph over the Crescent the Pope's task was accomplished. He died on May 1st of the following year, deeply regretted by the Roman people and by all the friends of the Church.

If Pius V. was unable to carry every one of his undertakings to a successful termination, were it only by reason of the shortness of his pontificate, his successors were able to reap where he had sown. This is particularly true of Gregory XIII., who enjoyed a fairly long reign (1572-1585). Equally remarkable as a jurist, a diplomatist and an organizer, that Pope gave a practical turn to the reforms so happily initiated by his predecessor. His chief care was the training of a well-educated and blameless clergy. The real significance of his pontificate lies, however, in the fact that besides continuing the ecclesiastical revival, he lent support to the efforts for the recovery of large tracts of territory in northern, central and eastern Europe which had fallen away from the Church. Together with the Catholic reform he also strove for a Catholic restoration. Both movements were forwarded by Gregory XIII. with decision, energy, and on the big scale. In this task he made use of nuncios trained in the school of Borromeo and Pius V., as well as of the new Orders then in all their youthful vigour, more particularly the Jesuits, the Capuchins and the Oratorians of Philip Neri. Just then Loyola's foundation was enjoying a period of great splendour. In every Catholic country of southern, central and eastern Europe, Ignatius' sons devoted themselves indefatigably to the education of youth, the formation of the clergy, the cure of souls, and the recall of those who had strayed from the faith. By command of the Pope they undertook the most arduous diplomatic missions and penetrated as far north as Stockholm and Moscow. At the same time they were the pioneers both of Christianity and of civilization in Japan, China, India, Ethiopia and Constantinople, whilst in Spanish America their missions rivalled those of the Dominicans and Franciscans. Their devotion, prudence and adaptability to existing conditions were rewarded almost everywhere with magnificent results.

Whilst in this way the countries across seas offered a compensation for the losses caused by apostasy, Gregory XIII. by no means despaired of restoring in Europe the priceless heirloom of the past, viz. the unity of faith. In the end, however, he failed to achieve this lofty purpose, notwithstanding unceasing and truly heroic exertions. In vain the Pope sought to reunite Sweden and Russia with the Church; in vain also he strove to render Elizabeth harmless. In France, too, the struggle between Catholics and Calvinists remained undecided so that, notwithstanding the preservation of Spain and Italy from apostasy, it was still uncertain whether the third among the Latin nations would remain faithful to the religion of its fathers.

On the other hand Gregory XIII. had the satisfaction of witnessing the success of his efforts to help the Catholic cause to victory in the western and southern parts of the Low Countries, whilst in the vast Polish kingdom a stop was put to apostasy, and former Catholic territory was recovered. Gregory's activity on behalf of Germany truly marks an epoch. Internal dissensions had already weakened the force of the Protestant offensive. With great caution the Pope now sought to exploit so favourable a situation with a view to the preservation of the territories which had remained loyal to the Catholic Church. He sought to instil fresh vigour into them by applying the reforms of Trent, by putting a stop to further apostasies, and by recovering what had been lost. In these endeavours, in addition to the Jesuits, the Pope had the support of the two

Wittelsbachs, Albrecht V., and William V., whose energetic championship of the Catholic restoration gave to the little duchy of Bavaria almost the importance of a great Power. Among the ecclesiastical princes, the pontiff was likewise assisted by the Abbot of Fulda, Balthasar von Dernbach, the Bishop of Würzburg, Julius Echter von Mespelbrunn, the Elector of Mayence, Daniel Brendel, the Bishop of Paderborn, Theodor von Fürstenberg, and after the accession of Rudolph II. (1576) by the Habsburgs also. These efforts for a restoration could be justified by an appeal to the so-called " right of reform " (*cujus regio, ejus religio*) which had been granted to the Estates of Empire by the religious peace of Augsburg, but which had until then only been made use of by the Protestants. That right proved a two-edged sword. It was William V. who, with the support of Gregory XIII., saved the Catholic Church on the Lower Rhine and in Westphalia in the war caused by the apostasy of the Archbishop of Cologne, Gebhard Truchsess. In this way the progress of Protestantism in north-west Germany was checked once for all. In order to provide a rallying centre for the Catholic reform and restoration for the future also, nunciatures were established at Cologne, Vienna and in South-Germany. It is amazing to see the Pope, notwithstanding such wide and diverse activities, still able to think of repressing the Turks, reforming the calendar and promoting science and the arts.

For the space of nearly thirteen years Gregory XIII. steered the barque of Peter with no less prudence than energy. Only five years were granted to his successor (1585–1590). If the figure of the Franciscan Pope, Sixtus V., has nevertheless impressed posterity far more powerfully than that of his predecessor, the reason is that in him a man of unique greatness had obtained the tiara. His gifted personality exercised so powerful a fascination over his contemporaries that achievements were ascribed to him which were really the work of Gregory XIII., and legend busied itself with him. Grandeur characterized all the plans and undertakings of Sixtus V. By a pitiless repression of banditry he established public security in the Papal States, brought order into the finances, began the draining of the Pontine Marshes and promoted learning and the arts. He created a new Rome. To this day his fame is proclaimed by the magnificent halls of the Vatican library, the palaces of the Vatican and the Lateran, by aqueducts and new streets, by obelisks adorned with the emblem of the cross, the statues of the Princes of the Apostles on the columns of Trajan and Marcus Aurelius and the dome of St. Peter's which he nearly completed. The Pope also showed himself an organizer on a big scale. By demanding that Bishops should pay regular visits to Rome he paved the way for a closer contact of the hierarchy with the centre of ecclesiastical unity, whilst by giving to the College of Cardinals its definitive constitution, and by the establishment of the various Congregations, he founded that world-wide, uniform, calm and smoothly running government of the Holy See, the grandeur of which wrings admiration even from the Church's bitterest foes. The reform of the administration was of the utmost importance for the Catholic reform and restoration in the German Empire, in the Spanish Netherlands and in Switzerland, and Sixtus V. did all he could to promote both these movements.

Even so we have not exhausted the importance of this brief pontificate. Sixtus V.'s attitude in the crisis which France was then undergoing, was destined to influence the history of the whole world. This man of genius, the width of whose political outlook contrasts so strangely with his humble origin, in a grim struggle with Spanish imperialism, saved the political autonomy of France, made it possible for the Church to live on in that kingdom, and preserved the Holy See and Europe itself from the evils of Spanish Cæsaro-papalism.

The solution of the French problem, namely the reconciliation of Henry IV. with the Church, which Sixtus V. had initiated, was reached under Clement VIII., (1592–1605) who, in contrast with the reckless energy and bold initiative of his gifted predecessor, showed himself an exceedingly prudent and cautious politician. His prudence and moderation enabled him to discover, slowly but surely, a satisfactory compromise which secured the autonomy of France against

Spanish appetites and preserved that kingdom from the religious disintegration which had befallen Germany. It became now possible to initiate a religious renewal in a country so long devastated by wars of religion. Clement furthered the movement in every way so that it soon affected the widest circles. The era of reforming Bishops now opened and new Orders arose, chiefly devoted to practical purposes, viz. education and the care of the sick. The preservation of France for the Catholic faith secured at the same time the existence of the Church in the adjoining Spanish Netherlands and in the districts on the Lower Rhine.

The reconciliation of Henry IV. entailed a further consequence, one that Sixtus V. had also aimed at. The re-establishment of equilibrium between the two great Catholic Powers relieved the Holy See of the weight of Spain's patronage and restored to it that international pre-eminence which had enabled it to arbitrate between the nations of Europe throughout the Middle Ages. In this way Clement VIII., assisted by his nephew, Pietro Aldobrandini, was enabled to bring about peace between France and Spain in 1598, and in 1601 between France and Savoy. Fully realizing the importance for the Catholic restoration of concord between Paris and Madrid, the Pope longed for a family alliance between the two Courts.

One of the aims of the peace policy of the Holy See was the protection of the Christian religion and civilization from the attacks of the Turks who were pressing westward. In order to avert the peril that threatened from Islam, Clement VIII. sought to form a great coalition and his efforts to this end reached as far as Russia and Persia. One of the most glorious pages in the history of his pontificate is the part played by him in the defence of Hungary. Notwithstanding the deplorable condition of his finances, he contributed considerable sums of money, and on three separate occasions sent papal troops into that country. However, success was only partial, and in the end, owing to the disorders in Hungary and Transilvania, the situation became more perilous than ever.

Clement VIII. was likewise to experience bitter disappointments in Holland, England, Scotland and Ireland, where

Catholics were being most grievously oppressed. The failure of the attempt to restore religion in Sweden was likewise most painful to him. As against these failures it was possible to register decisive progress of the Church in Poland. " If at the beginning of the reign of Clement VIII., it looked as if Protestantism would exterminate the Catholic religion in that kingdom, now the ancient Church is in the act of burying heresy "—thus the Polish nuncio Malaspina in the year 1598. Great hopes could likewise be founded on the return to the Church of the schismatic Ruthenians which came about in 1595, as well as the first stirrings of a new Catholic vitality in Germany, the Spanish Netherlands and Switzerland. In the latter country the Pope found choice instruments for his efforts on behalf of a reform in the persons of Peter Canisius and Francis de Sales.

The great change which had taken place within the Catholic world in the second half of the sixteenth century was splendidly revealed during the universal jubilee of the year 1600. A hundred years earlier the Rome of Alexander VI. had given a tremendous shock to pilgrims. Now they beheld the Pope imitating the humility of the Saviour by washing the feet of pilgrims and hearing confessions like an ordinary priest. A million pilgrims who came to Rome for the jubilee, returned to their homes edified and full of enthusiasm for the faith. No less than the success of the jubilee, the news which the Pope received from missionary countries also raised the highest hopes. The Jesuit, Matteo Ricci, a man of genius, had opened the Kingdom of the Middle for the Gospel, and the Church made progress in the Philippines, in Persia, Abyssinia, western Africa and in Central and South America. Thereupon Clement VIII. took a step wholly in keeping with the universal character of the Church when he established in Rome a centre for this world mission. This he did by founding a special Congregation, the forerunner of Propaganda.

Like most of the Popes of the reform period—Paul IV. and Pius V. being the only exceptions—Clement VIII. also showed himself a keen patron of learning and art. He did much for the development of the Vatican library and the Roman university, and whenever there was question of promotions, scholars were given the preference. The clearest proof of his interest in learning is the elevation by him to the sacred College of Bellarmine and Baronius, the two greatest scholars of the period.[1] The name of the Aldobrandini Pope is also connected with Torquato Tasso in whose poem, *Gerusalemme liberata*, the revival of Christian sentiment may be clearly felt.

It is a rare occurrence in history to meet with a continuous line of rulers pursuing a common aim with so much energy and determination as that of the great Popes of the period of the Catholic restoration. The uniform aim of recovering the lost Catholic ground which inspired the action of the occupants of the See of Peter, especially from the reign of Gregory XIII. onwards, is a marked peculiarity of the long pontificate of Paul V. (1605-1621); it reaches its climax in that of Paul's successor, Gregory XV. The Borghese Pope, whose one weakness was his excessive concern for his relatives, was, like his predecessors, tireless in promoting both the spread of Christianity in missionary countries and the Catholic revival in the various countries of Europe. Paul V., who completed St. Peter's, the mightiest architectural achievement of the period of the Catholic reform, was nowhere more successful than in France and in the Spanish Netherlands, where Catholic life experienced a wonderful revival and expansion, which, in the former country were rendered possible by the re-establishment of internal peace, and in the latter by the armistice of 1609 with the Northern Low Countries. Various factors contributed to the powerful revival of the Church in France, the foremost being the papal nuncios, the Jesuits, Bérulle, the founder of the Oratory of France, and lastly Francis de Sales and Frances de Chantal who between them inaugurated a new epoch in the history of female religious Institutes.

In the Spanish Netherlands the fresh vigour of Catholic life

[1] GOTHEIN (*Reformation und Gegenreformation*, II., Munich, 1924, 100), considers that " Protestantism has nothing to place side by side with Bellarmine's controversial writings ". The same may be said of the Annals of Baronius which earned for him the title of " Father of Modern Church History ".

was characterized by the extraordinary development of religious painting in the persons of Rubens and Van Dyck. In other Catholic countries also the religious regeneration was reflected in the arts. Just as in music Palestrina opened a way which led to the production of exquisite works, such as impressed even those who did not profess the faith, so did El Greco in Spain, the Caracci, Domenichino, Guido Reni, Sassoferrato, Bernini, Pietro da Cortona and countless others in Italy, express in their wonderful creations the religious ideals of the era of the restoration.[1] Baroque art, which only of late has met with adequate appreciation, emerged very gradually from the art of the renaissance. It embodies the new vigour of ecclesiastical life, and the glow of genuine religious enthusiasm which animated the great Saints of that period. To understand baroque art we must rightly appraise the peculiarities of the religious sense of those days, which in Ignatius and Francis Xavier resolved itself in an eager desire—sustained by the certainty of victory—to fight for Christ and the Church; in Philip Neri and Francis de Sales in quiet joy; in Teresa of Jesus in mystic ardour. The more deeply one penetrates into baroque art the more clearly one becomes aware of the powerful religious energy with which it is charged.[2] One of the most eloquent apologists of the new orientation thus concludes his pregnant remarks on the spirit of this art: "The baroque period took for granted a belief in a future perfection and transfiguration of life, and this faith, instinct with hope, so far from damping in any way its enjoyment of the natural life, precisely gave to that life its value and price. Hence the joyousness, the splendour, the flood of light

---

[1] Besides RANKE, *Päpste*, I.⁶, 322 seq., cf. HASE, *Vorlesungen*, III., 397 seq.; KREITMAIER, in the *Stimmen der Zeit*, CX. (1925/6), 456 seq., 461 seq. With regard to Rubens and Van Dyck cf. besides our Notes, Vol. XXVI., p. 101 seq., 108 seq., the Essay by R. GROSCHE, " Der Katholische Rubens," in *Hochland*, XXIV. (1926/7), 258 seq.

[2] See WEINGARTNER, *Der Geist des Barock*, Augsburg, 1925, 13, 18. Cf. KREITMAIER, loc. cit., 453 seq., and GROSCHE, loc. cit, 253 seq.

in which baroque art clothes even this earthly existence ; hence the cheerful affirmation of all reality, including that of matter ; hence the ease with which every natural means of expression was pressed into the service of religious art ; hence the disappearance of all strict boundaries between the world above and that below, since everyone was convinced that there was no gap between spirit and matter, between nature and the supernatural, between heaven and earth ; that, on the contrary, the one builds on the other, that, in fact, they complete each other. And the result was that all the positive forces of the civilization of that period, whether of a material, spiritual or a religious kind, worked together for the building up of this art, thus making of it a mirror of the harmonious culture of a whole period."[1]

The decay of religious art in Protestant countries clearly showed how much they had lost when they lost the ancient faith. In the north of Scandinavia, Catholicism was wholly extinct. In Holland, Great Britain and Ireland, Catholics still formed an important minority in the time of Paul V., though, like the Christians of the catacombs, they lived in constant danger and had to hear or say Mass in secret. Even in North-Germany the ancient Church was by no means dead ; there was grouped round the monasteries and isolated priests a diaspora which had not as yet fallen a victim to the violence of territorial ecclesiasticism. In South-Germany also there existed a diaspora, though there the situation was somewhat more favourable because Catholics were not so completely deprived of all contact with Catholic territories as were their North-German brethren. Here the Catholic restoration, furthered by Paul V., made satisfactory progress in many places. On the Rhine also and in Westphalia as well as in Bohemia the restoration progressed, though the outbreak, in 1618, of the Bohemian revolt seriously endangered it. Paul V. was very distressed when the revolt assumed the character of a war of religion, for everywhere the first aim of the Pope's action was the maintenance of peace.

[1] See WEINGARTNER, *loc. cit.*, 24. *Cf.* also DVOŘÁK, *Entwicklungsgesch. der barocken Deckenmalerei in Wien*, 5 seq.

From the first years of his pontificate Paul V. had worked for a reconciliation between the two great Catholic Powers, France and Spain, by means of a matrimonial alliance. Unfortunately, to his deep chagrin, negotiations to that effect yielded no other result except to strain still further the relations between the two Powers. In consequence of the struggle for the succession of Jülich (1609), the situation became so acute that there was reason to fear the outbreak of war between France and Spain. Paul V. did his utmost to prevent such a catastrophe. The assassination of Henry IV. gave a new turn to French policy. During the regency of Marie de Medici, the Pope's efforts for peace were crowned with success and a double Franco-Spanish alliance was successfully negotiated. The removal of the long-standing rivalry between the Houses of Bourbon and Habsburg was of decisive importance for the fate of the Catholic restoration in Austria and Germany.

The ecclesiastico-political conditions in those countries had become increasingly strained. Whilst under Rudolph II. and Matthias, Austria had to undergo an endless crisis, in the Empire all those who were still conscious of their Catholicism grouped themselves round the person of Maximilian of Bavaria. This was all the more important as Calvinist Protestantism, under the leadership of another member of the Wittelbachs, the Count Palatine, Frederick V., threatened to pull down all that the Catholic restoration had succeeded in building up. Against the Protestant Union of 1608, whose aim it was to decide the fate of Germany by the sword, a Catholic League was formed in the following year, under the leadership of Maximilian I. of Bavaria. However much Paul V.'s sympathies may have been with this defence league, he nevertheless adopted in its regard a cautious waiting policy. He would not commit himself to any step calculated to precipitate a war of religion. That catastrophe was provoked by the other side, when the Palatine allied himself with the Bohemian rebels. What these aimed at was sufficiently shown by the expulsion of the Archbishop of Prague and the banishment of the Jesuits from Bohemia and Moravia. Thereupon, and notwithstanding the bad state of his finances, Paul V. granted considerable subsidies to the Emperor and to the League. But it was of far greater consequence that he secured from Louis XIII. France's benevolent neutrality, with a view to the crushing of the Bohemian rising.

The victory of the combined army of the League and the Emperor, at the battle of the White Mountain, not only destroyed in one hour the " Calvinist Monarchy " of Bohemia, but also saved the Catholic Church in the east and west of the Empire, perhaps in the whole of Germany. The seventy-nine years old Pontiff lived long enough to witness " this immeasurable weakening of Protestantism in Germany " and he celebrated the tremendous turn of events with a joy that was all the greater as the sceptre of the Habsburg territories had passed into the hands of Ferdinand II. on whose solid Catholicism he could rely unreservedly. Thus, when the Borghese Pope died on January 28th, 1621, his pontificate had reached its zenith.

His successor, Gregory XV. (1621-3), a member of the Ludovisi family, was all eagerness to help the Catholics towards complete victory in the war which broke out in Germany after the Bohemian revolt. In this respect it was of great advantage to the aged Pontiff that in the person of his youthful nephew, Cardinal Ludovisi, he had at his side one who, like himself, had been a pupil of the Jesuits, one also who had but one purpose in view, viz., the spread and exaltation of the Church. To this end the Congregation of Propaganda was founded, so that the hitherto autonomous Catholic missions for the conversion of infidels and heretics were now placed under a central authority in Rome. This magnificent institution gave to Catholic missionary enterprise that solid and powerful unity which distinguished it so favourably from the divisions of the Protestant missions.[1] Propaganda's field of action was the whole world—the new world, discovered less than a century before, where a rich field offered itself to the

---

[1] WARNECK recognizes this (*Gesch. der protestantischen Missionen von der Reformation bis auf die Gegenwart*[10], Berlin, 1910).

missionaries; and the old world, in part torn away from Rome, which required even greater solicitude.

Gregory XV. gave strong support to the Emperor Ferdinand II., to Maximilian and to the League, and he exploited their victories systematically and in every direction, for the benefit of the Catholic restoration. To the Bavarian Duke the Pope gave both financial and diplomatic support. It was largely owing to his efforts that, notwithstanding Spanish machinations, Maximilian obtained the dignity of Elector Palatine. To mark his gratitude the latter presented the Pope with the valuable library of Heidelberg. The Duke of Bavaria had to put up a hard fight for his new dignity, for from Denmark and Sweden as far south as Venice, and from France to Transilvania and Constantinople, the most strenuous efforts were afoot for the formation of a vast coalition whose aim it would be to restore Frederick V. now under the ban of Empire. Once again events took a favourable turn for the Catholic cause, and the proposed coalition never came into being. To the astonishment of the whole world Frederick's brother-in-law, the Prince of Wales, was about to set sail for Spain with a view to a matrimonial alliance. England seemed on the point of contracting a close bond with Catholic Spain. It was of no less consequence that Gregory XV. succeeded in preventing a war between France and Spain which threatened in consequence of the question of the Valtellina. The Pope brought about an understanding between Paris and Madrid by the terms of which the strong places occupied by Spain were to be in part put under papal sequestration and in part evacuated until a final decision of the question should have been arrived at. In view of a situation so profoundly altered neither the King of Denmark nor the Estates of Lower Saxony dared to move. Mansfeld, Christian of Brunswick and the Margrave of Baden-Durlach, who took up arms on behalf of the banned Palatine, Frederick, were defeated by the League. The Catholic restoration was inaugurated in the re-conquered Palatinate of the right bank of the Rhine. Tilly pursued Christian into Lower Saxony and destroyed his wild hordes in the battle of Stadtlohn (August 6th, 1623), thus making

Maximilian the military master of the north-west of Germany. Gregory XV., who died on July 8th, 1623, did not live to see this triumph of the Catholic cause. The movement of restoration, of the enthusiasm and strength of which his Briefs speak in such burning terms, was now nearing its climax.

The new Pope, Urban VIII. (1623-1644), was only 56 years old. He was a scion of the house of Barberini on which he heaped countless favours. This highly cultured man had very much at heart the continuation of the protection which the Holy See had always bestowed on science and art. The good fortune which for his artistic plans gave him Bernini, the most gifted exponent of baroque, left him completely in the lurch in the political sphere. He was indeed full of goodwill and anxious to promote peace between the rival Houses of Bourbon and Habsburg with a view to opposing their combined strength to the Protestants and the Turks, but from the very beginning of his pontificate fresh clouds rose on the political horizon, the harbingers of a great war.

The question of the Valtellina threatened to lead to a conflict between Spain and Austria on the one hand and France on the other. The frustration of the hope of an alliance between England and Spain came as a further disappointment. The ill-success of the Prince of Wales' wooing caused England to break with the Habsburgs and to seek to win the help of Holland, the Estates of the circle of Lower Saxony, Denmark and Sweden for a proposed restoration of the Elector Palatine.

But an even more fateful turn of events took place in Paris where, in April, 1624, Cardinal Richelieu was entrusted with the conduct of the affairs of State. In his person one of the most ominous figures of modern history makes its appearance on the stage of the world. In his ardent patriotism and insatiable ambition Richelieu shrank from no means if thereby he might make of France the leading European Power in place of the House of Habsburg. The circumstance that his action threatened to destroy the unity of the Catholic world which was so essential for the prosecution of the Catholic restoration and the protection of Christendom from Turkish attacks, troubled him as little as the fact that his purpose could only be achieved with the help of the Protestant Powers. The Machiavellian guide of France's fortunes, who rejected no means however reprehensible, was determined to sacrifice the highest interests of the Church to the momentary advantages of his country. The attack on the Hispano-Austrian Power planned by him was more comprehensive than anything that had ever been attempted. To this end he leagued himself with Savoy and Venice, forcibly drove the papal troops from the Valtellina, and concluded alliances with Calvinist Holland and Protestant England. With a view to the restoration of the Palatine Frederick, who constituted the centre of European Protestantism, he secretly supplied Christian IV. of Denmark and the freebooter Mansfeld with money and troops. Thus a victory over the Habsburgs which would have rendered nugatory all the triumphs of the Catholic restoration seemed assured.

However the Cardinal had presumed to much. Whilst the Pope, and not the Pope alone but the whole of Catholic France as well, protested against his policy, Richelieu saw himself simultaneously threatened by a fresh Huguenot rising. Nothing so characterizes the Cardinal's unscrupulousness as the way in which he extricated himself from his perilous plight. He prevailed on Holland and England to lend their help against their own co-religionists ; but when they had done him this service, he abandoned them without remorse. Even the cautious Venetians were completely deceived. To the amazement of everyone, in March, 1626, France and Spain came to terms over the Valtellina affair by the treaty of Monzon. The Cardinal had excluded the Pope from the conference, but the latter had cause to be all the more satisfied with its result, inasmuch as by its terms security was also guaranteed to the Catholics of the Valtellina. Simultaneously with this *rapprochement* between the great Catholic Powers, relations between France and England grew worse, so much so that a rupture seemed imminent. Such an eventuality would mean the failure of the conditions agreed upon for the enterprise of Christian IV. and Mansfeld. The latter were but inadequately supported. with the result that they were defeated in 1626 by the strategy of Tilly and Wallenstein. In the following year the imperial and leaguist troops made themselves complete masters of northern and north-eastern Germany. Whilst it thus became possible to extend the Catholic restoration also to those parts of the Empire, prospects for the Catholic cause also improved in yet another direction.

Soon after the outbreak of war between France and England, Urban VIII. succeeded in winning over the great Catholic Powers for a combined attack on the Island Kingdom. In 1628 the project was the subject of lively discussion between Paris and Madrid. Once Louis XIII. had taken the Huguenot stronghold of La Rochelle, in October of that year, it lay in his power to restore complete religious unity in his kingdom. Rome expected it. Even greater hopes were raised by the defeat of Protestantism in North-Germany. It looked as if the moment had come, by one great stroke, to bring to a conclusion the Catholic restoration which, owing to the energetic co-operation of the nuncios of Cologne and Vienna, had made very considerable progress both in the Austrian territories and within the Empire. The feeling that victory had been achieved prompted the edict of restitution which enjoined the restoration to the Catholics of whatever the Protestants had illegally deprived them since the treaty of Passau.

Thus in 1628 was Protestantism grievously threatened in France, England and Germany. It owed its escape, not to its own strength, but to the circumstance that the Catholic world failed to remain united.[1] Above all, the *entente* between France and Spain should not have been troubled. However, its preservation would have entailed the abandonment by Richelieu of his plans for the destruction of the Habsburgs; but of this the Cardinal would not hear, for now, as before, he was bent on the prosecution of his imperialistic aims. In order to assure himself of a free hand for this policy he contented himself with the defeat of the Huguenots as a

---

[1] See RANKE, *Päpste*, II.⁶, 328, who thinks that if Catholicism had remained united, one cannot see how North-Germany could have withstood it in the long run. MAYNARD (IV., 4) is of the same opinion.

political party—he did not interfere with their religious liberty. In 1629 he concluded a treaty of peace with England in which he expressly bound himself not to intervene on behalf of English Catholics. But the adherents of the ancient faith in Germany were destined to suffer even more bitterly from the unscrupulous policy of the Cardinal who did all he could to prevent the war from coming to an end.

There can be no doubt that the man who allied himself with Gustavus Adolphus, and who urged even the Turks to attack the Emperor, must bear the chief responsibility for the failure of the complete Catholic restoration in Germany, and for the fact that the northern parts of the Empire remained for the most part Protestant. One of the most eminent of German historians justly observes that of all non-Protestants no man did greater service to Protestantism than the great French realist politician in Rome's own purple.[1]

Whilst on this point historians are of one mind, opinion is still very much divided as to whether Urban VIII. always adopted the right attitude towards the rival Catholic Powers amid the ever increasing political troubles caused by the storms of the Thirty Years' War. Must we blame him for not having, in effect, brought sufficient pressure to bear on Richelieu with a view to restraining him in his dealings with

[1] See RANKE, *Französische Gesch.*, II.², 514 seq. *Cf.* as well STIEVE, *Abhandlungen*, 207 ; VOSSLER, *Racine*, München, 1926, 43 seq.; MOMMSEN, *Richelieu*, 33, and SCHNITZER, 249, who justly remarks: " Even if Richelieu and P. Joseph did not desire the strengthening of German Protestantism, they nevertheless became responsible for it." KASER (" Das Zeitalter de Reformation und Gegenreformation von 1517 bis 1660," in L. M. HARTMANN's *Weltgesch.*, VI., 1, Stuttgart-Gotha, 1922) writes, p. 197 : " The statesman in Richelieu was stronger than the priest. He strove to rouse the whole of the Protestant world against the Habsburgs ; and he has done far more harm to that first line of defence of the Papacy than any Protestant ruler." MAYNARD, among French historians, has expressed himself very strongly on the injury done to the Catholic restoration through the Machiavellian policy of Richelieu (IV., 2 seq.). *Cf.* also DE MEAUX, *Luttes relig.*, II., 373 seq., and 416.

the Protestants, and for giving but inadequate financial support to the Emperor and the League, and for having injured the Habsburgs quite as much as he played into the hands of France's policy?[1]

Light can only be thrown on these questions, which indeed received varying answers from contemporaries, by a detailed account of the whole of his pontificate. Meanwhile recent research has clarified certain points and exposed the main lines of his policy as well as corrected not a few erroneous views. The Spanish assertion that the Pope looked with indifference on the ruin of the Catholic religion in Germany, has been shown to be a calumny. Of all Gustavus Adolphus' enemies Urban VIII. was the most irreconcilable, if not the most dangerous. Notwithstanding his French preferences he was by no means pleased with Richelieu's Protestant alliances; on the contrary, as soon as he had information of these agreements, he condemned them and worked for their dissolution.

In 1632 he mobilized all his diplomatists in order to prevent the raising of Gustavus Adolphus to the throne of Poland.[2] Nor can it be called in question that, in the full consciousness of his duty as the common Father of Christendom, he strove to pursue an impartial attitude towards the rival Great Catholic Powers and did all he could to bring about a general pacification. Notwithstanding many disappointments papal diplomacy never wearied in its efforts for a conference which would lead to a compromise on the diverging interests of France and the Habsburgs and in this endeavour it never allowed itself to be discouraged.[3]

True, for these offices the Holy See received nobody's thanks. On the contrary, because the Pope always kept in view the common interest, and took pains, as became his high position

---

[1] G. WOLF, in his critique of LEMAN's work, *Urbain VIII, et la rivalité de la France et de la maison d'Autriche de 1631 à 1635* (Lille, 1920), in the *Zeitschr. für Kirchengesch.*, XLIV. (1925), 139 seq., says that this was indeed the result of Urban VIII.'s policy but certainly not its aim.

[2] *Cf.* LEMAN, 122 seq.

[3] *Ibid.*, v-vi. *Cf.* our notes in Appendix 1.

to hold himself above parties, he was viewed with suspicion by all of them. What was wanted was not an impartial mediator, but an ally who would obey unconditionally. Discontent with the Pope was all the greater at Madrid and Vienna inasmuch as there people had counted on a continuation of the plentiful subsidies which had been granted with particular lavishness by Gregory XV. However the situation was changed, for though the religious motives, which during the first period of the Thirty Years' War had given it the character of a struggle against Protestantism, were still strongly operative, they were nevertheless gradually falling into the background. If from the beginning, the faith was not the chief motive for which the mercenaries fought, so that in every army Catholics and Protestants fought side by side, in course of time the Catholic commanders enrolled an ever growing number of Protestant officers and men under their banners.[1] The war, in which from the first, questions of property and power had been mixed up with the interests of religion, put on, in the course of its progress, mainly a political character and transformed itself into a struggle of European high politics on the grandest scale.[2]

Richelieu was anxious to represent the war purely as a struggle for the interests of the State, and here he was in a position to complain that notwithstanding a great show of zeal for religion, the Spaniards were giving support to the Huguenots in France.[3] Philip IV. and Ferdinand II. claimed that the struggle was purely a war of religion. Urban declined to accept such a differentiation. In order to induce the Pope to support the Catholic princes of Germany, the Secretary of State, Cardinal Barberini, wrote to the nuncio in Vienna, in the spring of 1632, that it was enough to know that the Catholic religion was in danger, and that it mattered little whether the

---

[1] See KLOPP, *Gesch. Ostfrieslands*, II., 441, and *Das Restitutionsedikt im Nordwestlichen Deutschland*, Göttingen, 1860, 84. *Cf.* HURTER, *Zur Gesch. Wallensteins*, 69.

[2] *Cf.* STEGEMANN, *Der Kampf um den Rhein*, Berlin, 1925, 214.

[3] See the *Relation of the Secretariate of State of 1631, in *Vat.* 6929, Vatican Library; *cf.* LÄMMER, *Analecta*, 38 *seq.*

war sprang from religious rather than from political causes.[1] However, in view of the inextricable intermingling of political and ecclesiastical interests, every political change was bound to work itself out in the religious sphere. Urban VIII. was not unaware of the fact, but there can be no doubt that he, like many Catholics in Germany, greatly underestimated the danger which threatened from the fact of the intervention of Gustavus Adolphus. He was also mistaken when he encouraged the alliance of Bavaria with France, for this reason, among others, that he hoped thereby to detach Richelieu from his league with the German Protestants.

The French Cardinal knew only too well how to entangle the Pope in his net, to deceive him with regard to his schemes and to feed him with illusions; above all he knew how to revive ever anew the fear which existed in Rome, of encirclement and oppression by Spain.

The Pope had always instinctively tended to support the small Powers against the great ones. Owing to the fact that he owned more than one-half of Italy, the King of Spain had, in some measure, come to occupy towards the Holy See, both in secular and ecclesiastical matters, the position held by the Emperors of the twelfth and thirteenth century. In view of the overwhelming preponderance of the territorial possessions and the far-reaching civil and ecclesiastical pretensions of Spain, the Pope was compelled to look for a counterpoise by which to ensure his freedom and autonomy as Head of the Church. This situation Richelieu exploited to the full. Against his skill was pitted the clumsiness of the imperial statesmen and their offensive attitude towards the Holy See, which they irritated repeatedly in sundry petty ways. The disputes to which this gave rise, the very unsatisfactory state of the papal finances, and the squandering of money on the part of the imperialists [2] account for the reserve with which Urban VIII.

[1] *Cifra, of April 24, 1632, Nunziat. di Germania, 123, p. 124, Papal Secret Archives. Cf. PIEPER, in the Hist.-polit. Blätter, XCIV., 476.

[2] Complaints arose about this as early as 1634; see DUHR, II., 2, 699.

met the Emperor's constant demands for subsidies. There can be no doubt that papal assistance was not equal to the immense need; it was however larger than is generally admitted.[1] If the Pope granted no more he could justly say that, in addition to famine and plague, the defensive measures which he had been compelled to take in view of the Mantuan war of succession had drained his exchequer.

It was nothing short of a disaster that Ferdinand II. allowed himself to be drawn by Philip IV. into the warlike confusion of Upper Italy, which brought the great Catholic Powers into sharpest opposition to each other at the very moment when the Catholic restoration in Germany was within an ace of complete success.[2] A further extension of the Habsburg sphere of influence and power in Italy, which was the object of the contest, was deemed intolerable by France as well as by the Italian States, more particularly by the Holy See. The splendid military triumphs of the Emperor in Germany, and certain threats uttered in the imperial camp, had fanned afresh in Rome the fear of Hispano-imperial Cæsaro-papalism which was never allayed, but was kept alive by various intrusions into the ecclesiastical sphere. It was this fear which, in the first instance, decided Urban VIII.'s line of conduct; the States of the Church were only a secondary concern. It is false to say that the Pope put temporal interests before spiritual ones. Assuredly Urban VIII. attached great weight to the preservation of the States of the Church and the freedom of Italy, but these worldly considerations were closely connected with his legitimate efforts for the preservation of the freedom of the Holy See, which the Papal States were meant to ensure.[3]

The experience of his predecessors had made clear to

[1] See PIEPER, *loc. cit.*, 480.

[2] *Cf.* RUSSO, *La politica del Vaticano*, 28, and P. NEGRI, *La guerra per la successione di Mantova*, Prato, 1924, 2.

[3] *Cf.* DE MEAUX, *Luttes relig.*, II., 427. Also NEGRI, who strongly emphasizes the " preoccupazioni d'indole temporale e perciò strettamente nazionali o italiane ", yet adds that they influenced Urban VIII. " più o meno inconsciamente "; see *Nuova Riv. stor.*, V. (1922), 185.

Urban VIII. the great danger for the Church of a Spanish preponderance in the Italian Peninsula, hence his attitude towards the occupation of Mantua by the imperialists was a foregone conclusion. The danger that threatened from the Spanish-Habsburg power was so evident that in February, 1632, in a conversation with the French envoy, the Marquis de Brézé, Gustavus Adolphus made the remark that, but for his intervention, the Pope would be reduced to the rôle of chaplain to the Spaniards.[1] But—and herein lay the seriousness of the situation—precisely at the moment of acute tension between the Holy See and the Habsburgs, the King of Sweden, who was by far the most dangerous enemy of both, threatened in very alarming fashion not only the Emperor's interests in Germany but those of religion as well. Rome did not fail to grasp this fact. Both in the lifetime of Gustavus Adolphus and after his death, the most pressing exhortations were sent to the Paris cabinet in the hope of obtaining the dissolution of the Franco-Swedish alliance. These requests fell on deaf ears. As for Spain's demand that Urban VIII. should excommunicate the King of France for having entered into an alliance with heretics, the Pope would not entertain the idea in view of bitter experiences with England and more recently with Venice, all the more so as he was aware of Richelieu's threat, uttered as early as June, 1628, which was to the effect that if the Pope lowered himself so far as to be no more than Spain's chaplain, France would break with Rome. This threat was a contributory cause to Urban's refusal to join in a league of all the Catholic States which the Emperor and Spain had planned together. That which finally decided the Pope in this question was the fact that the league was to be used not only to stem the progress of the Protestant King of Sweden, but likewise to further the political aims of the Habsburgs against France. As Head of the Church and common Father, the Pope would not have anything to do with such a scheme.[2]

[1] See the message from M. de Brézé of February 14, 1632, in LAUGEL, Gustav-Adolphe et Richelieu, 408. Cf. also PUFENDORF, De rebus Suecicis, II., 62.

[2] See PIEPER, loc. cit., 481.

From a like motive he had refused to join a league planned by France in 1629.

When death removed Gustavus Adolphus, by far the most dangerous enemy of the Catholic cause, Richelieu nevertheless adhered to his alliance with Sweden. All the Pope's efforts to detach him from it proved in vain ; Paris deemed it more advantageous to prosecute the war by means of its allies, the Swedes and the German Protestants. But this did not discourage Urban VIII. in his endeavour to put an end to the struggle. When, in view of the successes of the Emperor in 1635, Richelieu changed into an open war the covert attacks which his Protestant allies, at his instigation, had been making on the Austro-Hispanic power, the Pope redoubled his efforts on behalf of a reconciliation of the great Catholic Powers. More insistently than ever his nuncios cried : Peace ! Peace ![1] However, heedless of the injury they were doing to the Catholic restoration, both Richelieu and his successor, Mazarin, went on fanning the flames of war, and keeping open the religious breach in blood-drenched Germany.

It is a tremendous tragedy that two Cardinals of the Roman Church should have decisively helped to wrest from her the final triumph for which she had fought for nearly a hundred years, and that so momentous an event in the history of the world should have been brought about by France, so dear to Urban VIII., and for whose well-being Sixtus V. had offered his life.

The consequences of a policy of force, unrestrained by any religious consideration, were much more than a mere paralysis and the eventual failure of the Catholic restoration in Germany. Until now the Holy See had maintained, in some measure at least, the commanding position which it had held throughout the Middle Ages, and which made of it a unifying centre for the nations, not only in moral and religious questions, but also in political and diplomatic ones. This historic rôle, which the religious upheaval had already severely shaken, was finally upset by the clever and crafty statesman who made of France

[1] See SCHNITZER, 250.

the leading European power and the seat of absolutism. He found many docile pupils : henceforth purely secular considerations were to inspire the policy of the other great Catholic Powers.

If we consider the manifold failures of Urban VIII. it is not surprising that he should have been described as one of the most unfortunate Popes. But a comprehensive view of his pontificate shows that he also achieved considerable triumphs. These he won, not in his capacity as a diplomatist, nor as a secular ruler, but as the Father of Christendom.[1] Though fated to witness the failure of the Catholic restoration in Germany, he was able to forward the movement of religious renewal in other Catholic countries. The strength of that movement was far from spent. In France it produced a Vincent de Paul, and in other countries similar selfless apostles, more particularly such as proclaimed the religion of the Cross to the furthest ends of the earth. It is a comforting spectacle to see how, whilst Christianity in Europe, in the reign of Urban VIII., was being torn and laid waste by cruel wars, the Church's mission to the world, which the Pope promoted with the utmost zeal and perseverance, extended its influence over an ever wider area.

[1] *Ott*, in the *Catholic Encyclop.*, XV., 220, draws attention to this.

CHAPTER I.

Election, Antecedents and Character of Gregory XV.—
The Ludovisi.

In the course of the sixteen years of Paul V.'s pontificate the composition of the Sacred College had undergone a substantial change. Among the older Cardinals those appointed by Sixtus V. were only represented by five survivors [1] and Clement VIII.'s Cardinals had shrunk to seventeen, whereas the number of those created by Paul V. amounted to forty-six. However only fifty-two of the seventy members of the Church's Senate were able to reach Rome in time. Of the five French

[1] Besides these, there remained one Cardinal of Gregory XIII. (Fr. Sforza) and one of Gregory XIV. (Od. Farnese); see " *Informatione distinta dello stato, numero e qualità de cardinali che si trovano nel s. collegio sino questo giorno 28 Gennaio 1621 fatta da Msgr. Ab. Cornaro, chierico di Camera in Roma " (in 1623 Fed. Cornaro was made Bishop of Bergamo and Cardinal in 1626), *Cod*. C. 20, of the Boncompagni Archives at Rome. From the *Risposta dell'oracolo cortegiano a signori cardinali nella sede vacante di Paolo V., in *Cod*. CCCCXI, in the Library of S. Croce in Gerusalemme, which is also to be found in *Cod*. I.b, 55, p. 291 *seq*. of the Servite Library at Innsbruck, Lämmer (*Zur Kirchengesch.* 21) has given five specimen verses on Bellarmine, Dietrichstein, Borromeo, Barberini, and Medici. The following may also be noticed :—

    Aldobrandino — fu troppo imperioso il tuo dominio.
    Delfino — non vuol S. Pietro a Marco star vicino.
    Zapata — la nation ti toglie la giornata.
    Doria — tu sei mezzo Spagnuolo s'hai memoria.
    Araceli — ne Scipio ne i Spagnuoli hai tra fedeli.
    Rochefaucauld — Monsieur sei francese e non si puo.
    Rivarola — Romagna fa che non ne sia parola.
    Borgia — non che alcun duca Valentino risorga.
    Camporeo — domandane a Pasquino et a Marforio.
    Roma — io so che Roma non conosce Roma.

Cardinals not one took part in the election, of the four Germans only Madruzzo[1] and none of the Spaniards, except Zappata and Borgia.[2]

In these circumstances the influence of the great Catholic Powers was bound to be greatly diminished. The Spanish cabinet, whose interests coincided with those of the Emperor, hoped to benefit greatly from its relations with Cardinal Borghese which Cardinal Cennini had originated. Borghese's intimate friend, Cardinal Pietro Campori who, together with Cesare Speciani, had at one time made a stay in Spain and Germany, was entirely acceptable to the cabinets of Vienna and Madrid. Ludovisi, Aquino, Cobelluzio and Villini, all of them Spain's nominees, belonged to the party of Paul V".s nephew. Ginnasio and Galamina were excluded by the Catholic King.[3] Aquino was France's candidate.[4] In view of the fact that it was necessary to reckon with the early demise of that Prince of the Church, Marshal d'Estrées, known as Marquis de Cœuvres, in conjunction with the representative of Savoy, did his utmost to bring about the election of Cardinal Alessandro Ludovisi, an election which Pietro Aldobrandini

---

[1] Ferdinand II., immediately upon first news of Paul V.'s sickness, ordered Cardinals Dietrichstein and Zollern to Rome, and commissioned the former to represent the necessity for the continuance of papal subsidies; however, neither of the two Cardinals arrived at Rome in time; but the Emperor's representative in Rome, Prince Savelli, knew the position sufficiently to take up, even without precise orders, the Borghese party interests with the Spanish ambassador Albuquerque, and to remind Madruzzo that the interests of the Emperor and those of his Catholic Majesty demanded that they should support Campori; see WAHRMUND, *Ausschliessungsrecht*, 122, 270 seq.

[2] At first, sixty electors were expected; see the *dissertation on the College of Cardinals in *Cod.* I.^{b}, 55, p. 303, of the Servite Library, Innsbruck. The " Informatione " of Cornaro of January 28, 1621, quoted above (note 1), only reckons fifty-five.

[3] *Cf.* PETRUCELLI DELLA GATTINA, III., 9, 36.

[4] This is reported by ESTRÉES in his *Relation du conclave, où fut élu Grégoire XV.* (s. l. et a.), reprinted in PETITOT, *Mém.* 2, Series XVI., 362.

desired and towards which a young Roman, Domenico Cechini, rendered important services.[1]

Whilst Cardinals Sforza, Farnese, Medici and Este maintained at first an independent attitude, the others formed three parties.[2] The smallest was that of Montalto, disposing as it did at most of six votes, and even these were not altogether reliable.[3] Nor could Cardinal Aldobrandini, the leader of the second group, depend definitely on the thirteen Cardinals of Clement VIII., his uncle. Only nine stood firmly by him, namely Bandini, Cesi, Bevilacqua, Bellarmine, Deti, Ginnasio, Delfino, Sannesio and Pio.[4]

The strongest group was that of Borghese. It included Barberini, Millini, Lante, Leni, Tonti, Verallo, Carafa, Rivarola, Filonardi, Serra, Galamina, Centini, Crescenzi, Ubaldini, Muti, Savelli, Ludovisi, Aquino, Campori, Bentivoglio, Priuli, Cobelluzio, Valiero, Roma, Ghirardi, Scaglia, Pignatelli, Capponi and Orsini. However the Cardinal nephew of the late Pope was by no means sure of these twenty-nine votes for there were not wanting in his party such as were dissatisfied.[5] Besides Zappata and Borja, Madruzzo, Sforza,

---

[1] See *Vita e successi del card. Cecchini descritta da lui medesimo, in Cod. 39 D, 17, p. 31 seq. Corsini Library in Rome. Cf. SIRI V., 253.

[2] Cf. for what follows see Note 1 of p. 29 for the previously quoted *Informatione, of Cornaro, and the relation in the Conclavi, I., 375.

[3] Among them there were, as Cornaro points out in his *Informatione, loc. cit., "tre pretendenti al papato" who would only proceed with caution. Besides this, Cornaro believed that Borromeo would not declare himself against the Spaniards, especially as he also was " in qualche predicamento ".

[4] Concerning the other Cardinals of Aldobrandini's party, CORNARO remarks in the *Informatione : " Zappata, Madruccio e Doria vanno con la fattione Spagnola. Peretti con Montalto et Este vuol esser libero all'inclusione et esclusione di chi piacerà a lui." (loc. cit.).

[5] See Conclavi, I., 375 ; CORNARO, *Informatione, loc. cit., and concerning the " malcontenti ", see the next note. Servite Library, Innsbruck.

Sauli, Doria, Este, Carafa, Aquino, Tonti, Roma and Orsini were reputed to have Spanish leanings. The Florentines (Medici, Monte, Barberini, Capponi, Ubaldini and Bandini) constituted a group of their own, and yet another party was made up of men holding strict principles in all that concerned the Church, Borromeo Dietrichstein and Sourdis being among those who were absent, whereas among those of the group who were in Rome there were Bellarmine, Galamina, Orsini and Cobelluzio.[1]

As usual many names of likely candidates for the supreme dignity were discussed, for instance from among the Cardinals of Sixtus V., those of Sauli, Giustiniani and Monte; from those of Clement VIII., Bandini, Ginnasio and Madruzzo and, lastly, those of Millini, Carafa, Galamina, Centini, Ludovisi, Aquino, Campori and Cobelluzio.[2] However a closer examination soon showed that in reality only a very few among them had any prospect of success.[3] Among Paul V.'s Cardinals Ludovisi and Aquino were the only ones who had a real chance.

[1] " *Vi sono alcuni che nelli passati conclavi si sono chiamati li spirituali : Borromeo, Bellarmino, Dietrichstein, Sourdi, Araceli, Orsino, S. Susanna. Questi sono gli cardinali, che in qualchemodo s'uniscono in fattioni. Hora si devono notare in genere gli contrarii loro et prima si dice che alla fattione nova per propria imputatione suol essere contrario il collegio vecchio. Alla fattione di Montalto sarà tam poco amica l'Aldobrandina. All'Aldobrandina poco amorevole la di Montalto et inimica la di Borghese. Alla Borghese sarà contraria l'Aldobrandina et forsi anco non saranno totalmente sott'una squadra gli cardinali che di Borghesi si chiamano malcontenti : Tonti, Serra, Crescentio, Ubaldino, Filonardi, Capponi, Orsino ne tam poco la Fiorentina gli sarà molt'amico." Cod. I.^{b}, 55, p. 304, of the Servite Library, Innsbruck.

[2] See CORNARO, *Informatione, loc. cit., and the *Avvisi of January 30 and February 1, 1621, Urb. 1089 B, Vatican Library.

[3] See CORNARO's *Informatione of January 28, 1621, Cod. C. 20, Boncompagni Archives, Rome, and the *report, printed in Appendix I. from the Servite Library, Innsbruck. In a MS. in the Boncompagni Archives, Rome, Cod. C. 20, a *Discorso de cardinali papabili nella sede vacante di Paolo V l'a. 1621, discusses the Cardinals singly, and much gossip that cannot be

Ludovisi's was the name most frequently mentioned.[1] Paul V.'s favourite, Cardinal Campori, though strongly supported by Spain, was unpopular with many of the supporters of the nephew, as well as with those of strict ecclesiastical feeling ; and he had to reckon with the opposition of Orsini. To this must be added that the French ambassador and Aldobrandini had agreed on his exclusion.[2] The prospects of Clement VIII.'s Cardinals were almost equally hopeless in view of the determined opposition of Borghese ; at most it was deemed possible that, out of regard for Spain Paul V.'s nephew might decide in favour of Madruzzo. It was much more likely that Borghese would adopt one of Sixtus V.'s Cardinals if none of his own set succeeded in coming to the top. In that eventuality, it was

verified, is reported. The following only is of interest : The unknown author, though no friend of the Jesuits, remarks about Bellarmine that he would have a chance if he were not deaf and a Jesuit, " se non fosse sordo e Giesuita. È anco tanto semplice e buono che si dubitarebbe d'un Papa Celestino." As to Ludovisi, it is said here : " Ludovisio non crede che resti altro che Ludovisio, al quale s'oppone che non sia conosciuto e che li suoi pensieri non si penetrino bene, forse vogliono dire che sia Bolognese, ma del certo l'esser vissuto tant'anni in questa corte et nella minor fortuna, nella quale si scoprono meglio li costumi e li vitii, ha dato saggio di contrario. Vi è chi dice che sia da pucco ; questo ancora non ha molto bon fondamento, perchè l'auditorato di Rota esercitò con molta esperiena et il negotio di Savoia ha fatto conoscere che sa trattare co'principi ancora. . . . Una sol cosa li potrà dar fastidio : il riveder Roma piena di Bolognesi superbi, imperiosi et sopra modo insolenti. Questi machierono il pontificato santissimo di Gregorio XIII."

[1] " *Ludovisio è in concetto di signore molto buono e piacevole. I Spagnuoli lo portano e Borghese non ha occasione alcuna di difidar di lui, anzi mostra d'inclinarsi assai et per esser vecchio et non molto sano, si crede sia soggetto molto facile a riuscire et la corte sin adesso ne parla più di nessun altro." *Informatione* of CORNARO, in *Cod.* C. 20, Boncompagni Archives, Rome.

[2] The author of the *Biografia del card. Campori* (Modena, 1878), 19, 29 *seqq.*, shows that violent accusations directed against Campori by his political opponents, were unfounded.

thought, he might feel inclined to give his support to Giustiniani, rather than to Sauli or Monte.[1] However, Giustiniani, though the object of the encomiums of the Spanish ambassador and the support of Montalto, was unacceptable to Sauli and to a number of Cardinals, especially the two Genoese, Rivarola and Serra. In a report of January 30th, 1621, the Mantuan envoy expresses the opinion that however unusual it may be to choose a Pope from the Cardinals of his immediate predecessors, the elevation of Ludovisi was nevertheless possible inasmuch as he possessed many, not to say all the necessary qualifications.[2] According to a report of the same envoy dated February 6th, the same papabili were still in the foreground in court circles.[3] In a letter of the same day Jacomo Cohelli states that out of all the personalities that could be considered, Ludovisi's prospects of securing the tiara stood the highest.[4]

Campori remained Borghese's real candidate, notwithstanding much opposition among the Cardinals of his party.[5] For his elevation, which was also favoured by Albuquerque, the Spanish ambassador, he secured the support of Zappata, Este, Montalto, Farnese, and Medici. But this candidature met with the opposition of Orsini, Ubaldini, Pio, Bevilacqua,

[1] See CORNARO, *Informatione, loc. cit., and in App. no. II the report about the " papabili ", Servite Library, Innsbruck.

[2] See the *Letter of FABRIZIO ARAGONA, January 30, 1621, Gonzaga Archives, Mantua.

[3] See the *report of F. ARAGONA, of February 6, 1621, loc. cit.

[4] See Arch. Rom., X., 293.

[5] CORNARO remarks in the *Informatione, of January 28, 1621: " Campori è il prediletto di Borghese e se fosse possibile vorrebbe far ogni cosa per lui, ma con questa ultima promotione (cf. the present work, Vol. XXV, Ch. VII., p. 338 seq.) nella quale sono entrati molti soggetti protetti di lui e si può dire fatta a posta per lui, invece di giovarle gli ha pregiudicato assai, perchè essendosi scoperto la intentione e la mira di Borghese, molte creature del med^{mo}. Borghese si dichiaravano di non volerlo in alcuna maniera e credesi che li sarà fatta l'esclusione a posta da Orsino, da Aldobrandino e dalli Francesi." Cod. C. 20, Boncompagni Archives, Rome.

Tonti, Crescenzi, and Filonardi, as well as that of Aldobrandini who desired the elevation of Ludovisi, and that of the French ambassador who was joined by Cardinal Bonsi.[1] All this simplified the relative position of the parties. On the one side was Borghese allied with the Spanish ambassador, Este, Medici and Farnese, and on the other Aldobrandini supported by the French ambassador together with Ubaldini and Orsini.[2] Borghese's party was without a doubt the strongest; without it an election seemed impossible. Many people were of opinion that Borghese disposed of a few votes in excess of the necessary two-thirds majority.[3] In effect Borghese felt at first so sure of success that he troubled but little about the counter-manœuvres of the opponents of Campori.[4]

[1] *Cf.* besides the *report of F. ARAGONA of February 6, 1621 (*loc. cit.*), *that of B. PAOLUCCI, of February 10, 1621, State Archives, Modena, and above all, " **Conclave per la morte di Paolo V. nel quale fu eletto Gregorio XV.*, scritto del card. Barberini," in *Barb.* 4676, pp. 1-22, and *Ottob.* 2481, p. 366 *seq.* (Vatican Library), hereafter quoted as the report of Card. Orsini. A fine bust of Cardinal Orsini, dated 1621, is to be found in the court-yard of S. Salvatore in Lauro.

[2] "*Erano dunque due le fattioni principali: Borghese, Montalto, Spagnuoli, Farnese, Este, Medici formavano con le loro seguaci la prima e più potente, Aldobrandini, Francesi, Orsini, Ubaldino con le creature di Clemente (VIII.) constituivano la seconda più debile." AG. MASCARDI, *Scrittura intorno all'elettione in S. Pontefice del card. Ludovisio*, Cod. C. 20 (continued in *Cod.* C. 13) of the Boncompagni Archives, Rome. Copies of this document also in *Barb.* 4680, p. 26 *seq.*, and 4695, p. 148 *seq.*; Vatican Library; also in *Cod.* 6581, p. 152 *seq.*, of the State Library, Vienna, and in the State Archives, Modena. The reprint of FR. L. MANNUCCI, in the *Atti d. Soc. Lig.* XLII., 542 *seqq.*, is from the latter MSS. See *ibid.*, 93 *seq.*, for the provenance of this document.

[3] See the report of the Venetian *obbedienza* ambassadors in BAROZZI-BERCHET, *Roma I.*, 115. *Cf.* SÄGMÜLLER, *Papstwahlbullen*, 230, note 4.

[4] See the report of the Venetian *obbedienza* ambassadors, *loc. cit.* *Cf.* the opinion of A. Tassoni in the relation published by STORNAJOLI (*Miscell. Ceriani*, Milano, 1910).

Nothing could have surpassed the ardour with which Orsini worked for the exclusion of Campori. In him he saw an old enemy of his family who had deeply offended him personally by some biting remarks. He could be sure of Aldobrandini's Cardinals who were as opposed to Borghese as he could have wished, and he could likewise hope to bring over to his side some of Borghese's own adherents.[1]

When on the morning of February 8th, 1621, after the customary discourse on the papal election delivered by Agostino Mascardi, a man who enjoyed a great reputation as a preacher, the fifty-eight electors [2] entered the conclave prepared in the Vatican, Orsini thought he would easily succeed in excluding Campori.[3] To prevent this Borghese did all that lay in his power. His efforts were energetically seconded by his friends, especially by Savelli and Pignatelli, by Zappata also and Este, and by the representative of the Emperor, Prince Savelli, and the Spanish ambassador, Albuquerque. The above named were indefatigable in their efforts to keep the adherents of Campori together and to win new friends for him. The task was an arduous one because Campori was very unpopular and many felt that a continuation of the paramount position of Borghese, which would follow on Campori's election, was more than they could stand. Este endeavoured, though unsuccessfully, to win over for Campori both Bevilacqua and Pio. Pignatelli sought to convince Bellarmine that he was bound in conscience to give his vote to so deserving a man. If that was really the case, Bellarmine replied, it should hardly be necessary to set up so unusual an agitation, even before the Bulls of the conclave had been read, as prescribed by law. Pignatelli was equally unsuccessful with Ubaldini. Zappata and the Spanish ambassador sought to influence Sforza and Madruzzo by threatening them with the displeasure of Philip IV. should they oppose Campori's elevation. However all these efforts were in vain. On the other hand the attempts of Orsini, seconded by Ubaldini, Pio and Bevilacqua, to win

---

[1] See the *report of CARD. ORSINI, *loc. cit.*

[2] See *Biografia del card. Campori*, Modena, 1878, 25.

[3] See the *report of CARD ORSINI, *loc. cit.*

Montalto, Medici and Farnese for Campori's exclusion, were equally unsuccessful.[1]

The struggle of the parties grew in tenseness as the day wore on. At one time the scales seemed to turn in favour of Campori. True, the attempts of the party of Borghese to induce Orsini to change his mind proved in vain, but the number of those who were for the exclusion of Campori fell from twenty-four, of whom Orsini imagined he could be sure, to sixteen.[2] However, eighteen votes were required for exclusion. As for Campori he felt so sure of his election that he made plans for his pontificate. An attempt by Delfino at that moment to win his countrymen, Priuli and Valiero, for Campori's exclusion failed, owing to the Venetian envoy, so it was thought, having left the conclave too soon. Instead, the French ambassador, the Marquis de Cœuvres, stayed all the longer. Though the governor of the conclave summoned him to depart, he only left the place of the election as a new day was breaking.[3]

That which had detained the French ambassador so long was the discussion with Cardinal Aldobrandini. The health of that prince of the Church had become so much worse that he had to keep to his bed. He was thus prevented from taking the lead in Campori's exclusion, as had been planned. Aldobrandini then advised Cœuvres to spring upon the assembled electors, in the name of the French King, the exclusion which would put an abrupt end to Campori's candidature. However, the

---

[1] *Cf.* the *report of CARD. ORSINI, *loc. cit.*, and the *relation of TASSONI, *loc. cit.*, 348 *seq.* MASCARDI says in connection with the opposition against Campori: " *Campori non era amato et alcuni non volevano vedere la continuatione del dominio in casa Borghese. Altri lo tenevano troppo inclinato all'accrescimento delle facoltà private, altri ascrivevano a lui solo tutti li disgusti havuti a Palazzo sotto Paolo V." Boncompagni Archives, Rome, *loc. cit.*

[2] See ORSINI's *report, *loc. cit.*, *B. Paolucci (*cf.* above, p. 35, note 1) gives the number of those excluded as seventeen. *Cf.* also C. CATANEO's report in COUDERC, *Bellarmin*, II., 304.

[3] See *ORSINI's report, *loc. cit.* *Cf. Conclavi* I., 384 *seq.*; SIRI, V., 255.

ambassador deemed this too dangerous a step, but he ended by obtaining from Aldobrandini, and the remaining Cardinals of Clement VIII., a promise in writing by which they bound themselves to exclude Campori and to vote for the elevation of Aquino or Ludovisi.[1]

The determined opposition which Campori's elevation encountered, especially Madruzzo's refusal to give him his vote, had made a profound impression on Borghese. Nor did it escape him that some of his most trusted followers were beginning to waver.[2] Hence he was afraid to attempt to bring off an election by adoration on the opening day. Even at the first scrutiny, on the morning of February 9th, he deemed it best not to come out into the open with his own candidate. On this occasion most of the votes—fifteen in all—fell to Bellarmine. The scrutiny was barely over when Orsini left the room. "Now we need no longer fear the elevation of Campori", he said to one of his intimates, "before the day is over another shall have the tiara."[3]

The conviction that Borghese would not be able to realize his scheme made way even with his own adherents. One of the first to perceive it was Cardinal Giustiniani and the idea took shape in his mind that with the help of Zappata and Madruzzo he might himself become Pope. But his hopes were promptly dashed for he was shown a letter of the King of Spain which expressly stated that he was not acceptable. Spain also

---

[1] See the *report of the French ambassador in PETITOT, 2nd Series, XVI., 369 *seq.*, and SÄGMÜLLER, *Papstwahlbullen*, 232 *seq.* *Cf.* M. D'ESTRÉES, *Mémoires*, p.p. Bonnefon, Paris, 1910, 345 *seq.* On account of illness, Aldobrandini was one of the first to leave the conclave, as reported in an Avviso of February 13, 1621 ; on reaching home, he died so soon as " alle 2½ hore di notte ". He had caught a chill on the hurried journey from Ravenna to Rome, which he accomplished in three days. *Urb.* 1089 B, Vatican Library.

[2] See *PAOLUCCI's report of February 10, 1621, State Archives, Modena.

[3] See *ORSINI's report (Vatican Library), which is also the chief source for that which follows.

excluded Cardinal Monte because of his dealings with the Grand Duke of Florence and with Venice. For all that, Medici now pushed the latter's candidature, for Borghese also had promised to give it his support if that of Campori should prove hopeless. All Campori's opponents expressed their readiness to vote for Monte, as well as Farnese, Este and the Florentine Cardinals of Borghese's party.[1]

Zappata informed Paul V.'s nephew of the danger of the situation and at the same time represented to him that he must make up his mind to exclude Monte if he wished to avoid a rupture with the Spaniards. Borghese happened to be in the cell of Cardinal Capponi at the moment when Zappata made this communication, which put him in a difficult position. If he opposed Monte, Medici could reproach him with disloyalty [2] and if he hesitated any longer there was a danger that the choice would fall on a man whose elevation might be extremely disagreeable to him. Of his own candidates, now that Campori's elevation had failed, there remained only Aquino and Ludovisi. Of the two, Borghese would have preferred the former had he not been laid low by a mortal sickness.[3] So there was nothing for it but to decide in favour of Ludovisi who had only come to Rome from Bologna on February 8th and who was very well aware of his prospects of the tiara.[4] Este, who also happened to be in Capponi's cell, likewise advocated this candidature.[5] As a matter of fact, by reason of his peaceable character, his blameless life and

[1] *Cf.* *ORSINI's report and that of *PAOLUCCI, *loc. cit.*
[2] See *PAOLUCCI's report, *loc. cit.*
[3] Aquino died on February 12, 1621. CIACONIUS, IV., 492.
[4] How certainly Ludovisi counted on success, and how little he feared the candidature of Aquino, but only that of Campori, is apparent from the account of DOMENICO CECCHINI, printed in *Arch. Rom.*, X., 291 *seq.*
[5] According to *PAOLUCCI's account, Este, supported by Capponi, induced Borghese to vote for Ludovisi. MASCARDI (*Scrittura, etc., Cod.* C. 13 of Boncompagni Archives, Rome) says he did not know who first proposed Ludovisi, whether it was Este who boasted of it, or Borghese : " Dell'uno e dell'altro è

his knowledge of the law, Ludovisi enjoyed universal esteem, the Spaniards wanted him, the French did not exclude him and he was popular with most of the Cardinals.¹ Borghese arranged with Zappata, Capponi and Este, forthwith to bring about the elevation of Ludovisi. Whilst Zappata informed the Spaniards of their resolution and Este similarly broke the news to Pio, Capponi called on the opponents of Campori and Borghese on Orsini who willingly fell in with his proposal. Together the erstwhile opponents, now reconciled, hastened to Ludovisi's cell, to inform him of his forthcoming elevation to the papacy. The remaining Cardinals soon foregathered in Ludovisi's room, except such of them as were impeded by ill health.²

The decision had been arrived at with surprising rapidity.³ Though Borghese had failed to push through his favourite candidate he had reason, nevertheless, to be satisfied that the election had fallen on one of the late Pope's Cardinal's and one he had had in view from the beginning, even though only as a third candidate. None the less everybody was surprised that Paul V.'s nephew, commanding as he did, so many adherents, had not made a serious effort to get his favourite through when the opponents of Campori were short of two votes to enable them to exclude him. Some ascribed his conduct to Borghese's weakness and inexperience, others to the circumstance that he did not feel quite sure of his followers.⁴

credibile perchè in ambeduoi concorrevano motivi efficaci di tal nominatione." Later accounts name Borghese; see GINDELY, *Gesch. des Dreissigjährigen Krieges*, IV., 349.

¹ See PAOLUCCI's report, *loc. cit.*

² See *ORSINI's report and that of PAOLUCCI, which was written immediately after the election.

³ "In termine poco più d'un quarto d'hora," is F. Aragona's assertion in his *report of February 10, 1621, Gonzaga Archives, Mantua. See also MAGNI PERNEI, *De efficacia divinæ gratiæ ex electione Gregorii XV.*, dedicated to the Pope, *Barb.* 3271/72, Vatican Library.

⁴ See *ORSINI's report. According to the *report in the State Archives at Simancas, which was used by GINDELY (*Gesch. des*

The shadows of night had already fallen upon the Vatican when the two senior Cardinals' Deacons escorted Ludovisi to the Cappella Paolina where his election and the first homage of the Sacred College took place.

The news called forth extraordinary joy in Rome. An immense concourse of people flocked to St. Peter's. Many penetrated into the conclave itself and only by the threat of severest penalties could they be persuaded to withdraw.

The Pope spent the night in Borghese's cell, the conclavists, as the custom was, having plundered his own. On the following morning (February 10th, 1621) Gregory XV.—Ludovisi took the name in memory of his countryman, Gregory XIII.—said Mass in the Sistine Chapel and only then was the newly-elected Pope escorted to St. Peter's where the people hailed him with joyous acclamations.[1] He was not unknown in Rome and by his agreeable manner he had made many friends there. The Sacred College also expressed its satisfaction for not only the Cardinals of Paul V. but those also of Sixtus V. and Clement VIII., took into account that those Popes had had a share in the rise of Gregory XV.[2]

Dreissigjährigen Krieges, IV., 349 *seq.*), Borghese, who only lacked two votes for a two-thirds majority (thirty-five), had contemplated, at the very beginning of the conclave, to secure the tiara for Campori by adoration; but this plan fell through, chiefly because too many others pressed into the election hall, and the rows of Cardinals were broken through, so that, when they finally remained alone, the late Pope's nephew no longer felt sufficiently determined to carry out this device, though even now it was not too late to do so. The Venetian *obbedienza* ambassadors affirm that Borghese commanded at first six and later three votes above the two-thirds majority, but could not make up his mind to act, as he was not sure enough of his supporters. BAROZZI-BERCHET, *Roma*, I., 115.

[1] See *Conclavi*, I., 395; *Report of the Venetian *obbedienza* ambassadors, in BAROZZI-BERCHET, *Roma*, I., 116; *Avviso of February 10, 1621, *Urb.* 1089 B, Vatican Library. For the names of the conclavists in *Bull.* XII., 497 *seq.*

[2] *Cf.* GIUNTI, *Vita del card. Ludovisi*, Corsini Library, Rome; see appendix no. IV. Numerous letters of congratulation to

The man who had thus risen to the highest dignity after a Cardinalate of only four years, sprang from a Florentine family which had settled at Bologna in the twelfth century and which could boast a great many distinguished men.[1] Gregory XV.'s mother, Camilla Bianchini, wife of Count Pompeo Ludovisi, also belonged to an old Bolognese family. Alessandro Ludovisi, as the new Pope was called, was born at Bologna on January 9th, 1554.[2] He came to Rome at the beginning of the reign of Pius V., in the autumn of 1567, to enter the Collegium Germanicum conducted by the Jesuits. That establishment, which enjoyed a high reputation, was at that time attended by a number of Italian noble youths. Ludovisi remained two years as a *convictor* and during that time studied humanities at the Roman College. In this way his classical studies were made in a Christian atmosphere. Besides the pagan authors the young Bolognese was a keen student of the Fathers of the Church. His favourite author was St. Jerome and he knew by heart numerous passages of the Saint's writings.[3] As one of the best students it fell to the lot of Ludovisi to deliver a panegyric of the great Apostle of India, St. Francis Xavier, in presence of

---

Gregory XV., especially from Bologna, are in *Cod. E. 70. 71*, of Boncompagni Archives, Rome. The election of Gregory XV. was celebrated with special festivities at Mantua ; see ADEMOLLO, *La bell'Adriana*, Città di Castello, 1888, 267 seqq.

[1] See P. Sc. DOLFI, *Cronologia delle famiglie nobili di Bologna*, Bologna, 1670, 461 ; MORONI, XL., 104 *seq.*

[2] See ACCARISIUS, *Vita Gregorii XV*. This work based on good authorities (see appendix no. V), the original MS. of which I found in the Boncompagni Archives, Rome, supplements considerably the meagre information obtainable until then on the antecedents of the Ludovisi Pope ; it is the source of the statements made hereafter.

[3] Ludovisi's tutor, Hieronymus Crucius, wrote in a *letter quoted by ACCARISIUS (*loc. cit.*) from the archives of the Collegium Romanum : " Comiti Alexandro Ludovisio meo in humanioribus litteris discipulo proprium hoc est, ut s. Hieronymi epistolas memoria promptas habeat earumque verba ac sententias saepius pro re nata, quod mirum est, fidelissime experteque subiiciat."

the Cardinal Protector of the college. Alessandro's delicate health, of which the paleness of his face was a symptom [1], was not equal to his ardour for study, hence the physicians sent him back to Bologna to recuperate. Though only barely restored to health, Ludovisi was soon back in Rome. From 1569 to 1571 he read philosophy and theology at the Roman College. During that time he became thoroughly acquainted with Protestant controversy. Here also he distinguished himself in a public disputation, in presence of the Cardinal Protectors, when he skilfully defended a number of theses. On the completion of his theological studies Alessandro returned to his native city in order to attend the lectures on law at the university there. He showed equal keenness in this branch of learning in which more than one of his ancestors had earned great renown. The Doctor's hat and licence to teach rewarded his application in 1575. Only now, and after consulting with some older friends, he made up his mind to become a priest, and since meanwhile his countryman Ugo Boncompagni had become Pope, he returned to Rome. Gregory XIII. made him chairman of the College of judges on the Capitol. Nor did the gifted young priest escape the attention of Sixtus V. When Cardinal Ippolito Aldobrandini went as legate to Poland, in 1588, the Pope's choice of a companion fell on Alessandro Ludovisi though an attack of illness prevented his making the journey.[2]

In view of Ludovisi's extensive knowledge of the law, Gregory XIV. named him a member of the commission for the examination of the escheat of Ferrara.[3] When the papal commissary general in France, Girolamo Matteucci, fell ill, Clement VIII., who as a Cardinal had taken Ludovisi under his patronage, thought of appointing in Matteucci's place the Bolognese priest who was as learned as he was pious. However Matteucci recovered, whereupon the Pope appointed Ludovisi referendary

[1] " Modicus enim virium fereque semper suppallida facie apparebat." *ACCARISIUS, lib. I., c. 2, *loc. cit.*
[2] *See *ACCARISIUS, lib. I., c. 5, *loc. cit.*
[3] *ACCARISIUS (*loc. cit.*) saw Ludovisi's report in the Papal Secret Archives.

of the *Segnatura di giustizia e grazia*, and, later on a substitute of the Cardinal Vicar of Rome in civil questions.¹

As referendary of the *Segnatura*, Alessandro Ludovisi was entrusted with the most difficult cases and his skill in solving them soon became proverbial.² When in 1595 the Pope was called upon to appoint a fresh occupant of the see of Toledo, a problem which had been greatly complicated by the testamentary dispositions of the deceased Cardinal Quiroga, and by the demands of Philip II., Clement VIII. had recourse to Ludovisi's services and on his advice he appointed Cardinal the Archduke Albert as Primate of the Church in Spain.³ If on this occasion Alessandro Ludovisi rendered an important service to the house of Habsburg, he also put the Bourbon dynasty under obligation by what he did for the absolution of Henry IV.⁴ These excellent relations stood him in good stead in his efforts to compose a scandalous dispute between the ambassadors of France and Spain, when he relieved Clement VIII. of no small anxiety. Ludovisi showed like prudence and moderation when the Pope charged him, together with Maffeo Barberini, with the duty of settling with the Viceroy of Naples the conflict over Benevento. On this occasion he dissuaded the Pope from inflicting the penalty of excommunication and in the end he composed the dispute in amicable fashion.⁵

Ludovisi's action as mediator and peacemaker was even more important on the occasion of the troubles caused by the Farnese in August, 1604.⁶ It was he who soothed Clement VIII.

---

¹ See MORONI, XCIX., 173 ; CIACONIUS, IV., 442.

² "Si nodus inexplicabilis accidit, enimvero is soli Alexandro nostro, ut calamo, non gladio dissolvat, reliquendus," Clement VIII. is reported to have said. *ACCARISIUS, lib. I., ch. 6, *loc. cit.*

³ According to *ACCARISIUS, lib. I., ch. 7, Domenico Tosco and Franc. Mantica also belonged to the commission for the affair of Toledo.

⁴ "Benignum oportet esse Pontificem Maximum, cum ecclesiae catholicae benignae fidelium matris sit sponsus," Ludovisi is reported to have said ; see *ACCARISIUS, lib. I., ch. 8, *loc. cit.*

⁵ See *ACCARISIUS, lib. II., c. 1.

⁶ *Cf.* present work, Vol. XXIII, 259 *seq.*

and secured a hearing for Duke Ranuccio Farnese and pardon for Cardinal Odoardo Farnese.[1] The Pope's confidence,[2] which had already been shown by Ludovisi's appointment as auditor of the Rota for Bologna,[3] now rose so high that his elevation to the Sacred College was believed to be imminent. However the death of the Aldobrandini Pope destroyed that prospect.

In other ways also fortune refused to smile on Ludovisi. Paul V.'s intention to entrust him with a mission to the Emperor was again frustrated by the bad state of his health. However, the Pope was unwilling to be wholly deprived of the services of so excellent a man, so he named him vicegerent of the Cardinal Vicar of Rome. In this position Ludovisi gave further proof of his skill as a mediator and peacemaker, especially in the disputes between Bishops and Regulars, which were frequent in those days.[4] In Paul V.'s conflict with Venice Ludovisi also worked in the direction of an amicable understanding.[5] Proof of the Pope's esteem was his appointment to the see of Bologna, on March 12th, 1612. Ludovisi signalled his taking of possession by a beautiful pastoral letter.[6] However, he was unable, at first, to devote much attention to his diocese owing to the fact that the Pope had

---

[1] See *ACCARISIUS, lib. II., ch. 4.

[2] " *Hinc Pontifex Maximus familiarius cum Alexandro versari, arcana pectoris ei fidentius aperire, immo vero obstrusiores deliberationes cum eo familiarissime communicare. ACCARISIUS, loc. cit.

[3] A. Ludovisi was considered one of the most distinguished members who had ever belonged to the Rota ; see MORONI, LXXXII, 272 seq. Cf. Decisiones S. Rotae Rom. coram Al. Ludovisio nunc Gregorio XV. cum annot. Ol. Beltramini, Romae, 1622, and Venetiis, 1638, and CERCHIARI, S. Romana Rota, II., Romae, 1920, 130. A *" Repertorium utriusque iuris ab Alex. Ludovisio exaratum dum S.R. Rotae auditoris munus obibat," in Cod. H. 15–17, Boncompagni Archives, Rome.

[4] See *ACCARISIUS, lib. II., c. 8.

[5] See ibid.

[6] Cf. CIACONIUS, IV., 468.

pressing need of his services. In the difficult question of Montferrat, which caused Paul V. grave anxiety, he thought that he could not do without Ludovisi's assistance as a peacemaker between Duke Charles Emmanuel I. of Savoy and Philip III. By the zeal he displayed in this matter, both in Milan and in Turin, Ludovisi won the highest regard of the parties to the dispute as well as that of the Pope.[1] On September 19th, 1616, the purple rewarded his exertions.[2] Both the court of Madrid and that of Paris thanked the Pope for the appointment: an act which represented a most exceptional agreement![3]

Towards the close of 1618 Ludovisi came to Rome where in the consistory of November 20th, he received the red hat and in that of December 3rd, the title of the church of Santa Maria in Transpontina.[4] He remained in Rome until the end of 1619. It was generally believed that he would succeed Paul V., so much so that the Venetian envoy courted his good will in conspicuous fashion.[5] The remainder of Paul V.'s pontificate was spent by Ludovisi in his native city of Bologna, discharging his duties as Archbishop in the spirit of the Tridentine reform, and applying himself in particular to the formation of a model clergy.[6]

---

[1] See *ACCARISIUS, lib. II., ch. 11. *Cf.* present work, XXV. Ch. IX., p. 422.

[2] See present work, Vol. XXV., Ch. VII., p. 337.

[3] See *ACCARISIUS, lib. II., ch. 12.

[4] See CIACONIUS, IV., 443.

[5] See BAROZZI-BERCHET, Roma I., 129.

[6] Quippe solitum dicere accepimus, nihil tam populis perniciosum quam clericorum licentiam (*ACCARISIUS, lib. II., ch. 10). *Cf.* TOMBA, *Arcivescovi di Bologna*, Bologna, 1788; CASSANI, *L'espiscopato Bolognese*, ibid., 1859; TAROZZI, *De archiepisc. eccles. Bonon.*, ibid., 1885. Aless. Ludovisi wrote from Bologna on December 21, 1619, to his nephew Ludovico: "La corte è piena di malignità e li Romaneschi oltre la buona qualità della corte hanno quella del paese; nelle cincie di Bologna bisogna far puocha riflessione (original in *Cod.* E. 67, of the Boncompagni Archives, Rome). As a sign of his affection, Gregory XV. later

His love of the arts is revealed by the extraordinary interest he took in his famous countryman, Domenichino, whose financial condition was deplorable. On one occasion he urged his nephew Ludovico, who lived in Rome, to support the master's demand for payment by the Apostolic Camera.[1]

In political questions Cardinal Ludovisi had always remained strictly neutral, first of all because he disliked disputes and party intrigues, and secondly because he was aware that, ever since his elevation to the archbishopric of Bologna, there was question of his election to the papacy.[2] The following incident is a characteristic example of his prudence. After his successful mediation between Spain and Savoy the Spanish Government offered him a pension of fifteen hundred scudi. However, he hesitated to accept it inasmuch as he did not wish to antagonize the French. On the other hand, to refuse would have deeply offended the Spaniards. At last he saw a happy way out. Through his confidant Domenico Cecchini he so successfully dispelled every suspicion from the mind of the French ambassador that he was able to accept the pension. Contact thus established with the representative of France

sent the Chapter of the Metropolitan Church at Bologna " imagini d'argento " which had been used during the last Canonization, see " *Lettera d'Agucchi alli canonici e capitolo della Metropolit. di Bologna, on May 16, 1622, Cod. X., V. 31, Casanat. Library, Rome.

[1] On April 11, 1620, Cardinal A. Lodovisi wrote from Bologna to his nephew: " *Il Domenichino vi si raccomanda ; è mal trattato costi e qui ; ha bisogno che il tesoriere e la Camera lo spedischino o dentro o fuori ; raccomandatelo caldamente a questi sig^{ri} camerali per la speditione a nome mio." On April 14 to the same : " *Il Domenichino sta molto travagliato per la causa sua ; bisogna pregare il tesoriere che vogli spedirlo o dentro o fuori." On April 25 : " *È stato bene a cominciare di raccomandare alli chierici di Camera la causa di Domenichino ; a mi piace che habbiasi scorta in essi buona voluntà di favorirlo per giustitia." Original in Cod. E. 67, of the Boncompagni Archives, Rome.

[2] See *Vita e successi del card. Cecchini, Cod. 39, D. 17, p. 30, Corsini Library, Rome.

proved of great consequence because the latter kept his eye on him as a likely candidate for the papacy.[1] It was of the utmost importance that plans of this kind should have the support of Montalto and Aldobrandini. With the latter Ludovisi came into close contact, because Domenico Cecchini was a distant relative of the Aldobrandini. True, Ludovisi's opponents objected that he lacked independence, that he was ignorant of politics and that his great goodness degenerated into weakness. But this did not prevent the fact that, as early as 1618, Ludovisi was one of those who might hope for the papacy. Though at Bologna feelings were in favour of France rather than Spain, the Cardinal showed no preference for either Power.[2]

Such reserve was in keeping with the quiet, placid nature of the new Pope who, whilst he was a man of few words, showed the greatest cordiality to all and sundry. The great skill displayed by him in the conduct of affairs and his prudence

---

[1] " *Volendo li Spagnuoli per la sodisfattione che mostravano havere havuta nel suo negotiato fare seco qualche dimostratione gli havevano costituita una provisione di ducati 1500 stava irresoluto il cardinale se dovesse pigliarla o piutosto ricusarla dubitando in pigliarla di dispiacere ai Francesi, mentre riceveva beneficio da Spagnuoli, et in ricusarla dispiacere alli stessi Spagnuoli, è deliberato alla fine che fosse meglio pigliarla e procurare di fare capaci li Francesi che questa era una mercede se li dava per la nuntiatura e secondo lo stile che si era usato con altri cardinali ; pensò che io mi valessi di Mons. Bunozetto, auditore di Rota Francese, che ne'negotii dell'ambasceria di Francia nella corte di Roma haveva grandissima parte et era amicissimo di marchese di Covere ambasciatore sapendo quanto grande fosse l'amicitia che passava tra di me e detto Monsignore e quanto di lui mi poteva promettere ; nè fu anche vano il pensare poichè Mons. Bunozetto fece l'officio in tal maniera che non solo i Francesi deposero ogni sospetto, ma il marchese di Covere quando venne l'occasione del conclave fu uno di quelli che per quanto pote promosse l'esaltatione del cardinale al pontificato. *Vita e successi del card. Cecchini*, p. 30[b], *loc. cit.*

[2] See *Discorso de cardinali*, of 1618, Boncompagni Archives, Rome.

had enabled him to obtain what he wanted quietly and without attracting undue attention.[1] His was an upright nature and he abhorred every form of duplicity—nothing could have induced him to utter an untruth.[2] His mode of life was abstemious and ordered by a strict rule: he was fond of exercise.[3] The outward appearance of Gregory XV., which the youthful Bernini perpetuated in a magnificent bronze bust,[4] had nothing of the imposing figure of his predecessor.

[1] See the report of the Venetian *obbedienza* ambassadors in BAROZZI-BERCHET, *Roma*, I., 117.

[2] See ACCARISIUS, *Vita Gregorii XV.*, lib. III., ch. 21.

[3] See the report of the Venetian ambassadors, *loc. cit.*

[4] Preserved in the Stroganoff Collection, Rome. See *Pièces de choix de la Collection du Comte Grégoire Stroganoff à Rome par L. Pollak et A. Muñoz*, II., Rome, 1912, 138, and plate XIV. Cf. MUÑOZ in *Vita d'arte*, VIII. (1911), 183; *L'Arte*, XIX. (1916), 104. The Pope's hair is very thin, his beard is cut short, his face expresses fatigue; whereas on his tombstone he seems quite strong. Poor copies of this masterpiece, which was rewarded with the Order of Christ (see FRASCHETTI, *Bernini*, 32), in which the young artist already shows his full powers, are in the Museo Civico, Bologna, in the Palace of Prince Doria, Rome, at Sangiorgi's and Simonetti's, in the Jacquemart André Museum, Paris (derived from the Borghese family), and finally a small one in the Palazzo Massimi, Rome. The whereabouts of a seventh copy which was sold from the Bandini Collection, 1899, and went to London, is unknown; see KROHN's essay on a bust in the Museum of Sculpture at Copenhagen, in the *Tidskrift för Konstvetenschap*, Copenhagen, 1916. Other busts of Gregory XV. are in the church of Propaganda (see FORCELLA XI., 455). The bust in the collection Barsanti, Rome, differs from these (see POLLAK, *Bronzi ital.*, Rome, 1922, 149, and plate 49). In 1913 a bronze bust of Gregory XV. was bought by L. Pollak from the Ludovisi Collection; it is a Roman contemporary piece of work: the Pope is represented in ordinary indoor dress with the biretta on his head, his brow is deeply furrowed and his beard sparse. For Algardi's bust of Gregory XV. see POSSE in *Jahrb. der preuss. Kunstsammml.*, XXVI., 194. The two marble busts of Gregory XV., both modelled by Bernini, have disappeared (see BALDINUCCI, ed. Riegl 74). With regard to the miniature bust of Gregory XV. in the Chiesa

Short and slender of stature, he had a deeply furrowed brow and thin beard. His blond hair became prematurely white so that he looked older than he was. This impression was further heightened by his pale and sickly complexion.[1]

Strenuous exertions and repeated illnesses [2] had tried the strength of Gregory XV. to such an extent that he felt compelled to look for someone who would help him to cope with affairs. This assistance he found in the eldest son of his brother whom he raised to the Cardinalate as early as February 15th, 1621, one day after his own coronation,[3] and whom he

---

Nuova see Muñoz in the *Atti d. Accad. di S. Luca*, II. (1911), 44. There is also a bust of Gregory XV. in the cathedral at Bologna. Likenesses of the Pope are to be found in the engravings of *Lukas Kilian and Peter Isselburg*, see *Portrait Index*, ed. by W. COOLIDGE LANE and NINA E. BROWNE, Washington, 1906, 616; a copy of the engraving by Isselburg is in WINTER, *Gesch. des Dreissigjährigen Krieges* (1893), 259. An engraving by Chris. Greuter, of Augsburg, is in the collection of the Munich Pinakothek. Statues of Gregory XV. on his tomb by Le Gros and in the Collegium Romanum; see *La Canonizzazione*, 33; *ibid.*, 31, also a copy of the oil painting of Gregory XV. in the Villa Aurora, Rome, in the possession of the Prince of Piombino. For the characteristic portrait of Gregory XV. in the Seminario Romano Maggiore, see CASTELUCCI, 169. *Cf. Il Pontif. Seminario Romano*, Rome, 1914, 23. For the miniatures of Gregory XV., see MARTINORI, *Zecca di Roma, 1621-1644*, Rome, 1919, 12 *seq.* Here also, page 7 *seq.*, information on the papal coins. *Cf.* also SERAFINI, *Le Monete del Museo Vatic.*, II., Rome, 1912, 175 *seq.*

[1] " In vultu color gilvus quique ad mellis similitudinem maxime vergebat fere semper apparuit " (*ACCARISIUS, *loc. cit.*). *Cf.* the *report of A. POSSEVINO of August 13, 1621, Gonzaga Archives, Mantua.

[2] *Cf.* above, p. 43. In the letters to his nephew, Ludovico, mentioned on p. 52, n. 2 (Boncompagni Archives, Rome), Cardinal A. Ludovisi often speaks of his gout.

[3] See *Acta consist.*, *Barb.* 2985, Vatican Library. For the Majordomoship under Gregory XV., see MORONI, XLI., 264; " *Ruolo di famiglia di Gregorio XV*. in *Cod.* H., II., 42, of the Chigi Library, Rome.

now entrusted with the management of the most important affairs, both spiritual and secular. The appointment created a good impression because it was known that the nephew was animated by the same gentle and humane spirit which had always been admired in the Pope himself.[1]

Ludovico Ludovisi,[2] the son of Count Orazio and Lavinia Albergati, was born at Bologna on October 27th, 1595, but had come to Rome in his childhood with his parents.[3] One of his uncles was an auditor of the Rota at that time. The promising lad received an excellent education at the hands of the Jesuits, in the Roman College. In the dramatic representations which form part of the customary school curriculum of the Jesuits, he shone by his eloquence and his excellent memory. Notwithstanding repeated illnesses and a disease of the eyes he completed his studies in the prescribed time. When Ludovico's uncle became Archbishop of Bologna in 1612, his nephew betook himself thither in order to study for the bar at the university. He pursued his studies with such ardour that he was able to take his doctorate in February, 1615.[4] In the autumn of the following year he became arch-

---

[1] " In quanto al presente pontificato s'aspetta ognuno uno ottimo governo si per la bontà e somma prudenza di S. B^{ne} nota a tutti come del nipote, l'un l'altro di natura molto mite e piacevole." *Report of F. ARAGONA on February 17, 1621, Gonzaga Archives, Mantua.

[2] For what follows see the *Biography of the Cardinal by L. A. GIUNTI, Corsini Library, Rome. *Cf.* Appendix no. IV.

[3] GIUNTI (*loc. cit.*) says : *A pena fuori delle fascie uscito da suoi genitori fu condotto in Roma, dove dimoravano molt'anni con Mons. Ludovisi all'hora auditore di Ruota.

[4] "A 15 febraro 1615 sostenne le sue publiche conclusioni, le quali furono da lui dedicate al card. Borghese et in lode del suo valore furono fatti gl'infrascripti versi." These end with the words :—

" Ludovice domus Ludovisiae nobile germen,
    Spes patriae, Themidis lux nova fatidicae,
  Dum patrum unanimi consensu insignia sumis
    Virtutis, per te crescit honoris honos.
A 25 dell'istesso mese di febraro 1615 riportò il conte Ludovisio

priest of the metropolitan church of Bologna. Afterwards he accompanied his uncle in his diplomatic missions to Turin and Milan, in the course of which he rendered him such splendid service as to earn the Legate's fullest satisfaction and confidence. In the summer of 1618, illness brought Ludovico to the verge of the grave.[1] At the close of 1619 he entered the Roman prelature. He maintained his former good relations with the Jesuits, worked with the greatest application in the Congregation of the *Segnatura di giustizia e grazia* and from the beginning of December, 1620, in that of *del buon governo* as well. With his uncle in Bologna Ludovico was in constant and lively epistolary correspondence,[2] and he did all he could to further the latter's prospects of the tiara.[3]

On the death of Monsignor Guevara, Ludovico Ludovisi took his place in the *Consulta*—January 5th, 1621. A little over a month later, in consequence of the change in the occupancy of the Apostolic See, which put his uncle on the throne of Peter, he became head of that Congregation and a member of the Sacred College. The youthful Cardinal gave proof of a truly ecclesiastical spirit—for which, as a matter

il grado di dottorato e l'aggregazione al collegio dei giudici, prerogativa, che si concede a quelli solamente che per nobiltà e scienza se ne rendono degni. Non molto doppo fu honorato d'una pubblica lettura nell'istessa sua patria potendosi raccogliere da un volume di lezioni fatte da lui, che si conserva fra suoi manoscritti." *GIUNTI, *loc. cit.*, Corsini Library, Rome.

[1] " *A 18 d'Agosto 1618 cadde infermo in Milano, dove pati una lunga e pericolosa malatia, nella quale ricadde poi anche in Bologna in maniera che si tenne morto " (GIUNTI, *loc. cit.*). Cesare Egnatio, the physician who treated Ludovisi at the time, wrote him a *letter of congratulation on the election of his uncle to the Papacy, dated Todi February 10, 1621 ; original in *Cod.* E. 70, Number 10, of the Boncompagni Archives, Rome.

[2] The originals of these very numerous but not very important letters, of the years 1619 and 1620, are in *Cod.* E. 67, Boncompagni Archives, Rome. On May 27, 1620, Cardinal Ludovisi wrote to his nephew from Bologna " *Mi rallegro, che il card. Barberini vi favorisca proteger nella maniera che scrivete."

[3] See *GIUNTI, *loc. cit.*, p. 5.

of fact, his education by the Jesuits had prepared the ground—by immediately taking priest's orders and by the choice of the Jesuit Giacomo Minutoli for his confessor. It was universally remarked that his rapid rise had not altered his genial manner. Now, as before, he was considerate to everybody, his servants included, and ever ready to render service. This is the character given to him by Lucantonio Giunti, a familiar of long standing and his subsequent biographer.[1]

Giunti cannot say enough in praise of the Cardinal nephew. The Cardinal, he relates, was so indefatigable in giving audiences that he would rather have foregone his meals than refuse to listen to anyone who might be waiting in his antechamber. The ambassadors were delighted to deal with so skilful and cautious a statesman. His outward appearance was imposing,[2] and though the nephew displayed the splendour that befitted his rank, he did not become haughty. When distinguished personages had to be entertained, the luxury of the period was not wanting, but when the Cardinal took his meals alone, his table was quite plain. At no time was he carried away by passion; never did he shock anyone. If someone happened to upset him, he was easily calmed; even those who offended him deliberately found him ready to forgive, for he was himself the first to seek a reconciliation. But the Cardinal had a special horror of double-dealing and deception. He loved to speak frankly and freely, without ostentation and boasting.[3]

Even though it may be necessary to deduct somewhat from these encomiums so lavishly bestowed by a loyal and grateful retainer, there remains enough that deserves praise and to which other observers also bear witness. The Venetian *obbedienza* ambassadors admired Ludovisi's distinction, pru-

---

[1] See GIUNTI, " *Vita e fatti di L. card. Ludovisi*, in Cod. 39, D. 8, of the Corsini Library, Rome. *Cf.* Appendix IV.

[2] There is a very fine full-length picture of the Cardinal in the possession of the Prince of Piombino in the Villa Aurora, Rome, reproduced in *La Canonizzazione*, 83.

[3] See *GIUNTI, *loc. cit.*, 10^b seq.

dence, and indefatigable application to work.[1] Even his declared enemies, such as Renier Zeno, who was as quarrelsome as he was unscrupulous, were compelled to acknowledge Ludovisi's ability in the conduct of government affairs: his talents, his energy, and his general aptitude which enabled him to find a way out of the most involved situations.[2] Already, on May 28th, 1621, Antonio Possevino of Mantua remarked that the youthful, amiable Cardinal nephew was endowed with a natural gift for political questions.[3]

No wonder, then, that Ludovico should have gained very great influence over his uncle whose goodwill he had enjoyed even before his elevation. He supplemented his uncle in happiest fashion, for the nephew possessed abundantly the strength that the sickly Pontiff lacked. Whereas, especially in the last period of Paul V., the latter's caution and the pedantic slowness of Cardinal Borghese had frequently prevented energetic action, the youthful Secretary of State gave a fresh and vigorous impetus to papal policy from which the cause of the Catholic restoration was to derive extraordinary benefit.

True, the position of the Cardinal nephew was not without the usual drawbacks. Rome was, unfortunately, to witness a repetition of the painful spectacle from which it had suffered under Clement VIII. and Paul V. Ludovisi was loaded with honours, dignities, and the most lucrative ecclesiastical offices and benefices in a measure exceeding all bounds. Immediately after his elevation to the Sacred College he was given the archdiocese of Bologna and, in consequence of the death

---

[1] See BAROZZI-BERCHET, Roma, I., 117.

[2] See *ibid.*, 160. With regard to R. Zeno's quarrelsomeness see DENGEL, *Palazzo di Venezia*, 117 seq. R. Zeno bribed officials of the State Secretariate to betray State Secrets. He cynically recounts this himself in his relation, in BAROZZI-BERCHET, Roma, I., 187.

[3] See the *dispatch of POSSEVINO in Gonzaga Archives, Mantua. *Cf.* also the opinion of the envoys of Lucca in *Studi e docum.*, XXII., 205 seq.

of Pietro Aldobrandini, the office of Camerlengo which yielded a revenue of 10,000 scudi, the legation of Avignon and numerous other benefices, among them some very wealthy abbeys.[1] By May Ludovisi's income from these sources amounted to 80,000 scudi a year.[2] Subsequently it rose considerably,[3] for Gregory XV.'s liberality towards his beloved nephew proved inexhaustible.[4] Thus it came about that Cardinal Ludovisi, who, in May, 1622, had paid the sum of 39,000 scudi for a palazzo of the Colonna situated in the piazza SS. Apostoli,[5] was able to proceed, in the autumn of the same year, to a far more important acquisition.

Pier Francesco Colonna had been obliged to meet such enormous debts incurred by his father that he saw himself compelled to sell the duchy of Zagarolo, with the *castelli*

[1] *Cf.* the *Index of GIUNTI in Appendix no. IV. The nomination to the archbishopric of Bologna took place on February 18, 1621 (see GAMS, 677 ; UGHELLI, II., 53), the appointment to the CAMERARIATUS on March 17, 1621 (*Acta consist.*, Vatican Library). On May 2, 1621, Ludovisi was consecrated Bishop in the Sistine Chapel (*Avviso of May 8, 1621), *Urb.* 1089 B., *ibid.*).

[2] See the *letter of A. POSSEVINO of May 13, 1621, Gonzaga Archives, Mantua.

[3] A *note in *Barb.* 4592 (Vatican Library) unfortunately without date, estimates the sum at 118,270 scudi per year.

[4] See the *report from Lucca in *Studi e docum.*, XXII., 207, and GIUNTI, *Vita, loc. cit.* P. Contarini reckoned later that Ludovisi received during the pontificate of his uncle 800,000 scudi *Luoghi di Monti*, and 1,200,000 Scudi of ecclesiastical benefices. BAROZZI-BERCHET, *Rome*, I., 202.

[5] *Cf.* the *Avvisi of February 26, May 18 and 28, 1622, *Urb.* 1091, Vatican Library. After Ludovisi had become Vice-Chancellor he decided to transfer to the Cancelleria. The palace of the Colonna was now re-acquired by Pier Francesco Colonna for the same price, " oltre al rifare le spese fatte del cardinale nella fabrica nuova " (*Avviso of June 28, 1623, *loc. cit.*). Concerning this palace, which finally came into the possession of the Odescalchi, *cf.* SCHREIBER, *Villa Ludovisi*, 5, n. 4 ; ASHBY, in *Papers of the British School at Rome*, VIII., and *Arch. Rom.*, XLIV., 387 seq.

of Colonna, Gallicano and Passerano. For the sum of 860,000 scudi Cardinal Ludovisi acquired this ancient, magnificent family estate, twenty miles in extent and situated south of Rome. It included most productive territories, famous vineyards, well-stocked hunting grounds, and yielded an annual revenue of 25,000 scudi. Gregory XV. sanctioned the transaction by a decree of September 27th, 1622, invalidating all previous dispositions to the contrary.[1] Thus did the Colonna family forfeit its oldest possessions and the place from which it derived its name. The main line of the Colonna impugned the validity of the sale. The dispute came before the Rota and was ultimately settled by a compromise.[2] The inhabitants of the duchy were perfectly satisfied with the change, for their new lord showed himself as benevolent as he was beneficent.[3] On his very first visit in October, 1621, the Cardinal was received with great demonstrations of joy.[4] He at once resolved

[1] Cf. MORONI, CIII., 368; *Papers of the British School*, IX. (1920), 69. Out of the price, 600,000 scudi were used to pay the debts of Colonna; see *Avviso of October 1, 1622, Urb. 1092, Vatican Library. It is a serious blunder to say, as RANKE does, (*Päpste*, III.³, 14) that the Dukedom of Zagarolo was bought from the Farnese.

[2] Cf. the *Avvisi of October 15 and 29, November 5, and 12, December 3 and 24, 1622; January 18, February 1 and 15, 1623, Urb. 1092, 1093 A., Vatican Library. As mentioned in an *Avviso of June 24, 1623, the report was current at that time that Ludovisi proposed to sell the duchy of Zagarolo once more to the Colonna; the rumour arose out of certain transactions between the Cardinal and the Spanish King, concerning the purchase of the duchy of Aquila, which was to cost two million gold florins. If Gregory XV. had lived eight or ten days longer, says an *Avviso of July 8, 1623 (*loc. cit.*) the repurchase of Zagarolo would have been carried through for 200,000 scudi.

[3] Cf. GIUNTI, *Vita di L. card. Ludovisi, Corsini Library, Rome.

[4] See the *Avvisi of October 8 and 12, 1622, Urb. 1092, *loc. cit.* The *DIARIUM P. ALALEONIS reports: " Oct. 3. 1622 Papa ivit ad Zagarolam ; 4 Oct. ivit ad Gallicanum ; 5 Oct. ad Columnam ; 9 Oct. redivit Romam." *Barb.* 2818, Vatican Library.

to put up new constructions at Zagarolo for which Carlo Maderno supplied the plans.¹

For a summer residence Cardinal Ludovisi bought from the Duke of Altemps the beautiful villa at Frascati which had been at one time the property of Cardinal Galli.² In May and September, 1622, Gregory XV. spent a few days there.³ His nephew considerably enlarged and embellished this country seat. His model was the celebrated Villa Aldobrandini with which the spot, with its waterworks, terraces and gardens could well stand comparison.⁴

A third magnificent domain was the vast summer residence which Cardinal Ludovisi prepared for himself not far from the Villa Borghese but well within the walls of Rome, on a site at one time occupied by the gardens of Sallust. The heart of the artistically laid out domain which, however, lacked creative originality,⁵—precisely because it grew by degrees—was the Villa of Giovanni Antonio Orsini, close to the city wall, which Ludovisi bought on February 5th, 1622, for the sum of 15,000 scudi. The property was further enlarged in the course of the ensuing months by the acquisition of the vineyards of Cardinals Capponi and Monte.⁶ As early as June 19th, 1622, and again on August 1st of the same year, the Pope honoured his nephew's Villa with his presence, and he took his midday

---

¹ See *Avviso of October 22, 1622, *Urb.* 1092, *loc. cit.*

² See GIUNTI, *Vita, loc. cit.*, and SCHREIBER, *Villa Ludovisi*, 5.

³ According to the *Diarium P. Alaleonis*, the Pope was at the villa in Frascati from May 27 to June 2, and he visited it again on September 28, 1622 (*Barb.* 2818, Vatican Library). *Cf.* also the *Avviso of May 21, 1622, *Urb.* 1091, *ibid.*

⁴ See FALDA, *Le Fontane nei Giardini di Frascati*, II., 12 seqq.; MORONI, XL., 109, and GOTHEIN, *Gartenkunst*, I., 337 *seq.* The Villa came later into the hands first of the Conti and subsequently into those of the Torlonia.

⁵ See GOTHEIN, I., 353.

⁶ See SCHREIBER, *Villa Ludovisi*, 4. The information concerning the purchase of the Vigna Monte, which is missing in this work, I have taken from the *Avviso of August 6, 1622, *Urb.* 1091, Vatican Library.

meal there.[1] When, on May 3rd, 1623, Gregory XV. paid yet another visit to the Villa,[2] he witnessed great alterations by which the north-eastern part of the Pincio had assumed a new appearance. Under the direction of the painter Domenichino,[3] who was also architect to the Pope, a new palace arose close to the entrance to the Villa, whilst on a hill in the western, park-like section, a summer-house was erected which, by reason of the wonderful view one enjoyed from it, became known as the Belvedere.[4] This small central building, surrounded by statues, was approached from all sides by broad alleys which spread like the rays of a star and all terminated in some splendid ornamental piece visible from a great distance, such as an antique sarcophagus or a colossal statue of Alexander Severus.[5] Guercino, who at that time was at work on his gigantic painting of St. Petronilla, destined for St. Peter's, undertook, with the assistance of the perspectivist Agostino Tassi, the decoration of the ceilings of the summer-house. His work displays extraordinary technique and the brilliance of his colour scheme is magnificent; however, both as regards design and delineation of form, his fresco is far below Guido Reni's soffit. In Guercino's picture on the ground floor of the summer-house, Aurora also scatters flowers, but how ponderous are the horses of her chariot! On the upper floor Guercino created a magnificent figure, wrongly styled

[1] " *19 Junii 1622 Papa pransus est ad vineam s. viridarium card. Ludovisi apud Portam Pincianam." Again, August 1, 1622, (*Diarium P. Alaleonis, Barb.* 2818, Vatican Library). *Cf.* *Avviso of June 22, 1622, *Urb.* 1091, *ibid.*

[2] See *Diarium P. Alaleonis, loc. cit.*, and *Avviso of May 10, 1623, *Urb.* 1093 A., *loc. cit.*

[3] The Brief of nomination of Domenichino, April 1, 1621, is in BERTOLETTI, *Art. Bologn.*, 127 *seq. Cf.* BAGLIONE, 385.

[4] It is now called, after the chief picture, Casino dell'Aurora and escaped destruction in 1885. For Domenichino's part, see BAGLIONE 386; BELLORI, II., 89. Besides Guercino and Domenichino, Giovan Luigi Valesio, Alessandro Algardi, Giovan Battista Viola and others took part in the decoration of the buildings of the Villa; see SCHREIBER, 4.

[5] See GOTHEIN, I., 352.

"Fame", for it is a masculine figure holding in its hands a torch and a bouquet of flowers.[1] Landscapes by Domenichino complete the decoration of the summer-house. To the right of the main entrance to the Villa, near the Porta Salaria, there was another summer-house with a gallery of statues. In front of it a long alley, terminating in a great statue, led to the city wall. From here one had a good view of the whole expanse of the Villa which, in this section, was covered with numerous copses, in the same way as the Villa Borghese. Water was furnished by the Acqua Felice.[2] If the visitor, on entering, turned to the left, he was faced by a piazza adorned with a fountain of Tritons and wide enough to allow for the manœuvring and stationing of the many carriages that had to be dealt with on festive occasions. In front of the beholder this space was limited by the private garden (*giardino segreto*), in the centre of which there was an aviary, as in the Villa Borghese. Along the right side ran pergolas, the so-called labyrinth, adorned with antique statues, busts, sarcophagi and columns; to the left rose the main building, behind which there came a second special garden for flowers and rare plants. The main building was approached by a terrace of the height of the first story which cut across a sunk garden adorned with two fountains.[3] In the lower

[1] *Cf.* PHILIPPI, *Kunst der Nachblüte*, 95 seq.; BERGNER, 120 seq.; KRAUS-SAUER, 795; SCHMERBER, *Ital. Malerei*, 197 seq.; KUHN, III., 2, 817; BERTEAUX, *Rome*, 129; ROSE, *Spät-Barock*, 217 seq.; *Jahrb. der preuss. Kunstsamml.*, XL. (1919), 149. In the letters of the President DE BROSSE (II., German trans., Munich, 1922, 54 seq.) the frescoes of Guercini receive the greatest praise (equally, recently, POSSE, SACCHI, 20, and W. WEISBACH, *Die Kunst des Barock*, Berlin, 1924, 42); VENTURI criticizes them sharply in the *N. Antologia*, 3, Series XXXII. (1891), 413 seq.

[2] An *Avviso of April 1, 1623, mentions a Papal Brief in which Cardinal Ludovisi was granted " la communicatione degli aquidotti dell'Acqua Felice per condurre alla sua vigna 44 once ". *Urb.* 1093 A, Vatican Library.

[3] See GOTHEIN, I., 352, where Falda's views of the Villa are reproduced. *Cf.* SCHREIBER, 4-13, and DAMI, 42. Piranesi gave very picturesque views.

rooms of the building, as well as in the Belvedere and the other garden house, a selection of the best statues had been brought together to constitute a gallery.

Keenly interested as he was in literature, Cardinal Ludovisi was even more enthusiastic as regards art.[1] How much he understood the value of the relics of antiquity is proved by a decree of March 2nd, 1622, which threatens with the severest penalties the destruction of ruins for the purpose of using them as building materials, and all unauthorized digging for treasure or statues.[2] The Cardinal was a keen collector and the fact was well known, hence with a view to winning his favour he was presented with numerous works of art of every description.[3] If the inexhaustible soil of Rome yielded some antique object, the Cardinal made haste to acquire it. For the sum of 120 scudi he bought from the finders, together with some smaller antique objects, a sarcophagus of uncommon size which had been dug up before the Porta S. Lorenzo and on which was represented a battle between Romans and Barbarians; it still retained traces of gilding. A big find of pottery near S. Francesco Ripa yielded the colossal terra-cotta vases which were set up in the Piazza in front of the Belvedere.[4] Cardinal Ludovisi likewise acquired numerous antique objects from private collections in Rome, especially from the Cesarini and the Cesi. With the assistance of the Pope who revoked the testamentary clauses which stood in the way, he was able to acquire, on August 6th, 1622, from Giovanni Federigo Cesi,

---

[1] For the Cardinal's Academy in the papal palace, see below, p. 69; cf. RENAZZI, II., 131 seq.; ibid., 92 seq., for the call of the celebrated physician Vincenzo Alsario Croce and p. 107 for the call of the poet Marini to Rome. Cf. also La Canonizzazione, 82. For Ludovisi's dealings with Tassoni, see TIRABOSCHI, VIII., 310. Cf. Giorn. stor. d. lett. ital., XLIX., 406.

[2] See SCHREIBER, Villa Ludovisi, 5. Under Gregory XV., in 1621 the Arch of Severus was again disinterred; see REUMONT, III., 2, 755.

[3] A. POSSEVINO reports on this in his statement of May 13, 1621, Gonzaga Archives, Mantua.

[4] See SCHREIBER, 8 seq., 27.

Duke of Acquasparta, twenty statues, five torsos, and fifty smaller fragments of statues, eleven vases, a few bronze fragments and pedestals, in all 102 pieces.[1] The acquisition was valued at more than 20,000 scudi.[2] It included the famous colossal head of Hera, the majesty of which impressed Göthe like a canto of Homer. In accordance with the taste of the period this magnificent work, like so many other antique sculptures, served to adorn the spacious gardens.[3] The colossal statue of Athene Parthenos, which, according to the inscription it bears, is the work of Antiochos of Athens, was also set up in the gardens. The head in profile of the "Dying Medusa" was used to adorn the exterior of the great palace.[4] The palace itself housed the most valuable pieces of a collection which Winckelmann rendered famous throughout the world, namely, "Mars asleep," the magnificent group generally understood to represent Electra and Orestes, the work, according to its inscription, of Menelaos, a pupil of Stephanos; the statue of the Gaul who, when about to be made a prisoner, slays his faithful wife and turns the weapon against himself; the "dying gladiator", belonging to the same group but which under Clement XII. was transferred to the Capitol.[5]

The incomplete inventory of the possessions of Cardinal Ludovisi, drawn up on January 12th, 1633, only a few months after his death, enumerates, without counting bronzes and mere fragments, 216 statues, ninety-four heads and busts, twenty-one columns, two basins, eleven tombstones, thirteen reliefs, four sarcophagi, and nineteen vases.[6] Besides the collection of antiques, perhaps the most splendid that Rome

---

[1] See *ibid.*, 7 *seq.*, 27 *seq.* For Cardinal Cesi's garden and his antiques see now the excellent monographs of HÜLSEN, *Römische Antikengärten des 16. Jahrh.*, Heidelberg, 1917, 1 *seq.*, 11 *seq.*, 41 *seq.*

[2] See *Avviso of August 6, 1622, Urb. 1092, Vatican Library.

[3] See SCHREIBER, 123.   [4] *Ibid.*, 125 *seq.*, 131 *seq.*

[5] *Ibid.*, 82 *seq.*, 89 *seq.*, 112 *seq.*

[6] See *Inventarium bonorum repertorum post obitum fel. rec. Ludovici card. Ludovisii (Arm.* 9, *Prot.* 325, n. 1, Boncompagni Archives, Rome) used in SCHREIBER, 14 *seq.*; *ibid.*, 28 *seq.*, is

had ever seen,[1] the Villa Ludovisi also contained modern works of art of great value, such as Bernini's "Pluto's Rape of Proserpina", a present of Cardinal Borghese; two female heads, a bust of Gregory XV., and a "Child bitten by a Snake". As a contrast to this piece the young Alessandro Algardi, who had been charged with the restoration of the antique pieces, of which many were in very bad condition, created the statue of a boy playing a rustic flute. Among the modern sculptures the following deserve mention: a "Cleopatra", by Cristoforo Stati, and a "Venus", by Giovanni da Bologna. Two bronze busts are ascribed to Michelangelo. The group catalogued as "Dead boy on a dolphin", without indication of the artist's name, is probably the marble figure spoken of in connexion with Raphael: it is now in the Eremitage at Petrograd.[2]

The extent of the art collections of Cardinal Ludovisi may be gauged from the fact that he also owned a large picture gallery which ranked among the most valuable in Rome. The exquisite art galleries, the delightful pergolas, the peaceful grottoes, the waterworks, the magnificent ilexes and cypresses whose sombre foliage constituted the foreground for the varied vistas of the city and the mountains beyond and, lastly, the incomparable panorama of Rome and the campagna which opened from the summer-house, invested the Villa Ludovisi with an enchanting fascination. Though the Villa d'Este at Tivoli, which Gregory XV. restored to the d'Este,[3] maintained its ancient reputation,[4] many people thought the summer

printed from the same archives, "*Inventario delle massaritie, quadri et altro, che sono alla vigna del principe di Venosa a Porta Pinciana rivisto questo dì 28 Gennaro 1663.*" *Cf.* L. G. PELISSIER, *Un inventaire inédit* (Corsini Library, Rome) *des collections Ludovisi à Rome*, Paris, 1894.

[1] See MICHAELIS, *Entdeckungen*, 6.
[2] See SCHREIBER, 15, 50, 68 *seq.*, 129.
[3] See F. X. SENI, *La Villa d'Este in Tivoli*, Roma, 1902, 17.
[4] See no. VII. in Appendix, A. POSSEVINO's enthusiastic description in his letter of August 14, 1621, Gonzaga Archives, Mantua.

residence of Gregory XV.'s nephew the most beautiful of all Roman villas.[1] Those whose good fortune it has been to walk in the shady grounds recall with sorrow the memory of the magnificent park limited on the north side by the picturesque walls of the city, which in the year 1885 fell a victim to the modern speculative builder. Apart from a few fragments[2] in the garden of the palazzo Boncompagni-Piombino (now Regina Margherita) built in 1886-90, nothing has been preserved of the Villa except the summer-house. The protests raised against the devastation of this Paradise proved only too justified. Rome lost " a park fit for Kings and Sages, so enchanting and so solemn that Horace and Virgil, Marcus Aurelius and Dante might have walked with religious awe in the shadow of its laurel groves and its alleys of cypresses ".[3]

Whilst the memory of the Villa Ludovisi survives only in the name of one of the districts of the city, the magnificent church of St. Ignatius in Rome bears eloquent witness, even at this day, to the piety of the papal nephew. For the completion of this splendid sacred edifice, which was begun in 1626,[4] he set apart the total sum of 200,000 scudi.[5]

[1] See in App. no. IV. *GIUNTI's opinion. For later judgments cf. specially that recorded in *Evelyn's Diary*, p. 98, in 1644. For the latter fortunes of the Villa and the dispersion of individual pieces of the collection of antiques, which were bought in 1909 for 1,400,000 lire by the Italian Government and for a long time most unsatisfactorily housed in the Museo delle Terme Diocleziane, see SCHREIBER, 15 *seq.*; HELBIG, II.³, 75 *seq.*

[2] For a reproduction of the magnificent fountain in the old garden, see GOTHEIN, I., 353.

[3] See *Allg. Zeitung*, 1886, no. 80; the preface to GRIMM's *Life of Raphael* (²1886) and GREGOROVIUS, *Kleine Schriften*, III. (1892), 42.

[4] See CIACONIUS, IV., 477. For *O. Grassi, architetto di S. Ignazio*, cf. *Civ. Catt.*, 1922, Aprile 1.

[5] Cf. GIUNTI, *Vita, Corsini Library, Rome, and *Sommario del testamento del em. card. Ludovisi fatto in Roma l'a 1629*. The MS. was bought by me in Rome in 1911. See also RINALDI, *La fondazione del Collegio Romano*, Roma, 1914, 119.

The Cardinal's intention to erect a church in honour of St. Francis Xavier, on the Quirinal, was not carried out.[1] In the summer of 1623, he built a new church for the Barnabites, in the Piazza Colonna,[2] and contributed to the erection of S. Eufemia in the forum of Trajan and to that of the adjoining orphanage.[3] Outside Rome the erection of the church of the Oratorians at Casale and that of another in the Valtellina were also due to the Cardinal.[4] He made presents to various churches, especially to those of the Jesuits in Rome and Bologna. Without considering that the Villa Ludovisi would be spoilt thereby, he cut off a large piece of ground and gave it to the Capuchins for their new convent.[5] At Zagarolo the Cardinal erected a chapel in honour of St. Ignatius in the church of St. Sebastian, and at Bologna he beautified the cathedral and bestowed rich gifts upon it, the most valuable being a painting for the reredos of the high altar representing the Holy Trinity and one of Guido Reni's masterpieces.[6]

If these activities by themselves reconcile us in a measure to the wealth piled up by Cardinal Ludovisi, we are even further inclined to condone it when we consider the liberality of the nephew of Gregory XV. towards the poor, the sick, the hospitals, the charitable institutions of every description, and the convents within the Eternal City. According to an accurate account supplied by his biographer, his yearly expenditure on charitable and pious purposes amounted to 32,882 scudi.[7] This does not include the alms he was wont to distribute on special occasions. The interest which this busy

---

[1] See GIUNTI, *Vita, loc. cit.

[2] See *Avviso of January 17, 1623, *Urb.* 1093 A, Vatican Library. The church of the Barnabites erected in 1596 in the Piazza Colonna had been burnt down in 1617; the new one disappeared when the Curia Innocenziana was erected; see ARMELLINI, *Chiese*, 500.

[3] See GIUNTI, *Vita, loc. cit.

[4] *Ibid.*

[5] *Ibid.*

[6] *Ibid.*

[7] *Ibid. Cf.* App. no. IV.

man took in the welfare of the numerous charitable and pious institutions of which he was official protector, was wholly admirable.[1] The Cardinal's energetic intervention in cases of necessity was seen at its best when, in the summer of 1622, Rome was visited both with a scarcity and an epidemic. From the month of May of that year onwards the nephew had bread and vegetables distributed to the poor both morning and evening and in the hospital near the Lateran he had 150 beds prepared for the sick, at his own expense.[2] He entrusted the supervision of these charitable undertakings to persons on whom he could rely, among them being Sebastiano Poggio, Bishop of Ripatransone, and the Jesuit Pietro Gravita; these never asked in vain for his help. In the Papal States he caused Mgr. Lorenzo Magalotti to make generous distributions of grain wherever the need arose.[3]

It was in keeping with the humane and sympathetic character of the Cardinal that he lived in perfect harmony with his relatives; consequently, during the reign of Gregory XV., history has nothing to relate of the mutual conflicts between the papal nephews which were so frequent during some other pontificates.

The Pope's brother, Orazio Ludovisi, came to Rome from Bologna on March 13th, 1621, accompanied by his wife Lavinia, his son Niccolò, and his daughter Ippolita. They were received with princely honours. Six Cardinals, the envoys of the Emperor and those of the King of Spain and many nobles escorted the travellers to the palazzo Orsini in the Campo de' Fiori. The Pope received them in audience that

---

[1] GIUNTI reports on this in detail, *Vita, loc. cit.

[2] See *Avviso of June 22, 1622, Urb. 1091, Vatican Library. Cf. G. B. MEMMI, Relaz. de' provvedimenti presi in Roma a beneficio de' poveri nella carestia del 1622, Roma, 1764.

[3] See GIUNTI, *Vita, loc. cit. The letter in which L. Magalotti congratulates the Pope, dated Ascoli, February 15, 1621, is in Cod. E. 71 of the Boncompagni Archives, Rome. Magalotti became commissario generale of the States of the Church, see MORONI, XLI., 233.

same evening.¹ A few days later Orazio was appointed General of the Church. His son, though an immature youth, was given the title of castellan of the Castle of S. Angelo and governor of the Borgo.² No less a sum than 200,000 scudi were spent on the purchase for Orazio, from the Sforzas, of the duchy of Fiano.³ His son Niccolò, was to be married to a daughter of the Colonnas,⁴ but the plan miscarried. At the end of May, 1622, Niccolò became engaged to Isabella Gesualdo, a niece of the Cardinal of the same name.⁵ The bride came to Rome on November 23rd, 1623, and seven days later the wedding took place in the Vatican.⁶

¹ See *Diarium P. Alaleonis, Barb.* 2818, Vatican Library; *Avvisi of March 6 and 17, 1621, *Urb.* 1089 B, *ibid.*; Gigli, in MORONI, XL., 107. Already on May 8, 1621, Gregory XV. was able to address a letter of thanks to the Doge, A. Priuli, for accepting Orazio Ludovisi and Cardinal Ludovisi, " *in patriciorum Venetorum ordinem* ", Brevia, in *Arm.*, XLV., 23, Papal Secret Archives.

² See PAGLIUCCHI, *I Castellani del Castel di S. Angelo*, II., Roma, 1928, 62, and the *Avvisi of March 20 and April 3, 1621, *Urb.* 1089 B., Vatican Library. The letter of congratulation from Niccolò Ludovisi to Pope Gregory XV., dated Bologna, February 12, 1621, is in *Cod.* E. 70 of the Boncompagni Archives, Roma.

³ See the *Avvisi of June 9, August 28, and September 8, 1621, *Urb.* 1089 B, 1090, Vatican Library.

⁴ See *Avviso of August 28, 1621, *Urb.* 1090, *ibid.*

⁵ See the *Avvisi of March 2, April 30, and May 28, 1621, *Urb.* 1090, *ibid.*

⁶ See *Diarium P. Alaleonis, loc. cit.*, and the *Avvisi of November 23, 26, and 30, 1622, *Urb.* 1092, *loc. cit.* Niccolò Ludovisi married as his second wife, Polissena Mendoza and thereby became lord of the principality of Piombino (Investiture by Philip IV., 1634, see MORONI, LXXVIII., 43), which later was inherited by the Boncompagni. Hence many documents concerning Cardinal Ludovisi and Gregory XV, came to be in the family archives of the Boncompagni, Rome. The letters addressed to Cardinal Ludovisi during the pontificate of Gregory XV. fill no fewer than thirteen large volumes in these archives (*Cod.* E. 70-82); those written to him later (1623-1632) fill sixteen

Niccolò's sister, though she was anything but a beauty,[1] also made a brilliant match. She was betrothed to Giovanni Giorgio Aldobrandini, nephew of Clement VIII.[2] On April 25th, 1621, the Pope himself officiated at the nuptials in the Cistine chapel.[3] Aldobrandini was granted all the privileges of a papal nephew, consequently, the first place also in the papal chapel after Orazio Ludovisi.[4] In April, 1623, though he was already Prince of Rossano, the Pope created him Prince of Meldola and Duke of Sarsina,[5] and when his son was born, Gregory XV. acted as godfather.[6]

Niccolò Ludovisi's marriage with the niece of Cardinal Gesualdo, a notorious Hispanophil, caused a good deal of anxiety lest Gregory XV. should come under Spanish influence in view of the fact that the lady was heiress to the principality of Venafro situate in the Kingdom of Naples. One of the immediate results of the kinship thus established between the Ludovisi and the Aldobrandini was that all the Cardinals of

---

volumes (*Cod.* E. 84–99). The letters of Lavinia Albergati-Ludovisi to her son, the Cardinal, 1623-1632, are in *Cod.* E. 100 The archives also contain a copy of the Briefs of Gregory XV., (*Cod.* E. 68 and 69). I have made use of the collection of the Papal Secret Archives ; *cf.* WIRZ, XXVI.

[1] " La sposa è bianca, del resto pigliarei più tosto le gioie che porta che lei," writes A. POSSEVINO, May 22, 1621. Gonzaga Archives, Mantua.

[2] See the *Avvisi of March 27 and April 1, 1621, *loc. cit.* The bride's dowry amounted to 100,000 scudi. The alliance had already been mentioned in an *Avviso of February 27, 1621. *Urb.* 1089 B, *loc. cit.*

[3] See the *Diarium P. Alaleonis, loc. cit.* The *Avvisi of April 28 and May 1, 1621, supply further information about the bride's rich jewels, which were valued at 150,000 scudi. *Urb.* 1089 B, *loc. cit.* For the wedding banquet, see REGIN, 804, p. 18 *seq*, Vatican Library.

[4] See the *Avvisi of May 15 and 22, 1621, *Urb.* 1089 B, *loc. cit.*

[5] See the *Avvisi of April 15, 1623, *Urb.* 1093 A, *loc. cit.*

[6] See the *Avvisi of January 26 and February 2, 1622, *Urb.* 1091. *loc. cit.*

Clement VIII. now joined the party of the Cardinal nephew.[1] They were a strong support against the Cardinals of Paul V. among whom Bentivoglio in particular created many difficulties for Ludovisi by reason of his relations with Sillery, the French ambassador.[2]

However generous Gregory XV. may have been towards his relations, he nevertheless would not allow them to interfere with affairs of State. Lavinia, the Pope's sister-in-law and an unusually gifted woman,[3] was greatly esteemed by Gregory XV., in fact she had exercised so much influence over him whilst he was still a Cardinal that in this respect there were widespread misgivings,[4] which, happily, proved groundless. When, in November, 1621, Lavinia Ludovisi, through her son, the Cardinal, attempted to obtain the red hat for nephew Albergati, the Pope flatly refused and in none too gracious a tone.[5] Otherwise, also, Lavinia failed to obtain the slightest thing from the Pope.[6] Orazio Ludovisi, a man of quiet and simple tastes,[7] and one wholly free from all ambition,[8] made no attempt to meddle with government

---

[1] See the *report of A. POSSEVINO of May 28, 1621. He writes on June 25, 1621: "*È tanta l'unione di Ludovisi et Aldobrandini che non si può dir più." Gonzaga Archives, Mantua. *Cf.* also the report from Lucca in *Studi e docum.*, XXII., 206.

[2] Ludovisi expresses himself frankly on this point in the letter sent by Agucchi to the nuncio Corsini, July 12, 1622, Cod. X., VI., 16, of the Casanatense Library, Rome.

[3] See the *report of the Venetian *obbedienza* envoys, in BAROZZI-BERCHET, *Roma*, I., 118.

[4] *Cf.* the *Discorso de cardinali 1618 in Cod. C. 20 of the Boncompagni Archives, Rome, and the *report of Fr. Aragona of January 30, 1621, Gonzaga Archives, Mantua.

[5] According to the *Avviso of November 13, 1621, Gregory XV. is supposed to have said: "Sinchè Papa Gregorio XV. viverà, casa Albergati non havrà cardinali," *Urb.* 1090, Vatican Library.

[6] See the report of the Lucca envoys in the *Studi e docum.*, XXII., 206. *Cf.* also the *report of A. POSSEVINO of May 22, 1621, Gonzaga Archives, Mantua.

[7] See the report of the Venetian envoys, *loc. cit.*

[8] See the report of the Lucca envoys, *loc. cit.*

business. This lay exclusively in the hands of Cardinal Ludovisi,[1] and besides him the learned Cardinal Bandini was also frequently consulted.[2] Ludovisi applied himself wholeheartedly to his manifold duties. In addition to ecclesiastical affairs he had also to deal with civil questions.[3] People praised his administration of Justice.[4]

Intercourse with writers and scholars, many of whom dedicated their works to him, was the chief recreation of the Cardinal Secretary of State.[5] For their benefit he founded the *Accademia dei virtuosi*—a literary society similar to that founded by Charles Borromeo under Pius IV.[6] The first meeting took place on Sunday, June 20th, 1621, at the Quirinal palace, in the rooms of the Cardinal opening on the garden. Scipio Pasquale, Bishop of Casale, opened it with an address.[7] Thereafter the meetings were always held in the summer months and on Sundays. They were attended by a number of Cardinals and prelates, often as many as eighty,[8] the subject

---

[1] *Ludovisi è caput rerum facendo tutto, massime che nè il fratello nè la cognata (Lavinia) possono cosa alcuna di momento," A. POSSEVINO reports, June 15, 1621, and again July 9 : " *Ludovisi agit et fert cuncta." Gonzaga Archives, Mantua.

[2] For the influence of Bandini, *cf.* the *Relatione di Roma*, 1624, Papal Secret Archives, II., 150, no. 3.

[3] On May 1 he was appointed a member of the Congregazione delle strade ; see *Avviso of May 1, 1621, Vatican Library.

[4] See GIUNTI, *Vita, loc. cit.* For the punishment of Paul V.'s Chief Treasurer, Pier Maria Cirocchi, see *Relatione della vita del card. Cecchini*, in *Cod.* 39, D. 17, of the Corsini Library, Rome, and in part in RANKE, *Päpste*, III., 166. *Cf.* our account in Vol. XXV., Ch. I., 57.

[5] See CARDELLA, VI., 222. *Cf.* also GIUNTI, *Vita, loc. cit.*

[6] *Cf.* our account, Vol. XVI., 308 *seq.*

[7] See *Avviso of June 26, 1621, Vatican Library.

[8] TIRABOSCHI (VIII., 23) reports that sometimes Gregory XV. took part in the meetings. In the *Avvisi where the meetings and their members are mentioned, this is not recorded, as indeed it is also omitted in GIUNTI (see Appendix no. IV). The suspicion entertained by PALATIUS (an author who wrote seventy years after the death of Gregory XV.) that Cardinal Ludovisi

of the discussions being passages of Holy Writ or some question of general interest.[1]

In the transaction of business Cardinal Ludovisi was loyally assisted by his countryman, Giovan Battista Agucchi. Next to the Cardinal, his was the most important personality.[2] Thirty years' work at the Curia had been an excellent preparation for the important duties which this old servant of the Aldobrandini who desired to take over the affairs of State without the knowledge of the Pope, induced him to spend his time in academic conferences —a suspicion which BROSCH (I., 374) repeated—is certainly an invention and proved to be so, were it only that the meetings were only held on Sundays.

[1] See the *Avvisi dated July 7, 1621 (exegetic themes), July 21, August 4 (Girolamo de' Preti, a nobleman in the Ludovisi household, " upon good and bad princes "), August 18 (The Dominican P. Mosto, " exegetic themes "), September 1 (the Servite Bolognetti, " Sopra la buona et cattiva fortuna in sensi morali "), September 15 (Monsignor Venturi, " on the Agape "), October 20 (Mgr. Spinola on the words of Job), June 8, 1622 (Mgr. de Rosis, sopra l'adulatione), July 13 (discourse on curiosity), July 27 (Cor regis in manu Domini), August 10 (on Osee), August 24 (on Job), September 7 (on Wisdom ; the battle of David with Goliath), May 31, 1623 (Creation of Light), June 14 (on the happiness of princes, especially the necessity of philanthropy), June 28 (magnanimità del principe). Urb. 1090, 1091, 1092, 1093. A meeting of the Academy, at which Mgr. de Rosis spoke on ingratitude, is mentioned by B. PAOLUCCI, in his report of June 14, 1623, State Archives, Modena. For the Marinist Girol. de' Preti who, however, strongly disapproved of Marini's lasciviousness, see FANTUZZI, VII., 122 ; Giorn. stor. d. lett. ital., XXXII., 227 seq. ; BELLONI, Seicento, 88 seq., 480.

[2] See the report of the Venetian obbedienza envoys, BAROZZI-BERCHET, Roma, I., 130. The nomination of Agucchi, who had been major-domo to Cardinal Aldobrandini, followed on the evening of this same day (February 10, 1621). (*Avviso of February 13, 1621, Urb. 1089 B, Vatican Library). Giov. Ciampoli, celebrated as a lyrical poet and letter writer, was the secretary for Briefs ; more will be said of him later on under Urban VIII.

was now called upon to discharge.¹ Agucchi, of whom Domenichino has left us an excellent portrait,² was chiefly occupied with the correspondence with the the nuncios. For this the main lines were given him by the Pope himself with whom he had an audience every morning, except on the day of the *Segnatura*. Briefs were signed by the nephew, and in the event of the latter's illness, by the secretary.³

Gregory XV. was so pleased with Agucchi's services that it was generally believed that, had the Pope lived longer, he would have bestowed the purple on him.⁴ Cardinal Bentivoglio also, though he had complained that Agucchi's style was not natural enough, praised the uncommon ability with which the secretary dealt with the most difficult situations.⁵ Giunti, Cardinal Ludovisi's biographer, relates that the nephew reserved to himself the making of the rough draft of the Instructions of the nuncios after consultation with the Pope, but that Agucchi gave them their final shape.⁶

Naturally enough criticism of the all-powerful nephew was not wanting. But this was only justified in so far as Ludovisi, fearing that the pontificate of his uncle would be of short duration, was too keen on enriching himself. The conduct of affairs left nothing to be desired, in fact, Ludovisi applied himself to it with so much ardour that in February, 1623, he suffered from eye trouble.⁷ The judgment passed on the

¹ *Cf.* our information in Vol. XXIII, 53. See also BONAMICUS, *De claris script*, 285 ; *Rev. d'hist. et de litt. relig.*, VII. (1902), 487. G. LENZI, *Vita di G. B. Agucchi*, Roma, 1850.

² Two copies of the portrait are in existence, one is in the Corsini Gallery, Rome, the other in the Uffizi, Florence. See SERRA, *Domenichino*, 11 seq. *Cf.* also BAYERDORFER, *Leven*, 94.

³ See LÄMMER, *Melet.*, 275-6. *Rev. de l'hist. ecclés.*, XI., 733.

⁴ BENTIVOGLIO, *Memorie*, 180.

⁵ *Ibid.*

⁶ See GIUNTI, **Vita*, in the Appendix no. IV.

⁷ See the *report of BALD. PAOLUCCI to Cardinal Este, February 15, 1682, dated from Rome ; State Archives, Modena. Ludovisi's handy copy of " Declarationes decret. et canon. S. Conc. Trid. a S.R.E. card. congreg. eiusdem concilii ad diversos episcopos missae singulis suis senioribus et capitulis ordine

nephew by so sharp an observer as Antonio Possevino deserves attention. Only those could complain of him, he says, who imagined that they might attain to the highest honours because of a previous casual acquaintance with the Cardinal. The Cardinal honoured true merit, but he was not interested in people actuated by vanity.[1]

The attacks on Ludovisi and the other nephews did not spare the Pope himself, who was represented as a nonentity. Antonio Possevino styles these pasquinades the unworthy offspring of idiots. Gregory XV., he says, was a most devout Pontiff and even those who were not in sympathy with him paid homage to his excellent sentiments.[2]

If by comparison with the Pope the younger and more lively Cardinal nephew was apparently more to the fore, the explanation was that Gregory XV. was greatly weakened by

---

accomodatae" with the note "Card^{lis} Ludovisii" was sold in 1906 by the Munich antiquary Rosenthal to the State Library at Trent, where it is now preserved as *Cod.* 2878.

[1] See the *report of A. POSSEVINO of May 28, 1621, Gonzaga Archives, Mantua.

[2] See App. no. VI. for POSSEVINO's *report of July 16, 1621, *ibid.* An *Avviso of September 4, 1621, reports an edict, which had appeared on the previous day against the author, copyist and publisher of " libelli famosi infamatori " (*Urb.* 1090, Vatican Library). How unfair these attacks were is shown by the quite untrue statement that in Rome, not enough was done for the poor ; had it not been for Paul V.'s provision of corn, the people would have died of hunger ; *Studi e documenti*, XXII., 207 seq. The Pope did what he could to secure corn. On November 12 and again on December 22, 1621, he *wrote to Philibertus, ducis Sabaudiae filius (*Brevia, Arm.*, XLV., 22, Papal Secret Archives) with a view to importing wheat from Sicily. In the following year *two letters with the same content went to the *Prorex Siciliae*, dated June 8 and December 1, *ibid.*, XLV., 24. An *Avviso also of October 20, 1621, records that the Pope had spent much money on the provisioning of Rome with wheat ; and that he had sent for corn from Piedmont to feed the Papal States. *Urb.* 1090, Vatican Library.

sickness and age.¹ However, this fact was enormously exaggerated in the pasquinades mentioned above and otherwise also. " Here in Rome, where people are always anxious for a change, every groan of the Pope," Possevino wrote as early as May, 1621, " is looked upon as a sign of his early death." ² When it became apparent that these expectations were premature, the Pope's enemies hinted at his irresponsibility, a fact, they said, which Ludovisi carefully suppressed.³ In point of fact, at the time when these rumours were circulating, Gregory XV. was applying himself with his wonted ardour to the duties of Government. Thus he presided over the Congregation of Propaganda and received the Archbishop of Lyons who had been dispatched to Rome in connection with the war against the Huguenots.⁴ What truth there was in the alleged mental debility of the Pope even in time of sickness is best shown by the deservedly famous admonitions which he addressed to his nephew in April, 1622.⁵ They honour

¹ Thus an *Avviso speaks, February 12, 1622, of Gregory XV.'s *Podagra*. An *Avviso of April 9, 1622, says that the Pope had been ill eight days, and was suffering from kidney trouble, fever and sickness. An *Avviso of July 30, 1622, says that the Pope was labouring under " dolori di fianchi e inappetenza " ; notwithstanding this he was giving audiences to the envoys ; " la nocte muta stanza e letto e sta molto fastidioso e malinconico." *Urb.* 1091, 1092, Vatican Library.

² See the *report of May 28, 1621, Gonzaga Archives, Mantua.

³ See the letter of R. ZENO of October, 22, 1622, in BROSCH, I., 374, who gave unqualified credence to this hostile and scandal-mongering reporter, although RANKE (III., 126) had accurately described his propensity to exaggeration.

⁴ See the *Avvisi of November 9 and 19, 1622, *Urb.* 1092, loc. cit.

⁵ *Avvertimenti dati da P. Gregorio XV. in voce al sig. card. Ludovisi, dal quale poi in questa forma sono stati scritti et notati questo di 1° d'Aprile, 1623 (in the margin, " steso da Mr Aguchio), Barb. 6908, pp. 1-10, Vatican Library. Other copies, some of which have the title " Ricordi ", *ibid. Barb* 4632, p. 35 *seqq.* ; 4606, p. 66 *seqq.* ; 5893, p. 195 *seqq.* ; *Ottob.* 2206, p. 1 *seqq.* ; 2487, p. 81 *seqq.* ; 2718, p. 61 *seqq.* ; in the Bibl. Bolognetti, 167,

both him who gave them and him who received them and who took care to preserve them as a precious heritage. At that time rumours were circulating that the state of Gregory XV.'s health was desperate and that the end was at hand. Taking the warning contained in this gossip for his text, the Pope took advantage of the leisure forced upon him by illness to engage his nephew in a prolonged conversation. The gist of this discourse the latter set down in writing on the same day, and later gave it a more polished form.

The Pope began with a high eulogy of the Secretary of State, praising Ludovisi's well tried devotion to the Holy See, his zeal for its honour, his moderation in the exercise of power, his business ability and his obedience to the smallest hint of the Pope. He then went on to give him advice, as if it were a last recommendation, for his future conduct, particularly for the time when the papal uncle would be no longer among the living. The Pope's words are remarkable. In them we hear the experienced old man freely pouring out his heart to one who stood nearer to him than anyone else in the world, and revealing to him what he himself had learnt whilst living at the Roman court. At the same time these confidential counsels allow us a glimpse into the depths of Gregory's soul. They lay bare the motives that guided him and the genuinely Christian conception of life that animated him. His first words are characteristic. Gregory begins by warning the busy Secretary of State not to forget God and the salvation of his own soul amid the turmoil of

Papal Secret Archives; in the Casanatense Library, X., V., 22, p. 293 *seqq.*; in *Fond. Gesuit.*, 120, p. 1 *seqq.*, Vittorio Emanuele Library, in *Cod.* AE. XI., 76, of S. Pietro in Vincoli Library (see LÄMMER, *Zur Kirchengesch.*, 23). Copies outside Rome: in Berlin, Royal Library, *Inform. polit.*, 20; Brescia, Bibl. Quirin., C., III., 2; Colmar, Municipal Library; Florence, State Archives, *Carte Strozz.*, 227, p. 114 *seqq.*, and Bibl. Magliabecchiana; Paris, National Library, *Ital.* 10416 (*cf. Marsand*, I., 474 *seq.*); Perugia, Town Library, E. 17; Rimini, Bibl. com., D. IV., 178; Rovigo, Bibl. d. Accad. dei Concordi, 8, 4, 16; Stockholm, Bibl. Hist. Ital., 4.

business and the absorbing cares of politics : " We remind you, more than that, we admonish you, nay we conjure you in the first place and before all else to make of the fear and love of God your supreme political wisdom, your rule of government and your most trusted counsellors." In good fortune and in bad we need a solid foundation. The fear and love of God are the twin guiding stars to which the nephew should ever look up in the stormy sea of this wretched life so as to avoid shipwreck and to reach the harbour of salvation.[1]

Just as this principle is an explicit rejection of the more or less worldly policy of the Popes of the renaissance period, the warning that follows is likewise a condemnation of a purely worldly conception of the higher ecclesiastical offices : " Bear in mind," we read, " that from the fact of your having been raised to a position which surpasses all others in loftiness and dignity, there arises for you the duty to be a leader, a model, and a subject of edification to all." [2] In point of fact, all eyes are upon us : men are prepared to pass a severe judgment upon our smallest action, to weigh the least word we utter. They scrutinize with utmost keenness your thoughts, your passions and tendencies, fully prepared as they are to follow the example you set them. And if it is certain that the episcopate is a more perfect state than that of a religious who consecrates himself to God by three solemn vows, since a Bishop needs for his office a higher perfection and charity, seeing that God has raised him to be a luminary in His Church, how much are you bound to excel all others by the brightness of a spotless life, the unblemished purity of your morals and the splendour of every virtue, you a Bishop, an Archbishop, a Cardinal and one to whom so many offices are entrusted ! Impress it well upon your mind that everything about you must be like so many living words by which the people are reminded of their duty, for the virtues of a prelate of your eminence must benefit not merely himself and his

[1] *Avvertimento no. 1 ; see LÄMMER, *Zur Kirchengesch.*, 23.
[2] *Avvertimento no. 2 ; see LÄMMER, *loc. cit.*

family, his countrymen and his diocesans, but the whole world."[1]

With great tact the admonition points out to the nephew that his present prestige would end with the death of Gregory XV. "It gives us much pleasure to see that you are free from the usual stupidity of papal nephews who foolishly imagine that their momentary good fortune will last for ever." Nevertheless the Pope deemed it advisable to give his nephew a hint with regard to the coming papal election and the future Pope. In this connexion Gregory XV. speaks of his Bull on the papal election, of the advantages which he hopes would result from it, of the dispositions which he expects from the electors and those which moved him to publish it. Upon entering into the conclave, the Pope tells the Cardinal, he should submit his will to God's will in all things. "Cast aside all personal interests, stifle your own desires, renounce every friendship, curb all petty jealousies, shut your ears to all unwholesome counsels and keep but one aim and purpose before your eyes, viz. the glory of God, the advantage of Holy Church and with it that of the whole world."[2] Such sentiments would procure him happiness and honour, for, if it be the will of God, whoever may be elected Pope would remain his patron and benefactor; in any case such dispositions could never go unrewarded. On the other hand, it would be the height of folly to set oneself against God in the conclave, to raise a kind of tower of Babel against Him and to endeavour to make the Holy Ghost subservient

[1] "Le virtù del prelato eminente, quale voi sete, devono essere indirizzati non a benefitio suo solo, o de suoi cari, o de compatrioti, o de diocesani solamente, ma di tutto il mondo." *Ibid.*

[2] "*Quando dunque serà il tempo, che doverete applicare necessariamente l'animo all'elettione et a negotii del Conclave, subbito rassegnate in tutto e per tutto la volontà a Dio benedetto, spogliatevi di tutti gl'interessi, quietate tutti i vostri desiderii, renuntiate a tutte l'amicitie, smorzate tutti i rancori, serrate l'orrecchie a tutti li consigli non sani, ne habbiate altr'oggetto che la gloria di Dio, il servitio di s^{ta} Chiesa con il beneficio universale del mondo." *Ibid.*, no. 3.

to one's own selfish designs. For the rest, the Pope hoped that his new regulations for the papal election would remove past abuses. Henceforth, in the meetings, discussions, and canvassings of electors, those who fancy that they are the Pope-makers may, indeed, boast of the number of votes which they command, but when it comes to the actual election they will be disappointed.[1] Hence Ludovisi must not mind the conduct and attitude of any one because the working of the Bull had not as yet been put to the test. " Even as we have put the will of God before our personal advantage so we cannot sufficiently urge you to sacrifice all self-seeking to the glory of the divine Majesty and the honour of this Apostolic See." Let Ludovisi use all his influence to secure compliance with the Bull and let him oppose those who would attempt to make a breach in this bulwark of the vineyard of the Lord.

Gregory XV. then speaks of the fall of any nephew which must inevitably follow the death of a Pope : " There is no more difficult and dangerous transition than that. We have seen many instances of men who in every other situation were deemed prudent and cautious, but who failed very seriously when they had to step down from their former position."[2]

[1] " *Ci confidiamo alla divina bontà che poichè ella ci spirò, per levar gli abusi introdotti in negotii che con tanta Santità devono maneggiarsi, a far la bolla dell'elettione, le cose anderanno in altra maniera per l'avenire, o che potrebbero farsi coloro che si vogliono far arbitri del Conclave, gloriarsi d'haver le congregationi et i consigli et le pratiche loro piene di voti ; ma alli scruttinii ne rimaneranno delusi. Perciò non vi prendiate pensiero degli andamenti d'alcuno, perchè non hanno ancora conosciuto per prova la forza della constituzione ; ma si come noi habbiamo anteposto il servizio di Dio a quello del nostro sangue, et il publico al privato, non possiamo comandarvi a sufficienza, che non solo non habbiate tentato di dissuadervene, ma sacrificando ogni vostro interesse alla gloria di Sua Divina Maestà et al bene di questa Sta Sede et habbiate fatta continua et ardente instanza per la speditione d'essa etc." *Ibid.*, no. 3.

[2] " *Non vi è passo ne più difficile nè più pericoloso di questi di nepoti de' Papa dopo la morte di loro zii, havendone veduta l'esperienza in molti, i quali ancorchè in altri tempi fussero

If, then, a Pope is selected who shows to the Cardinal both affection and confidence, perhaps one who had at some time received favours from himself or from Gregory XV., Ludovisi must carefully avoid any semblance of wishing to share the pontificate with him, or of meddling unduly in affairs of State when he is not consulted. He must not endeavour to retain offices which usually fall to the Pope's relatives or display such magnificence as to throw the Pope in the shade. On the contrary, modesty in his conduct will be the best way to preserve the prestige he had acquired, and moderation in the enjoyment of favours received the surest means to secure fresh ones; in any case the familiarity of earlier days must in no way diminish the reverence due to the new status of the former friend. But should the new Pope not be friendly, an insolent attitude would be as much out of place as excessive fear which would cause him to run away at once. Should the latter supposition be verified, the best thing for him was to appear as if he did not notice that he had been set aside, not to take up an irreconcilable attitude, to refrain from finding fault with the government, to avoid even the shadow of an intrigue, in a word to give no opening to his opponents. His best policy, however, would be to leave Rome and to retire into his archdiocese of Bologna.

Gregory XV. alludes to yet another difficulty. Since at the Pope's death Ludovisi would cease to be Secretary of State, he would find himself in a most embarrassing situation, for he would still remain the head and heart of the Cardinals created by the late Pope and as such he would retain an outstanding position even with regard to the other Cardinals or the foreign Princes. In the course of his long life the experienced uncle had closely studied the chief difficulties and dangers that must arise from such a situation and he was well able to warn the Cardinal on this point also. Towards the Cardinals created by himself, the Pope said, the Cardinal should avoid a patronizing or domineering air; on the contrary he should show both affection and respect for their persons,

stimati prudenti et accorti, non di meno nel scender gradi sono sdrucciolati pericolosamente." *Ibid.*, no. 4.

put them under obligation to himself by his favours and win their confidence by his regard for them. Let him avoid partiality, and refrain from distinguishing, as it were, between real sons and step-sons, and let him beware of following the example of those who sow discord among the " creatures " in order to assert their authority the more easily. Apart from all other considerations such conduct would be fraught with disastrous consequences for himself.[1] If in the conclave or elsewhere, he does not meet with the gratitude he might expect, he should not forthwith open hostilities, so to speak, but rather shut his eyes to the slight.

Towards the other Cardinals, dignity should be combined with courtesy. Here also he should take no notice of possible slights but rather render good for evil. " All the Cardinals have had so many favours showered upon them that they must admit that they have received more benefits from us in sixteen days than from others in sixteen years." For all that, the Cardinal should not be perturbed if some of them show themselves utterly ungrateful, for such conduct, for one thing, is natural to this climate where men only think of the present moment and completely forget the past: the wonder would be if they acted otherwise.[2] He should maintain good relations with foreign princes, less for the sake of their favour than to prevent them from injuring him and with a view to an increase of his own prestige in consequence of his good relations

---

[1] " *Nè seguitate mai l'esempio d'alcuni che si sono studiati con raporti e con mal'ufficii di mantenerli tra di loro divisi per dominarli più facilmente, perchè oltre vi dilungarete dalla pietà, scopertosi il reo artificio corresti risico non s'unissero contro di Voi." *Ibid.*, no. 5.

[2] " *Nè vi da fastidio ch'essendo ciascun cardinale stato beneficato da noi così largamente che confessino haver ricevuto più gratie da noi in sedici giorni che d'altri in sedici anni (an allusion to the sixteen years of Paul V.'s reign), " vi si dimostrino poi alcuni così ingrati ; poichè tal è la proprietà di questo cielo, tanto amico dell'interesse presente, e tanto contrario alla gratitudine del passato, che sarebbe più tosto da maravigliarsi se loro facessero il contrario." *Ibid.*, no. 5.

with them. The goodwill of princes may be won by two means; the first was for the nephew to take advantage of his present position in order to further their interests, meeting their ambassadors half-way, and obtaining favours for them; the second means was his personal qualities, that is, his constancy, prudence, sincerity, liberality, business ability, knowledge of affairs and, lastly, a virtuous life.[1]

Not a few of these counsels must seem obvious. Yet how many men only learn by a bitter experience how difficult it is to apply these simple rules and how easy it is to overlook them amid the stress and pressure of life! Often the Pope's remarks throw light on conditions then obtaining at the Roman court, on the spirit that permeated Rome at the time of the Catholic reform, as well as on the personality of Gregory XV. himself who, in the midst of the turmoil of affairs, viewed the situation with serene eyes and drew his own conclusions.

The same may be said of some further instructions concerning the papal nephew's attitude towards his relations, his servants, and his callers. With his kinsfolk, especially the Aldobrandini, Ludovisi should at all times live in charity and concord and bestow special care on the education of his younger brother.[2]

Some of the great lords may have attached but small importance to their relations with their domestic staff. Not so Gregory XV. He is of opinion that if a man knows how to govern his household, he has given the highest proof of circumspection and has at the same time closed the door to many annoyances. Ultimately servants have in their hands the life, the goods and, most of the time, also the good name of their master, for the good or bad reputation of a prince rests before all else on the testimony of the persons of his household, which always meets with ready acceptance, especially when it is an unfavourable one. Hence, Ludovisi must be careful in the choice of his servants and know how to keep them occupied once he has engaged them, and treat them kindly. From time to time he should reward them above their

[1] *Ibid.*, no. 6.
[2] *Ibid.*, no. 7.

just wages, for free gifts are more highly valued. And since the majority of those who offer their services to the Cardinals do so in the hope of future promotion, Ludovisi should meet their wishes. Those who have held the more important posts, and the more deserving among them, should have higher recognition ; but let him be on his guard lest he should have an all-powerful favourite who would pass for his idol in the opinion of the world, somewhat after the manner of Sejanus, or some recent examples " that we have before our own eyes ". The consequence would be that the court would consider the Cardinal as a weakling, one unable to know his own mind, and everyone would turn to the favourite instead of his employer. No one should be under any uncertainty that merit was the only road to the nephew's favour.[1]

In his relations with the world, the Cardinal should be courteous and affable towards everyone, modest yet dignified and dignified though genial ; let him be sparing of his promises and generous in keeping them, and avoid above all things the semblance that his pledged word is but a mockery if not a deliberate deception. Only persons of merit should be among his intimates ; this will be to his advantage and will enhance his prestige. He should not readily admit anyone into the number of his friends ; on the other hand let him stick to a tried friend, come what may.[2] After these general observations Gregory XV. turns once more to the special conditions then obtaining in Rome. Any amount of charm of manner, he tells his nephew, will not guarantee his peace if he does not restrain the passion for innovation which is peculiar to Rome. Rome appoints its rulers by means of an election and normally the choice falls on a Cardinal of advanced years. Consequently the Curia lives in constant expectation of a speedy change : prophecies, gossip, intrigues concerning the future pontificate, are the order of the day. It was so already in ancient Rome, even when the Emperors were in the prime of life. Whether this be in the very nature of things or a peculiarity of the climate, it seems impossible to prevent the Curia from revolving

[1] *Ibid.*, no. 8.
[2] *Ibid.*, no. 9.

round these things as if they were its natural axis and all else were subordinate to them. Whilst rumours are spread of the speedy demise of one whose death is expected to usher in a new epoch, respect and esteem for him and his family grow less, obedience suffers, the administration is upset, public affairs receive inadequate attention, friends are alienated and rivals gain power. Such rumours are especially circulated at the beginning of a new pontificate by those who view with jealous eyes the rise of a new family, for people are more quickly envious of a rising family than of one already established, because the original condition of the former is still fresh in every memory. It was so in bygone centuries; hence there is no need to worry if the same is experienced to-day, for all such talk is silenced as the years succeed each other.[1]
" As for our own life," the Pope proceeds, " we have committed it to divine Providence and we only desire its prolongation in order to devote it to God's glory by serving the Church

---

[1] " *Essendo questo un principale elettivo posto quasi sempre in persona di grave età si appoggia di continuo la Corte alle speranze delle mutationi, e se ne sta sopra li pronostichi e discorsi della novità e su le pratiche del Pontificato, e pur si vede che anticamente, benchè l'Imperadori fussero giovani, Roma era involta in simili pensieri, onde o sia per natura delle cose, o sia per quello del Cielo non se può fuggire che la Corte medesima non s'aggiri intorno a ciò, quasi intorno all'oggetto e fine de' suoi pensieri, al quale tutti gli altri interessi vengono drizzati. . . . Mentre si sparge l'opinione della breve vita di colui, la morte del quale cambia lo stato di tutte le cose, manca verso di esso e di suoi più cari lo rispetto e stima, si scema la autorità, si intorbida il governo, li negotii pubblici si precipitano e se ne vanno alienando gli amici, et accrescendo gli emoli, il vigore per ciò tutti li Pontificati e massime nel principio d'essi si spargono volontieri simili voci, da chi volontieri non vede la crescente fortuna d'una nuova famiglia, perchè la invidia s'esercita maggiormente contro le si fatte, che contro le si stabilite, essendo ancora troppo fresca la memoria delle precedenti conditioni loro. Per ciò quello che nell'andati secoli si è successivamente veduto, non vi ha da recar noia se hoggi si faccia il medesimo perchè alla fine tali voci svaniscono gli anni tuttavia correnti . . ." *Ibid.*, no. 10.

and the advantage of all men. Hence we may feel confident that He will preserve it amid all dangers, and notwithstanding the wishes of foolish men, for as long a time as shall profit our own salvation and that of others."[1]

As for any malicious gossip of which he may be the butt, let the Cardinal pay no attention to it. Anyone occupying a lofty position is exposed to the eyes and the tongue of all. Rome has always had an itch for news; when there is none it invents it.[2] There was only one remedy against calumny, especially when it was unfounded, namely to despise it, not to betray any feeling, not to justify oneself. "A blameless life and conduct such as becomes a Prince of the Church are of themselves the best refutation of calumny."[3]

The Pope concludes his long list of counsels with some warning concerning ecclesiastical revenues. He had abundantly provided his nephew with these with a view to enabling him to keep up his high dignity and to show liberality, and in order that he might give full play to the talents with which God and nature had endowed him. He then enters into some details as to the use the nephew should make of his wealth. Among other things he advises him at least to tie the hands of his calumniators if he cannot restrain their tongues,[4] to support the "creaturae" of his uncle or else to explain to them that his income is insufficient to enable him to make provision for all the adherents of the house of Ludovisi. The servants of his house also would hardly thank him if, to show

---

[1] " *Quanto alla nostra vita havendola noi raccomandata alla divina providenza, ne per altro desiderandola che per impiegarla a gloria sua in servizio della Chiesa et anco a benefitio universale de tutti, dobbiamo confidarci che la conservarà . . ." *Ibid.*

[2] " *Questa città fu sempre avida di cose nuove e quando non ve ne sia, le trova e partorisce martirii e sinistri rapporti." *Ibid.*, no. 11.

[3] *Ibid.*

[4] " *E se non potete impedire le lingue, legate almeno le mani altrui, poichè per ligarle all'istessa invidia che non vi ferisca, non vi rimane altra più sicura via che di scuoprirle a voi medesimo con prudente larghezza et christiana libertà." *Ibid.*, no. 13.

his appreciation, he only opened his mouth but not his hand. But the Pope insists even more earnestly upon the spirit in which ecclesiastical revenues should be used. If wrongly used, Church property became an unbearable burden, by reason of the strict account to be given one day, but if rightly used it was a source of joy amid the troubles of life and a comfort in grief. Church money was "the patrimony of the poor".[1] The axiom was a hint as to how such money should be apportioned. It represented the purchase money lent to us by God Himself, with which we purchase heaven.[2] Hence, the Pope hopes that the Cardinal will not use his wealth to satisfy a love of vain display, luxury, or caprice, but as becomes an Archbishop and a Cardinal. Church money is meant to be distributed, not to be piled up, thereby robbing the treasury of Christ, perhaps under the specious pretext that at death one would leave it for the good of the Church: this was merely an excuse for hidden avarice. Money, Gregory XV. adds, perhaps in allusion to an old Christian proverb,[3] is unwilling to remain in a man's hand, unless it be the hand of one in need or that of a compassionate almsgiver. Gregory XV. had made his nephew Commendatory Abbot of many monasteries, with the intention that whilst he drew their revenues he should also interest himself in their churches. He should strive to fulfil at least the strict obligations laid down in the papal Bulls. "For this reason we could not applaud

[1] For the origin of this description see BRAUNSBERGER, *Epistulae Canisii*, IV., 92.

[2] " *Li beni ecclesiastici riescono di intollerabil peso a chi mal se ne serve, perchè oltre modo aggravano la coscienza dovendosene rendere strettissimo conto, ma di grande alleggerimento sono nelle humane gravezze e conforto alle tribulationi, a chi religiosamente l'adopera, sono però patrimonio dei poveri ; et eccovi la più giusta et aperta via da dispensare l'avanzi, che sono prezzo del cielo, che Dio vi presta per comprarlo. E quindi apparisce la grandezza della divina bontà che non solo ci addita l'eterna felicità, ma ci apporge il modo di farne acquisto con il suo proprio danaro, contentandosi ancora che la christiana nostra dispensa sia ad ogni loro prezzo et constitutione." *Avvertimento* no. 13.

[3] Cf. *Zeitschr. für kath. Theologie*, XXVI. (1902), 779.

certain people who built large churches in Rome, perhaps in order to make a name for themselves, but who allowed the Abbeys and the churches attached to them to go to ruin." [1] We blame no one for erecting churches, colleges, and pious foundations, on the contrary ; but we attach far greater value to those good works on which there falls not a shadow of vainglory and which are more deeply instinct with true charity and give it a fuller expression. "Buildings of lifeless stone must not cause a Prince of the Church to forget the true temples of the Holy Ghost, that is, the poor both of the religious and the secular state who, for the most part, bear with patience the miseries of this life, and who deserve to be supported by alms lest they should perish through human frailty."

The whole of this series of counsels given in an intimate conversation with his nearest relative and at no time intended for a wider public, is an irrefragable proof of Gregory XV.'s deep religious feelings, of his wisdom and mental alertness. It also shows in striking fashion how powerfully the spirit of the Catholic reform had impregnated the whole Church, until it had reached those who held the highest positions. Nearly a hundred years had gone by since the death of Adrian VI., a Pope animated by the same noble sentiments, had provoked in Rome an explosion of wild joy. Then there seemed to be no hope whatever for a transformation of the Eternal City and of the Church, as desired by the pious Dutchman, yet now, notwithstanding every obstacle, the reform had won through. It was one of the most remarkable proofs of the astounding power which is peculiar to the Catholic Church, that of always renewing itself from within and of showing forth, within a short time, a youthful vigour even after a period of seemingly hopeless lethargy.

[1] Perhaps Alessandro Farnese is meant ?

CHAPTER II.

GREGORY XV.'S ACTIVITY WITHIN THE CHURCH—CREATIONS OF CARDINALS—BULL ON PAPAL ELECTION—CANONIZATIONS—FURTHERING OF THE ORDERS.

IN the person of Gregory XV., for the first time, a pupil of the Jesuits had been raised to the See of Peter. Ludovisi, the Cardinal nephew, who was as influential as he was energetic, had received his education and formation in the same school. Consequently, the two men who now guided the destinies of the Church, were filled with the new religious spirit in the rise of which the Order founded by the knight of Loyola had played a leading part. This spirit showed itself in everything the Ludovisi Pope undertook in the internal government of the Church, more especially in the care with which the Pontiff filled the vacancies in the Sacred College.

The first great promotion of Cardinals, on April 19th, 1621, met with universal approval. The men who were raised to the supreme Senate of the Church on that occasion were eminently worthy of that honour.[1] A particularly good impression was created by the fact that among the new Cardinals there was not one Bolognese, though the Pope's native city did not lack suitable candidates, among them being a kinsman of Gregory XV., viz. the nuncio of Cologne, Albergati. It had been thought at Court that the latter would surely receive the purple, but it was precisely this circumstance that induced Gregory XV. to refrain from such a nomination.[2] The first among the new Cardinals, Antonio Caetani, had held under Paul V. the post of nuncio in Germany and Spain with conspicuous success, and had afterwards become Archbishop of Capua. There was great joy in Rome at his return to the

---

[1] See the *report of F. Aragona of April 21, 1621, Gonzaga Archives, Mantua.

[2] See the report of the Lucca envoys, in *Studi e Docum.*, XXII., 205.

Curia. He furthered literature and founded the *Accademia degli Umoristi*, a title which points to the one fault for which Caetani could be blamed, namely, the sarcasm into which his love for witticism often degenerated.[1]

The next Cardinal, Francesco Sacrati, also founded an Academy, this time a theological one. A scion of a noble family of Ferrara, he had opened, under Clement VIII., a line of auditors of the Rota all of whom originated from his native city. He carried out his duties with so much distinction that Paul V. was much criticized for failing to admit him into the College of Cardinals. Gregory XV., who had long known and esteemed Sacrati, made him his *Datarius* and gave him the see of Cesena. His elevation was generally applauded in Rome where Sacrati stood in the highest esteem by reason of his modesty, the purity of his life and his learning. Like Caetani he died prematurely (September 6th, 1623). For his resting place he had chosen the German national church of S. Maria dell'Anima, and his predilection for Germany further showed itself by his leaving his choice library to the German College.[2]

The two other Cardinals appointed on April 19th, 1621, were relatives of former Popes. Francesco Boncompagni belonged to the family of Gregory XIII. Though only 20 years old he was deemed worthy of the purple because to a wide knowledge of theology, the law and the classical languages, he added a deep piety and an extraordinary purity of life. By this nomination Gregory XV. also wished to discharge a debt of gratitude to the Pope who, in his time had called him to Rome.[3] In 1626 Boncompagni became Archbishop of Naples where he set a splendid example by the stern asceticism of his life and his great liberality. His alms at

---

[1] See **Vita del Card. Caetani*, in *Barb.* 6030, Vatican Library ; CIACONIUS, IV., 479 ; CARDELLA, VI., 222 *seq.*

[2] For F. Sacrati, *cf.* BAROZZI-BERCHET, *Roma*, I., 122 ; CIACONIUS, IV., 479 *seq.* ; CARDELLA, VI., 223 *seq.* ; SCHMIDLIN, *Gesch. der Anima*, 491.

[3] See **Relatione di Roma*, 1624, Papal Secret Archives, II., 150, no. 3.

Naples are calculated to have amounted to 240,000 scudi, and to his prayers the people attributed the preservation of their magnificent city on the occasion of the terrible eruption of Vesuvius in 1631. When he died he left his choice library to the Gregorian College in Rome. The fourth of the prelates who received the purple in 1621, Ippolito Aldobrandini, was also credited with excellent qualities, with learning and purity of life. Urban VIII. expressed the opinion that he possessed all the good qualities and none of the defects of his uncle, Cardinal Pietro.[1]

As early as July 21st, 1621, the Sacred College was increased by two new members. Under Clement VIII. the Neopolitan, Lucio Sanseverino had successfully administered the archdiocese of Rossano, and under Paul V. that of Salerno; he had subsequently acted as nuncio in the Netherlands. He was an excellent Bishop as well as a distinguished theologian. His early death (December 25th, 1623) was a great loss to the Church. Marcantonio Gozzadini of Bologna, a relative of Gregory XV. and a jurist of mark, also died in 1623, at the early age of 49. His first episcopal see was that of Tivoli where he held a synod; subsequently he became Bishop of Faenza. In Rome he restored and beautified his titular church of St. Agatha.[2]

In his biography of Gregory XV., Accarisius relates that in the choice of Cardinals the Pope examined with the utmost care the qualifications of the candidates; also that he kept a list of those who had a claim to the purple, and that he was much preoccupied with it.[3] Hence princes did not find it easy

---

[1] *Cf.* CIACONIUS, IV., 479 *seq.*; CARDELLA, VI., 224 *seq.* " *Del card. Aldobrandini suol dire il Papa che ha tutte le buone qualità, ma non le cattive del card. Pietro suo zio. È stimato signore ingenuo, affetuoso verso i amici* " (*Discorso di Roma*, 1626, in *Cod.* C. 20 of the Boncompagni Archives, Rome). For the Boncompagni Library see SERAPEUM, II., 322.

[2] See CIACONIUS, IV., 480 *seq.*; CARDELLA, VI., 228 *seq.* F. ARAGONA speaks of Sanseverino, with high appreciation of his merits, in his *report of July 21, 1621, Gonzaga Archives, Mantua.

[3] See ACCARISIUS, *Vita Gregorii XV.*, Boncompagni Archives, Rome.

to get their proposals for nominations accepted in Rome. Even the Emperor Ferdinand II., whom Gregory XV. held in the highest esteem because of his strict Catholic principles, failed to secure, in 1621, the nomination of a candidate whose promotion he had greatly at heart.[1] However, in the long run the Pope could not refuse to yield to the prayers of the Catholic princes.[2] He met their wishes in the promotion of September 5th, 1622.[3] Ottavio Rodolfo owed his elevation to the Sacred College to the recommendation of the Emperor; he had deserved it by his work for the Catholic reform in his capacity

---

[1] See the *Brief to the Emperor Ferdinand II., of April 19, 1621, *Arm.* XLV., 23, Papal Secret Archives. *Ibid.*, 22, a *Brief to Duke Charles Emmanuel of Savoy, December 25, 1621, putting him off with promises with regard to the promotion of the Archbishop of Turin to the cardinalate.

[2] *Cf.* the note of Agucchi to Card. Sourdis, April 29, 1622, *Carte Strozz.*, I., 2, 87 *seq.*

[3] See *Acta consist.* The address of the Holy Father which we quote, is as follows: " Ven. fr. Postulant dudum a Nobis Caesar et Galliae, Hyspaniae et Poloniae reges, ut in ipsorum gratiam aliquos in Collegium cooptemus. Quorum tantum et Nobis carissimorum principum precibus, quantum cum D^{no} possumus, satisfacere cupientes, praesertim cum eos viros Nobis commendent, quos vestro ordine dignissimos censemus, decrevimus, si vobis videbitur, quattuor cardinales creare, qui sunt isti: Cosmus de Torres archiep. Adrianopol., Rom., Pol. Nunc., Ludov^{ci} card. de Monreale, fr^{is} filius, qui fidem et prudentiam suam in hoc munere egregie Nobis probavit; Amandus s. Armandus Io. Du Plessis de Richelieu, episc. Lucion., Gallus, vir generis nobilitate, omni doctrinae genere, maximarum rerum usu et zelo religionis insignis; Octav. Rudolphus episc. Arian., Florent., non minus virtute quam sanguine nobilis, qui et in pastorali munere et pluribus praefecturis multa cum laude se gessit, et cuius familia superiori saeculo amplissimum habuit cardinalem; Alphonsus de la Cueva, prothonot. apost. Philippi regis cath^{ci}, in Belgio orator, qui claris natalibus ortus et amplissimis legationibus perfunctus magnam ingenii, prudentiae et pietatis laudem est consecutus," *Barb.* 2926, Vatican Library.

as Bishop of Ariano.¹ The King of Spain received satisfaction with the promotion of Alfonso della Cueva, a member of the Order of Alcántara and one of his diplomatists,² and Louis XIII. with that of the youthful Bishop of Luçon, Armand de Richelieu, though a party at the French court had sought by various intrigues in Rome to frustrate the nomination.³ Sigismund III., King of Poland, had made vain efforts with Gregory XV., as he had done with Paul V., to secure the red hat for the ambitious Rangoni.⁴ But to avoid offending so good a Catholic prince, Gregory XV. bestowed the purple on Cosimo Torres, an excellent man in every respect, and who was nuncio in Poland at the time.⁵

Gregory XV. made no further nominations though they would have been very much to the advantage of his nephew. For the biographer of Ludovico Ludovisi this is a proof that the Cardinal only considered the interests of the Church.⁶

¹ *Cf.* CIACONIUS, IV., 489 *seq.*; CARDELLA, VI., 235 *seq.*; BOGLINO, *La Sicilia e i suoi cardinali*, Palermo, 1884, 57 *seq.*

² For Cueva, see PIRENNE, IV., 353 *seq.*

³ The threads of this intrigue have been carefully unwound lately by DEGERT, in the *Rev. hist.*, CXVIII. (1915), 225 *seqq.* The evasive *replies of Gregory XV. to the requests of Louis XIII. and Marie of Medici, dated July 1, 1621, for the cardinalate for Richelieu, are in *Brevia Arm.*, XLV., 22, Papal Secret Archives. It is stated there : " *De cardinalibus creandis minime hoc tempore cogitamus, quia nuper clarissimorum virorum electione s. senatum supplevimus." However, hopes are held out for the future. *Ibid.*, 24, a *Brief dated April 2, 1622, to Marie de Medici, who induced the unwilling Louis XIII., after the death of Card. de Retz, to change his mind ; see HANOTAUX, *Richelieu*, II., 448 *seq.* The appointment was announced to Louis XIII. by a *Brief of September 5, 1622. *Cf.* ZELLER, *Richelieu*, 311 *seq.*; *ibid.* the *Brief to Richelieu, though both are wrongly dated. The *letter of Ludovisi to Richelieu, of September 5, 1622, is in *Cod.* X. V. 31, of the Casanatense Library, Rome.

⁴ See the *Briefs to Sigismund III., of August 25, 1621, and February 5, 1622, Papal Secret Archives, *loc. cit.*

⁵ For Cosimo Torres, see CIACONIUS, IV., 485 ; CARDELLA, VI., 230 *seq.*; and BOGLINO, *loc. cit.*, 58 *seq.*

⁶ See GIUNTI, *Vita*, Corsini Library, Rome.

This is probably too favourable a view ; in any case, the fact that Gregory XV. made no better provision for the interests of his nephew in the next conclave shows the baselessness of the assertion that the Pope was no more than " a helpless tool " in the hands of Ludovisi. Such a possibility was further excluded by the fact that Gregory XV. allowed the Cardinals to discuss affairs with him and to state their views with the utmost freedom.[1] This action, which, together with the kindly, conciliating manner of the new Pope, which was in sharp contrast with that of Paul V.,[2] as well as the distribution of offices and the apportioning of benefices to outstanding Cardinals created an excellent impression.[3]

Among the older members of the Sacred College, Ubaldini, Orsini and Maurice of Savoy, who had come to Rome after the conclave, were most in favour with the Pope.[4] Maurice attached himself closely to Cardinal Ludovisi, but he left Rome in July, 1621.[5] Cardinal Borromeo was honoured

[1] See the *report of the Venetian ambassadors, in BAROZZI-BERCHET, *Roma*, I., 122.

[2] *Cf.* the *report of A. Possevino of May 28, 1621, Gonzaga Archives, Mantua.

[3] *Cf.* the detailed account of GIUNTI, in his *Vita d. card. Ludovisi*, Corsini Library, Rome.

[4] See the Venetian report quoted in note 1. For Maurice di Savoia, *cf.* *the report of A. Possevino of May 22, 1621, Gonzaga Archives, Mantua. Cardinal Eitel Friedrich of Hohenzollern also came to Rome. Gregory XV. expressed his pleasure at this to the Emperor Ferdinand II., in a *Brief of December 1, 1621 (*Arm.*, XLV., 22, Papal Secret Archives). For Cardinal Eitel Friedrich, see *Mitteil. des Hist. Vereins für Hohenzollern*, XXXI. and XXXII., and G. HEBEISEN, *Die Bedeutung der ersten Fürsten von Hohenzollern und des Kard. Eitel Friedrich von Hohenzollern für die kath. Bewegung Deutschlands ihrer Zeit*, Hechingen, 1923. For his election to the see of Osnabrück, in April, 1623, see *Mitteil. des Vereins für Gesch. von Osnabrück*, XXIV. (1899), 156 *seq. Cf.* also STÜVE, *Osnabrück*, III., 19 *seq.*

[5] Cardinal Ippolito Aldobrandini wrote on July 24, 1621, from Rome, to the Duke of Savoy : " E universalmente dispiaciuta la partenza di questa corte del sig. card. Maurizio, figliuolo di

with a laudatory Brief.¹ Cardinals Bandini and Cobelluzio also stood high in the Pope's esteem.² Bellarmine was asked to take up residence in the Vatican, but he did not remain there long. The strength of that splendid man, now almost an octogenarian, who had always been an ornament of the Sacred College, was utterly spent, as he himself felt. Like Baronius, Bellarmine also wished to die among his brethren in religion. Pleading his failing health he obtained leave to retire to the Jesuit novitiate house where he took up residence on August 25th. A violent fever soon compelled him to take to his bed. He expired on September 17th, 1621. The Pope had paid him a visit on September 1st. In his will Bellarmine had expressed the wish to be buried in some Jesuit church in the still hours of the night, and for his obsequies to be celebrated by the Jesuits alone, without participation of the Cardinals. However, with the consent of the Pope, the General of the Society of Jesus refused to comply with such a request and arranged for the obsequies to be celebrated in the church of the Gesù, in the presence of the Sacred College. In conformity with the wish of the illustrious dead his mortal remains were provisionally laid to rest in the crypt of the professed house ; a year later they were transferred to the grave in which the body of St. Ignatius had at one time reposed.³ To the right of the high altar a monument was erected in honour of this outstanding defender of the Holy See ; figures of Religion and Wisdom, carved by Pietro Bernini, adorn the monument.⁴

Both Gregory XV. and Cardinal Ludovisi had greatly at heart the liberation of Cardinal Klesl, whom, since 1619, the Emperor had held in honourable but strict confinement in

---

V. Altezza " ; see PASSERINI, *Alcune lettere del card. Ipp. Aldobrandini a Carlo Emmanuele, duca di Savoja* (Nozze Publ.), Roma, 1881, 4.

¹ *Brief of May 21, 1622, *Arm.* XLV., 22, Papal Secret Archives.

² See the **Relatione di Roma*, 1624, in the Papal Secret Archives, II., 150, no. 3.

³ *Cf.* REUSCH, *Selbstbiographie*, 294 seq. ; COUDERC, II., 312-378.

⁴ See FRASCHETTI, *Bernini*, 33 seqq.

the remote Tyrolese monastery of Georgenberg.¹ When Carlo Carafa entered on his Vienna nunciature in the spring of 1621, he was instructed to work for a termination of the sufferings of the prisoner, as his faults were now obsolete. Carafa must at least obtain greater freedom for the Cardinal within the monastery itself. The objections made to the transfer of the Cardinal to Rome were declared incomprehensible.² If the Emperor's representatives in Rome imagined that Gregory XV. would ever cease to demand Klesl's liberation ³ they were mistaken. On the contrary, when Verospi was dispatched to Vienna, in January, 1622, as envoy extraordinary, with mission to congratulate the Emperor on his marriage to Princess Eleanore of Mantua, he was directly charged to demand Klesl's extradition in the name of the Pope. Even if Klesl was guilty, decorum should have been better safeguarded in the eyes of the world, as Paul V. had already pointed out, and it was not right that the Cardinal should be held in captivity in the territory of the princes who had caused his arrest. Verospi was instructed to do his utmost to induce the Emperor and the Archduke Leopold to consent to Klesl's transfer to Rome, where he would be less dangerous to them than anywhere else.⁴ Ferdinand II. was

¹ *Cf* our account in Vol. XXVI., p. 326 *seq*. In the very detailed works of HAMMER-PURGSTALL and KERSCHBAUMER there is nevertheless nothing about the question whether Klesl took part in the Conclave of 1621. A special Congregation of Cardinals was instituted on this point (see the *report of ABBATE ALFONSO PICO to Emperor Ferdinand II., dated Rome, February 2, 1621, State Archives, Vienna). How it dealt with the difficulty can be seen from the *letter of F. Aragona of February 6, 1621, Gonzaga Archives, Mantua. According to this a letter, *pro forma*, was sent to Klesl, " senza obligarvi però ad aspettare altra risposta sapiendosi molto bene che non sarà liberato dall'Imperatore et che in tanto non può l'eletione del pontefice patire dilatione."

² See *Barb.* 5232, Vatican Library.

³ Thus Alfonso Pico reports to the Emperor in his *account of August 7, 1621, State Archives, Vienna.

⁴ See KERSCHBAUMER, *Klesl*, 314 *seq*. The *Instruction for Verospi quoted here is also in *Cod. Celsius* H 323 of the Library

not unwilling to grant such a request, but he did not wish to do anything without the consent of the Archduke Leopold in whose power Klesl was. At first the Archduke made many difficulties, but the Roman diplomat ended by overcoming his objections, and securing his consent to the extradition. On October 23rd, 1622, the Cardinal, now nearing his 70th year, was able to set out for Rome with Verospi.[1] Gregory XV. warmly thanked Ferdinand II. for this proof of his piety and devotion to the Holy See.[2] Klesl reached Rome on November 27th, 1622, and was taken to the castle S. Angelo. On the evening of the third day he was privately taken into the presence of the Pope who received him with the greatest kindness. For the time being the Cardinal remained in the castle of S. Angelo, where he occupied the beautiful rooms on the upper story. Otherwise also his confinement was of the mildest, since he was allowed to receive the visits of Cardinals and ambassadors.[3] The victories won in Germany gave Klesl an opportunity, on December 24th, 1622, to offer his congratulations to the Emperor. At the same time he appealed to the goodness and mildness of the monarch which surely would not suffer a German Cardinal, one who was a natural subject of his majesty and who owed his elevation to his predecessors, to die in prison, to the great shame of the German nation. He attested before God and his conscience that he had always honestly striven to serve the Church, the Emperor, and the noble House of Austria, to the best of his ability. True, he was but a man and not an angel, hence he could make mistakes; for these reasons he pleaded for pardon, seeing that he was now 71 years old, and worn out by his labours and fatigues.[4] In Rome the Venetian and Spanish ambassadors did all they could on behalf of Klesl together

at Upsala. *Cf.* GROTTANELLI, *La Riforma e la guerra de trent'anni. Ricordi studiati sulla corrispondenza degli ambasciatori Toscani,* Florence, 1899, 115 *seq.*

[1] See KERSCHBAUMER, 315 *seq.*
[2] *Cf.* HAMMER, *Urk.,* 964.
[3] See KERSCHBAUMER, 321 *seq.*
[4] *Cf.* HAMMER, *Urk.,* 963.

with the Protector of the German nation, Cardinal von Zollern. At first the Emperor demanded that Klesl should resign the Sees of Vienna and Wiener-Neustadt and forgo all claim to the money confiscated by the Emperor Matthias for the benefit of the imperial exchequer at the time of the Cardinal's arrest. However, he soon dropped that demand. The Capuchin Giacinto da Casale also did his utmost to obtain Klesl's pardon. On June 16th, 1623, the imperial ambassador, Savelli, was instructed not to oppose Klesl's liberation if the above conditions were fulfilled, but that he was to remain in Rome. Gregory XV. was quite satisfied with this solution and wrote his thanks to the Emperor on the same day. On June 18th, Cardinal Ludovisi, accompanied by the imperial envoy, personally repaired to the castle of S. Angelo in order to set Klesl at liberty and to conduct him to the Quirinal. The two Cardinals dined together; afterwards Klesl was received in audience by Gregory XV. to whom he expressed his gratitude.[1] The Pope assigned to him the apartment in the Vatican which Cardinal Galamina had at one time occupied.[2]

An act of violence resembling that committed against Klesl had occurred in Spain against Cardinal Lerma. The latter had been all-powerful under Philip III., but in 1618 he was compelled to retire into his estates, when his son, the Duke of Uzeda, became prime minister and obtained the offices and the influence at one time enjoyed by his father.[3] However, the change did not put an end to the misgovernment of Spain. The Venetian ambassador, Pietro Contarini, who confirms this statement, was of opinion that the fallen Cardinal would never recover his former power. For one thing he was too old, and he had been abandoned by all, even by those who had been most beholden to him. Philip III. died on March 31st

---

[1] See KERSCHBAUMER, 324 seq. The *Brief of June 16, 1623, is in HAMMER, Urk., 971. For the influence of Giacinto, see VENANZIO DA LAGO SANTO, 267 seq.

[2] *Avviso of July 1, 1623, Urb. 1093 A, Vatican Library.

[3] Cf. RANKE, Osmanen und spanische Monarchie⁴ (1877), 173 seq.

1621, and his successor, Philip IV., yielding to the pressure of Lerma's many enemies, caused a judicial examination to be made into his previous conduct. The Cardinal was found guilty of having enriched himself by unlawful means and condemned to repay a large sum of money into the public treasury.

Cardinal Lerma had been interned as soon as the judicial procedure began. The news greatly perturbed both the Pope and the College of Cardinals. On September 9th, 1621, Cardinal Ludovisi instructed the Spanish nuncio to express to the King the Pope's astonishment and indignation at such an injury to ecclesiastical indemnity, one that could not fail to lower the cardinalitial dignity in the eyes of the people.[1] In Rome they never expected such conduct on the part of the Catholic King. Should Spanish ministers quote the fall of Cardinal Klesl, the nuncio was to explain that that case was quite different, were it only for this reason, that the Austrian Cardinal had been accused of gravely imperilling the public good, whereas Lerma was only reproached with having unlawfully pursued his private advantage. Moreover, the evils that had befallen the House of Austria were surely a consequence of the unjust persecution of which Klesl had been a victim. No secular power, however great, had the right, under any pretext whatsoever, to condemn a member of the Sacred College. If princes presumed to do so, they fell under the severest penalties of the Church and the anger of God himself.[2] The scandal occasioned by the action against Lerma

[1] See the *letter to the Spanish nuncio, Alessandro de Sangro in the *Registro delle lettere di Msg. Agucchio*, Cod. 33 D of the Corsini Library, Rome.

[2] " *Niuna podestà terrena per grande che sia nè per qualunque cagione o sotto qualsiasi pretesto ha ragione o legitima autorità di giudicare le persone de cardinali, e se alcuni principi l'hanno tal'volta fatto, o siano per farlo, sono tanto grave le censure e le maleditioni date loro da sagri canoni e concilii e constitutioni apostoliche, che ben è mestieri, che sia grande la divina misericordia verso di loro a non permettere che i flagelli delle pene temporali non li perseguitano." *Cod.* 33 D. 23, Corsini Library, Rome.

must be removed. If the Catholic King began to interfere with the liberty of Cardinals what might not other Powers do ? If his Majesty had reasons to proceed against Lerma, which the Pope hoped was not the case, he must have recourse to the true and only judge, the Pope. Should the Cardinal be found guilty he would punish him as he deserved, just as his predecessors had done in similar cases.[1]

At this very time Rome had to complain of some further encroachments of the Spanish Government. The conflict of jurisdiction which had broken out at Milan under Paul V. had become so acute that in a letter of September 8th, 1621, to the Spanish nuncio, Cardinal Ludovisi remarked that it appeared as if the officials meant to lay hands on the whole government of the Church, so much so that the heretics of the neighbouring countries were in high glee over the conduct of the representatives of the Spanish King. The Pope was deeply grieved at their behaviour and hoped that Philip would put an end to the scandal.[2]

The very position of the Spanish nuncio was causing the gravest alarm, for, not only had he to contend with the arbitrariness and the jealousy of the State, but he had even to cope with the suspiciousness of certain ecclesiastical bodies.[3]

---

[1] A second *letter of Ludovisi to Sangro, September 9, 1621, adds : " If Lerma really appears to be guilty, the King, in order to be able to proceed against him, must request permission from the Pope by letter or through his ambassador, whereupon he would receive a reply, after, as was customary, a congregation of Cardinals had reported on the subject." " Aveva S.Stà prima che si ricevessero le prime lettere di V.S. delli 10 Agosto scritto un breve in raccomandatione del cardinale, che si è fatto assai temperato come vedrà V.S. dalla copia di esso " (*Cod. Corsini, loc. cit.*). Ibid., a *letter in cipher to Niccolò Tighetti, fiscale in Spagna, in which it is stated : " Si è scritto in maniera in favoure del sig. card. di Lerma che non si poteva far più, ne S.Bne si è mossa tanto per commiseratione della fortuna di lui quanto per sostegno della dignità cardinalizia e della libertà e immunità ecclesiastica."

[2] *Ludovisi to Sangro, September 8, 1621, *Cod. Corsini, loc. cit.*

[3] *Cf.* MEISTER, in *Röm. Quartalschr.*, VII., 466.

The difficulty of the situation in Spain appears from the Instruction to the new nuncio, Alessandro de Sangro, Patriarch of Alexandria, which bears the date of April 5th, 1621.[1] The nuncio is advised to be moderate in the use of his faculties, which were far more extensive in Spain than in other Catholic countries. When granting benefices and ecclesiastical dignities he should consider the most deserving as well as the most needy, and in the concession of dispensations he must strictly conform to the decrees of the Council of Trent, for these are the very foundation of ecclesiastical discipline. Special caution is required when there is question of the reform of male and female religious Orders. Notice should be given to the civil authorities, with a view to preventing interference on their part. The enclosure must be strictly observed. Permission for the setting up of private oratories, against the too easy concession of which Paul V. had already had occasion to protest, must now be stopped altogether.

[1] The important and interesting *Instruction for Sangro, is to be found in MS. in widely scattered places : Berlin, State Library, *Inf. polit.*, XI., 477 *seq.*; Vienna, State Library, 5580^b, p. 48 *seq.*, and 6837, p. 56 *seq.*; Rome, *Ottob.* 2721 (Vatican Library); *Varia Polit.*, 117, Papal Secret Archives. Angelica Library, T., 3, 13, p. 1 *seq.* LÄMMER has already quoted an extract from the latter MS. (*Zur Kirchengesch.*, 70 *seq.*). This has been overlooked by MEISTER in his interesting essay, " Zur spanischen Nuntiatur im 16. u. 17. Jahrh." (*Röm. Quartalschr.*, VII., 448 *seq.*) hence he regarded the part of the Instruction quoted by him from *Ottob.* 2206, p. 137 *seq.*, as addressed to Sangro's successor, Mgr. Massimi. The part of the Instruction which regards the affair of the Valtellina had already been published in *Arch. stor. Ital. N.S.*, VII., 1, 8–9, in 1858. The nomination of Sangro was communicated to the Spanish King by Gregory XV., in a *Brief of April 3, 1621; see *Epist.*, in *Arm.*, XLV., 23, Papal Secret Archives. Sangro left Rome, April 7, 1621; see *Avviso of April 7, 1621, *Urb.* 1088, Vatican Library. For the prehistory of the nomination, see the letter of CARD. DI SUSANNA (Card. Ludovisi) of February 10, 1621, in which we read : " N.S^{re} non ha anchora risoluto della persona del Nuntio di Spagna. Io li propongo Mons. di Bregni." There follows a eulogy of him. Original in *Cod.* E. 70 of the Boncompagni Archives, Rome.

Naturally enough a large part of the Instruction deals with the government's interference with ecclesiastical jurisdiction and the pretension of the royal council to examine all papal documents. From this document we learn that the government went so far as to claim for itself the right to enforce the Tridentine reform decrees, an abuse against which the nuncio was told to protest. Then there were the usual infringements of the liberty of the Church in other spheres. With regard to the disputes between Bishops and Chapters, which were very frequent in Spain, the nuncio should see to it that the former did not push too far their right of supervision, nor the latter the limits of their liberty. Both sides should exercise restraint, the Bishops exercising their authority without oppressing the Chapters, and the latter not abusing their exemptions. Some general directions dealt with the manner of transacting business at the Spanish court and the obligation of observing the stringent ceremonies in use there. The Instruction also insisted on a reliable service of information. It likewise dealt with the nuncio's duties and obligations in his capacity as a Collector General. As such, it was his duty, with the aid of assistant collectors, to gather the dues (*spoglie*) and tithes. In this sphere conflicts were all the more frequent as men are wont to be particularly sensitive where money is concerned. Prudence and justice must be the guiding stars of the nuncio. On October 6th, 1621, Ludovisi pointed out to Sangro the importance of his rôle as a judge besides that of nuncio, both for the authority of the Holy See and for the preservation of ecclesiastical jurisdiction. The latter had suffered many breaches in France and Germany owing to Concordats and other concessions, and the heretics had inflicted heavy damage to the authority of the Holy See and to the Catholic religion itself. If the nuncio showed himself too yielding to the ministers of the King, the latter's fiscal officials would not fail to restrict the competence of the nunciature.[1] On October 15th, 1621, the Capuchin, Giacinto da Casale, then on a mission to Spain, was urged to support the nuncio to the best of his

---

[1] **Cod.* 33 D. 23, of the Corsini Library, Rome.

ability in his conflicts on questions of jurisdiction.[1] Unfortunately Alessandro de Sangro proved wholly inadequate to his arduous task. The encroachments of the Spanish Government grew steadily worse and it was in vain that Gregory XV. complained to the King.[2] Sangro was recalled on June 24th, 1622, and replaced by Innocenzo de' Massimi, Bishop of Bertinoro.[3] However, he too failed to fulfil the hopes set on him.[4] A letter of Gregory XV. to Philip IV. dated January 4th, 1623, complains bitterly of the interference of the secular power.[5] In these circumstances it was not surprising that there was great tension in the Pope's relations with the Spanish ambassador, the Duke of Albuquerque.[6]

[1] See the *letter of AGUCCHI to Giacinto da Casale of October 15, 1621, *Cod.* 33 D. 23, Corsini Library, Rome.

[2] See the *Brief to Philip IV., of March 5, 1622, *Arm.*, XLV., 24, Papal Secret Archives.

[3] See the *Brief to Philip IV., of June 24, 1622, *ibid.* Canon Paolo Tronci of Pisa was Major-domo to Massimi ; *cf.* his *letter to his sister in *Cod.* S. 5 of the University Library, Pisa.

[4] *Cf.* " Cagioni che indussero la S^{tà} di N.S. Gregorio XV. a levare la nunziatura di Spagna al patriarca d'Alessandria Msgr. Sangro et abusi al tempo di Msgr. de Massimi suo successore," *Barb.* 5316, p. 1 *seq.* and *Ottob.* 2415, p. 404 *seq.*, Vatican Library, in *Cod. Bolognetti,* 61, Papal Secret Archives, and *Inf. polit.*, XVIV., 398 *seq.*, of the State Library, Berlin. A fifth copy in the Corsini Library, Rome, *Cod.* 33 A. 19, was used by MEISTER (*Röm. Quartalschr.*, VII., 464). For the case of Covarruvia, quoted here, in which even Massimi adopted an altogether mistaken attitude, *cf. Barb.* 3560, p. 1 *seq.*, Vatican Library ; *Veto on the pamphlet of *Antonio de Covarruvia, canonico de Sevilla,* 3 *seq.* ; *Censura* of this document by IOH. DE MIRANDA, 13 *seq.* ; " *Relazione di quanto ha fatto Msgr. Patriarca de Sangro et Mons. de Massimi Nunzio nella causa del sudetto Covarruvia e dei torti che per questo ha ricevuto la giurisdizione apost.*" *Cf.* also the *account of AGUCCHIO to the Spanish nuncio, October 26, 1621, in *Cod.* 33 D. 23, of the Corsini Library, Rome.

[5] A similar *Brief was sent on January 4, 1623, to Olivares, both are in *Arm.*, XLV., 24, Papal Secret Archives.

[6] See *Studi e Docum.*, XXII., 209.

But the rights of the Church were even more grievously injured by that Italian State which constituted the political antipodes of the Catholic King, namely by Venice. After the successes it had won under Paul V., and acting on the advice of Paolo Sarpi, the Catholic Church's bitterest enemy, the republic obstinately held to its former Church policy. Though Paul V. had made frequent remonstrances he had avoided an open conflict. After his death, the Signoria, from political motives, showed some willingness to conciliate the new Pope,[1] so much so that in Rome a hope was born of better relations with Venice. These feelings inspired Gregory's Instruction to Laudivio Zacchia, Bishop of Montefiascone, who was appointed nuncio in Venice on May 12th, 1621.[2] That able diplomatist, who also sought full information from his predecessor, Gessi, was commissioned to regain the lost ground, but at the same time to proceed with the utmost caution,[3] to precipitate nothing, always to wait for the right moment and not to lose heart if he met with opposition. Above all he was to appeal to the political shrewdness of the Venetian government, and represent to them that their own political interests demanded the re-establishment of good relations between Rome and Venice, for assuredly the prestige of the republic could not be enhanced if it set at nought the laws of the Church and entertained strained relations in the ecclesiastical sphere with the Head of Catholicity and the ruler of the Pontifical States. Such a situation must be fatal even to the political interests of the republic of St. Mark. It was

[1] This was shown by the dispatch of a ceremonial embassy to offer homage (cf. BAROZZI-BERCHET, *Roma*, I., 111 seq.) and by the reception of the papal nephew as a patrician of the Republic (cf. above, p. 66, note 1).

[2] The *credentials to the Doge A. Priuli, May 12, 1621, are in *Arm.* XLV., 23, Papal Secret Archives. For L. Zacchia, whose magnificent bust by A. Algardi, is preserved in the Museum at Berlin, cf. the essay by POSSE, on A. Algardi, in *Jahrb. der preuss. Kunstsamml.*, 1905, 3 Ser.

[3] See the text of the Instruction in *Arch. stor. ital.*, VII., (1858), 13 seq.

thought in Rome that representations of this kind would not fail to impress the elder Senators, all the more so as at that time the question of the Valtellina, which touched the republic of Venice so closely, hung in the balance. Gregory XV.'s gravest fear for Venice was Protestant propaganda. He was filled with anxiety when he saw how, for reasons of trade, heretics and schismatics were allowed to take up residence in the City of the Lagoons, and how the danger of a disruption of the unity of the faith was still further increased by the fact that Venice maintained permanent embassies in wholly or partially Protestant countries such as England, Holland, Germany, and Switzerland. In these circumstances the official surveillance which in Venice sought to limit the action of the Inquisition as much as possible, seemed exceedingly dangerous.

Gregory XV. had already given expression to his anxiety on this score to the four Venetian *obbedienza* ambassadors. On that occasion he had likewise complained of the insidious machinations of Paolo Sarpi, who stood in the highest esteem with the Signoria, though in 1620, his deadly hatred of the Church had been unmasked when his history of the Council of Trent became known in consequence of an indiscretion on the part of Marcantonio de Dominis. The envoys met the Pope's complaints with a denial of the existence in Venice of any danger to the faith, and by protesting the Catholic sentiments of their countrymen. As for Sarpi, they affirmed that he lived in complete retirement and had no influence whatever with the government.[1] Gregory XV. saw clearly that as regards Sarpi nothing could be obtained from the Signoria; his only comfort was that that irreconcilable enemy was now so advanced in years that he could not long continue his underground activities. Consequently the nuncio was instructed that it was enough to see to it that Sarpi left no followers behind him.[2]

The best antidote against Sarpi's plots in Venice, and the

---

[1] See *ibid.*, 22, note 20. *Cf.* BAROZZI-BERCHET, *Italia*, I., 128.
[2] See *Arch. stor. ital.*, VII., 1, 22, note 20.

Protestant propaganda in general, Zacchia's Instruction adds, would be the return of the Jesuits to Venice. The Pope had expressed this wish to the *obbedienza* envoys, but his request had met with instant and strong opposition. Even a middle course, that of allowing the Jesuits to return, if not to Venice itself, then at least into the territory of the republic, had been rejected. For all that, Zacchia was instructed to continue his efforts for the repeal of the law of banishment against the Jesuits, and not to allow himself to be discouraged by any difficulty whatsoever.

The Instruction also draws the nuncio's attention to the sad state of the monasteries in Venice in which Sarpi had numerous adherents and where discipline had become very relaxed. There was pressing need of a reform. As regards the correction of the secular clergy, let the nuncio have recourse to the Bishops and urge them to observe the decrees of Trent. Without an improvement in this direction, and unless evil counsellors were displaced by good ones, there was no prospect of any improvement with regard to the frequent injuries done to ecclesiastical jurisdiction. The nuncio is urged not to allow himself to be discouraged by opposition and never to cease from energetic protests until conditions should be at least what they were previous to the reign of Paul V.

Apart from the ecclesiastical conflicts, purely political ones had likewise arisen between Rome and Venice. They concerned navigation in the Adriatic and the determination of frontiers opposite Ferrara. In both questions Gregory XV. showed a yielding disposition,[1] for he was much more anxious for a favourable solution of the ecclesiastical problems. But it was precisely here that the government of Venice showed the least goodwill. Sarpi's death, on January 15th, 1623, delivered the Pope from his fears of the friar's machinations. Though he had completely broken with the teaching of the Church, Sarpi had played his hypocritical part until the end. He had said Mass as late as January 8th, though he had

---

[1] See *ibid.*, 29 *seq.*

described it as idolatry.[1] On August 14th, 1621, Gregory XV. had sent a special Brief to the Doge to secure the repeal of the decree banishing the Jesuits.[2] The Brief paid a high tribute to the Society. The Pope referred to previous discussions with the Venetian envoys and pleaded for a repeal of the unjust banishment of the Jesuits from Venice. Even if individual members should have erred, the whole of the Society should not be made to suffer. The Signoria presented a painful exception among all the Catholic States.[3] Since the Jesuits were accused of excessive sympathy for Spain he would not speak of that country, but would only mention the high esteem enjoyed by their Order in France. As for Germany, the Society had saved the faith in that country. The calumnies of apostates against the Jesuits redounded to the Fathers' honour. They had rendered immense services in spreading Christianity in pagan lands. Nor had they deserved less well of Italy and as in most Italian cities, there must be many inhabitants of Venetian territory also, who could bear witness to all they had done to raise the tone of ecclesiastical life and to promote the education of youth.[4] However, though French diplomacy also intervened on behalf of the Jesuits,[5] the appeal of the Pontiff fell on deaf ears. Shortly before his death, Gregory XV. saw himself compelled to protest to the Doge against an act of

[1] For Sarpi's last days see the report of ZACCHIA in *Arch. stor. ital.*, 4 Ser., IX. (1882), 146 *seq.*, according to which Sarpi asked for the Last Sacraments. Whether the unhappy man was sincerely converted at the last cannot be ascertained.

[2] *Arm.*, XLV., 22, Papal Secret Archives.

[3] " *Europam universam animo percurrite, catholicorum principum suffragia numerentur, periculum erit, ne vos uni male de tam praeclara societate sentire reperiamini." *Ibid.*

[4] " *Nam sacra accuratius coli, iuventutem sapientius institui, pietatis studia frequentius exerceri Iesuitis in eam rem alacrius incumbentibus, et pleraeque huius provinciae civitates testificantur et non pauci etiam vestrae ditionis homines palam fatebuntur." *Ibid.*

[5] See *Arch. stor. ital.*, loc. cit., 22, note 20. Cf. ZELLER, *Luynes*, 239 *seqq.*

infringement of the Church's jurisdiction by the civil authorities of Padua.[1]

As regards the Roman Inquisition,[2] we have no information of any proceedings against heretics during the pontificate of Gregory XV.,[3] evidently because there was no occasion for action. The Pope's watchfulness to prevent all danger of heretical infection is shown by his severe prohibition, which was itself based on a similar decree of Clement VIII., of heretics taking up residence in Italy under any pretext whatsoever.[4] Thus, at the close of 1622, we see the Pope insisting with the representative of Lucca on the removal of some Germans who were staying in that city for the purpose of learning the Italian language.[5]

Whilst beyond the Alps, and especially in Germany, trials for witchcraft and burnings of witches were at their height, Rome was spared such horrors under this pontificate as during the preceding ones, for in this respect the practice of the Roman Inquisition was much milder than that of the secular tribunals in Germany, for it only handed over to the secular arm obstinate delinquents or recidivists, whilst such as recanted, or were accused for the first time, escaped with imprisonment. However, a decree of Gregory XV. of March 20th, 1623,

---

[1] See the long *letter to the Doge A. Priuli of April 1, 1623, *Arm.*, XLV., 21, Papal Secret Archives.

[2] The members of the Roman Inquisition were then Cardinals Bandini, C. Madruzzo, Millini, Verallo, Borgia, Centini, Cobelluzio, Scaglia, Ludovisi and Lavalette ; see L. DIANA, *Coordinatus*, 577.

[3] In Bologna, on November 27, 1622, four persons were executed for outrages to pictures of Saints ; see R. CAMPEGGI, *Racconto degli eretici iconomiasti giustiziati in Bologna*, 1623, and BATTISTELLA, *S. Officio*, Bologna, 1905, 114 *seq.*, 191 *seq.* The names of the Great Inquisitors in DIANA, v.

[4] Constitution of July 2, 1622, DIANA, 555 *seq.* ; *Bull.*, XII., 708 *seq.*

[5] See the *report in *Studi e docum.*, XXII., 207. For the Spanish sect of the Alumbrados, against whom Cardinal Pacheco had to proceed in the diocese of Cadiz and Seville, see *Freiburger Kirchenlex.*, IV.[2], 796 *seq.*

prescribed a greater measure of severity.¹ It stated that if any person was convicted of having made a pact with the devil, thereby apostatizing from the Christian faith, and by sortileges had so injured one or more persons as to cause death, the culprit must be handed over for due punishment, viz. execution, to the secular arm, even if it was his first offence ; but one who, by means of a pact with the devil, had only caused sickness or considerable injury to cattle, or to the crops, was to be sentenced to immurement, viz. lifelong imprisonment.²

Gregory XV. showed extraordinary mildness towards Marcantonio de Dominis, a former Archbishop of Spalato, who, during the pontificate of Paul V., had apostatized in London, and since then had violently attacked the Catholic Church.³ The Pope had at one time been friends with the unhappy man, and now that he seemed to be in earnest in his desire to return to the bosom of the Church, the Pontiff, assisted by Cardinal Ludovisi, facilitated in every way the realization of his resolution.⁴ The negotiations were conducted through the Spanish ambassador in London ⁵ and the nuncio of Cologne, Antonio Albergati.⁶ Having received a safe-conduct, de Dominis repaired to Antwerp where he abjured

---

¹ DIANA, 567 seq. ; Bull., XII., 795 seq.

² See PAULUS, Hexenwahn, 268 seq., who shows that Döllinger and Hinschius are mistaken in seeing a modification of the penalty in the decree ; ibid., 257 seq., for the proof that immurement (Muro claudi) meant " life imprisonment ", which, however, generally only lasted a few years. That the sentence was less severe than was customary in Germany is shown by MÜLLER, Kirchengesch., II., 354.

³ Cf. L. VEITH, E. Richeri systema confutatum. Acc. discursus de vita et scriptis M.A. de Dominis, Mechlinae, 1825 ; LJUBIČ, O Markantunu Dominisi, 2 vols., Zagrab, 1870. Cf. our account, Vol. XXV., 211 seq., 303 seq.

⁴ Cf. GIUNTI, *Vita del card. Ludovisi, Corsini Library, Rome.

⁵ See the *Brief to Count de Gondomar, the Spanish ambassador in London, August 21, 1621, in Arm., XLV., 22, Papal Secret Archives.

⁶ See NICOLETTI, *Vita d'Urbano VIII., Barb. 4731, Vatican Library.

his errors before the Bishop of that city,¹ a step on which Gregory XV. sent him his congratulations.² On his arrival in Rome, de Dominis was temporarily assigned a lodging in the Franciscan convent of Araceli. The Inquisition granted him his pardon on condition that he made a public abjuration and retracted his calumnies against the Roman Church by means of some printed publication. This appeared in Rome in 1622.³ When some prelates of the Curia found fault with so much leniency, the Pope remarked that since, up till then, little had been achieved by proceeding against heresy with fire and sword, he thought it right to try the way of leniency. However, should de Dominis relapse into his errors, he would not escape condign punishment.⁴

Gregory XV. renewed and extended the powers already granted by Pius V. to the Roman Inquisition against the abuse of the sacrament of Penance by a confessor who attempted to induce a penitent to commit a grave sin against the sixth or ninth commandment.⁵ The Pope was likewise in favour of greater strictness with regard to the Index. On December 30th, 1622, he revoked all previous concessions for the reading or keeping of prohibited books.⁶ As for excommunication, Gregory XV. held fast to the principles he had maintained under Clement VIII., viz. that the penalty of excommunication should only be used with discretion and moderation, otherwise, as experience had shown, it lost all its force. He was wont to say that the Church of

[1] See REUSCH, *Index*, II., 403. *Cf. Stimmen aus Maria-Laach*, IV., 82 *seq.*; for the safe conduct for de Dominis see *Cal. of State Papers*, XVII. (1621-3), 170.

[2] *Brief of January 6, 1622, *Brevia Arm.*, XLV., 22, Papal Secret Archives.

[3] See REUSCH, *loc. cit.*

[4] See ACCARISIUS, *Vita Gregorii XV.*, lib. III., ch. 13. Boncompagni Archives, Rome.

[5] *Bull.*, XII., 729 *seq.*

[6] *Ibid.*, 779 *seq.* For the books prohibited by the Congregation of the Index since 1621, see BAUMGARTEN, *Neue Kunde*, 235 *seq.*

Christ should rule her children by love rather than by terror.¹

Like his predecessor, Gregory XV. was also persistently urged by the King of Spain, Philip IV., to decide the old theological controversy concerning Mary's Immaculate Conception.² However, from the first the Pope made it quite clear that the reasons which had restrained Paul V. also, prevented him from coming to a decision.³ Now, as then, theologians were divided on the question; whilst the Dominicans persisted in their opposition, the Franciscans and the Jesuits were of another opinion. Gregory had the whole question examined once more by the Roman Inquisition. The result was a decree, published on May 24th, 1622, which extended to writings and private conversations ⁴ the prohibition by which Paul V. forbade the assertion in lectures and sermons that Mary had been conceived in original sin. Nevertheless, the Dominicans were given leave to expound the opinion of their Order amongst themselves, but not in presence of outsiders.⁵

Gregory XV.'s most important measure for the internal life of the Church was one that dealt with the election of the Pope. In the conclaves of the sixteenth century there had been

¹ ACCARISIUS, (*Vita Gregorii XV., lib. II, ch. 1), thus quotes the Pope's words: "Quemadmodum certissimum est, excomunicationis gladium nervum esse ecclesiasticae disciplinae, si sobrie adhibetur, ita si immodice et non accommodate exerceatur, experimento compertum est, eandem potius enervare—Ecclesiae Christi amore, non terrore venerationem intendi." Boncompagni Archives, Rome.

² Cf. L. WADDINGUS, Πρεσβεια s. Legatio Philippi III. et IV. ad Paulum V. et Gregorium XV. de definienda controversia Immacul. conceptionis B. Virginis Mariae, Lovanii, 1624.

³ See the *Brief to Margaretae a Cruce sanctimoniali regis catholici amitae, dated July 12, 1621, Arm., XLV., 22, Papal Secret Archives.

⁴ Bull., XII., 688 seq. Cf. the Brief to Philip IV., dated June 4, 1622, Arm., XLV., 24, and ibid., the Brief to the city of Seville, November 3, 1622, Papal Secret Archives.

⁵ Bull., XII., 717 seq.

REFORM OF PAPAL ELECTIONS. 109

plenty of undesirable features, but to the honour of the Popes it must be added that they never relaxed their efforts to remedy the evil. At the beginning of the century, Julius II. reacted against the intrigues which had marked the election of Alexander VI. with his stern Bull against simoniacal practices.[1] The two popes who issued from the most protracted and most stormy conclaves of the century,[2] viz. Julius III. and Paul IV., were the very ones who, by means of new electoral regulations, dealt sternly with those irregularities to which they themselves owed in part the tiara.[3] True, death prevented Julius III. from publishing his Bull, but the wish for a reform gained ground. Paul IV. energetically condemned all electoral intrigues during the lifetime of a Pope,[4] whilst Pius IV. attacked the evil at its root when he sought to circumscribe the influence of secular princes. Pius V. worked in the same sense as Paul IV., both by verbal exhortations and by his efforts for the religious renewal of the electoral College.[5] These efforts were not without effect, but much more remained to be done ; hence attempts at electoral reform were frequently renewed. Innocent IX. formed a commission to study the question.[6] Clement VIII. composed a draft for a new electoral Bull,[7] but since he had not had time to publish it, an election capitulation was agreed to, by the terms of which his successor was to publish such a constitution within six months.[8] Consequently, within the very first days of his short reign, Leo XI. appointed a new commission for the study of the question.[9] Paul V. also busied himself with the matter, on the basis of

[1] *Cf.* our account, Vol. VI., 440.
[2] *Ibid.*, Vol. XIII., 2 *seq.*
[3] *Ibid.*, Vol. XIII., 166 *seq.* ; Vol. XV., 66 *seq.*
[4] *Ibid.*, Vol. XVII., 153.
[5] *Ibid.*, Vol. XVII., 154 *seqq.* A similar warning by Gregory XIII., of June 26, 1573, is in SANTORI, *Diario*, 156 *seq.*
[6] L. WAHRMUND, in *Archiv. für kath. Kirchenrecht.*, LXXII. (1894), 203.
[7] WAHRMUND, *loc. cit.*, 204.
[8] No. 27, *ibid.*, 221.
[9] *Ibid.*, 205.

Clement VIII.'s draft,[1] though it was only granted to his successor, Gregory XV., to carry out the reforms.

Spain's meddling with papal elections had become intolerable. Philip III. persevered in the practice inaugurated by his father of seeking to manage the conclaves according to his pleasure. As a matter of fact, the occurrences at the conclave of 1605 showed the extent of Spain's interference, though in the end it achieved nothing. The conclave of Gregory XV. also was not free from numerous abuses, chiefly by reason of the non-observance of the regulations of Pius IV. The conduct of the French ambassador at that conclave could not fail to give fresh impetus to the desire for a reform of the papal election. Cardinal Federigo Borromeo and other Cardinals made strong representations to the Secretary of State. To them, and especially to Cardinal Bellarmine, the Cardinal nephew pledged his word that he would do his utmost in the matter.[2] As soon as the improvement in the Pope's health had disposed of the suspicion that the nephew's zeal for reform was only inspired by a desire to increase his own influence in a conclave that could not be long delayed, he submitted to his uncle a scheme for the abolition, at papal elections, of what was called election by " adoration " by the Cardinals.[3] Like many others, Ludovisi was of opinion that such a procedure, owing to its publicity, militated against freedom of choice,[4] for the electors were easily influenced by considerations of friendship, by fear of the princes and the more powerful among the Cardinals, and not a few joined in

---

[1] *Cf.* our account, Vol. XXV., 224 *seq.*

[2] Ludovisi to Borromeo, November 6, 1621, in WAHRMUND, 260 ; for the date see *ibid.*, 212. For Bellarmine's influence see BARTOLI, *Della vita di Roberto cardinale Bellarmino*, lib. 3, ch. 16, Torino, 1836, 214 ; LE BACHELET, *Auctuarium Bellarmin.*, 530.

[3] WAHRMUND, 261.

[4] *Ibid.* The reasons given by Ludovisi in his letter are repeated by GIUNTI. **Vita e fatti di L. card. Ludovisi*, 16, Corsini Library, Rome, 37 D. 8.

the collective acclamation solely in order that the election should not come off without them. In consequence of such a system it happened at times that the election of the Supreme Head of the Church was completed without due reflection, because the leaders of parties came forward with their proposals without previous warning; the decision was frequently left to the younger and less experienced among the Cardinals; a proper scrutiny became useless; a number of votes were given to young men of small ability, merely to save appearances, and at times the most deserving were barred from the papacy precisely because of their outstanding merit; moreover some of the electors were for ever tossed hither and thither between inclusion and exclusion and the fear lest an election should take place without their knowledge. The disorders which everyone expected to mark the election of a new Pope had as their result that, even before the conclave, the favour of the mighty counted for more than merit; ambition and adulation were rampant; the Cardinals no longer dared give free expression to their opinions, especially in questions concerning justice and the defence of the Holy See. With a view to strengthening parties, insignificant people were raised to the Church's highest senate whilst deserving men were excluded; the Cardinals lost all mutual esteem whilst they forfeited the respect of the princes and a pretext was given to the heretics for attacking the Church. Thus the way was paved for unholy bargains and agreements for, whilst the Pope was still alive, the question of his successor was already under discussion. Even the danger of a schismatical election was not excluded since it was not certain whether for an election by " adoration " the participation of all the electors was not required, and when the election was at last completed enmity continued to subsist between those who had practised exclusion and the one who had been its object, and idle folk had ample material for stories of the conclave which the enemies and calumniators of the Holy See took pleasure in reading and spreading abroad.

Gregory XV. greatly appreciated the lofty motives which prompted Ludovisi, though himself the most powerful of all the Cardinals, to tie the hands of the parties, his own included,[1] but he did not at once fall in with his suggestions. On September 9th, 1621, Ludovisi wrote that the Pope had as yet come to no decision.[2] Nevertheless, as early as September 11th, the imperial envoy, Abbate Alfonso Pico, informed his sovereign that the Pope had made up his mind to decree that a secret scrutiny would henceforth be the only lawful mode of election in a conclave.[3] Two days later the Secretary of State spoke to the imperial envoy about the forthcoming Bull; the Pope, he said, deemed it very useful, and was of opinion that it could only give satisfaction to the princes; meanwhile he did not intend to inform them of its nature.[4]

The Pope's proposals met with the approval of many Cardinals but also with some opposition; Cardinal Millini, in particular, earnestly warned the Pope not to alter a state of affairs which had grown out of the experience of the centuries.[5] Clement VIII. and Paul V., who had only planned to limit election by acclamation to certain hours and without abolishing it altogether, had in the end arrived at the conclusion that it was best to leave things as they were. The existing regulations of the conclave aimed at speeding up the election, and it was to this end that a subsequent " accession " to a vote as well as nomination by acclamation had been permitted. The influence which the heads of parties were allowed to wield was to the same end; without it a two-thirds majority would hardly ever be secured. True, it was claimed that in a secret vote everyone would follow his conscience. But even then it was possible to be actuated by passion; many things were perpetrated in secret which would not be done in public. The party leaders could only

---

[1] See WAHRMUND, 261.

[2] " La verità si è, ch'il Papa non è ancora risoluto di farla," (the Bull). To Nicoletti Tighetti, *fiscale in Spagna, Carte Strozze*, Ser. I., II., 86.

[3] "* levando ogni altra forma usata sin'a questo tempo." State Archives, Vienna. *Rom. fasc.* 49.

[4] *Pico to Ferdinand II., September 18, 1621, *ibid*.

[5] MEMMOLI, 42.

propose worthy candidates, for otherwise they would meet with no response, since at times even the most deserving men failed to secure sufficient support, and one who had not enough conscience to say "No!" when an unworthy candidate was put forward, was capable of anything in secret. Moreover, experience was not unfavourable to election by acclamation; of late only good Popes had been elected in this manner. Lastly, when there was question of innovations, it was impossible to calculate the consequences beforehand. Supposing that, for instance, after publication of the new Bull, agreement among the Cardinals became impossible, what then? There was no Pope to alter the Bull, and if the Cardinals were to change it on their own authority, the election might be contested, with disastrous consequences. Therefore, let the election be limited to fixed hours, and if the Pope was bent on abolishing nomination by acclamation, let him at least retain open accession to a vote.[1]

The Pope was greatly impressed with these objections: "They have robbed me of two nights' sleep," he told Millini at their next meeting, and he made him expound his views before the assembled Cardinals.[2] None the less, Ludovisi's views prevailed, though many saw in the latter's eagerness for reform no more than a desire to weaken the following of his chief opponent, Cardinal Borghese, at the next conclave.[3] As a matter of fact the latter also proved a decided opponent to the plans of the Cardinal nephew, though in a different manner from Millini's. No sooner had he had information of these plans than he approached the Spanish ambassador, the Duke of Albuquerque, with a view to getting the King of Spain to intervene. Albuquerque excused himself at first, on the plea that he had no instructions from his King in the matter, but he ended by asking the Pope to allow him to send a courier to Madrid whilst the Pontiff delayed publication of the Bull

[1] *Ibid.*

[2] *Ibid.*, 46.

[3] *Ibid.*, 43. Ludovisi on November 15, 1621, writes to the nuncio in Florence, of "artificii incredibili" in order to delay the Bull of the papal election. In WAHRMUND, 259.

until the messenger's return. Gregory, who at the moment had not yet made up his mind about the Bull, repressed his annoyance at the uncalled-for meddling and the thoughtlessness of the ambassador who seemed anxious to involve his government in complications with the Holy See. He answered quietly that a Bull of this kind was not the work of one day, so that the messenger might very well undertake his journey.[1] Madrid was slow in replying. Once more Albuquerque called on the Pope, only to receive practically the same answer as at the former interview.[2] Meanwhile the plan of an electoral reform had made considerable strides. On October 26th Ludovisi wrote that Gregory XV. would not alter his decision whatever Spain's reply might be. The draft of the Bull had been circulated among the Cardinals, but the Pope did not seek their opinion on the opportuneness of an electoral reform as such, but merely on particular details thereof. For the rest the majority of the Cardinals approved the resolution of His Holiness whilst a few who did not like it, nevertheless realized that here there was question of something very sacred. With the exception of the Spanish ambassador, all the other envoys so far from raising any opposition applauded the Pope's project.[3]

In preparation for the projected Bull numerous memorandums and other writings had been drawn up in the early months of Gregory's pontificate, especially by Cardinal Frederick Borromeo and the Jesuit, Benedetto Giustiani. There was a consensus of opinion against election by acclamation. When the first draft of the Bull was drawn up it was submitted to the Cardinals. The latter's observations were collected in a single paper which was first discussed by a

---

[1] Ludovisi to Niccolò Tighetti, September 9, 1621, *Carte Strozze*, Ser. I., II., 86 *seq.*

[2] *Ludovisi to Tighetti, October 26, 1621; see AGUCCHIO, *Registro di lettere*, Corsini Library, Rome, 33 D. 23.

[3] *Ibid.* Letter of thanks from twenty-one Cardinals to Ludovisi, October 24 to December 8, 1621, for sending them the draft of the Bull. WAHRMUND, 215, note 1.

commission of six, and thereafter, with the former's amendments and cancellings, by another commission of seventeen prominent members of the Sacred College, in presence of the Pope himself.

On November 15th, 1621, Gregory XV solemnly promulgated in a secret consistory his new regulations for papal elections.[1] The Bull bears the same date though it was only published on the 26th.[2] One of the proposals made whilst the Bull was in preparation would have altered the whole electoral system.[3] By its terms only five or six of those who had received most votes at the first scrutiny would have been considered in the second scrutiny and in the following scrutinies the number of those eligible was to be still further reduced until only two candidates remained at the fifth scrutiny. If in the fifth and sixth scrutiny the Cardinals could not agree on one of the two candidates, recourse was to be had to a compromise in the sense that three Cardinals chosen by lot would decide in favour of one or the other by a majority vote. In this way everything would be over within two days at most of the death of the Pope, and no time would be given to the secular princes for any unlawful interference. Moreover, in order to emphasize the gravity of the act as well as the transitoriness of earthly greatness, the election was to take place in presence of the Blessed Sacrament exposed, and before the dead body of the Pope. However, Gregory XV. could no more make up his mind to introduce a system which broke with all tradition and which debarred Cardinals living at a distance from participation in the election, than he could see his way to adopt the proposed ceremonial.

The Bull is instinct throughout with a sacred gravity and characterized by a circumspection which allows for every eventuality and alteration of circumstances. The chief innovation is stated at once : henceforth a papal election can only take place when the conclave has been closed, after the Mass of the first day, at which the Cardinals assist and communicate, and by a two-thirds majority of votes cast in

[1] LÄMMER, *Melet.*, 243 ; WAHRMUND, 217, note 2.
[2] *Bull.*, XII., 619, 627.
[3] WAHRMUND, 249-258.

a secret ballot. Nevertheless, in consequence of Millini's objections, two other modes were not excluded, viz. the nomination may be made by compromise, that is, by leaving the decision to a committee, or by a kind of inspiration when all the electors without exception and without previous agreement, declare themselves in favour of one and the same person.[1]

Another innovation is this, that no one may vote for himself,[2] for until then it had been lawful to do so at least in the subsequent declaration of " accession ".[3] If a candidate has received the exact two-thirds majority, steps must be taken to ascertain that he has not voted for himself. If more than one candidate has obtained or exceeded the two-thirds majority, and if the number of votes is equal, none of them is elected ; if, on the contrary, the votes are unequal, he is elected who has the greater number.[4] Before the electors cast their vote into the chalice, they must swear that they elect the person whom before God they feel bound to choose.[5] This oath was no doubt intended to stop the abuse which occurred at some conclaves when a certain number of votes were given to individual Cardinals merely by way of paying them a compliment.[6]

If the vote was to remain secret whilst control was possible in certain cases, everything depended on the shape of the ballot papers. The paper must not betray the name of him who

[1] § 1, *Bull.*, XII., 620.

[2] § 2, *ibid.*

[3] H. Singer, *Das c. Quia frequenter* : *Zeitschr. der Savigny-Stiftung für Rechtsgesch.*, XXXVII., *Kan. Abt.*, VI., p. 115 *eq.*, 52, of the reprint. *Cf.* also our notes, Vol. XIII., 17 *seq.* The above-mentioned, over severe ruling, had aimed at making it an obligation to vote for oneself in cases when only one vote was missing. The text given only in part by WAHRMUND (253 *seq.*) is printed in full in SINGER, 125. For Gregory XV., who opposed the " personal vote ", the circumstances of the 1592 Conclave were probably a determining factor (SINGER, 128, 131).

[4] §§ 4 and 5, *Bull.*, XII., 621.

[5] § 5, *ibid.*

[6] *Cf.* our account, Vol. XV., 20, 31 *seq.*, with regard to the Conclave of 1559.

cast it yet it must be possible to ascertain whether someone did not vote for himself or whether in the subsequent " accession " he did not vote twice for the same Cardinal. Hence the elector had to write his own name on top of the paper and at the bottom a number with a motto, for instance a text of Holy Writ. The paper was then folded both on top and at bottom in such wise that the name, the number and the motto were hidden by the folds which were sealed. In the centre of the paper the elector wrote the name of his candidate, in a disguised hand for choice. Whatever else there was on the paper must be in print or if that was not possible, it had to be written by the same hand. The Cardinals filled in the papers at separate tables lest any one should see what was being written.[1]

For the sake of a speedier agreement, Gregory XV. chose not to abolish the right of subsequent accession to a vote, but because the custom hitherto in use to declare oneself openly on such occasions would have once more enabled the heads of parties to exert their influence, he made provision for secrecy in this respect also. After every scrutiny that fails to yield a definite result, all the Cardinals at once fill in a fresh paper in which they declare whether they wish to " accede " to a candidate, and to which one.[2] Contrary to what had been done until then, not more than one name may be written on the ballot paper. In each scrutiny only one vote of accession may be taken and by it the electors do not withdraw the vote cast immediately before. After the declarations of accession the presidents, by opening the fold above the motto of the ballot paper, make sure that no one has given two votes to one and the same candidate. The fold above the name of the Cardinal is only opened if it chances that two electors hit on an identical number and motto. Special directions regulate the procedure to be followed when the votes of sick Cardinals have to be collected; here special precautions are taken to safe-guard the secrecy both in the collection itself and in the checking and counting of the votes. There must be two

[1] §§ 6-9, *Bull.*, XII., 621.
[2] § 10, *ibid.*

scrutinies daily. The Cardinals are strictly forbidden to enter into any pacts and conventions in view of the future election or the inclusion or exclusion of certain definite persons or groups of persons. Secret marks of identification on the ballot papers are also forbidden. Gregory XV. may have thought that by this prohibition he had restricted interference on the part of secular princes, if he had not stopped it altogether. In this he was mistaken. All that he secured was that the ambassadors who until then could work against unwelcome candidates rather by influencing their partisans by underhand means, henceforth had to proclaim exclusion openly and officially in the conclave.[1]

The Bull of November 15th, 1621 was followed on March 12th, 1622, by another[2] which fixes, down to the smallest detail, everything connected with the papal election. In the first assembly after the death of the Pope, the Cardinals must swear to abide by all the Apostolic Constitutions dealing with the papal election, among them the Bull of Gregory XV. There follow the obsequies of the late Pope, on nine consecutive days, the expenses of which, exclusive of the gifts distributed to the people of Rome, must not exceed 10,000 ducats. After the Mass of the Holy Ghost in St. Peter's and a sermon, the Cardinals go into the conclave where they swear once more to observe the papal constitutions on the election. After an address by the Cardinal Dean the cells are assigned by lot. In the evening the conclave is closed, but before this is done care must be taken to ascertain that no conclavist is in hiding who has no right to be present. On the following day, after the midday meal, there is another muster of conclavists in the chapel. It must likewise be ascertained whether all the Cardinals are at least in deacon's orders, and especially whether the conclave is really shut in on all sides. In view of the fact that strict

---

[1] Concerning "exclusion" and the controversy between Sägmüller and Wahrmund on that point, *cf.* the bibliography given by SÄGMÜLLER, *Lehrbuch des kath. Kirchenrechts*, I.[3], Freiburg, 1914, 404 *seqq.*

[2] *Bull.*, XII., 662 *seqq.* The date given is March 12, anno Incarn. 1621, which is equivalent to our 1622.

enclosure was made a condition of the validity of the election, there was a possibility that someone might use this very circumstance as a weapon with which to impugn the election. Gregory XV. provided against such an eventuality by means of certain explicit declarations.

As regards nomination by inspiration, compromise and vote, the second Bull contains nothing new, except that the regulations laid down in the first are here analysed and fixed with meticulous exactness. The result was that this legislation, so maturely pondered and carefully worked out, needed no reform until the days of Pius X.

On November 28th, 1621, Ludovisi wrote that up to date the secular princes had expressed their joy and satisfaction at the reform.[1] In conversation with Bentivoglio and Campori he promised himself the best results in the next conclave, and he expressed the opinion that the Bull was calculated to win friends for the Roman Curia in France also.[2]

A characteristic feature of Gregory XV.'s piety was his great confidence in the power of the intercession of the Saints. In a letter to Maximilian I. of Bavaria he declares emphatically that their help would be particularly effective in the struggle with the heretics.[3] This conviction induced the Pope to take into consideration the numerous requests which reached him

[1] " (N.S.) hebbe carissimo, che ciò fosse per essere grato a S.M. secondo che finora s'intende esser lodato da tutti li prencipi cattolici." To the Spanish nuncio ; see AGUCCHIO, *Registro di lettere, Corsini Library, Rome, 33 D. 23, p. 121.

[2] To the French nuncio, Corsini, November 23, 1621, in AGUCCHIO, *Registro, Casanatense Library, Rome, X., VI., 16. The " *Ceremoniale Ritus elect. Rom. Pontificis, was published by CINGOLI in Rome, 1621. The " *Glossemata ad Bullam Gregorii XV. de elect. Pontif." by the learned Dean of the Rota, J. B. COCCINI, are dedicated to Cardinal Ludovisi (Cod. 151) (128), University Library, Bologna—a copy from the Library of Benedict XIV. ACCARISIUS (see *Vita, lib. III., c. 17), published a justification of the Bull.

[3] See the *Brief of May 21, 1622, in which Gregory XV, answered the letter of thanks of Maximilian, concerning the canonization of March 12, Arm., XLV., 24, Papal Secret Archives.

from the most diverse quarters, for instance, from the Emperor, from the Kings of Spain and France, etc., begging him to proceed with the canonization of a number of *Beati*.[1] Accordingly the necessary inquiries and discussions were forthwith initiated. When the prescribed formalities had been completed in several consistories, during the months of January and February, 1622,[2] March 12th, 1622, was fixed for the canonizations. This honour was to be bestowed simultaneously—a rare occurrence in itself [3]—upon five heroic figures of outstanding character and originality : they were the two great founders of Orders, Ignatius of Loyola and Philip Neri ; the reformer of the Carmelites, Teresa of Jesus ; the apostle of the Far East, Francis Xavier ; and a plain and simple Spanish husbandman of the thirteenth century called Isidor, a man filled with extraordinary confidence in Divine Providence. Since four of the above-named were Spaniards, the Spanish colony in Rome and

[1] For the canonization of Ignatius Loyola, the Pope was first approached by Louis XIII., then by Maximilian of Bavaria and Isabella of Spain. *Cf. La Canonizzazione* (see the full title below, p. 121, note 4 *seq.*, where all else concerning the canonization of the founder of the Jesuits is discussed. Gregory XV., of his own accord, combined it with that of Francis Xavier). No mention is made here of the fact that Gregory XV. addressed *Briefs concerning this matter to Duke Ranuccio Farnese of Parma and Piacenza, November 20, 1621 ; to the Spanish King and Queen, December 1 ; to the Grandees of Spain, December 22, and to the Archduchesses Maria Magdalene and Christina of Tuscany ; see *Arm.*, XLV., 22, Papal Secret Archives. *Savelli reports on June 12, 1621, with regard to the Emperor's request for the canonization of St. Theresa that the Pope had expressed his special veneration for this great reformer. A *report of SAVELLI, July 24, 1621, deals with the request for the canonization of Ignatius and Francis Xavier. State Archives, Vienna.

[2] *Cf.* *Arm.*, XLV., 22, Papal Secret Archives ; *Acta Sanct. Iulii*, VII., 622 *seq.*, 630 *seq.* ; LÄMMER, *Zur Kirchengesch.*, 21 *seq.*, and *Melet.*, 306 note ; *Mon. Xav.*, II., 687-99 ; *La Canonizzazione*, 35 *seq.*

[3] See ACCARISIUS, *Vita Gregorii XV.*, lib. III., c. 16, Boncompagni Archives, Rome.

the city of Madrid undertook to bear the heavy cost of the decoration of St. Peter's for the occasion.¹ The painter and architect, Guidotti Borghese, displayed on this occasion all the splendour of baroque art, and he achieved truly fairy-like effects.² From the first Cardinal Ludovisi had given strong support to the wishes of his uncle with regard to these canonizations, and he did all he could for the splendour of the function. The Jesuits perpetuated the memory of the ceremony by means of a painting now to be seen near the sacristy of their church, the Gesù.³

The religious functions organized in various churches of Rome proved as splendid as the canonization itself.⁴ Solemn processions marked the translation of the pictures of SS. Ignatius and Francis Xavier to the Gesù, of that of St. Philip Neri to the Chiesa Nuova, that of St. Isidor to S. Giacomo dei Spagnoli, and that of St. Teresa to S. Maria della Scala in the

¹ See *Arm., XLV., 24, p. 27, Papal Secret Archives.
² Cf. the account of GIOVANNI BRICCI and the Theatrum in ecclesia S. Petri by PAOLO GUIDOTTI BORGHESE (mentioned in the *Avviso of March 16, 1622, Urb. 1091, Vatican Library) in La Canonizzazione, 43 seq., 56 seq.; ibid., 73 seq. the account of G. GIGLI and of the Avvisi.
³ See GIUNTI, *Vita del card. Ludovisi, Corsini Library, Rome.
⁴ See the detailed *report in Arm., XLV., 24, p. 27 seq., Papal Secret Archives. Cf. *Diarium P. Alaleonis, Barb. 2817, Vatican Library, and the splendid work, " La Canonizzazione dei Santi Ignazio di Loyola, Fondatore della Compagnia di Gesù, e Francesco Saverio, Apostolo dell'Oriente. Ricordo del terzo Centenario, XII. marzo 1622. A cura del Comitato Romano-Ispano per le Centenarie Onoranze, Roma, 1922 (Redattore principale : P. Pietro Tacchi Venturi, S.J.) A. POSSEVINO, though he has a tendency to exaggerate, says in his *account of July 22, 1621 (Gonzaga Archives, Mantua) that the canonization of Ignatius and Xavier would cost the Jesuits 40,000 ducats. In Bull., XII., 483 seq., 673 seq., there are only the Bulls for Isidor and Teresa. As the Bulls for Ignatius, Xavier and Neri had not been published, Urban VIII. issued them on August 6, 1623 (for Philip Neri, Bull., XIII., 11 seq., for Ignatius, ibid., 23 seqq., for Xavier, ibid., 33 seqq.). Cf. Mon. Xav., II., 704 seq.

Trastevere.¹ Special solemnity marked the celebration of the canonization of the two heroes of the Society of Jesus in the Roman College and in the Society's church of S. Fedele at Milan.²

On September 15th, 1622, Gregory beatified one of the most learned of German scholars, Albert of Lauingen, who by the twin splendours of virtue and learning had won for himself the glorious epithet of " The Great ".³ A similar honour had been bestowed on Peter of Alcantara on April 1st, 1622.⁴ The Pope also specially promoted devotion to St. Anne, St. Joachim, St. Joseph and St. Bruno.⁵ At the request of the

---

¹ See the *Avviso of March 16, 1622, Vatican Library. For the celebrations in the Gesù, see *La Canonizzazione*, 89 seq., 94 seq. For the magnificent celebration of the feast of S. Philip Neri in the Chiesa Nuova on the anniversary of his death, see the *account of B. PAOLUCCI in his letter of May 28, 1622, State Archives, Modena.

² *La Canonizzazione*, 102 seq., 130 seq. Cf. AMBROS, IV., 132 seq. For the celebrations in France see FOUQUERAY, III., 478 seq., for those in Ingoldstadt, *Sammelblatt des Hist. Vereins von Ingoldstadt*, fascicule 22.

³ Cf. MICHAEL, *Gesch. des Deutschen Volkes*, III., 111, where there is further bibliographical information.

⁴ See *Bull.*, XII., 685 seq. Cf. *Relatio canonizationis servi Dei fr. Petri de Alcantara*, in Cod. 107 of the Communal Library at Cuneo (with the arms of Gregory XV.). Cf. *Acta SS. Oct. VIII.*, 798 (Beatifications of April 18, 1622). See also the *Briefs to the King of Spain, December 21, 1621, in *Arm.*, XLV., 22, Papal Secret Archives. The beatification of Jacopo della Marca is mentioned in the *Brief to the Prince of Lusignano, September 25, 1621, and in another to the deputation of the town of Naples, February 5, 1622, ibid. The *Relatio Rotae ad Gregorium XV. in causa beatificat. Iacobi de Marchia*, is in Cod. H. 1 of the Boncompagni Archives, Rome.

⁵ Cf. *Bull.*, XII., 686 seq., 757 seq., 789 seq.; *Stimmen aus Maria-Laach*, XXXVIII., 296 seq. The feast of Ambrose of Siena had been granted by Eugene IV. to the whole *provincia Romana* and especially to the Dominican convent at Siena, in 1443. The Protector of the Order, Cardinal Borghese, obtained from Gregory XV.

General of the Jesuits, Vitelleschi, Gregory XV., by a Brief of October 2nd, 1621, granted leave to all priests to say the Mass of St. Aloysius Gonzaga on his feast day as that of the Saint of the day, in all the Jesuit churches and Jesuits were permitted to say the Saint's office.[1]

By a decree of March 12th, 1622, the observance of holy days in the Eternal City was once more inculcated.[2] The feast of Corpus Christi was celebrated with special splendour. On the day itself a procession, starting from St. Peter's, went through the Borgo, the Pope, the Cardinals and the whole Court taking part. During the octave there were processions in all the more important churches.[3] The clergy of S. Spirito in Sassia and that of the German church of Our Lady of the Campo Santo held theirs on the Thursday. On Friday there followed a procession

the extension of the privilege to the whole Dominican Order. Attestation of this by Card. Borghese is in *Acta SS. Marc.* III., 243 *seq.* On October 8, 1622, Gregory XV. permitted the veneration of John Capistran by the Franciscan Order. The Vicar General of the Fr. Min. Obs., ANT. STROZZI, *reported to the Emperor Ferdinand II. on the canonization of B. John Capistran : " Sanctissimus pater . . . in beatum Ioannem de Capistrano ob eius praeclara ac mirabilia gesta adeo se bene affectum praedemonstrat, ut cum . . . in sanctorum numerum referre iudicaverit." State Archives, Vienna.

[1] Paul V. had allowed the proper Office and Mass only to the four Roman houses (*Acta SS. Iun.*, V., 761, where the Brief of October 2 is printed). According to a *report of Savelli, of August 22, 1622 (State Archives, Vienna) the Emperor, through the General of the Jesuits, charged Savelli with the affairs of the canonization of B. Aloysius.

[2] See *Editto sopra osservanza delle feste,* March 12, 1622, Bandi V., 7, p. 47, Papal Secret Archives. For France, Gregory XV. ordered the observance of the Forty Hours' devotion in 1621 ; see *Bull.*, XX., 576 *seq.* A DE SANTI *L'orazione,* 222 *seq.*

[3] *Cf.* for what follows, the rare pamphlet : *Ragguaglio di tutte le processioni che si fanno ogn'anno da 50 chiese di Roma pe la solennità del Corpus Domini et sua ottava, poste per ordine dei giorni, che si fanno nel present' anno 1621 sotto il Pontificato di N.S.P. Gregorio XV.,* Roma, 1621.

from S. Maria sopra Minerva in which the Senator, the Conservators of Rome, many Cardinals, ambassadors and courtiers took part. On Saturday came the turn of the Augustinians of S. Maria del Popolo, the archconfraternity of the Sicilians of S. Maria di Constantinopoli, the Greek College and the confraternity of *S. Lucia alle botteghe oscure.* On Sunday no less than a dozen processions started from as many different churches, viz. the Canons and the archconfraternity of the Blessed Sacrament from S. Maria in Trastevere; the confraternity of the *pizzicaroli* (i.e. the gardeners and millers) from S. Maria dell'Orto; the Germans from S. Maria dell'Anima; the Spaniards from S. Giacomo in the Piazza Navona; the French from S. Luigi; the Chapter of the Lateran from that basilica; the Germano-Hungarian College from S. Apollinare; the Carmelites from S. Maria della Scala; the Somaschans from S. Biagio de Monte; the Barnabites from S. Carlo a' Catinari; the Canons of S. Nicola in Carcere and the confraternity of S. Giacomo Scossacavalli from their church. On Monday there were seven processions; the Servites from S. Maria in Via; the Franciscans Conventuals from SS. Apostoli; the Augustinians from S. Agostino; the Canons of S. Maria Rotonda (the Pantheon), the confraternity of the Blessed Sacrament of SS. Celso e Giuliano in Banchi, the confraternity of a Good Death of S. Maria dell'Orazione, and the confraternity of the fishmongers of S. Angelo in Pescaria. On Tuesday there were processions of the Carmelites from S. Maria Traspontina, of the Florentines from their national church of S. Giovanni, of the Regular Clerics of S. Lorenzo in Lucina, of the Canons and the archconfraternity of S. Maria del Pianto and S. Eustachio; on Wednesday a procession of the Minims of S. Francis de Paula from Trinità dei Monti, of the archconfraternity of Trinità dei Pellegrini and the archconfraternity of S. Cecilia in the Trastevere. On the Octave day, to conclude the solemnities, there were no less than fifteen processions, viz. of the chapter of S. Maria Maggiore, the Lateran Clerics Regular of S. Maria della Pace, the Jesuits of the Gesù, the Minims of S. Andrea delle Fratte, the Carmelites of S. Crisogono, the Breton and Roman lawyers of

St. Yvo, the Canons of S. Maria in Via Lata and S. Lorenzo in Damaso together with the archconfraternity of the Blessed Sacrament, the confraternity del Suffragio of S. Biagio della Pagnotta, the Venetians of S. Marco, the confraternities of S. Roch and SS. Simon and Jude, the parish of S. Salvatori ai Monti, the celebrated confraternity del Gonfalone of S. Lucia della Chiavica, and lastly the Chapter and the confraternity of the Blessed Sacrament of S. Peter's.

In this way strangers staying in Rome during the Octave of Corpus Christi were given a glimpse of the wealth and variety of the various Orders and confraternities at the centre of Christendom. Many of these were of recent origin. In 1621, Antonio Possevino reports that statistics show that during the last fourteen years, thirty-one new religious foundations had been made in Rome.[1] Two of the new Congregations, both devoted to education, that of the Clerics Regulars of the Mother of God, founded by Giovanni Leonardi and approved by Clement VIII., and the Clerics Regulars of the Pious Schools of Joseph of Calasanza, owe to Gregory XV. their elevation to the status of a religious Order with solemn vows, beside many other favours.[2] The Congregation of secular priests called the Pious Labourers (*Operarii pii*), founded at Naples by Carlo Carafa, which also devoted itself to education and subsequently to the work of popular missions, was confirmed by Gregory XV. The Pope also approved the Congregation of the Theatine nuns; that of the Theatine Hermit Sisters; the Brothers of St. Bridget, founded in the Spanish Netherlands; the French reformed Cistercians as well as the French Benedictine Congregation of St. Maurus which was to render imperishable services to learning.[3] Close to the church of

---

[1] " *Per mia curiosità esaminando il numero delle religioni quali lassai in Roma 14 anni sono quando venni a Mantova ho trovato che ne sono stato instituite 31 di nuovo tra riforme delle vecchie et nuove." Letter of August 6, 1621, Rome.

[2] See *Bull.*, XII., 608 *seq.*, 627 *seq.*, 650 *seq.*, 687 *seq.*, 749 *seq.*, 780 *seq.*, 790 *seq. Cf.* MORONI, XLIII., 92 *seq.*

[3] See HEIMBUCHER, I., 151, 229, 509; II., 255. The Constitution concerning the erection of the Congregation of St. Maurus,

St. Cecilia, in Rome, Gregory XV. erected a college bearing his own name, for the purpose of housing Benedictine monks temporarily in the eternal city for religious, scientific, or other purposes.[1] Some of Gregory XV.'s ordinances concerning the Franciscans were neither happy nor lasting. The Pope had been misinformed.[2] The Pontiff promulgated a number of decrees dealing with the reform of various Orders in France,[3] South-Germany,[4] and Poland.[5] A constitution of February 5th, 1622, regulated the position of the Orders with regard to the Bishops and the cure of souls.[6]

Gregory XV.'s strictly ecclesiastical spirit explains his strong preference for the new reformed Orders of the Theatines, Oratorians, Jesuits and Capuchins. The Theatines had their privileges confirmed.[7] For the Jesuits and the Oratorians the canonization of their founders was an event of considerable

---

May 17, 1621, in *Bull.*, XII., 533 seq. The French Benedictine sisters of Mount Calvary were raised by Gregory XV. to the status of an independent Congregation ; the Swiss Benedictine Congregation was exempted from episcopal authority ; see *Freiburger Kirchenlexikon*, II.², 349, 1727.

[1] See *Bulla apost. Gregorii XV. super creatione hospitii Gregoriani in Urbe pro univ. monachis sub regula s. Benedicti milit.*, Romae, 1621. *Cf. Bull.*, XII., 537 seq. *Ibid.*, 682 seq. on the Bonaventura College at Prague for the Franciscans Conventuals.

[2] More on this point in HOLZAPFEL, *Gesch. des Franziskanerordens*, 331, 337, 343. For the *Brief on the Portiuncula Indulgence, see *Freiburger Kirchenlex.*, X.², 201.

[3] *Cf. Bull.*, XII., 519 seq., 705 seq.

[4] *Cf.* the *Briefs to Maximilian I. of Bavaria, August 12, 1621, and June 11, 1622. A *Brief to the *Abbas monasterii Campidunen. ord. s. Benedicti in Suevia*, November 12, 1622, commands him to re-establish discipline. *Arm.*, XLV., 22 and 24, Papal Secret Archives.

[5] See the *letter to Sigismund III. of Poland, September 8, 1621, in THEINER, *Mon.* III., 364.

[6] *Bull.*, XII., 656 seq.

[7] *Constitution of October 16, 1621, BANDI, V., 15, p. 438, Papal Secret Archives. *Ibid.*, 440 : *Gregorii XV. prohibitio ambitus pro congreg. cleric. regul. Theatinorum.*

importance. By a constitution of April 15th, 1621, the Jesuits were empowered to establish in their churches or residences, in any part of the world, Sodalities in honour of the Annunciation of the Blessed Virgin, and to affiliate them to the Roman Sodality.[1] To this were added numerous other favours, many of which were in connexion with missionary activity outside Europe, a work which was chiefly exercised by the Society of Jesus.[2]

Cardinal Ludovisi, who like the Pope himself, cherished a great veneration for his former teachers, acted as their Protector; his zeal in this respect rivalled that of Cardinals Alessandro and Odoardo Farnese.[3] At the very outset of his administration he gave a clear proof of his enthusiasm for the Order when he said his first Mass in the chapel of the professed house of the Roman Jesuits.[4] He also bestowed rich gifts upon their churches in Rome and Bologna, and it was his intention to erect magnificent chapels of St. Ignatius at Bologna and Zagarolo.[5] We have already spoken of the splendid church in honour of the Saint erected by him in Rome, at his own expense. It was the Cardinal's intention to collect in a house adjoining the church all his religious pictures.[6]

But preference for his old teachers did not blind Cardinal Ludovisi to the merits of another reform Order, viz. the Capuchins, towards whom he had been attracted from his earliest youth. He assisted their Roman house by generous gifts of bread, meat, wine, oil, coal and wood, and encouraged the Order by every means in his power. When on the death of Cardinal Montalto he became Protector of the Capuchins, he declared that he valued this dignity above all the honours that had fallen to his lot.[7]

[1] See Synopsis, II., 293.
[2] See *Bull.*, XII., 554 *seq.*, 754 *seq.* : Synopsis, II., 291-304. *Cf.* below ch. 3.
[3] See Giunti, *Vita card. Ludovisi*, Corsini Library, Rome.
[4] *Cf.* Avviso of April 7, 1621, *Urb.* 1088, Vatican Library.
[5] See Giunti, *loc. cit.*
[6] *Ibid.*
[7] *Ibid.*

In his esteem for the Capuchins, Ludovisi was in full accord with Gregory XV. A papal constitution of December 9th, 1621, was of great importance for that Order. It renewed the prohibitions of Gregory XIII, and Gregory XIV. which forbade other Regulars to wear the same habit as the Capuchins or one similar to it. The Bishops, particularly those of Spain, France and Italy, were instructed to proceed with ecclesiastical sanctions against those who arrogated to themselves, on their own authority, either the name or the habit of the Capuchins.[1] Gregory XV. also showed his predilection for the Capuchins when he once more entrusted to the excellent and devout P. Girolamo da Narni (1565-1631) the office of preacher in the Apostolic Palace. The sermons which Girolamo preached in this capacity are out of the common, both as regards matter and form; the depth of his thought, the purity of his style and his powerful delivery called forth general admiration. Subsequently Cardinal Ludovisi saw to it that the sermons appeared in print.[2] Girolamo da Narni, whom his contemporaries compared to St. Paul, also had some share in the establishment of Propaganda, a work which by itself alone would suffice to immortalize the memory of Gregory XV.

[1] See *Bull.*, XII., 647 seq.
[2] See GIUNTI, *loc. cit.* Cf. FR. ZANOTTO, *Storia della predicazione*, Modena, 1899, 231.

CHAPTER III.

(1.)

FOUNDATION OF PROPAGANDA AND STATE OF THE MISSIONS—
POSITION OF CATHOLICS IN HOLLAND AND ENGLAND

THE period of the Catholic reform and restoration witnessed most wonderful successes in the mission field, by now greatly enlarged in consequence of the extensive discoveries of the time. However in consequence of the independent action of the Orders and the lack of unity between them, in consequence also of the abuse by Spain and Portugal of the right of patronage which had been granted to them, certain irregularities had crept in which imperatively demanded redress. Above all there was need of a firm and uniform organization which could divide up the field of work, choose suitable workers, settle disputes among the missionaries and set boundaries to the excessive claims of patronage by the colonizing Powers. This could only be realized through the creation of a supreme central governing body in Rome. The first steps in that direction were taken during the pontificate of Pius V. This great Pope, in order to place the missions in immediate relation with Rome and to free them from interference by the secular Powers, thought of creating the post of an overseas nuncio; but this project was thwarted by the opposition of Philip II. Instead of this first plan and acting on a suggestion of Francis Borgia, Pius V. erected in July, 1568, two Congregations of Cardinals for the Propagation of the Faith, one for Protestant countries, the other for those oversea.[1] His successor, Gregory XIII., created, in 1573, a Congregation for the spread of the Faith in the East, at the instigation of Cardinal Santori.[2] The turn of the century brought about an important development when Clement VIII., in 1599, called into being a Congregation of Missions which had the same

[1] *Cf.* our account, Vol. XVIII., 349 *seq.*
[2] *Cf.* our account, Vol. XIX., 60.

name, purpose and organization as Propaganda at a later period. During the lifetime of its Prefect, Cardinal Santori, the Congregation of the missions displayed great activity.[1] Under Paul V., this central directorate of the missions fell into abeyance,[2] although the idea of an institution of the kind was kept alive throughout his pontificate. Three men, whose names will ever be honoured by History, secured its realization : they were the Carmelites Thomas of Jesus and Dominic of Jesus Mary and the Capuchin Girolamo da Narni.

In his *Treatise on the Missions* published in 1613, Thomas of Jesus adopted and further developed the ideas of Santori and advocated the creation of a special Congregation for the Propagation of the faith. It was to consist of twelve apostolic men who, assisted by a few secretaries, were to meet in council on appointed days to deliberate how best to assist all the nations, to write to princes, bishops, and heads of Orders, in order to encourage and comfort them ; to translate and spread books and catechisms, to encourage and confirm wavering Catholics and those threatened by the heretics. All these activities were to be carried out in the name of the Pope. The various countries of the world were to be divided up among the secretaries.[3] Ever since the days of Paul V., Dominic of Jesus Mary and Girolamo da Narni, the Preacher of the Apostolic

[1] *Cf.* our account, Vol. XXIV., 266 *seq.*

[2] It is clear from B. CECI, that it still existed in the time of Paul V., *Relazione di Roma*, etc., in which it is specifically mentioned : " La Congregazione detta de Fide Propaganda. Qui si discorre e risolve del modo che si de' tenere in quei luoghi ove si sente che la fede cattolica habbia qualche principio e che vi sia chi cerchi istruirla e propagarla. Vi sono questi cardinali : Ascoli, S.ta Cecilia, Aldobrandino, San Giorgio, Paravicino, Arigonio, Visconti, Spinelli, Monopoli, Serafino, San Cesario " (*Urb.* 837, p. 464, Vatican Library). For its end through lack of means, which had always been the great difficulty, see P. A. SANTORII, *Annales*, in *Cod.* K. 7, of the Vallicelliana Library, Rome.

[3] See SCHMIDLIN, " Die Gründung der Propagandakongregation," in the *Zeitschr. für Missionswissenschaft*, XII. (1922), 2 *seq.* I was able to use not only this essay, but many other invaluable written accounts and notes of this learned author

Palace, had laboured with the same end in view, the latter having been confirmed in his office by Gregory XV.[1]

Gregory XV. and his Secretary of State, Ludovisi, who knew and appreciated the rigid and centralized organization of the Jesuits,[2] gave these plans special attention as there seemed to be then " doors opening wide for the conversion of unbelievers and heretics ".[3] The Sacred College shared their conviction that something special should be done for the missions. Some of the Cardinals laid particular stress on the rôle of the national Colleges which Gregory XIII. had supported with so much enthusiasm ; others were of opinion that the propagation of the gospel should be made the care of the nuncios.[4] Gregory XV. and Cardinal Ludovisi finally came to a decision in accordance with the plan of Thomas of Jesus, namely the creation of a Congregation which in its aims and general organization would be a revival of the institution begun under Clement VIII.[5]

of the " Missionsgeschichte ", for this chapter as also for the account of the missions under Urban VIII. and Innocent X., and I desire to express my sincere gratitude for them here.

[1] See SCHMIDLIN, *loc. cit.*, 4, notes 2 and 3. *Cf.* also ARENS, *Handb. der kath. Missionen* (1920), 4 *seq.* ; SCHWAGER, *Die Heidenmission*, I. (1907), 18 ; ROCCO DA CESINALE, II., 40 *seqq.* ; CASTELUCCI, 202 *seq.*, 208 *seq.*

[2] See MEJER, I., 57 *seq.*, 91 *seq.*

[3] See the circular to the nuncios of January 15, 1622, in the *Collectanea*, I., 1.

[4] These details, unknown until now, are in ACCARISIUS, *Vita Gregorii XV.*, lib. III., ch. 14. Boncompagni Archives, Rome.

[5] That Gregory XV. had the Congregation, instituted by Clement VIII., before him as a model, appears from a note not hitherto utilized, though printed by LÄMMER, *Zur Kirchengesch.*, 130. It occurs in the Instruction for the Polish nuncio, Lancellotti, December 14, 1622 : " È noto a V.S. che la S.$t^à$ di N.S. rinnovando o di nuovo instituendo La Congregazione de Propaganda Fide tanto importante per ampliare la fede, ordinata già da Clemente VIII. di f. mem. e poco appresso tralasciata, ha eccitato tutti i nuntii," etc. *Cf.* also the *Letter of Propaganda to Paolo Emilio Santori in Castelucci, 195, n. 1.

In 1622, on Epiphany Day, that most ancient festival which commemorates the call of the Gentiles to the faith and kingdom of Christ, the gigantic work of the *Congregatio de Propaganda Fide*, best known as *Propaganda*, was founded. The event was destined to become a landmark in the history of the missions. The annals of the newly founded institution have commemorated it in these simple words : " In the name of Christ. Amen. In the year 1622 after His birth, on the sixth day of January, our Holy Father in Christ, Gregory XV., by divine Providence, Pope, convinced that the chief duty of his pastoral office was the spread of the Christian faith whereby men come to the knowledge and worship of the true God, created a Congregation of thirteen Cardinals, two Bishops and a secretary, to whom he entrusted and recommended the duty and responsibility of the propagation of the faith."[1] Gregory XV. officially confirmed and published this measure in the chart of foundation of June 22nd, 1622.[2] In this document the Pope declared that it was his desire to continue with greater energy and vigliance the work of training labourers for the rich harvest which his predecessors had inaugurated with so much zeal. He points out that all Christians must be apostles, especially the Bishops, and the Pope in the first place, as the successor of Peter on whom the Lord had laid the special duty to announce the gospel to the nations even as he had commanded him alone to feed his flock. The *élite* of the Sacred College were nominated to the Congregation, namely Cardinals Sauli, Farnese, Bandini, Sourdis, Barberini, Millini, Borgia, Ubaldini, Eitel von Hohenzollern, Cobelluzio, Valiero, Ludovisi and Sacrati ; Bishops Giovan Battista Vives and Giovan Battista Aguchi ; finally, as secretary, a priest from Ravenna, Francesco Ingoli, who soon displayed a remarkable activity.

In the same document the members of the Congregation were given full powers and commanded to supervise all preaching and religious teaching in the missions, to appoint

---

[1] See *Collectanea*, I., 1 ; SCHMIDLIN, *loc. cit.*, 5, note 1 ; KOLLMANN, *Acta*, I., 3, note 6 ; CASTELUCCI, 123, note 1.

[2] See *Bull. S.C. de Prop.*, I., 26 seqq. ; *Collectanea*, I., 2 seqq. ; MEJER, I., 96 seq. ; SCHMIDLIN, *loc. cit.*, 9 seq.

and to dismiss missionaries, to deliberate on and to take action in everything that concerned the spread of the gospel in all parts of the globe. To this end they were to meet once a month in presence of the Pope and twice by themselves, in the house of the senior member. Only the most important matters were to be brought before the Pope; all else could be decided independently by the Congregation. To meet expenses they were to have, besides the personal offerings of the Pope and the faithful, a fixed income from the Apostolic *Camera*. Propaganda secured a permanent source of income when the sum of 500 gold ducats, which every Cardinal had to pay for his ring on his elevation to the purple and which until then had gone to the Lateran basilica, was assigned to it.[1] Subsequently further privileges followed: on November 12th, 1622, Gregory XV. empowered Cardinals Santori and Ludovisi to sign and seal contracts for the purpose of increasing revenues and providing for better management; on December 14th he granted the free drafting, registration and postage of all letters and papers of Propaganda by the officials of the Curia; finally on July 13th, 1623, he granted the Congregation the privilege of appointing a judge chosen from among its own members for the execution of business; this official also enjoyed the right of delegating his authority.[2]

The newly constituted body held its first sitting on January 14th, 1622, in the house of Cardinal Sauli. After thanking the Pope for his pious zeal and for this wonderful creation so worthy of him, they proceeded to draft the Bull of erection and to concert measures concerning finance. The missions had until then been chiefly manned by the religious Orders who had received faculties to that effect from the Pope. It was now decided to turn not only to the Generals of the Orders but also to the nuncios.[3] By January 15th, 1622, a cir-

[1] See *Bull.*, 1., 30 *seqq.*; IUS. PONTIF., I., 11 *seqq.*, also SCHMIDLIN, *loc. cit.*, 10 *seq.*

[2] See *ibid.*

[3] See SCHMIDLIN, *loc. cit.*, 5, according to the *Acta S. Congreg. de Prop. Fide*, in the Archives of Propaganda, Rome. *Cf.* CASTELUCCI, 124; KOLLMANN, *Acta*, I., 6.

cular letter had gone out to all the papal nuncios inviting them to report on the state and progress of the missions, to procure the support of princes, governors and Bishops. In order to allay all suspicion, especially on the part of heretical princes to whom it was sometimes insinuated that in these Congregations or other conferences dependent on them, conspiracies were afoot against their persons and their States, or that they were concerned with attempts to suborn their peoples, or other political schemes. They were to emphasize the fact that there was no question of erecting tribunals, or of exercising temporal jurisdiction, or of using any violent methods, but that their only aim was to convert unbelievers by gentle and kindly means, by sermons, instructions, fasting and alms, the Sacraments, prayers and tears—and all this without noise or clamour.[1] On January 7th the Generals of the Jesuit and other Orders were instructed to command their missionaries to send in reports from time to time on their respective missions. Towards the end of the year the Congregation addressed a circular to all the Bishops, including copies of their first letter, in which they were requested to emulate the zeal of the Supreme Pastor and to exhort the faithful to support the missions with money, advice and recommendations.[2]

The financial question, which was fully discussed at the second meeting, was happily solved through the generosity of the Pope. Besides the contribution from the tax on the Cardinals' rings, Gregory XV. assigned to his foundation other important sums from the *Camera* and from the taxes on canonizations, as well as numerous sums from his private purse—for instance on November 5th, 1622, 10,000 ducats, on December 21st 13,000 ducats. To this must be added the gift of a palace worth 10,000 scudi and the considerable alms collected by the Carmelite, Dominic of Jesus and Mary.[3] The business procedure of Propaganda followed, in the main, the same lines as to-day ; once or twice a month there was a discussion on the basis of correspondence

---

[1] See *Collectanea* I., 1 seqq.; KOLLMANN, *Acta* I., 1 seqq.
[2] See SCHMIDLIN, *loc. cit.*, 6 seq.
[3] See *ibid.*, 12, and *Zeitschr. für Missionswiss.*, 1924, 58.

received and the secretary wrote the answers after the decisions had been reached. He also received correspondence on its arrival, examined it and made some small notes on the back. If the matter was of small importance, he dealt with it himself, otherwise it was brought before the Congregation when the particular Cardinal concerned discussed it and the Congregation gave its decision in accordance with the faculties received from the Pope. If these were not adequate the matter was held over until the Congregation met before the Pope and was there dealt with. However the decrees of the Congregation of the Cardinals had, under certain conditions, the value of Apostolic Constitutions.[1]

How far did the competence of Propaganda reach according to the Bull of foundation ? It had the exclusive right to govern the missionary territories, though within certain limits. First of all there was the Inquisition which, from the very nature of the problem of missionary administration, had to intervene very frequently. The Datary was also concerned. Furthermore, the Congregation of Rites dealt with matters belonging to its competence. With regard to the other tribunals and Congregations of the Curia, Propaganda had received the widest faculties. The Secretary, Francesco Ingoli, remained the soul of Propaganda until 1648, whilst Cardinal Ludovisi became Prefect of the Congregation in succession to Sauli in the autumn of 1622.[2]

Already at the third meeting, on March 8th, 1622, a division of labour was made in the " provinces of the whole world ", in the sense that France was put under the nuncio of Paris ; Holland, England, Scotland, Ireland, Denmark and Norway were entrusted to the nuncio of Brussels ; Switzerland, Alsace and South-West Germany to the nuncio of Lucerne ; North-West Germany to the nuncio of Cologne ; South-East Germany and Austria, Hungary, Transilvania, Moldavia and Wallachia to the nuncio of Vienna. The Polish nuncio looked after Poland, Prussia, Pomerania, Sweden and Prussia ; the southern

[1] *Cf.* KOLLMANN, *praef.*, v. seqq.

[2] See SCHMIDLIN, *loc. cit.*, 7. For Ingoli *cf.* KILGER, in the *Zeitschr. für Missionswiss.*, XII., 15.

Slav countries were under the nuncio of Venice. The Spanish nuncio was placed over all the possessions of that kingdom, including the missionary colonies and territories, especially the West Indies. The Portuguese Collector took charge of the possessions of that kingdom together with the missions of the East Indies. Special patriarchal Vicars were appointed for the Balkans, Asia Minor and Northern Africa with residence, respectively, in Constantinople, Jerusalem, and Alexandria. These territories, in this same order; were later assigned to individual Cardinals of the Congregation.[1]

So many blessings for the whole of the missionary world have proceeded from Propaganda that its foundation has justly been described as an Act of Providence.[2] The Congregation became the centre of the Catholic missionary movement which is unique of its kind in the world. Its own work became as universal as that movement. The archives of Propaganda contain the result of all these labours, and they are superior even to the Papal Secret Archives as regards completeness, and, next to them, they are the most important of all Roman archives. Here we find preserved in thousands of volumes accounts of inestimable value, though often one-sided and in great part not yet utilized; without them a definitive history of the missions cannot be written.[3] The chief aim of this

[1] See PIEPER, in the *Röm. Quartalschr.*, I., 263 seqq.; SCHMIDLIN loc. cit., 8; KOLLMANN, *Acta*, I., 9 seq.

[2] See HUONDER, in the *Kath. Missionen*, 1922, 66.

[3] PIEPER was the first to write in detail on the Archives of Propaganda (comprising about 6,000-7,000 vols.) in the *Röm. Quartalschr.*, I. (1887), 80 seq., 258 seq.; after him came a number of research workers, chief of whom were: CAUCHIE (*Sources mss. à Rome*, Bruxelles, 1892, 10 seq.), SCHMOURLO (in *Roma e l'Oriente*, I., 101 seq.), I. KOLLMANN (in *Casopis musea Kral. Céskeho*, LXVI. (1892), 423 seqq., and *Mitteil. aus dem Landesarchiv des Königreichs Böhmen*, I. (1906), 51 seq.), FISH (*Guide to the mat. of American Hist.*, Washington, 1911, 111 seqq.), BROM (*Archivalia in Italië*, III. (1914), lx. seqq.), SCHMIDLIN (in *Zeitschr. für Missionswiss.*, XI. (1921), 142 seq.), and last of all, KOLLMANN, in an exhaustive work, never published, but of which I had a privately printed copy, i.e. *Tomus prodromus*

" Pontifical Ministry of Missions " was to give a uniform and truly religious character to the missions, to link and bind them as closely as possible to the Holy See and to free them from the bondage of the secular Powers and the colonizing States which threatened to strangle them.[1]

For all these reasons Propaganda was determined to take affairs into its own hands, itself to send out missionaries, to watch over them, to regulate their activities, and to divide up missionary territories. Consequently on February 20th and June 24th, 1623, it demanded from all Superiors of the religious Orders a list of all their subjects engaged in the work of spreading the faith and the place of their activity, to the end that, after due inquiries, they might receive their missionary credentials from the Congregation. On their part they were to report every year, under pain of ecclesiastical censure, on the state, the prospects, and the resources of their missions.[2] True, this decree was never completely carried into effect and the ideal was only realized after a long and bitter struggle with the Spanish and Portuguese Colonial authorities. But from the beginning it was envisaged by the Holy See and fought for with the utmost tenacity until final victory was secured.[3] In this way, at least in principle and in germ, and after infinite resistance also in actual practice, the Holy See was in a position to improve and spiritualize missionary methods, to extend and to give greater autonomy to the

of the *Acta S. Congreg. de Prop. res gestas Bohem. illustr.* The opening up of the Archives of Propaganda was due to Leo XIII.; owing to the vast amount of information that has appeared since, especially the publication of *Ius pontif.* and the *Collectanea*, the work of Mejer, based, in part, on wholly unreliable sources, has become quite out of date. Pieper speaks, *loc. cit.*, 84, of the losses suffered by the archives in their transit to Paris. In the confusion of those times some documents were taken to Vienna and embodied in the State Archives, 73 vols. in all, and covering the years 1566-1809; they have recently been returned to Propaganda.

[1] See HUONDER, *loc. cit.*, and KILGER, *loc. cit.*
[2] See *Ius Pontif.*, II., 10, n. 8, and *Collectanea*, I., 5, n. 6.
[3] See KILGER, *loc. cit.*, 20 *seq.*

missionary hierarchy, to increase the supply of labourers by calling on the resources of other nations as well as on the secular clergy and to increase the number and to improve the education of the native clergy and other auxiliaries.[1]

During the whole of this first period, Propaganda busied itself less with the missions to the pagans than with those to the Oriental Churches and the very difficult missions in Protestant countries where the cure of souls met with even greater obstacles than in the schismatic East.[2] In the first year of Propaganda, among the subjects discussed were the missions of the Jesuits and the Dominicans in Denmark and Norway; also Ireland, the English College in Lisbon, the Apostolic Vicariate of Holland, the Jesuit College at Douai, the Jesuits in Hamburg, the seminary of Sitten, and the assassination of the Capuchin Fidelis of Sigmaringen in Ratia, the ecclesiastical situation in Bohemia and the seminary of Prague, a report by the Bishop of Strasbourg, the Hungaro-Slavonic mission, a visitation of Hungary, a mission to the Ruthenians with a view to their reunion, the bishoprics and Bishops of Aquilea, Sofia, Scutari, Narona, Skopia, etc.; the cure of souls in Constantinople, an embassy to Aleppo, the Armenian mission, the Carmelite mission in Persia, letters and petitions from Persia, Syria and Palestine.[3] From the very first the Congregation, with the effective support of the Pope, directed its special attention to the Colleges and educational institutions in Rome and out of Rome. On April 15th, 1652, it constituted a special commission for the Colleges in Rome, that is, the German, English, Scots, Greek, Maronite and Armenian Colleges, with a view to examining whether they fulfilled the end for which they had been founded, and if this were not so, with the intention of intervening.[4] Another important step was the canonical visitation of all Roman and foreign Colleges which was decided upon at a meeting of

---

[1] See HUONDER, *loc. cit.*, 66 seq.
[2] *Cf. Zeitschr. für Missionswiss.*, XI. 143.
[3] See SCHMIDLIN, *loc. cit.*, 9, note 1.
[4] See *ibid.*, 13.

March 21st, 1623, by the express order of the Pope.[1] Propaganda also commanded the Generals of Orders to set up schools of languages and controversy for missionaries destined for the East, whilst at the same time it made provision in Rome for the teaching of Arabic and the printing of Arabic Bibles.[2] A Decree of Propaganda of September 12th, 1622, ordered the institution of seven schools of controversy in Rome to train missionaries for heretical countries.[3]

The particular interest of Propaganda in the East was well justified because there the missions were greatly hindered and injured by the hatred of both schismatics and heretics.[4] The reports which came in from the Bishops specially delegated to Hungary, Serbia, Bulgaria, Bosnia and Albania drew a very dark picture of religious conditions in those countries. Only in Albania were Catholics in the majority; everywhere else ground had been lost.[5] Nevertheless even in the most

---

[1] See KOLLMANN, *Acta*, I., 298 seq. *Cf.*, the *Visite dell'1622-4, I., Propaganda Archives, Rome, first used in that work. There we find the *Visitatio collegii Braunsberg. of August 16, 1623. The Greek College was given back to the Jesuits on October 31, 1622; see DE MEESTER, in *La Semaine de Rome*, 1909, 452.

[2] See SCHMIDLIN, 13. A *Brief to *Milethius, archiep. Alepi Syriae* of June 24, 1622, deals with *de fide in Oriente propaganda* in connexion with Propaganda. The Pope had sent him Arabic and Greek books. "Arabicae linguae gymnasia in hac orbis patria et nationum omnium domicilio constitui iussimus, ut theologos vestri idiomatis peritos quamprimum ablegare istuc possimus." He promises further help: " cupimus enim pontificatus nostri memoriam cath. fidei propagatione et divini cultus incremento in Oriente commendari." He is to continue courageously. *Arm.* XLV., 24.

[3] See *Ius pontif.*, II., 1, n. 2.; SCHMIDLIN, *loc. cit.*

[4] For the difficult position of the Franciscans in the Holy Land and the help given to them by Propaganda, see LEMMENS, *Acta s. congreg. de Prop. fide pro terra sancta*, I., II., Quaracchi, 1921-2.

[5] See *Visite*, I., 99 seqq. (Propaganda Archives, Rome): " Visitatio Constantinopolitana episc. Santorin." (Pietro de Marchis). *Report from Constantinople, November 12, 1622, especially concerning the activity of the Dominicans and

difficult circumstances the Latin missionaries of the Franciscan, Dominican, Capuchin, Carmelite and Jesuit Orders continued

Conventual Franciscans in Pera and Constantinople. *Report of November 26, 1622 : in Pera 9, in Constantinople two churches, four convents (*Predic. Min. conv., Min. oss., Giesuiti.*) " Quelle chiese sono tenute tutte pulite e honorate come a Roma stessa." The services are held regularly and with open doors, without any interference (therefore there was more freedom than in any Protestant countries), " et ben spesso alle prediche sono Greci heretici et anco Turchi, forse per curiosità, ma con gran silentio, e facendosi la cerca, danno essi ancora l'elemosina " ; in Pera about 580 souls. The Greek Patriarch rejects confession. " La plebe del rito greco è ignorante assai et li sacerdoti poco sanno et la gente vile odia la gente nostra latina et sol dire queste parole : più tosto Turco che Franco. Li Turchi naturali moralmente sono di buona natura et cortesi." The attacks came mostly from renegades. There follow the decrees of the Visitor. *Report of P. de Marchis, dated Smyrna, July 27, 1623 : In Gallipoli there are no Latins, except one Franciscan and there remains one Latin church. In Smyrna, sixty souls " of the Latin rite " ; the church recently rebuilt by the Venetians—*Report, dated Chios, August 9, 1623 ; Visitation. Necessity of a *Vicario generale* for Smyrna.—*Report from Chios, September 18, 1623 : detailed visitation in Chios where there are still twelve churches (fourteen formerly, two turned into mosques). In the district one hundred old, abandoned churches, 7,000 souls. The Visitor continued his activity under Urban VIII.—*Relatione della visità fatta da Pietro Masereccho, sacerdote Albanese, eletto visit. apost. della Ungeria, Bosna, Servia e Bulgaria l'a 1623 (*Visite, I., 66 *seq*., Archives of Propaganda). (1) *Bulgaria:* In Sophia two Catholic families, one chapel. Scattered Catholics everywhere. " Infinità de Bulgari scismatici, incapaci di conversione." (2) *Serbia:* Hostility of the numerous schismatics towards the Pope. " Come la Servia, Bulgaria e Grecia è piena di scismatici, così la maggior parte dell'Albania è piena di cattolici." An Albanian College in Rome is necessary. (3) *Hungary:* In Belgrade, which properly belongs to Serbia, 12,000 Catholics. Visitation of *Pannonia inferior* where there are Calvinists, Lutherans and Arians : similarly in Transilvania. It was necessary to send a Bishop to Sirmium. (4) *Bosna:* " De Turchi saranno tre parti et a pena de cattolici

to strengthen those in communion with Rome, to recall the schismatics and to win over the infidels.[1] In 1622 the Jesuits had obtained leave from Gregory XV. to found a College in Jerusalem but the plan could not be carried into effect owing to the opposition of the local Franciscans who were nearly all Italians.[2] On the other hand in 1623 the Jesuits were able to establish themselves in Constantinople whither they accompanied an imperial embassy. The Peace of Vienna in 1615 had already made it possible for Catholic priests to build churches and to carry out religious functions.[3] It was a source of deep sorrow for Gregory XV., who had used all his influence to bring about the reunion of the Ruthenians,[4] that the Greeks

una, scismatici saranno per la metà di cattolici. I cattolici di Bosna buoni et devoti." Seventeen convents but only one was visited. A *Frate* would be the most suitable Visitor.—*Report of the Bishop of Scutari to the Pope, 1623 (*Visite*, I., 93 *seq.*) : shows with what energy he tried to establish order.—The mission of the Minorite Andreas Bogoslavichus, Min. S. Francisci, for the support of the Catholics in Wallachia, Moldavia and Bulgaria is dealt with in the *Briefs to the Princes of Wallachia and Moldavia, May 15, 1623, *Arm.*, XLV., 21, Papal Secret Archives.

[1] See SCHMIDLIN, *Missionsgesch.*, 219.

[2] See LÜBECK, 50.

[3] *Cf.* C. DE MUN, in *Rev. d. quest. hist.*, 1903, 163 *seqq.* A decree of Propaganda of January 22, 1622, calls the ecclesiastical differences of the Latins in Constantinople and Pera to Rome ; see *Ius pontif.*, II., 9. A *Brief to the French ambassador in Constantinople, September 2, 1622, commends the local Christians to him. *Arm.*, XLV., 22, Papal Secret Archives.

[4] The Latin Bishops of Poland imagined that the Ruthenians would be more securely attached to the Church if their Rite were accepted (*cf.* the *Instruttione a Msg. Lancellotti, vesc. di Nola, destinato da N.S. nuntio in Francia*, used by RANKE, III., 122* *seq.*, but quoted without place or date ; it is to be found, dated December 14, 1622, in *Cod.* 471, p. 164 *seqq.* of the Corsini Library, Rome ; in *Cod. Barb.* 5564, of the Vatican Library, and *Inf. polit.* 10, of State Library, Berlin) ; they reported in this sense to Rome, where the proposal was seriously considered, but in the end it was decided to uphold the Union at the Diet against the attacks of the schismatics (see *Relacye*, II., 165 ;

of the Ottoman Empire, together with the Russians and the LIKOWSKI, 226 seq., 228). Gregory XV. implored King Sigismund III. in 1622 and 1623 to protect the Uniates, and he gave the same command to the Archbishop of Gnesen (see LIKOWSKI, 238). The nuncio Lancellotti was instructed to defend the Union at the Diet of 1623 (see *ibid.*, 274). Gregory XV. promised the King of the Poles, by a *Brief of August 7, 1621, money for the war against Turkey (THEINER, *Mon. Pol.*, III., 364), a promise which he kept, according to the Accounts (see ACCARISIUS, *Vita Gregori XV.*, lib. III., c. 10). In other ways also he endeavoured to protect Poland against the Turks ; see *Instruttione a Msgr. Torres arcivescovo di Adrianopoli, Nuntio destinato da N.S. in Polonia*, dated May 30, 1621, Cod. X., V., 15, p. 375 seq. of the Casanatense Library, Rome ; Cod. Barb., LIX., 186, Vatican Library; Cod. 6837, n. 3, of the State Library, Vienna, and Cod. V., 3, F. 96, of the Library at Salzburg. Correspondence about this nunciature in the Dragonetti Archives, at Aquila. *The Instruction for Cosmo de Torres who held the Polish nunciature until 1622 (see BIAUDET, 289), outlines a detailed programme for the development of the Catholic restoration in Poland. As, in this matter, a great deal—almost everything—depended upon the co-operation of the king, Torres is instructed to make good the misunderstanding that had arisen under Paul V. The king, on whose attachment to Rome the Pope counted, is above all to continue to exercise his right of nomination to numerous posts (about 26,000), strictly in favour of the Catholics, and to suppress Protestant worship in the royal towns (see RANKE, II., 259, who, neither here, nor in III., 121, quotes the source of the Instruction). In the second place, Gregory XV. counted upon the co-operation of the Bishops and the clergy in general : " Se tali fossero i pastori quali dovrebbero essere, chi non si prometterebbe in breve la conversione di tutti gli eretici ? . . . Contro l'heresia conviene principalmente opporre i buoni curati et buoni predicatori et gli incitatori diligenti della fanciullanza et gioventù." The Bishops should arrange for missions to be given and make use of the religious Orders, especially the Jesuits who had two provinces in Poland and were working most successfully : they should also introduce the " utilissimo esercitio della dottrina christiana che nelle parochie in Italia si fa ", and provide for catechisms, spiritual books, and Catholic hymns. In the third

people of the Balkans remained obstinate in their schism. In 1623 the Jesuits settled at Smyrna and in the Isle of Chios.[1] place, the reform of the religious Orders is insisted upon and the fourth explains the scope of the work of the nuncios: " V.S. anderà mantenendo con tutti i prelati una perpetua corrispondenza et cercherà d'havere in ciascuna città o diocesi o paese alcuna persona eccles.^{ca} amorevole che la faccia avvisata di quanto quivi accaderà di momento." At the Diets the nuncio must oppose all anti-Catholic efforts including those against *giurisdittione, immunità et beni* of the Church. Furthermore, he was to work for the preservation of ecclesiastical discipline, especially for the execution of the Tridentine decrees with regard to seminaries. For the ecclesiastical as well as the political effectiveness of the nuncio, whose position was nowhere so much appreciated as in Poland, everything depended on " che egli di tal carico si mostri degno, ma portì più la sua dignità nella persona che nell'uffitio, perchè tutti li pongono gli occhi adosso et prendono ancora esempio da santi costumi ". He is therefore, not to take part in the banquets customary in Poland, however useful these meetings might be for his purposes. The nuncio is to keep a watchful eye on the persons of his household, who must lead religious and moral lives, and accept no presents. From the Instruction for Lancellotti, it appears that Torres, in accordance with a wish of Propaganda, was to get the Bishops to send in reports about their dioceses: Lancellotti was instructed to admonish the Bishops who had not yet done so (see LÄMMER, *Zur Kirchengesch.*, 130). The Czartoryski Museum at Cracow preserves in *Cod.* 1211, a magnificent manuscript in which, on page 5, between the Arms of Gregory XV. and Poland, the following inscription is found:—

   Istud Breviarium manuscriptum
  fuit Urbani Papae Quarti qui sedit anno MCCLXI
   et a Cosmo de Torres Archiep. Adriã.
  ac Sm̃i in Christo Patris Gregorii Papae XV.
     Nuntio
  Sermõ Principi Sigismundo III. Polon.
  ac Sveciae Regi Potentissimo ad signi-
   ficandum singularem animi sui devo-
  tionem dono datum Varsaviae 26 Octobris 1621.

[1] See SCHMIDLIN, *Missionsgesch.*, 220. To the time of Gregory XV. belong the *monographs " *De unione Graecorum ad ecclesiam*

The Maronites of Lebanon distinguished themselves for their loyalty to the faith. Many Syrians were reconciled to the Church through the efforts of the Patriarch Simeon.[1] For the Armenians, who were under the care of the Dominicans of the archdiocese of Nakshevan, Gregory XV. founded a College in that city.[2] Besides the foundation of this seminary Propaganda, at a meeting of January 10th, 1623, at which the Pope was present, decided to send four Dominican missionaries under Santinellus to Armenia, to have the Catechism of Bellarmine and the Florentine Instruction translated, to summon to Rome the ignorant Archbishop and to exhort the schismatic Patriarchs to reunion.[3] Among the Chaldeans the Patriarch Simeon of Urmia was in communion with Rome, and Elias II. of Mosul had made his submission at the Synod of Diarbekr.[4] In Persia the Carmelites worked with such success from their centre in Ispahan that many were converted and numerous churches and congregations arose.[5]

A report to Propaganda by the Collector of Portugal, Albergati, in the spring of 1623, gives an account of the situation of the missions in the Portuguese colonies. If at this time, he relates, in countries formerly blessed with so many conversions, more backsliding than progress had to be registered, this was partly due to the fact that the Portuguese colonists ill-treated the natives, and partly to the bad conduct of many religious and their connivance at the vices of the Portuguese as well as to the circumstance that only Portuguese missionaries were admitted, who seemed chiefly concerned to acquire

Dei (the comments of a pilgrim to Jerusalem) and *De statu conversionis ad fidem Christi gentis Paulinorum in Graecia* (Bulgaria), in *Ottob.* 2536, p. 325 seqq., 330 seqq. (Vatican Library, cf. LÄMMER, 46. *Analecta*, 46.

[1] See SCHMIDLIN, *loc. cit.*

[2] *Brief to Math. Erasmus archiep. Nachevanensis of February 4, 1623, *Arm.*, XLV., 24, Papal Secret Archives. Jubilee for Armenia in *Bull.*, XII., 787 seqq.

[3] *Ius pontif.*, P. II., n. 6.

[4] See SCHMIDLIN, *Missionsgesch.*, 221.

[5] *Ibid.*, 222. Cf. *Bessarione*, V. (1898-9), 506, 508. See also the report in *Spicil. Vatic.*, I., 97 seq.

wealth for their relatives. Hence it was necessary that good religious of other nationalities should also be sent out. He had insisted on the removal of unsuitable subjects and procured the dispatch of eight Italian Jesuits. He asked Propaganda to send out only zealous and courageous messengers of the faith, not to promote religious to bishoprics, to warn superiors against commercial undertakings and to settle existing disputes. As for Africa, Albergati continues, he had proposed to the King the creation of two dioceses for the West and the East, better provision for the cure of souls in the Congo, and the erection of a College at Loanda ; he had also recommended the exploration of the Upper Nile in order to establish communications between the African missions of the West and the East, and asked that four missionary expeditions should be sent to Sierra Leone, Cape Verde, São Thomé and the Congo.[1]

These suggestions were well founded for on the one hand the Jesuit missions in the kingdom of the Congo, which dated from the sixteenth century, had come to an end, and on the other hand the Italian Capuchins [2] whom Gregory XV. had sent out, had not yet arrived, so that notwithstanding the uninterrupted succession of Bishops in the see of San Salvador, there was an almost complete lack of priests in the country, to the great sorrow of its pious ruler [3] ; Angola alone was still being served by the Jesuits.[4] The Jesuit missions on the coast of Upper Guinea had also come to an end with the exception of those of the islands of Cape Verde and Sierra Leone which were served from Santiago.[5]

In South Africa the Jesuits, according to their report to Propaganda, continued to evangelize the Kaffirs from their

[1] See Kilger, in the *Zeitschr. für Missionswiss.*, XII., 18 seq.

[2] See the *Brief to *Alvarus, rex Congi* of March 19, 1621, *Arm.*, XLV., 23, Papal Secret Archives.

[3] See the *Brief to *Alvarus, rex Congi*, of March 5, 1622, *Arm.*, XLV., 24, ibid.

[4] See Kilger, *loc. cit.*, 16. In 1622 the future queen Zinga of Matamba, had herself baptized at Loanda, under the name of Anne.

[5] See Kilger, *loc. cit.*

centres at Mozambique, Sena and Tete. They even planned to penetrate again into the country of Monomotapa and the adjacent territories where their missions, like those of the Dominicans, had fallen into decay.¹ Some years earlier a Jesuit mission, under Fr. Mariana, had set out for Madagascar but it failed owing to the overweening behaviour of the Portuguese with the consequence that the son of the King, who had had a Christian education at Goa, was left to his own resources. Fr. Mariana did what he could by visiting the island once a year from Mozambique.² In Ethiopia the Jesuits, though working under the greatest privations, were full of hope as a result of the conversion of the Emperor Socinius which was sealed, in 1621, with a public confession of faith. Many pagans of the neighbouring districts also accepted Christianity.³ As regards India, Albergati recommended that, with a view to greater freedom, missionaries should be sent via Aleppo. He also urged resumption of work among the fisher folk of the Indian coast which had been almost completely abandoned and the dispatch of reinforcements to China where prospects were most favourable. He begged for help for Japan where the missions were in great straits, and for reinforcement of the clergy of the Philippines.⁴ For the Franciscans in India, who at this time did but little for the conversion of the pagans, Gregory XV. had erected a special Province under the patronage of the Mother of God in addition to the existing Province of St. Thomas.⁵ The Vicar General, Rangel, in his memorandum to Propaganda, dated December 24th, 1623, requested the erection of a similar Province for the Dominicans of India.

---

¹ *Ibid. Cf. Zeitschr. für Missionswiss.*, VII., 101 *seq.* In 1624 the Jesuits mention eight stations with about twenty missionaries in the Zambesi district ; Father Mariana conceived a scheme for communications with Abyssinia by sea. According to the report of Fr. M. Rangel, the Emperor of Monomotapa begged for Dominican missionaries. See KILGER, *loc. cit.*, 17.

² *Cf.* SCHMIDLIN, *Zeitschr. für Missionswiss.*, XII., 197.

³ See KILGER, *loc. cit.*, 16.

⁴ *Ibid.*, 18 *seq.*

⁵ See MÜLLBAUER, 321 *seq.*

Their congregation of seven convents and fourteen vicariates had the care of 300 parishes, which it provided with priests. These instructed the children day by day and trained the adults to holiness of life by means of confraternities, but they were greatly hindered by the lack of labourers, by the slave trade, and by the hostility of the heretics, the Mohammedans and the pagans.[1] The Augustinians possessed in India eighteen convents and twenty-one parishes with 30,000 souls; in 1622 they erected a school for the sons of Brahmins in Mura.[2] The Carmelites also were able to complete their convent at Goa, in 1623, notwithstanding the opposition of the Portuguese, but their mission at Ormuz was destroyed in 1622.[3]

The Jesuits administered with great success eight parishes on the Island of Salsette near Bazaim; twenty parishes with 70,000 Christians on the peninsula of Salsette near Goa; ten in Ceylon and as many in Bengal, notwithstanding the hostility of the secular clergy; they also had another sixty parishes in Manar and Travancore.[4] In the kingdom of Coromandel many conversions had been obtained by means of their two Colleges; in Goa they were still baptizing great numbers and from there they had sent two Fathers into the kingdom of Idalkhan (Bejapur).[5] In the north of the kingdom of the Mogul six Jesuits were still at work under the protection of the Emperor, although for want of means they had been

---

[1] See KILGER, loc. cit., 17; also MÜLLBAUER, 333 seq.

[2] See MÜLLBAUER, loc. cit.

[3] See MÜLLBAUER, 345 seq. Cf. HENRION, Hist. gén. des miss. cath., II., 243.

[4] Cf. KILGER, loc. cit., 16. Along the coast, as the result of a dispute among the Paravese, a storm arose against the Jesuits; see MÜLLBAUER, 293 seq. The conversion of the peninsula of Salsette was completed in 1623; ibid., 277.

[5] The king allowed the Jesuits to settle there in 1622; see MÜLLBAUER, 278. On the East Coast there were colleges at Meliapur and Negapatam; ibid., 296. For the baptisms in Goa in 1618/19, according to the Litt. ann. of 1621, see KILGER, loc. cit., 16, note 3.

constrained to abandon two stations.[1] In the Province of Cochin they brought back to the unity of the Church 10,000 schismatic Christians of St. Thomas.[2] In Madura two Fathers devoted themselves to the difficult mission to the Brahmins but their prospects, so a report tells us, were dependent upon the Pope's willingness to tolerate the caste insignia which the former absolutely refused to renounce.[3] Gregory XV. complied with this request in his Bull of January 21st, 1623, in so far as, after having heard the Inquisition, he granted to the Brahmins and other neophytes, permission to wear the girdle and tuft of hair as a sign of nobility or of office, also the custom of anointing themselves with sandal oil and the practice of ablutions for purposes of cleanliness, but he commanded that strict precautions should be taken so as to eliminate any idolatrous act or intention from these practices. In this way the Pope gave his approval to the principle of accommodation which de Nobili had recently put in practice in Madura and which he had defended against all opposition in his detailed apology.[4]

As to the achievements and prospects of the missions of Further India and Hindustan, Propaganda had detailed information from Bishop Sylva of Malacca.[5] In that report Malacca appears as the starting point for the different religious

---

[1] The Great Mogul was constantly wavering between friendship and dislike of the Jesuits, but they received permission to settle at Patna in 1621 ; MÜLLBAUER, 280 seq.

[2] See MÜLLBAUER, 152 seq., 296 seq.

[3] See the reports of the Jesuits of Goa in KILGER, loc. cit., 16. The Litt. annuae of Nobili speak of barely a hundred Christians, as many had apostatized or had been murdered ; famine and caste quarrels were additional causes of loss ; for this reason Nobili pressed into the interior in 1623 and laid the foundations of the communities of Tiruchirapalli and Selam ; see DAHMEN, R. de Nobili (1925), 45 seq.

[4] See Ius pontif., I., 15 seqq., n. 8. Cf. MÜLLBAUER, 195 ; BERTRAND, La mission du Maduré, II., Paris, 1848, 195 seqq., 401 seq. ; DAHMEN, 45 seq.

[5] See KILGER, loc. cit., 16 seq.

Orders which sought, in the first instance, to establish themselves in Pegu (Burma). On several occasions Dominicans and Jesuits had penetrated into Siam and Cambogia; since 1615 the Jesuits had thrice entered Cochin China under Fr. Buzoni; six in number they worked in two residences thus paving the way for the more famous Alexander Rhodes.[1] Similar missionary attempts were undertaken by the Franciscans on the large islands of Celebes, Java and Sumatra.[2] Ten Jesuits worked in the Moluccas, their base being at Malacca,[3] and as many Dominicans came from Solor. In the latter place there were so many demands for baptism that a hundred missionaries would scarcely have been sufficient according to a statement of the Superior of the Dominicans, Rangel, in his memorandum of December 24th, 1623. In the Island of Rotti, where Luis d'Andrade had made many conversions since 1618, two Fathers now served the two churches.[4]

About the year 1622, in the Philippines, besides numerous Augustinians, Franciscans and Dominicans, some 118 Jesuits were working for the conversion of the inhabitants who were still pagans and for the moral formation of the converts. A hierarchy was established in 1621.[5]

In China where Ricci, as a consequence of his conciliatory methods, had opened fair prospects for the gospel, there were working, according to a report from Goa of the year 1622, a score of Jesuits scattered over six towns. They had made many converts even among the Mandarins.[6] The Portuguese

---

[1] *Cf.* SCHMIDLIN, *Missionsgesch.*, 251 seq.; PACHTLER, *Das Christentum in Tonkin und Cochinchina*, 27 seq.; KILGER, *loc. cit.* 16.

[2] In 1622 the martyrdom of Fr. Palominus took place in Manados, where a king had been baptized and churches built; see SCHMIDLIN, *Missionsgesch.*, 255. *Cf.* also KILGER, *loc. cit.*

[3] See KILGER, *loc. cit.*

[4] See BIERMANN, in the *Zeitschr. für Missionswiss.*, XIV., 30 seq., 38.

[5] See *Die katholischen Missionen*, 1880, 207; Astráin, V., 670, 572, 674.

[6] See KILGER, *loc. cit.* According to THOMAS (*Hist. de la mission de Pékin*, I. (1923), 401) there were, according to the catalogues

Jesuit Antonio d'Andrade was preparing to start from Agra on an expedition into Tibet, which led to the foundation of the mission of Tsaperang, in 1624.[1]

In Japan, notwithstanding the persecutions, Franciscans, Dominicans, Augustinians and Jesuits had remained at their posts in order secretly to comfort and strengthen the hard-pressed Christians.[2] The persecution reached its height in 1622. Over 120 Christians, among them sixteen priests and twenty lay-brothers of the four different Orders sealed their faith with their blood. On September 10th, 1622, on the "Holy Mountain" near Nagasaki, the so-called "Great Martyrdom" took place in which ten Dominicans, nine Jesuits, three Franciscans and thirty-two laymen suffered death for Christ amidst appalling tortures. The description of them recalls the ancient Acts of the Martyrs. Again in the following year, 1623, the blood of martyrs was shed in great abundance.[3]

In recognition of the work accomplished by the Jesuits in Japan, China and all India, Gregory XV., in a Bull of November 5th, decreed that their houses and colleges should be exempt from payment of tithes and semi-tithes, which in accordance with the Brief of Paul V. of the year 1613, they had to pay in the countries subject to the Portuguese crown.[4]

In America, at the time of the foundation of Propaganda, the work of evangelization was for the most part finished; however, there were in the Spanish South many zealous apostles from various Orders as, for instance, the Franciscan Luis de Bolanos who converted 20,000 Indians and founded several

of 1621, at first thirteen and in 1626 only eighteen Jesuits working in China, see KILGER, *loc. cit.*, 17.

[1] See SCHMIDLIN, *Missionsgesch.*, 275; WESSELS, *Early Jesuit Travellers in Central Asia* (1924), 43 seq.

[2] *Cf.* KILGER, *loc. cit.*, 16.

[3] *Cf.* DELPLACE, II., 153 seq., 167 seqq.; PAGÈS, 337 seqq.; Freib. *Kirchenlexikon*, VI.², 1250 seq.; *Anal. Boll.*, VI. (1887), 52-72 (Carlo Spinola); FERRANDO-FONSECA, I., 649 seq.; PEREZ, in *Arch. Ibero-Americ.*, XXI., 5; *Rev. d'hist. eccles.*, XX., 101.

[4] *Ius pontif.*, I., 8 seqq.

Reductions [1]; the Jesuit Peter Claver who from Carthagena as his centre, gained about 300,000 negroes for Christianity by his sermons, catechisms, and by tending the sick.[2] In Uraba the Augustinian Alphonsus of the Cross obtained many conversions.[3] Very promising also was the harvest which, through the care of the Jesuits, was maturing in the Reductions of Paraguay, notwithstanding the incursions of the slave-traders.[4] According to Miraeus there were then 116 Jesuits in Paraguay, 70 in Peru, 300 in New Granada, all of them exercising a most beneficial activity by means of schools and colleges, and after 1621 through their University at Quito.[5] Jesuits were also found at work in Mexico by the side of Franciscans, Dominicans and Augustinians.[6] The sons of St. Francis multiplied their foundations in the neighbouring territories also, especially in New Mexico from 1598, and in Florida from 1621 converting hosts of savages to the Christian religion and to civilization.[7] In Portuguese Brazil 180 Jesuits saw not only to the spiritual needs of the white population in the towns but to those also of the numerous Indian neophytes. They had also baptized 100,000 negroes in the sugar factories, and had penetrated into the newly-discovered Province of Maranhoa.[8] The larger isles of the Antilles were already Christian and Spanish Trinidad was occupied by Franciscan missions, and

[1] See SCHMIDLIN, 311.

[2] See ASTRÁIN, V., 479 seqq.

[3] See SCHMIDLIN, 304.

[4] See ASTRÁIN, V., 595 seq., 542 seq.; SCHMIDLIN, 310.

[5] See MIRAEUS, *Politiae ecclesiast.*, Lugd., 1629, 280 seq., 340 seq. Miraeus reckons there were in the Spanish missionary field, 1,026 members in fifty-one houses; see KILGER, *loc. cit.*, 16, note 6. Cf. also L. PAZ, *La Universidad Mayor de S. Francisco Xavier de la Capital de los Charcas*, Sucre, 1914, in which, p. 87 seq. is quoted the Brief of Gregory XV. on the foundation of the University of La Plata at the Jesuit College.

[6] For the more recent Jesuit missions of Cinalos, Rio Mayo, Hiaquis, Tepahuanes, Taraumaras, and Sonora see ASTRÁIN. V., 326 seqq.

[7] Cf. SCHMIDLIN, *Missionsgesch.*, 347, 351.

[8] *Ibid.*, 329. Cf. KILGER, *loc. cit.*, 16.

not long after the sun of Christianity was to rise also in the French islands, 1625.[1]

In North America the French Recollects of the Paris Province had been in Canada since 1614; those from the Province of Aquitaine had been in Nova Scotia since 1619, and they were constantly being reinforced by fresh arrivals. Unfortunately the colonists often defeated their efforts among the pagans.[2] That side by side with these achievements and glorious triumphs there were many dark shadows in the picture of the missions as it presented itself to Propaganda from its creation, is shown, especially as regards the Indies—more particularly the West Indies—by a memorial presented to that Congregation by Gregory of Bolivar, a Franciscan Observant, who, about 1621, had personally evangelized the Chuncos, the Motilones, and the Chiriguanes of Peru.[3] The document complains that though there were six archbishoprics and forty bishoprics, far too little had been done for the conversion of the pagans, firstly, on account of the lack of priests fully qualified for work in the Indian mission, seeing that students coming from the seminaries were exclusively trained for work in the Christian parishes and even many religious competed for those benefices; secondly, owing to the greed of the Bishops who exacted a quarter of the income of the clergy; thirdly, because of the prevalence of the vice of gambling which ruined the priestly spirit; fourthly, because of the trade in Indian slaves and in liquor which was practised both by the secular and the regular clergy—with the exception of the Jesuits—the result of which was that the natives were taught the vice of drunkenness and many other evil habits; fifthly, because most of the parochial posts were filled with religious instead of secular priests.[4] Accordingly the secretary of Propaganda, Ingoli, in his enumeration of the abuses in the missions of the Indies, notes that the chief cause of them was on the one hand the greed of many missionaries and on the

---

[1] See SCHMIDLIN, 295 seq.
[2] Ibid., 353 seq.
[3] See MARCELLINO DA CIVEZZA, VII., 2, 73 seq.
[4] See KILGER, loc. cit., 19 seq.

other their endless quarrels among themselves, with the hierarchy and with the civil authorities, which gave occasion to persecutions and scandals which account for the utter barrenness of missionary effort. To remedy these evils he recommends in addition to the prohibition of trading and of a previous examination of all missionaries, the dispatch of nuncios or delegates, the multiplication of dioceses and the appointment of secular priests as Bishops, the formation of a native clergy instead of the practice hitherto followed of barring the ecclesiastical career to the Indians.[1]

In these proposals we already perceive the lofty ideal of which the newly created Congregation never lost sight and which it realized, though after many a bitter struggle, namely the self-sufficiency of the missions by means of a native clergy. The aim of the missions was not to Europeanize other continents but to christianize them, whilst preserving as far as possible their cultural characteristics and their racial autonomy.[2]

(2.)

Among the missions to which Propaganda and the Pope devoted their attention, those in the North of Europe occupied the first place. As soon as the opportunity offered itself, the nuncio of Brussels, Giovan Francesco Guido del Bagno, sent two Dominicans, Jacob de Brower and Nicholas Jansenius, on a reconnoitring journey through North-Germany and Denmark. Even before the arrival of their report,[3] Propaganda on April 11th, 1622, as a result of an appeal by Cardinal Eitel von Hohenzollern, decided to send eight Jesuits to Denmark and Norway.[4] The Pope recommended these missionaries to

[1] *Ibid.*, 21 seq.

[2] *Ibid.*, 23, and HUONDER, *Der einheimische Klerus in den Heidenländern*, Freiburg, 1909.

[3] See MÜNTER, *Magazin für Kirchengesch. des Nordens*, II., 4, 31 seq.; PIEPER, *Nordische Missionen*, 2 seq.; DE WEDEL-JARLSBERG, *Une page d'histoire des Frères-Prêcheurs. La province Dacia*, Rome, 1897, 243 seqq.

[4] See PIEPER, *loc. cit.*, 9.

the protection of the King of Spain in a Brief of June 4th, 1622.¹ In November, 1622, the efforts of the nuncio of Cologne to obtain for the Catholics of Hamburg the free exercise of their religion were successful, but already in the summer of 1623 this liberty was frustrated by a brutal act of violence.² The mission of the Jesuits to Denmark, though begun under excellent auspices, also came to a sad end.³ A royal decree of February 28th, 1624, forbade all Catholic priests and religious to reside in the country under pain of death.⁴ A similar fate befell the mission in Sweden where there were still many Catholics, among them the secretary of Gustavus Adolphus, George Ursinus, and the Burgomaster Zacharias Anthelius. The Jesuit Henry Schacht, whom Propaganda dispatched to Sweden in 1623, got in touch with these when, after many difficulties and disguised as a hawker of mousetraps, he succeeded in reaching that country. At Gripsholm he called on George Ursinus and Anthelius engaged him as his servant. However the authorities discovered everything and all three were condemned to death.⁵

Holland, England, Scotland and Ireland were under the authority of the nuncio of Brussels. The Pope's representative and the Pope himself were obliged to give special attention to these countries since the position of the still numerous adherents of the ancient faith had become much worse.⁶

¹ *Gregory XV. recommends the missionaries who have been sent to " Norwegium, Daniam et finitima septentrionis regna. Eos illuc ducturus est Nicolaus Hermannus Danus." The Pope emphasizes : " Nos intelligentes nullam esse adeo a nobis dissitam in Oceano regionem, quam pontificiae caritatis bracchia complecti non debeant." *Arm.*, XLV., 24, Papal Secret Archives.

² See PIEPER, 9–10 ; DUHR, II., 1, 137 ; METZLER, *Apost. Vikariate des Nordens* (1919), 12.   ³ See PIEPER, 10–11.

⁴ H. FR. RORDAM, *Danske Kirkelove*, III., Kobenhavn, 1889, 104 seq. ; METZLER, *loc. cit.*, 14 seq.

⁵ See PIEPER, 12–15 ; METZLER, 14.

⁶ In Denmark, which was also assigned to the Brussels nuncio, foreigners were the only adherents of the ancient faith ever since the confiscation of property of those suspected of Catholicism, a measure enforced in 1613.

In view of the circumstance that the armistice between Spain and Holland was to terminate on April 9th, 1621, the nuncios in Brussels and Madrid were informed that, contrary to all expectation, the oppression of the Dutch Catholics had markedly increased during the period of the armistice. Cardinal Ludovisi recalled the fact that the towns of Utrecht, Amsterdam, Haarlem, Leyden and others, on adopting the Dutch side, had been guaranteed the preservation of the Catholic religion but that this promise had not been kept any more than the guarantees given in his time by Henry IV. For this reason the renewal of the armistice was not regarded with favour in Rome and the nuncios of Brussels and Madrid were instructed to press for the renewal of hostilities; the opportunity was favourable, for the Dutch were weakened by internal dissensions; they could expect no help from Protestant Germany, neither would the English Government give them much support, nor, indeed, the French, for their King was probably about to attack the Huguenots. If, however, negotiations for an armistice or a treaty of peace actually took place, the nuncio was not to countenance them; in any case he should seize the opportunity and do all he could for the betterment of the lot of the Dutch Catholics. The nuncio of Paris received similar instructions. Whatever happened, the Brussels nuncio, Giovan Francesco Guido del Bagno, was commissioned to watch over the spiritual needs of the Dutch Catholics, especially those in Utrecht, Amsterdam, Haarlem, Leyden, and Gouda, where they were still very numerous and held faithfully to their religion. He was to support the Vicar Apostolic, Francis Rovenius, whom Paul V. had appointed Archbishop of Philippi, and the secular clergy under his jurisdiction; he was to counteract the excessive severity of Rovenius, and above all to restore peace between the Dutch secular clergy and the Jesuit missionaries. In this task Gregory XV. concurred with all his energy.[1]

[1] See CAUCHIE-MAERE, 114 seq. Cf. KNUTTEL, 71 seqq.; Archief. v. h. Aartsb., Utrecht, XXXII., 390 seqq.; Bull. de l'Institut Belge à Rome, I. (1919), 139. For statistics of the Dutch Catholics and the ministration to them, RANKE quotes (Päpste,

In England too, the old internal disputes among Catholics were by no means ended at the time of Gregory XV.'s election. The Benedictine Thomas Green, and more particularly his brother in religion, Thomas Preston, who had defended his opinions in writing during the pontificate of Paul V., still maintained the lawfulness of the oath of allegiance. Preston wrote a submissive letter to Gregory XV. but continued to defend his personal opinion.[1] The great desire of many English priests to have a Bishop amongst them continued under Gregory XV. As late as 1619, the Brussels nuncio was instructed from Rome not to listen to such requests, which for very good reasons had so far always met with a refusal.[2] When the persecution of Catholics had to be suspended owing to the negotiations for the Spanish marriage, all the old hopes revived. The office of the Archpriest, who had hitherto been the leader of the Catholics, happened to be vacant, for Blackwell had died in 1607 and both his successors, Birkhead and Harrison, had also died in 1614 and 1621; but shortly before his death Harrison had sent the priest Bennett to the Eternal City, on the pretext of forwarding the Spanish marriage, but actually to obtain a Bishop from the Pope—an aim which had never been attained, notwithstanding the support of the nuncios Barberini at Paris and Bentivoglio at Brussels. Even now views were divided on this point in Rome. Cardinal Bandini supported the efforts of Bennett and his companion

---

II.[6], 313) a *Compendium status in quo nunc est religio catholica in Hollandia et confoederatis provinciis* of December 2, 1622, without stating where this MS. is to be found. More authentic than this anonymous document is ROVENIUS' " *Descriptio status in quo est religio catholica in confoed. Belgii provinciis* ", addressed at the beginning of 1622 to the Brussels nuncio (see *Archief. v. h. Aartsb.* Utrecht, XIV., 180), preserved in *Barb.* 2431, 3047, Vatican Library. For the Dutch mission see also BROM, *ibid.*, XXXI., 321 seqq.

[1] CAUCHIE-MAERE, 171 seqq. Preston wrote under the name of Roger Widdrington, therefore, not altogether under a *nom de plume*. Cf. TAUNTON, in the *Engl. Hist. Review*, XVIII. (1903), 119.

[2] CAUCHIE-MAERE, 93; cf. 50, 69.

Farrar; he insisted that, by the will of Christ, every Church ought to have its own Bishop at its head. The vexatious quarrels among the English missionaries, the conspiracies against the State, would probably have been avoided had there been a shepherd at the head with full powers. If the Pope maintained his opposition, it was to be feared that the Gallican Bishops of France would, on their own authority, try to give a chief shepherd to the English Catholics: the Archbishop of Rouen had already shown signs of taking such a step. On the other side, Cardinal Mellini maintained that a Bishop was not absolutely necessary for the maintenance of a particular Church; that the presence of one in England would give rise to a fresh persecution of Catholics, and that the association of England with France might expose the English Bishops to the contagion of Gallicanism. Bennett found support from the French and Spanish ambassadors, and Gregory XV. seemed inclined to give ear to his requests. However the convert, John Matthews, a son of the Archbishop of York and a former member of Parliament, reported these negotiations to the Royal Council, and James I. informed the Pope, through the Spanish ambassador, that he would never tolerate a Catholic Bishop in his realm. None the less, Gregory XV. did nominate a Bishop—not four, as he had at first intended—his choice falling on William Bishop who perhaps commended himself in the eyes of the government in that in 1602, he and twelve other priests had signed the oath of allegiance to Elizabeth.[1] In Rome this was indeed no recommendation. Furthermore, in view of the fact that he had studied at the Sorbonne, Bishop was suspected of Gallicanism, so that his appointment was to be revocable at any time.[2] Moreover, so as not to stir up Protestant feeling, he was not given an English see, but was to have the title of Bishop of Chalcedon. The French nuncio, Ottavio Corsini, whose duty it was to watch over the interests of the Church in England

[1] BELLESHEIM, *Scotland*, III., 434 [Engl. Transl.]. *Cf.* our notes, Vol. XXIV., 36.

[2] By Propaganda March 23, 1623; his episcopal consecration at Paris, June 4, 1623 (BELLESHEIM, *Scotland*, III., 434 *seq.*).

and Scotland,[1] at the request of the new Bishop, drew up a set of instructions for his future guidance.[2] In the first place stress was laid on the maintenance of unity which was a more vital issue for English Catholics than any others. Corsini likewise enjoined obedience to the sovereign and the civil authority—respect for the king together with a higher standard of piety and conduct should be the distinguishing marks between Catholics and heretics. Should he fall into the hands of the pursuivants, let him stand firm for the faith, but let him observe moderation and modesty before his judges, so as not to give them a pretext with which to cover their barbarity; meekness should be one of the distinguishing marks of a Catholic. As to the direction of the priests under him, Bishop should use all diligence to prevent opposition between the secular and regular clergy, hence he should be conciliating towards the regulars, especially the Jesuits; on the other hand he must not forego any of his prerogatives.

Just then the Church in England was threatened by external enemies rather than by internal dissensions. During Gregory XV.'s reign hatred of Catholicism reached its climax. Events such as Babington's conspiracy and the Gunpowder Plot were most adroitly exploited by the Government, and gave rise throughout the country to a disposition to regard every Catholic as a dark conspirator and a born criminal, and every Protestant and opponent of Catholicism as a blameless champion of virtue.[3] Quite recently Frederick, the Elector

---

[1] *Ibid.*, 148; LEMAN, 45 *seq.*, note.

[2] Of July 15, 1623 (BELLESHEIM, III., 435 *seqq.*).

[3] According to GARDINER, not even the nation's representatives in Parliament seemed capable of a more impartial judgment. "Black and white were the only colours on their canvas. To them every Protestant was a model of saintly virtue; every Catholic a dark conspirator against the peace and religion of the world. . . . As they could see nothing but light on one side, they could see nothing but darkness on the other." The King of Spain was in their eyes: "the aspirant by force and fraud to universal empire for his own bad purposes, the restless, ambitious, insatiable vicegerent of Satan upon earth."

Palatine, had been acclaimed with enthusiasm by Protestant England as a champion in the fight against Rome, and the Bohemian insurrection had been hailed with enthusiasm as the first step to the downfall of " Babylon ". But the utter frustration of these hopes by the battle of the White Mountain caused the hatred of Catholicism to blaze up afresh, for a new danger to Protestantism seemed to be looming on the horizon. Of all the Catholic kingdoms Spain was considered as the home of darkness, its King the very Vicar of Satan on earth, and now there was question of the marriage of the Prince of Wales which would bring a Spanish lady to the royal throne of England, and with her the old religion would once more return to the country.

Nevertheless the King stuck to his plan of winning the Spanish Infanta for his son and her ducats for his own empty purse. With Rome he went on playing all his wonted tricks. Three days after the opening of Parliament, James I. had an interview with the Spanish ambassador, Sarmiento, lately made Count Gondomar. The King pointed out to him that at his reception at Westminster the whole service had been sung in the Latin tongue, i.e. according to Catholic usage. Gondomar replied he hoped to see the King returning altogether to the old Church. James answered that if the matter could be discussed dispassionately a compromise could surely be arranged. As far as he himself was concerned, he would be ready to acknowledge the Pope as the spiritual Head of the Church, and to allow the English Bishops the right of appeal to him, provided the Pope did not interfere with the temporal government and ceased to claim the right to depose temporal rulers at will. If in his writings he had called the Pope " Antichrist " it was on account of the power over princes which he had arrogated to himself, not because the Pope claimed to be the Head of the Church. Gondomar knew the value of such assurances. He asked the King to shake hands to prove that he was serious. James shook hands and requested, for obvious reasons, that the ambassador would report this conversation to Madrid. Gondomar fulfilled this commission, but his account shows no sign of his placing any reliance on the royal handshake. " At one time, whilst still a novice in his profession, he might have attached some importance to the conversation," Gondomar wrote, " but at present he would only say that nothing was impossible with God ! "[1]

In his speech at the opening of Parliament James could not refrain from alluding to the Spanish marriage. Fears had been raised, he said, that such a marriage would lead to a policy of toleration towards the Catholics ; but he would do nothing that might be detrimental to religion or dishonourable to the nation.[2] The King secured nothing by these generalities. As far as hatred for the Spaniards and Catholics was concerned, Parliament continued to hold the views of the common people. In the very first debate, Perrot asked that the House should receive the Lord's Supper in a body, so as to make quite sure that no Catholic had clandestinely sneaked into its ranks. The suggestion met with approval and provided an opportunity for a spate of virulently anti-Catholic speeches. It was asserted that the Catholics had lighted bonfires at the news of the defeat of the Palatine Frederick ; that they were assembling in great numbers in London and were perhaps at this moment planning another Gunpowder Plot.[3] It was imperative to take sterner measures against the recusants.[4] To this James I. would, however, not consent. He replied [5] that there were laws enough and it was against his character to be too severe in matters of conscience. He was constantly receiving requests to plead with foreign princes on behalf of the persecuted Protestants in their lands. How could he do that if he persecuted the Catholics in his own land ? Parliament was dissatisfied with his reply, and it was said that if Supplies had not already been voted, they would not have been granted.[6]

Public opinion had not, so far, greatly busied itself with James' quarrels with his Parliament, hence it had scarcely

[1] GARDINER, IV., 25 *seq.*
[2] *Ibid.*, 25.
[3] *Ibid.*, 28.
[4] *Ibid.*, 30.
[5] On February 17, 1621, *ibid.*, 34.
[6] *Ibid.*

ever been necessary to inflict any penalties for the offence of political criticism. However, everything was suddenly changed when the king's son-in-law saw himself compelled to fight for his throne and his realm, as it was thought, on account of the Spaniards. In this way the populace's hatred for the southern rival found fresh fuel; but the King was of opinion that he must take Spain under his patronage on account of his prospective daughter-in-law.[1] A certain London preacher, Everard by name, was committed to prison for having expatiated on the cruelty of the Spaniards in the Indies. Ward, a colleague of his at Ipswich, not only suffered the same fate but was forbidden to enter the pulpit in future for having created a sensation by means of a drawing which represented in the centre the Pope and the Cardinals in council with the king of Spain and the devil, whilst on either side were to be seen the wreck of the Armada and the discovery of the Gunpowder Plot.[2] As the Spanish ambassador was being carried down Fenchurch Street in his litter, a young apprentice called out: "Here comes the devil in a dung-cart." When one of the ambassador's servants threatened the rabble, he was laid out in the gutter by a blow of the fist. King James, in defiance of the people, insisted on the offenders being flogged; one of the youths died under the whip.[3] The rising discontent led to a fresh conflict between the monarch and his Parliament. Rumour had it that an aged Catholic lawyer, Floyd by name, who was lying in the Fleet, in his joy at the defeat of the White Mountain, had made some caustic remarks about Frederick the Elector Palatine and his consort, asserting that the Elector had no more right to the Bohemian Crown than he himself. This terrible crime, which was wholly uncorroborated and which Floyd denied, came up for discussion in Parliament, where it occasioned a scene such as can hardly be conceived. One member outdid the other in suggesting punishments for the old man who had not been convicted of any crime. Phelps demanded that Floyd should be made to ride through London with his face towards

[1] *Ibid.*, 117.
[2] *Ibid.*, 118.
[3] *Ibid.*

the horse's tail and with the inscription on his hat : " A wretched papist who has insulted His Majesty's children " ; after that he should be thrown into the horrible dungeon of Little Ease and treated as harshly as was possible without endangering his life. The remark of Roe and Digges that the matter was not one for Parliament at all, but for the Lords of the Privy Council, only added fuel to the storm. " If there is no precedent, " cried George More, " we will create one. Let Floyd be flogged all the way back to whence he came and then handed over to the Lords of the Council." " Have his rosary hung round his neck," shouted Francis Seymour, " and deal him as many blows as there are beads on it." " Let him stand in the stocks at Westminster and be whipped," suggested Edward Giles. " The stocks twice and whipping twice," clamoured Francis Darcy. Others demanded that his tongue be pierced with red-hot irons ; that his tongue or his ears and nose be cut off ; that he be branded on the forehead, or that he be compelled to swallow his rosary, etc. At last Sandys somewhat calmed the fury of the storm with the remark that by such penalties they would make a martyr of the man ; moreover, it was not right to whip a gentleman. In the end the House contented itself with sentencing Floyd to three periods in the stocks ; to ride through the streets, his face to the horse's tail and with an inscription on his hat ; and to pay a fine of 1,000 pounds. On the following day the King sent a message of thanks to Parliament for defending his honour, but he demanded a reply to two questions, viz. How was it that the house adjudicated upon offences that had not been committed against Parliament itself ? and how could judgment be passed without sworn witnesses ? Coke, who had acted for the prosecution at Garnet's trial, was not at a loss to prove the competence of Parliament in the matter. A daughter, he said, was part of her father, hence an insult to the Countess Palatine was an insult to the King ; now the King belonged to Parliament, hence whosoever offended the Countess, offended Parliament.[1] However, the House felt unable to identify itself with the famous and learned judge's reasoning. After much discussion

[1] GARDINER, IV., 123.

in this sense and in that, it was resolved to defer the matter to the Upper House. There Floyd's fine was raised from 1,000 to 5,000 pounds; he also saw himself deprived of his civic rights and condemned to be whipped all the way from London Bridge to Westminster and to imprisonment for life. The wretched man was spared the whipping at the intercession of the Prince of Wales.

At the final sitting of Parliament, on June 4th, 1621, the most burning question of the day came up again, namely, the restoration of the Elector Palatine. Perrot insisted that the true faith must be upheld; abroad it was in a parlous plight and in danger even at home. Let them declare, before the prorogation of Parliament, that, on reassembling, they would be prepared to sacrifice possessions and life itself for the cause of God and the King's children. The suggestion was hailed with enthusiasm and much waving of hats, and a resolution to that effect was drafted. James I. gave orders for its translation into the chief European tongues, although the reference to the danger to religion in England plainly referred to the King's Spanish policy.[1]

Parliament reassembled on November 20th, 1621. In the debate on the King's financial requests, the House gave unmistakable expression to its aversion for Spain and everything Catholic. Phelps, on November 21st, informed his colleagues that England's enemies were the Catholic States, and her natural allies the Protestant countries of Europe. It had been said that the King of Spain was a friend, but everyone was aware that he presided at the council of war which decided upon the occupation of the Palatinate, and that the attacking forces were paid with his money. He felt that God was angered because the Elector had been allowed to lose the Bohemian Crown. Trade was bad at home, and the hearts of the Papists beat for the Spanish King. They had waxed so bold that they spoke of the Protestants as a mere "party", and openly discoursed on matters of religion. The House of Commons must protect England from such dangers.[2]

[1] *Ibid.*, 128-31.
[2] *Ibid.*, 236 *seq.*

Next day it was Coke's turn to pour out the over-flowing vials of his wrath on the Catholics and the Jesuits. He declared that under Elizabeth the Pope had dispensed her subjects from their oath of allegiance, whereupon the Jesuits had instigated one conspiracy after another against the Queen, and had attempted to poison or murder her in some other way. Every evil came from Spain. From Spain came the Armada; from Spain came the sheep scab which had caused such extensive damage; from Spanish Naples came the worst form of plague that had ever visited Europe; Catholics flocked to the house of the Spanish ambassador, and England would be in danger so long as she nurtured Papists at her breast.[1]

These speeches produced their effect. The committee whose business it was to discuss in detail the monetary grants for the King, was instructed to draft a petition for the execution of the laws against the Catholics. At the committee meeting a speech by John Pym prepared the way for the petition; Pym declared that there were errors which led to a false worship of God and others whose consequences were disastrous for the life of the State; it was the duty of the authorities to suppress not only the fruits of rebellion, but the seeds thereof. The same rule of faith from which Papists derived the superstitious elements of their religion, imposed on them opinions which involved grave perils for non-Catholic princes and nations. Hence the laws against Catholics were not designed to punish their beliefs and opinions, they were only concerned with their actions. Once Catholics obtained indulgence, they pressed for toleration, then for equality, then for privileges, and finally for the suppression of all other religions. Hence it was necessary to introduce an oath of loyalty with a view to the safety of the King's Majesty and the execution of the laws which aimed at consolidating true religion. This oath must be taken by all loyal subjects; the King should likewise publish a special decree for the suppression of the recusants.[2]

A petition to James I., on the lines advocated by Pym, was

---

[1] *Ibid.*, 241 *seq.*

[2] GARDINER, IV., 242 *seq.*; Gardiner's justification of the speech, *ibid.*, 243-6.

drawn up and accepted by Parliament. It states that the aim of the King of Spain was universal temporal power, and that of the Pope, universal spiritual power. Papistry was built upon diabolical principles and teachings. There followed a description of the position of the Protestants abroad where their united Papist enemies were supported by the armies of the Spanish King. At home the project of the Spanish marriage and the privileges enjoyed by the Spanish ambassador had emboldened the Catholics; they went openly to the Embassy chapels, they flocked in vast numbers to the capital, they sent their children to Papist seminaries on the Continent. Their property, though forfeit to the State, was being restored to them; their books circulated unhindered; their priests were everywhere. If nothing was done against them they would not rest until, with the help of foreign princes, the downfall of the true religion had been attained. Therefore let His Majesty take his sword and rally the Protestant nations to his person against Spain. A commission should attend to the execution of the laws against Catholics; the heir to the throne should marry a princess of his own faith; Catholic children must be educated by Protestant schoolmasters; and attendance at seminaries overseas and the restoration of forfeit property must be strictly forbidden.

Unfortunately for the petitioners, the Spanish ambassador, who knew how to handle James I., heard of the proposed petition and immediately wrote to him a letter such as a ruler of Great Britain can have received but rarely from a foreign ambassador. Gondomar explained that he would have left the country at once had he not been convinced that the King would condemn the impertinence of the House. He then pointed out that such behaviour on the part of Parliament might constitute a *casus belli* and that the time had come for the King to show who was master in the realm.[1]

Thus Parliament's declaration of war against Spain was countered by Spanish pride and repaid in its own coin. Thereupon, in his message to Parliament, the Solomon of the North gave the House a little homily on the limited intelligence of

[1] *Ibid.*, 249.

subjects. Some hotheads, he informed the assembly, had ventured to discuss and criticize matters which were far beyond the limited scope of their understanding, and had thereby impinged upon his royal honour. The House was therefore informed that it was no business of its members to meddle with matters of Government or to concern themselves with the mysteries of statecraft. The Spanish marriage was not to be discussed, nor was a word to be spoken against the honour of the Spanish monarch.[1]

To the King's annoyance, the reply to his homily to Parliament was a fresh petition, which was presented by a deputation of the House on December 11th, 1621. " Fetch chairs for the ambassadors," cried James, when the deputation appeared before him, as a hint that his Parliament arrogated to itself royal privileges. On December 14th the King's answer was read to Parliament; it gave rise to strong opposition.[2] Consequently, on December 30th, James I. repaired in person to the House, demanded the book in which the protest had been filed, and with his own hand tore out the page on which it was written.[3] On January 6th, 1622, Parliament was dissolved.[4]

James I., therefore, stuck to his friendship for Spain. One preacher was imprisoned for uttering libels against Spain; another for repeating Coke's dictum about the Spanish sheep scab; another who had expatiated on a nation that worshipped the Beast and its image (Apoc. xiv., 9) escaped with a censure.[5] On the other hand, in August, 1622, at Gondomar's intercession, hosts of Catholic prisoners were released from the prisons; the ambassador boasted in Spain that their number amounted to 4,000.[6] Shortly before this, the Keeper of the Great Seal had received instructions to grant to all Catholics,

---

[1] *Ibid.*
[2] *Ibid.*, 261.
[3] *Ibid.*, 265.
[4] *Ibid.*, 267.
[5] *Ibid.*, 346.
[6] LINGARD, VII., 240.

under the Great Seal, a free pardon for non-attendance at Church, provided they applied for it within the next five years.[1] At no time, wrote Valaresso, the Venetian envoy, had the Catholic religion enjoyed greater freedom.[2] Nevertheless the joy of the Catholics was a very subdued one, because the recusants thus freed from prison had to take an oath that they would present themselves again if requested to do so, and in order to calm Protestant fanaticism Williams declared that though the prisoners were freed, " they had still the shackles about their heels." [3]

Whilst Parliament, as well as the Protestant populace, gave unmistakable expression to their aversion for Spain, the King continued his efforts for an Anglo-Spanish marriage. Immediately after Philip III.'s death on March 21st, 1621, inquiries came from England to his son and heir with a view to sounding him on the subject. Philip IV. answered that he would do his best to further it.[4] Some time before the death of Paul V.—January 28th, 1621—the Dominican Diego de la Fuente, acting as Spanish envoy, and George Gage, an English Catholic, had met in Rome for the purpose of obtaining the necessary papal dispensation. Gregory XV. appointed a commission to study the matter, and on September 1st, 1621, Gage was able to report to Digby that the papal permission

[1] *Ibid.*, 240.
[2] August 9, 1622 (GARDINER, IV., 349).
[3] LINGARD, VII., 240. The King's order was carried out badly : " Per esservi intervenuti certi giudici ordinari del paese (senza i quali non si potevano liberare dett'incarcerati conforme allo stilo e usanza di questo regno) non si crederebbe mai quanti dilatorii e scappatorii li detti giudici trovassero, e come per lo spatio quasi d'un anno intiero non si potesse mai ottenere che si eseguisse l'ordine del Rè in favore di quell'incarcerati " (Letter from London, 1623, in AREZIO, 66). " Non sono passati otto giorni che per ordine espresso di Rè si sono fatti cercare le camere di tre sacerdoti incarcerati, e si sono stati levati con grandissima insolenza e crudeltà di un certo Crosse, più infame sbirro che sia, due calici, alcuni paramenti di altare e tutt'i libri " (*ibid.*, 67).
[4] GARDINER, IV., 190.

for the marriage would be granted as the price of freedom of religion for English Catholics.[1]

Nevertheless negotiations were protracted beyond all expectation. In 1622 the English ambassador in Madrid, in conversation with Zúñiga, remarked that after two years' efforts in Rome de la Fuente had obtained nothing so far. Zúñiga referred the ambassador to King Philip IV. The latter expressed his great satisfaction at the proposed marriage. Digby even tried to influence the Infanta. He obtained an audience with her, when he spoke of the love and longing of the successor to the English throne, and begged her to favour his aspirations. " I thank the Prince of Wales for the honour he does me," was all she said, and with that the audience was at an end.[2]

Actually the matter could not be forwarded in Spain until Rome had spoken. As early as August 11th, 1621, Gregory XV. commissioned four Cardinals to consider the terms of the marriage treaty as they had come from Madrid.[3] The Cardinals declared them to be unacceptable, for though the religious needs of the Infanta and her household were sufficiently safeguarded by them, nothing definite was laid down for the benefit of English Catholics in general. The Pope could only grant the dispensation that was being asked for if the position of the Catholic Church in England would thereby be materially improved. The vague promises of James I. during the previous year, to the effect that the Penal Laws would not be applied, were totally inadequate. Nothing less than the grant of complete liberty of conscience for Catholics could be regarded as a sufficient ground for the dispensation, and by way of a

---

[1] Ibid., 230. The personality of De la Fuente made a very good impression in Rome : " È riuscito et a questi miei Signori Illustrissimi et a me persona così destra, discreta e prudente e piena di ottime maniere che ne siano sodisfattissimi." Cardinal Ludovisi to the nuncio in Madrid, April 12, 1623 (in AREZIO, L'azione, 67).

[2] Ibid., 333 seq.

[3] Cf. our notes, Vol. XXVI., 196 seqq.

pledge more would be required than the mere word of the King.[1] The answer which Gage received from Cardinal Bandini on July 4th, 1622, was to the same effect. The Cardinals had been told that full freedom of conscience for Catholics would best be guaranteed by a personal enactment on the part of the King. They therefore hoped that James would state how much he was prepared to do for his Catholic subjects.[2] Several important alterations in the marriage contract were demanded even at this stage. The future Queen's household must be wholly Catholic; the churches assigned to the Queen and her retinue must be open to everybody; the priests were to have a Bishop at their head and were to be exempt from all laws, with the exception of those of their ecclesiastical superiors. The education of her children must be reserved to the Infanta; the girls were to remain under her care till they reached the age of twelve, the boys until they were fourteen.[3]

James was, of course, extremely dissatisfied when Gage, on his return to England on August 25th, 1622, informed him of these conditions. The Cardinals might have known, so he wrote to Digby,[4] that he could not grant an open church; that the exemption of priests from the civil law was not even granted in all Catholic countries; he would allow the children to be under their mother's care until they were seven years old and even longer if their health required it. As to the general position of Catholics, he had gone as far as he possibly could in his letter of April 27th, 1620; the existing laws might be softened by the manner in which they were applied. These were his proposals; if they were not accepted he would break off negotiations. A covering letter from Buckingham to Gondomar, who had returned to Spain, contained the threat that if Spain proved obstinate, the Penal Laws against Catholics would be enforced once more.[5]

[1] GARDINER, IV., 350 seq.
[2] Ibid., 351.
[3] Ibid., 352.
[4] September 9, 1622, ibid., 353.
[5] Ibid., 353-7.

Madrid, too, was annoyed at the stricter conditions of the marriage. Zúñiga and Gondomar assured the English envoy, Digby, that their King would bring the Pope to reason,[1] and after Zúñiga's death, his successor, Count Olivares, expressed the same opinion.[2] At the council which discussed the marriage contract, Gondomar maintained that it was not necessary to make such extraordinary demands in order to obtain the conversion of England.[3]

Notwithstanding the threats on the part of England, opinion in Madrid did not doubt the happy issue of the matter. Neither did the King of England take his own threats too seriously. Digby, who had recently become Earl of Bristol,[4] was commanded,[5] in the event of an unsatisfactory answer by the Spanish Court, not to leave the country. James I. even tried to win over the Pope for his plans. On September 30th, 1622, he addressed a personal letter to the Pontiff in which he said that His Holiness would perhaps wonder that, notwithstanding their divergences on matters of religion, the King should be the first to greet His Holiness by letter. However, such was the anguish of his mind, by reason of the unhappy conflicts and the shedding of blood which had of late years brought so much misery on the Christian world, and so great was his daily anxiety and endeavour to put a stop to these ever-growing evils, that he could remain no longer silent, but must plead earnestly and in a friendly spirit that it would please His Holiness to co-operate with him in a task so eminently religious and so worthy of a Christian prince. He made this request in view of the fact that both parties worshipped the same Triune God and hoped for salvation by no other means but the Precious Blood and the merits of the one Lord and Saviour Jesus Christ.

Though it was not mentioned, the affair of the marriage appears to be at the back of this document. James's reasoning

---

[1] Digby on September 13, 1622, ibid., 373.
[2] GARDINER, IV., 380.
[3] Ibid., 383.
[4] Ibid., 364.
[5] October 4, 1622, ibid., 374 ; cf. 378.

was evidently to the effect that if the Pope granted the dispensation, a political *rapprochement* between Spain and England would ensue, consequently also the restoration of the Palatinate, and with it the end of bloodshed and a general peace.

Meanwhile the two young people whose proposed marriage was keeping the Courts of Rome, Madrid and London in breathless suspense, had reached an age when they could speak for themselves. The Infanta Maria, whose outward appearance has been perpetuated by Velasquez,[1] was now seventeen years of age. People admired the dignity and affability of her manner and her profound piety. Each day she spent two hours in devotional exercises and received the Sacraments twice a week. The young princess had a special devotion to the Immaculate Conception of Our Lady,[2] viz. to the special prerogative whereby the Mother of God, in view of the future merits of her Divine Son, was preserved from all taint of original sin from the first moment of her existence. This was a Spanish national devotion ; Philip III. had often implored the Pope to define the doctrine of the Immaculate Conception as a dogma of faith,[3] and it is well known with what enthusiasm Murillo, at a later period, devoted his art to the glorification of this special prerogative. It was none the less a proof of nobility of soul that this young princess should have felt so strongly attracted towards such an ideal of purity and utter sinlessness. Her piety was more than a matter of sentiment. She did not spend her pocket-money on pleasures, but on the poor. Her self-control, especially over her tongue,

---

[1] Portraits are in the Prado and the Berlin gallery ; see JUSTI, " Die spanische Brautfahrt Karl Stuarts," in the *Miszellaneen aus drei Jahrhunderten spanischen Kunstlebens*, II., Berlin, 1908, 303 seq., 306 seq.

[2] GARDINER, IV., 378.

[3] Πρεσβεια sive Legatio Philippi III. et IV. Catholicorum Regum Hispanorum ad SS. DD. NN. Paulum PP. V. et Gregorium XV. de definienda controversia Immaculatae conceptionis B. Virginis Mariae, Lovanii 1624. See L. FRIAS, in *Razón y Fe*, X. (1904), 21 seqq. ; CAUCHIE-MAERE, 84 seqq., and our account, Vol. XXV., 252 seqq.

was well known. From her piety arose a very great distaste for marriage with a heretic; she was supported in her opposition by her confessor and by the Archduchess Margaret, a daughter of the Emperor Maximilian II., who lived as a Carmelite in Madrid.[1]

The Prince of Wales was likewise a young man of lofty character. His appearance was both manly and handsome[2]; he was an adept in all bodily exercises, acquainted with music and the plastic arts, and his moral conduct was irreproachable. He blushed like a young girl at any unseemly remark, and women of a certain character thought it wiser to cast their nets in other directions.[3] At first he was but little disposed towards marriage with the Infanta. When he came to see her likeness he expressed the customary admiration, out of consideration for the bystanders, but, when out of their hearing, he remarked to a confidential friend: "If it were not a sin, a king should have two wives, one for the sake of his politics and one for his own sake."

However, by degrees his disposition changed, probably because he felt that by an alliance with Spain he would be of use to his beloved sister, the Electress Elizabeth. He therefore got into closer touch with Gondomar, and on his recommendation he appointed Walter Savage, a Catholic, as one of the controllers of his household, although Savage had refused to take

---

[1] GARDINER, IV., 389.

[2] See the portraits in JUSTI, *loc. cit.*, 313, 333.

[3] GARDINER, IV., 366; KHEVENHILLER, X., 258. According to a report of 1622: "*Relatione fatta alla Congregazione di Propaganda Fide da Dionisio Lazzari sopra alcune cose d'Inghilterra che possono essere di servizio alla s. fede cattolica*," Charles was "d'indole molto ingenua, di costumi assai generosi, molto sobrio in detestar li cattolici." Of James it is said, "Per la pratica che ho di lui, lo stimo indifferente in qualsivoglia religione." Buckingham's wife was reputed to be clandestinely a Catholic (*Cod.* 35, B. 9, p. 48 *seq.*, of the Corsini Library, Rome). *Cf.* LÄMMER, *Zur Kirchengesch.*, 147 *seq.*; RANKE, *Päpste*, III.[8], 123. On the Catholicism of Buckingham's mother and wife, see W. H. HUTTON, *The English Church, 1625-1714*, London, 1903. 9.

the oath of allegiance.[1] Gondomar also was responsible for an idea by the execution of which the Prince caused enormous excitement throughout England. It was this: shortly before Gondomar left England, Charles promised that he would go in person to Madrid if on his return Gondomar recommended such a step.[2]

After that Charles could only think of the projected journey to Spain. Endymion Porter, a former servant in the household of Count Olivares and now in the service of the Prince and entrusted with Buckingham's Spanish correspondence, was dispatched to Spain to sound Gondomar with regard to his views on the Spanish journey. If Gondomar approved, the Prince intended to send a fleet to Spain to fetch the Princess, and he would personally go out with the fleet.[3] Just as Porter was about to leave,[4] Cottington arrived home from the British Embassy at Madrid. He was the bearer of a letter from Gondomar to James I., expressing the hope that by next spring the Infanta would be able to set out for England.[5] Thereupon it was decided to authorize the English envoy in Madrid, through Porter, to concede that the future children of the heir to the throne should remain under their mother's care up to their ninth, instead of their seventh year, although in the written articles of the contract the seventh year only would be guaranteed.[6] Porter arrived in Spain in the early days of November, 1622, and was soon able to report that the Prince of Wales would be welcome in that country.[7] Thus, after endless negotiations, it seemed as if the marriage treaty was about to be successfully concluded to the joy of the much-tried negotiators and to the dismay of the Infanta Maria. Her tears were not without making an impression on Philip IV., but on the other side there was Olivares to be reckoned with.

[1] Gondomar, January 31, 1622, in GARDINER, IV., 368 *seq.*
[2] Gondomar, May 16, 1622, *ibid.*, 369.
[3] *Ibid.*, 370.
[4] October 4, 1622, *ibid.*, 373.
[5] *Ibid.*
[6] *Ibid.*, 374.
[7] *Ibid.*, 383.

Her ordinary confessor was taken from her and others were instructed to paint in glowing colours the merit she would acquire if she were to bring back a lapsed nation to the true faith. In the end the Princess was prevailed upon to declare that for God's honour and in obedience to the King she was ready for any sacrifice. However, a few days later, she sent word to Olivares to say that she had herself cut the Gordian knot : she would not marry at all, but would enter the cloister.[1] After that Philip IV. refused to press his sister any further. He wrote to Olivares that on his deathbed his father had declared his preference for the Austrian marriage and the minister must find a way out of the business.[2] Olivares who, up to this point, had appeared to have been keen on the marriage, now avowed his real opinion in a memorandum. Philip III., he declared,[3] had never wished the English marriage to take place, unless the Prince of Wales became a Catholic. The negotiations had, however, been set afoot and drawn out in order to obtain better conditions and not to jeopardize their friendship with James I. Until the entanglement over the Palatinate had been cleared up, an alliance by marriage with England was out of the question, for Philip IV. could obviously not declare himself openly against the Emperor ; but a decision in favour of the Emperor meant war with England, consequently also with the Infanta as the future Queen of England ; to remain neutral was an equally impossible solution for Spain. But there was a way out of the complication ; it was that Prince Charles should marry a daughter of the Emperor, and that the son of the Elector Frederick should be brought up as a Catholic with a view to his securing the hand of one of the Archduchesses.

The Privy Council rejected this proposal and the negotiations for the English marriage went on. Even Olivares, who had informed the imperial ambassador of the tenor of his memorandum, acted as if he had made the views of the Council his own. Thus, on December 2nd, 1622, the reply to James I.'s

[1] *Ibid.*, 390.
[2] *Ibid.*
[3] *Ibid.*, 392.

objections to the articles of the contract were communicated to Bristol. By these Philip IV. was willing to give up the idea of a public church, accessible to all the Catholics of London. On the other hand he insisted that the priests should not be subject to English law; if they broke the law, James could deport them, and in a really bad case the Spanish King would offer no objection to their punishment. The proposal to leave the children with their mother up to the ninth year was accepted, with a rider that the addition of another year was much desired. As to liberty of conscience, Gondomar suggested that James should grant to Catholics the undisturbed exercise of their religion within their own homes. A written promise from the King and the Prince on this point would suffice, without mention in the articles of the contract.[1]

Bristol was not empowered to accept these alterations, but he offered no objections. On their part, the Spaniards promised to press the Pope to grant his dispensation by the end of March, or in the course of April; the marriage was to take place before the end of the spring.[2] Thereupon Gage returned to Rome and Porter to England.[3]

Meanwhile the additional year of the royal children and the point about the exemption of the priests from English law had been granted by James I. in a written document.[4] Thereupon both the King and the Prince of Wales signed the articles as well as another document in which they bound themselves not to persecute Catholics for their religion, or for receiving the Sacraments, so long as they gave no scandal and confined their religious practices within their homes. Nor were they to be compelled to take oaths contrary to their religion, or such as might appear contrary thereto. This document was to be kept back by Bristol until the dispensation should have arrived from Rome.[5]

In view of concessions of such importance, it was taken for

[1] *Ibid.*, 396.
[2] GARDINER, IV., 397.
[3] Porter arrived in London, January 2, 1623; *ibid.*, 398.
[4] To Bristol, November 24, 1622, *ibid.*
[5] *Ibid.*, 398 *seq.*

granted that the Holy See would withdraw its veto. All obstacles seemed to have been swept aside. Orders came from London to make ready a fleet of ten ships to bring the Infanta to England. Buckingham was to be in command of the ships.[1]

With the prospect of a great journey to the Continent before them, both the Prince and his favourite, Buckingham, soon wearied of delay. They decided not to wait until the fleet was ready but to go to Madrid overland, with only a few attendants, under assumed names so as not to betray their rank.[2]

The escapade was a risky one. Did not the heir to the British Crown thereby put himself in the hands of the Spaniards? But just as the scheme shows the thoughtlessness and the romantic love of adventure of the Prince and his favourite, so does the fact that permission for the journey could be extorted from James betray the lack of will power of the aging King more effectively than all the State papers of his latter years. James had long since become unable to say nay to his darling Charles.

With false beards and under the assumed names of Tom and John Smith, the Prince and Buckingham set out on March 2nd, 1623. Charles danced for joy when, after crossing the Bidassoa, he stood on Spanish soil. The pair reached Madrid in the evening of March 16th.[3] Gondomar at once communicated the news to Olivares, who informed the King. Turning towards the crucifix at the head of his bed, Philip IV. swore that the arrival of the Prince would not induce him, where religion was concerned, to take a single step beyond what had been determined by Christ's Vicar, the Pope, not even if he should thereby lose his whole kingdom.[4] He then wrote with his own hand to the Pope, begging him to grant a dispensation for a marriage with the heretic.[5]

The King, the nobility and the people of Madrid celebrated

[1] *Ibid.*, 409.
[2] *Ibid.*, V., 1 seqq.
[3] See JUSTI, *loc. cit.*, 309 seq. *Cf.* also GINDELY, " Eine Heirat mit Hindernissen," in the *Zeitschr. für allgem. Gesch.*, 1884.
[4] GARDINER, V., 11.
[5] *Ibid.*, 12.

the arrival of the English visitors, who had laid aside their incognito, with genuine enthusiasm,[1] but for the diplomatists the situation was embarrassing enough. The Infanta had been destined for Ferdinand, the Emperor's son; hence the imperial ambassador Khevenhiller, brought his heaviest gun into the field against the English marriage. There had never been any blessing on marriages with heretics, he declared. If the Habsburg line died out in Spain, the crown of the Catholic Kings would fall to the Calvinist English; James I. desired this marriage for political reasons, but Spain would only derive disadvantages from friendship with England. The Infanta herself would either become a Martyr in England, or, to the everlasting shame of the Habsburgs, a Calvinist. In the latter event all the hoped-for advantages for the English Catholics would come to naught. The Infanta was not an expert in controversy; it would be wiser to marry the Englishman to an imperial princess who would be better able to cope with the subtleties of heretics. The example of the Elector Palatine showed that the word and oath of Calvinists could not be relied upon, whilst the example of Henry IV. of France proved that, when necessary, they were even willing to hear Mass, to receive the Sacraments and to recognize the Pope.[2]

The arrival of the visitors caused even greater embarrassment to Olivares. To save at least appearances he was now obliged to make some show of zeal in the affair of the marriage. On the other hand for a wedding a bride is indispensable. Now Olivares knew very well that nobody was more averse from marriage than the Prince's chosen one, who was most unwilling to be handed over to a heretic for the sake of politics.[3] The minister needed all his astuteness if he was to extricate himself creditably from so complicated a situation.

One way out there was: "Let us," said Olivares to Buckingham, "settle the matter without Rome." "Splendid!", answered the latter, "but how?" "It's very simple,"

[1] A description of the celebrations is in KHEVENHILLER, X., 237 *seq.*; LINGARD, VII., 243; JUSTI, 310 *seq.*, 317 *seq.*

[2] KHEVENHILLER, X., 241 *seqq.*

[3] JUSTI, *loc. cit.*, 328.

said Olivares, " the Prince need only come over to the Catholic Faith ; we cannot conceive how he could have undertaken this journey unless that had been his intention." Buckingham denied that Charles entertained any such idea. " If that is so," said Olivares, " we shall have to appeal to Rome."[1] In effect he did write to Cardinal Ludovisi ; in his letter he expressed the hope that the dispensation would be granted without delay.[2]

However, the attempt to convert the Prince fitted too well into Olivares' plans for him to give it up in a hurry, for if Charles were really converted all difficulties would be at an end ; but if not, the minister would be able to say that the dispensation could not be obtained from Rome for that reason ; in that case all the odium of the unhappy issue of the business would fall on the Pope and no one would be able to blame Olivares.[3]

Added to this was the fact that the conduct of Buckingham and the Prince gave support to the hope of their return to the old Church. Throughout their stay in Madrid they never once attended the Protestant services at the British Embassy chapel.[4] Whenever Charles entered a church he bent the knee before the Blessed Sacrament. One day, as a procession passed the royal castle, the Prince, who was watching from a window, remained on his knees until the Blessed Sacrament had passed out of sight. When on the occasion of a visit to the Archduchess Margaret, Maximilian II.'s daughter, at her Carmelite convent, the latter expressed the hope that the Prince would also open similar holy houses in England, he answered that with God's help he hoped to do so.[5] Bristol himself thought

[1] GARDINER, V., 14.
[2] Ibid., 14 seq.
[3] Ibid., 16.
[4] Ibid., 28. Charles made at most but one exception. When a month later, Cottington set out for England, Charles commissioned him " to give His Majesty satisfaction in that His Highness hath not had the exercise of his religion in hearing sermons " (ibid., 37).
[5] GINDELY, in the Archiv. für österr. Gesch., LXXXIX. (1901), 63.

his conduct so remarkable that he proffered his services to the Prince if he really wished to be received into the Church.¹ For these reasons Olivares subsequently renewed his efforts to convert the Prince. Nothing was reported to London by Buckingham and Charles of any inclination towards the old religion, but they did seek information from the King as to how far they might use his name in the question of the recognition of papal supremacy. If they conceded that the Pope was the Supreme Head of the Church under Christ, then it was their view that the marriage might be arranged without a papal dispensation.² James replied that he could not concede anything beyond what he had stated in his book against Bellarmine: viz. if the Pope would "quit his godhead and usurping over kings he (James) would acknowledge him for chief bishop to whom all appeals of Churchmen ought to lie *en dernier ressort*".³ However, in the end Charles rejected the idea of conversion. Thus was frustrated Olivares' first attempt to extricate himself from his awkward predicament.

Thereupon he changed his tactics. If Charles would promise freedom of religion for the English Catholics, the Pope would probably consent to the marriage, and with the papal permission once granted the opposition of the Infanta would soon be overcome. Consequently Olivares questioned Buckingham on this point. The answer was that open toleration could not be granted to English Catholics without the risk of an

¹ GARDINER, V., 17. KHEVENHILLER, too, writes on June 8, 1623, to Vienna: "His Excellency the Count (Olivares), has given the English Prince a meed of praise: he does indeed deserve it; he is a modest, pious, intelligent, and virtuous gentleman, and one who seems to show some marked inclination towards the Catholic religion" (X., 258). KHEVENHILLER, had, however, written on April 17, 1623 (*ibid.*, 79), "The English make a great show of Catholicism and thereby create great hopes of conversion; they are great adepts at this kind of thing— the English here are the very *quinta essentia* of cunning!"

² Note of March 10, 1623, in LINGARD, VII., 244; GARDINER, V., 15.

³ Note of March 25, 1623, in LINGARD, *loc. cit.*; GARDINER, V., 16.

insurrection in which Catholics themselves would suffer most; the free exercise of their religion within the four walls of their homes was the utmost that could be promised.[1] This the papal nuncio, de Massimi, declared to be inadequate. The Pope, he told Olivares, would not go back on the decision of the Commission of Cardinals without very special reasons. His own opinion (the nuncio's) was that unless freedom of worship were promised the dispensation would not be granted. If the King of England could not bring himself to make such a concession now when he was so anxious to obtain the Pope's assent, how much less could he be expected to do so later on? If James was afraid of his own subjects because his power was limited by Parliament, how would he be able to maintain his promises after the arrival of the Infanta in England? Massimi even suggested that the Catholics should be given some strong places such as the Huguenots in France possessed.[2] To this proposal Buckingham replied that the position of the Huguenots in France was very different from that of the Catholics in England: the French Protestants had been found fully armed and in possession of these strongholds; the English Catholics, on the contrary, were in hiding, full of fear, and without prestige.[3] Thus Olivares had to register yet another defeat. He now decided to act as if he furthered the marriage, but secretly to render it impossible. On March 25th, 1623, he told Buckingham to lose no time in arranging for the departure of the Infanta. The Duke of Pastrana was sent to Rome to obtain the dispensation, but the ambassador was secretly instructed not to insist on the purpose of his mission, but rather to assure Rome that the dispensation was not desired at Madrid. In this way Olivares hoped to throw all the odium of the failure of the marriage plan on the Pope's shoulders, and to extricate himself from his difficulties. However, a fresh disappointment awaited the wily minister. Pastrana had scarcely left Madrid when the unexpected news arrived that Rome would not refuse the dispensation.

[1] GARDINER, V., 20.
[2] Ibid., 22.
[3] Ibid., 23.

Gregory XV. had heard with great joy of the Prince's journey to Spain.[1] If Henry VIII.'s divorce from his Spanish wife had been the occasion of England's separation from the Church, might one not cherish the hope that the present marriage with the Infanta would lead to her reconciliation with the ancient Church?[2] A Congregation of six Cardinals was appointed to study the question of the dispensation.[3] After hearing de la Fuente and Gage it decided unanimously that the Pope could and should give his consent to the marriage.[4] The possibility of the Prince's conversion to Catholicism, or at least the prospect of a marked amelioration of the position of English Catholics seemed to the Cardinals a sufficient reason for granting a permission which had been withheld by Paul V. in different circumstances. An instruction was drafted for the Spanish nuncio informing him in detail of the position of affairs. It stated that since direct relations with the King of England were impossible, the promises of the King of Spain were to be regarded as guarantees for the execution of the marriage treaty. By its terms both the English King and the Prince of Wales were bound to place in the hands of the Catholic King a written promise concerning the execution of the contract; this document, therefore, must first of all be handed over and an authentic copy thereof sent to the Pope. The document with the dispensation was not to be allowed out of the nuncio's keeping until Philip IV. had made the required promise on oath, as guarantor for James I.

The chief reason why Gregory XV. granted the dispensation was his hope for an amelioration in the position of English Catholics.[5] No hope for complete religious freedom could be

[1] *Cf.* the note of Ludovisi of April 12, 1623, in Arezio, 61 *seqq.*
[2] Gardiner, V., 35.
[3] They were Bandini, Barberini, Millini, Ubaldini, Cobelluzio, and Ludovisi. The instruction for the Spanish nuncio of April 12, 1623, is in Arezio, 72.
[4] Instruction, *ibid.*
[5] "non v'essendo cagione più efficace, che muova N.S. a concedere la dispensa, che la speranza del giovamento de'catolici medesimi" (*ibid.*, 74).

entertained in view of the Puritan's hatred for everything Catholic. But at least, the persecution and oppression of the Catholics must cease, and the nuncio was to press for this with all his energy. In the course of these matrimonial negotiations many such promises had been made, but reliable and recent information went to show that the persecution was still raging ; as a matter of fact it raged even more fiercely in Scotland and Ireland than in England.[1] Vanmala, the representative of the Infanta Isabel Clare Eugenie, was not a little astonished thereat, for if the King did not act with greater mildness now that he had no more than a hope of securing a Spanish daughter-in-law, what would he not do once she was in his power ? Therefore the Infanta Maria must not be allowed to be taken out of the country before the royal promises had been carried out ; and with a view to reassuring English Catholics, means must be found of acquainting them with the royal promises, and if the marriage did not come off, the King of Spain must publicly declare that the fault was not the Pope's.[2]

The demands of the Secretary of State were not meant to be taken too seriously. On April 18th, Ludovisi sent a document, dated April 12th, in which he demanded that James I. should grant to Catholics liberty of public worship, and that this grant should be confirmed both by the Royal Council and by Parliament,[3] whilst in a covering letter the Spanish nuncio was told that he was free to produce this document or not, at his discretion ; in any case it would enable him to protract the negotiations if necessary.[4] The hopes for a happy issue of the affair expressed in the Roman documents were, of course,

[1] " havendo noi relationi assai fresche e fidate, che tuttavia durano (i.e. the persecutions) ; e che nella Scotia si esercitano ancora con maggior rigore, che nell'Inghilterra, e nell'Irlanda nè piu nè meno " (*ibid.*, 74).

[2] *Ibid.*, 75 *seq*. On Rome's caution in dealing with James I. GARDINER says (V., 3) : " They were shrewd enough to suspect that, as soon as Charles was safe in England with his bride, he would forget all his promises."

[3] AREZIO, 76. [4] *Ibid.*, 78.

somewhat diminished, though they were not quite dashed, when it was learned that the whole business was not serious.[1] However, now as before, Rome avoided anything that might prejudice the negotiations. A number of letters concerning the matter were addressed to Philip IV., to Prince Charles, and to three influential ecclesiastics.[2] When the Prince complained in Rome of unfriendliness on the part of the Spanish nuncio, the latter was admonished not to hinder a greater good by being too exacting.[3]

When a preliminary communication from Cardinal Ludovisi on the subject of the dispensation reached the nuncio, the latter informed Olivares in the strictest confidence. But soon the whole world knew of it and congratulations were showered on the Prince as if all difficulties had been overcome.[4] Fresh attempts at conversion had been made, in the first instance, with Buckingham,[5] who patiently listened for hours to discourses on the truth of the Catholic religion, occasionally dropping a remark himself. A fresh discussion also took place with the Prince. Charles seemed impressed with the arguments in favour of papal supremacy when Buckingham jumped up, showed his contempt for the arguing monks by his gestures, threw his hat on the ground and angrily stamped on it.[6] This behaviour led to the termination of the interview more surely than any arguments.

On April 24th, 1623, the dispensation came into the hands of the nuncio. A papal Brief commending the English Catholics to the King accompanied it.[7] Olivares was now able to take cognizance of the full contents of the marriage dispensation.

[1] Ludovisi, April 18, 1623, *ibid.*, 77, 79.
[2] Ludovisi, April 19, *ibid.*, 80.
[3] Ludovisi, April 19, and May 1, *ibid.*, 79 seq., 83.
[4] GARDINER, V., 33.
[5] April 4, 1623, *ibid.*, 29, 31; GINDELY, in the *Archiv. für österr. Gesch.*, LXXXIX., 64 seqq.
[6] GARDINER, V., 34 seq.
[7] *Ibid.*, 37. An earlier *Brief to Philip IV., of February 24, 1623, in the *Epist. Greg. XV.*, vol. III., no. 69, Papal Secret Archives; *one to the King's confessor, *ibid.*, no. 70.

He protested against the unwelcome concession; the nuncio, however, declared that he was bound by his instructions from Rome. Willy-nilly the minister saw himself compelled to communicate the dispensation to the Prince and to inform him of the more stringent conditions.[1] Rome now demanded that the royal children should remain under their mother's care up to their twelfth year; the Infanta's church must be open to the public; and the oath of loyalty, the text of which the Pope himself was drafting for the future Queen's servants, was to serve for all the Catholics of England.[2]

After a barren discussion between Olivares and Buckingham, a commission of three Spaniards was set up to confer with Buckingham, Bristol, Aston and Cottington. The Prince himself appeared before this commission and declared that he and his father were prepared to promise under oath that the Penal Laws would not be carried out against the Catholics for the present; they would do their utmost to obtain from Parliament the confirmation of the conditions agreed upon, as well as the suspension of the Penal Laws, if it were not possible to get them repealed. When the Spaniards asked how long it would be before this was effected, Charles answered promptly: Possibly from three to six months, more likely a year, quite certainly less than three years. It is hardly credible that he believed this himself.[3]

On May 6th the Prince had an opportunity to state his reasons against the hardening of the marriage conditions. The provision that the Infanta's church was to be open to all was not called for, he said, since Catholics were to be allowed the free exercise of their religion within their own houses. But he would show consideration. To grant more would be to concede complete religious liberty, which his father had always resisted. The introduction of a papal oath for the Queen's retinue was superfluous, nor was it fitting that the Pope should dictate an oath to the King of Great Britain. As to the point concerning the age up to which the royal children were to

[1] GARDINER, V., 38.
[2] Ibid.
[3] Ibid., 39.

remain with their mother, he would speak to his father about it, but he would not guarantee the result.[1]

The Spanish Council of State declared the proposals of the Prince insufficient: the Roman conditions must be accepted or rejected in their entirety. The oath demanded from the King of Spain was a condition *sine qua non* of the marriage; under what conditions the King might take it was a matter to be discussed by a committee of forty theologians.

It would seem that Olivares now sought to render the conditions so difficult as to make a rejection of them by England a certainty. The King of England, he wrote to Philip IV., could not possibly mean his promises seriously, hence the Infanta must be kept in Spain until they were fulfilled. On May 7th he proposed the immediate celebration of the betrothal, but the Infanta was to remain in Spain until King James should have put his promises into execution—that is until the Privy Council should have agreed to, and Parliament confirmed, the repeal of the Penal Laws, and until some positions of trust should have been given to Catholics by way of a pledge. If such a procedure were adopted, Catholics would increase in number and in influence, the King would no longer be able to oppress them, and in the end he himself would have to embrace their religion.[2] However, these proposals did not meet with the approval of the Privy Council which hoped to obtain further concessions.

As a matter of fact, Charles now considered it a matter of honour not to return to England without the Infanta for whom he had gradually conceived a real affection. He watched " as a cat watches a mouse " for an opportunity to catch her eye; he turned verses which the chosen one could only have understood with the help of an interpreter.[3] One day, as the Infanta was taking the air in the garden, he climbed over the hedge, with the result that the young Princess screamed aloud and ran away.[4]

[1] *Ibid.*
[2] *Ibid.*, 40-41.
[3] *Ibid.*, 60.
[4] *Ibid.*, 52.

Olivares took advantage of Charles' complaisance constantly to raise his demands. He first of all inquired of the Prince what, in his opinion, would be a sufficient guarantee for the oath that was demanded of the King. Charles answered that his own oath and that of his father should be confirmed by the oath of the Privy Council. He would also do his best to get it confirmed by Parliament. Shortly afterwards he declared his readiness to make himself responsible that, in the presence of his future spouse, never a word should be spoken against her religion; on the contrary, if she desired it, he himself would be prepared to listen to the explanations of Catholic theologians.[1] However, the nuncio was not authorized to accept these promises as sufficient. In vain Buckingham discussed the matter with him for three hours, ending with the threat of a fresh persecution of Catholics. In vain did Bristol try his diplomatic arts upon him; negotiations came to a standstill. At last it was agreed that Philip IV. would once more appeal to Rome with regard to the conditions of the marriage, and that the Prince would consult London. As for the oath to be taken by the King of Spain, a junta of theologians would discuss it. At first Charles expressed a wish to return to England in order personally to bring pressure to bear on his father, but, yielding to Philip IV.'s friendly persuasion, he consented to remain in Spain.[2] In fact, he committed himself to even greater concessions—so much so that for a time any further discussions of the junta seemed superfluous. Secretly Buckingham let it be known that only one point caused the Prince difficulties, namely, the request for the suspension of the laws against English Catholics; but that his father would do his best in this respect. If James would do this, Olivares replied, then, in his opinion, all the necessary guarantees would have been given to enable Philip IV. to take the oath demanded by the Pope: but because the nuncio was of a different opinion, he must insist on the Prince's returning to London without the Infanta in order to obtain the fulfilment of the promises.

[1] GARDINER, V., 42.
[2] *Ibid.*, 46 *seq.*

This new delay made the Englishmen so angry that the nuncio withdrew his objection. As a matter of fact Charles was pretty well ready for almost anything, so long as he should not have to return to London without the Infanta. He agreed that the royal children should remain under their mother's care until the age of twelve; that the oath proposed by the Pope should take the place of the oath of loyalty; and that the Infanta's church should be open to the public. Both himself and his father were prepared to guarantee that the application of the Penal Laws would be suspended, and that Parliament would be requested to repeal them within three years.[1] In view of these far-reaching concessions, the King of Spain declared that if they met with James I.'s assent, he would take the oath demanded of him and allow his sister to leave for England.[2]

Thus the Prince's wishes seemed about to be realized. He had already instructed Cottington to carry the good news to London, when a fresh difficulty arose. A certain preacher, one Pedrosa, warned the King in a public sermon not to sacrifice religion to considerations of State. To marry the Infanta to a a heretic was a serious step, and to swear that a heretic would keep his word was an even graver one.[3] The consequence of this warning was that, after all, the junta of theologians actually met. On May 23rd, 1623, they gave their decision—it was unfavourable to the Prince. They were of opinion that for Philip IV. to take the oath with a good conscience, it would be necessary to demand that the Infanta should remain in Spain for a whole year after the wedding; and within that period a public proclamation must be made that the Penal Laws against the Catholics would no longer be carried out, and that the latter

---

[1] *Ibid.*, 47.

[2] *Ibid.*, 48.

[3] *Ibid.* As to the sincerity of the Prince's promises, GARDINER's opinion is as follows (V., 45) : " For months he lingered at Madrid, sacrificing his country to his love, making promises, into the full meaning of which he did not care to inquire, and satisfying himself with the prospect of being able to explain them away, if at any time they should prove inconvenient."

had been granted the free exercise of their religion within the four walls of their own houses. King James, Prince Charles, and the Privy Council would have to swear that these concessions would not be revoked. Finally, every attempt must be made to obtain the assent of Parliament.[1]

The Prince deemed these conditions excessive. The very next day after he had been informed of them he sent Cottington to the Court to request permission to return to London.[2] True, he did not mean this very seriously. When it was represented to him that he had promised first to place his father in possession of the facts, Cottington was told to hold himself in readiness to leave for London as soon as copies of the minutes of the latest negotiations should be in his hands. Charles himself remained in Spain where he attempted, through Bristol, to get the nuncio de Massimi and the theologians to change their minds.[3] Perhaps by more than anything else his desire for the Spanish marriage is proved by the fact that this time he went so far as to enter into a correspondence with the Pope himself.

In Rome the Prince's journey to Spain was regarded as a symptom of his attraction towards the ancient Church, and on April 23rd, 1623,[4] Gregory XV. wrote the following letter to Charles : " England," he begins, " which fills the old and the new world with the fame of her name, cannot fail to arrest also, and that very often, the Pope's attention ; indeed, during the first Christian centuries the Cross penetrated there before the Roman Eagles, and many of England's Princes are revered as Saints. Even now the English Royal House is distinguished by natural virtues which would be a joy to the Pope and an

---

[1] GARDINER, V., 50. The President of the Royal Council, Roco de Campo Frio, stated his objection to the marriage in writing (in KHEVENHILLER, X., 278–305) ; so did Francisco de Jesu (cf. ibid., 306 seqq.) ; another document to the Prince of Wales, ibid., 314–26.

[2] Ibid., 51.

[3] Ibid., 53.

[4] Printed in BELLESHEIM, Scotland, III., 426 seqq. ; KHEVENHILLER, X., 253 seqq.

honour to the Christian name, if only it were possible to add that it supported the true faith." Alluding to his own name, the Pope recalls that it was another Gregory—a Roman Pope also—who had instilled into the hearts of England's Kings and people the light of the Gospel and devotion to the Apostolic See. In imitation of this first Gregory, he too had the salvation of those realms very much at heart—especially now when the Prince's journey and his desire to be united in matrimony with a Catholic Princess seemed to open up the happiest prospects, for nobody who hated the Catholic religion, or desired the oppression of the Holy See, could be desirous of such a marriage. " We have therefore commanded that fervent prayer be offered to the Father of Lights, to the end that He may lead you, an ornament of the Christian world and the hope of Britain, into the possession of that inheritance which your ancestors acquired for you as the most precious patrimony, that is that you may protect the papal authority and beat down the hydra of heresy. Remember the days of old, ask your fathers and they will declare to you which is the road that leads to heaven and which is the road that mortal princes must follow. Look through the open doors of heaven and behold there those Kings of England who, under angelic tutelage, made pilgrimages to Rome in order to do homage to the Lord of Lords and to the Apostolic See of the Prince of the Apostles. Their actions and their example are the voice of God loudly exhorting you to stand firm by the principles of those whose throne you are one day to inherit. Could you really tolerate that men should be judged by heretics as ungodly, and by them cast down into the abyss of everlasting darkness, who according to the testimony of the whole Church reign with Christ in heaven, exalted far above all earthly principality? They stretch out their hands to you now from their everlasting abode, even as they have safely led you to the Court of the Catholic King, and desire to bring you back to the bosom of the Roman Church."

Accompanied by Olivares and other grandees the nuncio presented the letter to the Prince at a special audience.[1]

[1] May 24, 1623; see KHEVENHILLER, X., 253.

Charles received it with " great reverence ", and treated the nuncio with utmost courtesy. On June 23rd he sent a reply to the Pope,[1] which could only confirm the opinion prevailing in Roman circles as to the intentions of the Prince. The very address was significant : " Most Holy Father ! " The Prince went on to say how gratified he had been to be reminded of the example of his forefathers. He would " do his utmost to the end that peace and concord, so long banished, might return to the Church of God and to the Christian world. Since the father of dissension has sown the seeds of so many unhappy quarrels among those who believe in one and the same Christian Faith, we believe that the most pressing need is to advance the honour of our God and Saviour Jesus Christ." His father also was deeply distressed by the cruel massacres and the pitiable misfortunes which arose from the dissensions between Christian princes. " Your Holiness' opinion with regard to our desire to ally ourselves with a Catholic princely house and to marry a Catholic princess, has been inspired by your Holiness' affection and corresponds with facts. We should never feel such eagerness to unite ourselves by so close and indissoluble a bond with a mortal being, if we abhorred her religion. Hence, Your Holiness may feel assured that we shall always study moderation, for we abhor any act that might in any way show hatred for the Catholic religion ; on the contrary, we shall seize every opportunity to further the free course of events to the end that every evil suspicion may thereby be put out of the way. Then, even as we all acknowledge the one undivided Trinity and the same crucified Christ, so shall we be united in the harmony of one Faith and one Church. If we could realize so noble an ideal, we should consider our labours and our vigils, nay the loss of kingdom and life, to be but a small sacrifice."

Schism then is the work of the devil ! Catholics have nothing to fear from the future ruler of Great Britain ; Charles will do his utmost to restore unity—this was much more than had been expected in Rome.

[1] *Ibid.*, 267 *seq.*; the date is in BELLESHEIM, *Scotland*, III., 426.

Olivares sought to make the Prince still more submissive by openly and solemnly betaking himself, on June 7th, to Khevenhiller, for the purpose of promoting once more the Infanta's marriage with an Austrian. The ambassador thereupon procured from Vienna the necessary authority.[1]

Shortly after his letter to the Prince, the Pope also replied to James I.'s communication of September in the previous year.[2] Referring to some of the King's remarks, he praises his desire for the restoration of world peace. But it was even more important that the great masses should be in a peaceful frame of mind, and since the disunion of the nations arose from religious dissensions, James should labour for religious unity. As in his letter to the Prince, the Pope touches upon England's former relations with the Holy See. He prays that James would restore them. The restoration of the Catholic faith in England would be his greatest achievement, one comparable to that of Constantine : God, who had subjected three kingdoms to the King, would vouchsafe him His protection. At the very least let James grant to Catholics the free exercise of their religion. George Gage would be the bearer of further information.

Meanwhile Cottington had left for London on May 21st, 1623, where he arrived on June 14th. Everything now depended on the attitude which James would take towards the question of the marriage.

Outwardly the weak monarch had at first made a brave show. When he heard of Charles's arrival in Madrid he commanded that bonfires should be lit and church-bells rung.[3] Before that, when on the first intimation of the Prince's surreptitious journey, the Privy Council in its dismay begged him on their knees to tell them what was the truth of the matter, he had spoken reassuring words. Charles was only acting as his father and many of his forefathers had done, when

[1] KHEVENHILLER, X., 255 seqq., 261 seqq.

[2] May 2, 1623, in the *Epist. Greg. XV.*, vol. III., no. 78, Papal Secret Archives. *Ibid.*, an exhortation dated April 19, 1623, to Philip IV. and his confessor, Ant. de Sotomayor, to work for the conversion of the Prince.

[3] GARDINER, V., 54.

they had gone forth in person to win their brides; universal peace for Christendom would be the issue of this journey.[1] Public opinion, however, was not calmed by these assurances; in all the churches prayers were offered for the safe return of the heir to the throne.[2] To all appearances James refused to be alarmed. He was busy collecting the fleet that was to fetch the Infanta. He spoke of the chapel which he was obliged to build for her—though very much against his inclination—and Charles' companion, Buckingham, was made a Duke.[3] However, in reality, James was as worried as his subjects. " What do you think ? " he asked a confidant, bursting into tears, " shall I ever see the Prince again ? " Oppressed as he was by the fear that the Spaniards might keep back Charles by force, he was ready for any concessions. The Prince had asked that every concession made by himself in the name of the King should be carried out by him. The foolish father gave these ample powers,[4] which completely subjected him to the whims of his thoughtless son. When Cottington arrived in London, James shut himself in with him and Conway for two whole days. He then wrote to Madrid that if the Spanish ministers could not be induced to reverse " the decisions of their devils ", the Prince should subscribe to the marriage conditions as they stood, proceed with the wedding and come home at once. On June 22nd William Croft arrived at Madrid with these instructions.[5]

Charles acted with his wonted indecision. On July 6th Olivares informed him that his royal master was obliged to abide by the decision of the junta. There was only one concession he would make, namely, if the marriage should take place, say in September, the King would forgo the plan of

[1] *Ibid.*, 8.
[2] *Ibid.*
[3] *Ibid.*, 54.
[4] May 11, 1623. GARDINER, V., 55.
[5] *Ibid.*, 61. What James thought of the negotiations he had already told Gondomar earlier; if the marriage were concluded, the Infanta would do what her husband asked of her, notwithstanding all treaties (KHEVENHILLER, X., 282).

keeping the Infanta a full year in Spain after the Prince's departure. He would be quite willing for her to leave already in March. Charles replied that his father had instructed him not to leave the Infanta in Spain when he returned; he must therefore look on the negotiations as broken off. However when he presented himself before the King on the following day he had changed his mind once more and was ready to accept all the conditions.[1]

It looked as if the last remaining difficulties had been overcome. Philip IV. embraced the Prince as a brother. During four nights in succession the streets of Madrid were illuminated to celebrate the event. Lord Andover was dispatched to England with the good news.[2]

James was paying dearly for having allowed the final decision in regard to the marriage to be taken out of his own hands. In his name his son had agreed to the demands of the junta. Compliance with them required the King of England and his counsellors to take an oath in respect to the marriage conditions. James was hurt by the implied mistrust shown in the demand of an oath from his counsellors, over and above his own royal word and oath. Moreover he was not prepared to suspend the Penal Laws unconditionally and loathed the idea of personally getting Parliament to ratify such a measure. On the other hand he was convinced that his son would be kept by force in Spain if England's King broke his pledged word. In this dilemma James summoned his counsellors on June 13th, 1623, at Wanstead, when he laid the most recent events before them. He then left the room so that they might discuss the matter with complete freedom.

At first the distinguished gathering's wisdom seemed to have forsaken it. The only way out they could think of was the recall of the Prince before the oath was taken. But in the end the King's first minister, Williams, saved his master. He realized that James I., in order to free his son from the trap, would, in any circumstances, take the required oath, and that all he really wanted from his advisers was some decision with which

[1] GARDINER, V., 63.
[2] *Ibid.*

to cloak this step in the eyes of the people. Williams therefore explained that it was not possible to offer counsel until they knew whether the King felt some scruple of conscience against taking the oath. James I. replied that in regard to his conscience, he maintained his former standpoint, but he was ready to listen to reasons which might be urged in favour of another point of view. Williams now put such reasons before him. He knew very well, he began, how ill it became him to discuss a theological question with one as learned as His Majesty, but he must draw attention to the fact that the Prince had already agreed to the conditions of the marriage. Now Charles was as good a Protestant as any in the world, and, in his opinion, he had done the right thing. He had not been asked to neglect in future the spread of the true religion or to further the papal supremacy; all that had been demanded of him was that he should not attempt to root out the Roman religion.

James had now secured what he wanted. On July 16th he once more convened his Council. The Spaniards, he said with some emotion, had treated him hardly, but what could he do if he did not wish to lose the Prince? He now put it to the members of his Council, whether they would take the required oath. He would explain to the Spanish ambassador that he did not intend to assume the obligation of asking the approval of Parliament, and the safety of the State must come before any obligation to which he might commit himself with regard to the Penal Laws. Thereupon all declared themselves ready to take the oath provided that they were ordered to do so under the Great Seal. On the following Sunday, after church, the King, in the presence of the two Spanish envoys, Coloma and Inojosa, swore to the conditions of the marriage. After a banquet the counsellors also swore that they would observe the public articles of the treaty and not press in any way for the execution of the Penal Laws. Seven members of the Council were absent. Subsequently, James I., at the residence of the Spanish ambassador, swore to another four secret articles: viz. that the special laws against the Catholics should not be enforced; that freedom to practise their religion in the spirit of the treaty would be extended to Scotland and Ireland; that neither he nor his son would ever interfere in the slightest way with the faith of the Infanta; that they would both do all they could to obtain the ratification of these articles by Parliament; that they would ask Parliament to abrogate the Penal Laws; and that they would never give their assent to any fresh laws of that kind. However, James declared before Cottington and two secretaries that with regard to the assent of Parliament, he was only obliged to do his best to obtain it; and that he did not pledge himself unconditionally never again to enforce the Penal Laws.[1]

Meanwhile rumours of what was going on had come to the ears of the populace and had aroused no small excitement. A letter to the King, published under the name of Archbishop Abbot, gave vent to the general feeling. It represented to James that by his promise of religious toleration he was doing his best to restore the most damnable and heretical teaching of the Roman Church—the Babylon of the Apocalypse. The letter did not omit to threaten with the wrath of God.[2]

On August 21st the King wrote to his son in Madrid. Of the commotion throughout England the letter does not breathe a word, but it lays stress on the fact that the Spaniards must not be allowed to forget their promise of money, " for if they do, then, my dear Charlie, you and I are both bankrupt."[3]

Madrid was anxious to get the marriage contract finally settled. A draft of the document, which was laid before the Prince, contained four additional points besides the four that had already been sworn to. By these additional clauses the Prince promised the execution, within three years, of the marriage conditions—failure to do so would be a stain on his conscience and royal honour. The Prince undertook to do his best with a view to raising the age limit up to which the royal children were to be under their mother's care to twelve years; on his accession to the throne he would concede this age limit. Finally as soon as the Infanta demanded it, he would be prepared to listen to explanations of religious questions by

[1] GARDINER, 63-70; LINGARD, VII., 248, note.
[2] GARDINER, V., 71. *Cf.* BROSCH, VII., 71 *seq.*
[3] GARDINER, V., 73.

Catholic theologians. All these concessions were also to apply to Scotland and Ireland.

Olivares had hoped that these demands, in part quite impossible of fulfilment, would wreck the marriage at the last minute. He had yet to learn that all the wisdom of reasonable men will go down before a lover's recklessness.

Contrary to all expectations, Charles agreed to the terms of the document. When Olivares was informed of it, he was at first speechless. He then exclaimed : " I should have expected my own death rather than this ! "

In point of fact all the minister's diplomatic astuteness had been utterly defeated. Nothing that he could do without showing open opposition to the projected marriage, had he left undone ; but he was destined to see the successive miscarriage of every one of his cleverly conceived manœuvres. Things had now gone so far that for the conclusion of the marriage only one thing more was required, namely, the consent of the bride ; and Olivares himself was now forced to do his utmost to remedy that deficiency. With the help of his own wife he succeeded in persuading the Infanta. With many tears that much tormented woman consented to sacrifice herself for the liberty of English Catholics.[1] On July 5th, 1623, the marriage treaty was signed by the Prince and by Philip IV. The Princess was not to leave for England until the following spring. The marriage was to take place as soon as James I. should have sworn to the articles and the Pope given his consent. The latter condition proved the Infanta's salvation, for at the moment when it was drawn up, as was learnt shortly after, Gregory XV, was already a corpse. All they could now do was to hope for the best from his successor.

[1] " essendo stata tuttavia impressa, che grandissimo merito aquisterebbe appresso il Signor Dio con maritarsi con questo principe, perchè beneficava tanto la religione, si haveva ella accommodato l'animo, etc. *Corner* to the Doge of Venice, August 18, 1623, in GARDINER, V., 92.

CHAPTER IV.

Progress of the Catholic Reformation and Restoration in France, Switzerland and the German Empire—Death of Gregory XV.

(1.)

UNDER the Pontificate of Gregory XV. the wide, uniform and universal policy of the Holy See towards a complete Catholic restoration reached its high-water mark. The same world-wide view which inspired the organization of the work of the missions is likewise revealed in the effort to exploit the political situation in Central Europe which was most favourable to the Church, in order to recover lost ground. This aim is revealed with great clarity and preciseness in the Instructions to the new nuncios whom the Pope dispatched in the spring of 1621, to the imperial Court and to Madrid, Brussels, Paris and Lucerne. All the representatives of the Holy See are put under obligation to advance not only the internal reform of the Church, but its external restoration. " All your zeal and all your activity," so we read in the Instruction for Carlo Carafa who was dispatched as nuncio to the Emperor in April, 1621, " must have but one end, that of exploiting to the greatest possible advantage the happy revolution of fortune and the victorious state of things." [1]

From now onwards the historic struggle between the ancient Church and the religious innovators was no longer to be limited, as it had been in the time of Paul V., to defending that which had escaped the storm, but by boldly taking the offensive, a victorious decision must be sought on all the

---

[1] KOLLMANN, *Acta*, I., 57. For the renewal of the political efforts of the Holy See, *cf.* BIAUDET, 59, who, however, wrongly attributes this to purely personal considerations. The guiding motive was the determination to begin afresh and with greater boldness and energy, the movement for Catholic restoration.

threatened points.¹ It was of the utmost importance to exploit at once the victories of the Emperor and the Catholic League in Germany; at the same time, since the armistice with the Netherlands was about to lapse, it was imperative that an effort should be made to crush Calvinism both in Germany and in France. It was well understood in Rome that these great enterprises were only possible if peace was kept between the Catholic Powers.

One of the first tasks, therefore, that Gregory XV. set himself, was the preservation of peace between France and Spain which was imperilled by the question of the Valtellina.² The cabinet of Paris, which for a time had made common cause with Madrid in this matter, was getting greatly perturbed by the successes of its rival and showed no disposition to tolerate the permanent occupation of the Valtellina by the Spaniards. On February 9th, 1621, Bassompierre was sent as ambassador extraordinary to Madrid. In this diplomatic intervention France could rely on the support of Venice and that of the Protestant party in the Grisons.³

The danger that this collision of political interests between the two Catholic Powers, whose long-standing enmity had apparently been set aside by the marriage of Louis XIII. with the Spanish Princess Anne, might provoke even more serious complications, caused the greatest alarm to Gregory XV., for thereby not merely the peace of Italy, but the progress of the Catholic restoration would have been gravely endangered.

[1] The Instruction for *C. Carafa* states : " *Until now it was a question of preserving the remainder (*reliquie*) of the Catholic Church and to save it from the approaching storm, but now we may hope for more." Ma ci confidiamo che al tempo di S. M.tà non saremo cosi poveri di aiuti nè cosi costretti a stare sulle difese, anzi dobbiamo delle sue vittorie et della divina beneditione, che la cuopre et protege, sperare felicissimi avvenimenti " (*Barb.* 5232, Vatican Library). Then follows the passage, quoted by KOLLMANN, on the results already obtained (*Acta* 59).

[2] *Cf.* our notes, Vol. XXV., 441 *seq.*

[3] See ROTT, *Représent. dipl.*, III., 406 ; *cf.* ZELLER, *Le Connétable de Luynes*, 175 *seq.*, on Bassompierre's mission.

From the first Gregory XV. had made it clear that he was not prepared to be used by Spain as a mere tool of her policy. Soon after his elevation he had recognized the legal argument put forward by Venice in support of her claim to hegemony with regard to shipping in the Adriatic, and he insisted that nothing should be changed in the existing state of things. To the Spanish ambassador he explained that this was not the time for drawing down upon Christendom still greater calamities, and that water, not wood, should be thrown into a raging fire.[1] Although many people in Rome sought to restrain him from meddling with so dangerous a problem,[2] the Pope who, as nuncio, had seen with his own eyes the horrors of war in northern Italy,[3] resolved to make every effort for a compromise by peaceful mediation and to prevent the outbreak of hostilities.[4] To this end he appealed both to France and Spain. In Paris he had representations made on the necessity of prompt action against the Huguenots who were preparing an insurrection, for thus the French would be prevented from intervening in the Valtellina.[5] It may be that Gregory XV. hoped for success in this attempt, for it was known that at that time he inclined rather to France and Venice than to Spain.[6]

In order to gain the Madrid Government for a peaceful solution, the Pope addressed himself on March 3rd, 1621,

---

[1] See the *report of the Venetian *obbedienza* ambassadors in BAROZZI-BERCHET, *Italia*, I., 127. ZWIEDINECK-SÜDENHORST, *Politik Venedigs*, I., 201.

[2] See ACCARISIUS, *Vita Gregorii XV.*, lib. III, ch. 4, Boncompagni Archives, Rome.

[3] *Cf.* above, p. 46.

[4] *Cf.* the *report of Alfonso Pico to Ferdinand II., dated, Rome, March 12, 1621, State Archives, Vienna.

[5] See the report of Savelli, February 12, 1621, in SCHNITZER, *Zur Politik*, 167.

[6] *Cf.* the narrative of the Lucca envoys, in *Studie docum.*, XXII., 205. A. POSSEVINO, too, remarks in his report of June 4, 1621, concerning Gregory XV., " non e inamorato di Spagna." Gonzaga Archives, Mantua.

to the all-powerful Duke of Uzeda,[1] and a little later, on the advice of the Venetian ambassador,[2] he wrote directly to the King, addressing a long epistle, in his own hand, to Philip III., on March 26th, 1621. He began with a survey of the situation of the world as viewed from his lofty watch tower, a situation which he described in a few but striking sentences : Germany was filled with the din of war, the armistice in the Netherlands had almost lapsed, the Poles were threatened by the Tartars and the Turks, the northern Protestant Powers were on the look-out for an opportunity to attack the Habsburgs, France was troubled by the Huguenots, and now even the peace of Italy was seriously imperilled by the affair of the Valtellina. Thus at the beginning of his pontificate, he had more reasons for tears than for joy. But he trusted in the help of God and in the King of Spain's love of peace, a sentiment which, in point of fact, coincided with his interest. Firmly relying on His Majesty's pacific intentions, he begged and enjoined him to restore the independence of the Valtellina, as soon as possible. No other question, Gregory continues, was nearer to his heart at the beginning of his pontificate ; there was nothing with which the King could oblige him more than by yielding on this matter. He once more emphasises that the maintenance of peace in Italy was in the best interest of Spain herself and concludes by reaffirming his determination to use every means at his disposal to effect this end.[3]

The Pope's letter was dispatched to Cardinal Cennini, who up till then had been nuncio in Madrid ; it was followed with appropriate Briefs addressed to the more distinguished Spanish ministers. Cennini was charged to dispel any suspicion that the Pope's step might be inspired by reasons other than his solicitude for the interests of the Church and those of the King himself who, in view of the situation in Germany and the

[1] See *Quellen zur schweiz. Gesch.*, XXI., 502 seq.
[2] See BAROZZI-BERCHET, *Italia*, I., 130.
[3] See *Lettera al re cattolico* in Cod. 33 D. 23, Corsini Library, Rome, dated March 26, 1621, in *Cod. Strozz.*, CLX. (State Archives, Florence), March 16, 1621.

Netherlands could not fail to set great store by the preservation of peace in Italy.[1] In a letter in code dispatched at the same time, Cardinal Ludovisi reminded Cennini that the Pope was firmly resolved to settle the affair of the Valtellina in such a way that the Catholic religion would be assured in that territory, which would also recover its full autonomy and would cease to be alternatively a cause of jealousy or fear for certain foreign Powers. In this document the separate treaty[2] concluded on February 6th, 1621, between the Spaniards and the delegates of the Great Council, was entirely repudiated by the Pope, because it signified nothing else but the occupation of the territory by the Spaniards. The letter accurately prophesies that the other Cantons would not accept the treaty, and that France and Venice would never recognize it. Bearing this fact in mind the Cardinal was instructed to make it clear to the King that he could not possibly wage war, not only in Germany and the Netherlands, but in Italy as well.[3]

The purpose of these papal letters was to prepare the ground for the new Spanish nuncio, Alessandro de Sangro, who received his Instruction on April 5th, 1621.[4] In that document we read that Italy had good grounds for fearing that the peace would be broken through the affair of the Valtellina since the Spaniards had occupied the territory, were constructing fortifications and concentrating large forces there. On their part the Venetians were also arming, for they feared both for themselves and for their friends, the

---

[1] The *letter to Card. Cennini of March 26, 1621, is in the MSS. mentioned above, p. 200, note 3, Corsini Library, Rome.

[2] *Cf.* JECKLIN, *Materialen zur Standes und Landesgeschichte der drei Bünde*, I., Basle, 1907, no. 1373.

[3] This *note also is in the *Codex* quoted, Corsini Library, Rome.

[4] *Instruttione a Mgsr. Sangro, patriarca d'Alessandria, nuntio in Spagna*, April 5, 1621, Cod. J., III., 80, Chigi Library, Rome. Also in *Barb.* 5352 and 5588, Vatican Library; in *Cod.* 11257 of the Ossoliniana at Lemberg. and in *Cod.* XI., G. 31 of the National Library, Naples. In *Ottob.* 2725 the date is wrongly given as April 15.

French. The Pope's hope for the preservation of peace rested upon his expectation that the King of Spain would disavow the action of the Duke of Feria, Governor of Milan. If the nuncio joined his efforts to those of the French and Venetian ambassadors in Madrid, success was all the more likely as the lapse of the Dutch armistice would distract the Spaniards from the affairs of Italy. If Sangro, on his arrival in Madrid, found that the King was unwilling to restore its independence to the Valtellina and to issue to his representatives in Italy the necessary orders to that end, he was to act with the greatest firmness and "to speak plainly and strongly", for the Pope was determined to preserve the peace of Italy at all costs.[1]

The Instruction for the new nuncio in Paris, Ottavio Corsini, Archbishop of Tarsus, dated April 4th, 1621, also discusses in detail the question of the Valtellina and the possibility of war between Spain and France. Corsini was to prevent such a misfortune by every means at his command. The Pope was indifferent as to how he did it, so long as the Catholics of the Valtellina were assured of protection and the outbreak of war between the two Catholic Powers was prevented.[2]

The prospects seemed favourable enough, for Philip III., in opposition to Feria, would not hear of the annexation of the Valtellina.[3] So the Pope hoped for a favourable answer from Madrid.[4] However, the King died on March 31st, 1621,

[1] The passage from the *Instruction to Sangro is printed in *Arch. stor. ital.* N.S., VII., 1, 8 seq.

[2] See *Archiv. für schweiz. Gesch.*, XII. (1858), 194 seq. and ZELLER, *Luynes*, 280 seq.

[3] See ROTT, *Représent. dipl.*, III., 407.

[4] See the *Instruction for the Viennese nuncio Carafa, April 12, 1621, who was told to urge the Emperor to press Spain. About the Valtellina the Instruction says : " N.S.re desidera intorno a quello due cose, l'una che ci salvi colà la religione cattolica, l'altra che non si venga per la contesa di quel passo ad una guerra aperta che seco involva l'Italia, laonde parendo a sua S.tà che nè il Re di Francia nè li principi d'Italia siano per acquetarsi se non si lascia in libertà la Valle con l'atterrarsi i forti et che si

hence the Pope's letter of the 26th never reached him. As for the young King, Philip IV., it was very uncertain whether he entertained the same intentions as his father. The impressions of the French ambassador, Bassompierre, at his first audience, were such that he threatened him with a declaration of war unless Spain withdrew her troops from the Valtellina. Considerations of a general character, more even than these threats, and the firm attitude of Gregory XV., induced the Madrid cabinet to give way.[1] In this way, on April 25th, 1621, the treaty of Madrid was concluded between Spain and France, which guaranteed the return of the Valtellina to the Grisons on condition of a complete amnesty in connexion with recent events. As for the religious question, it was decided that all the innovations introduced after 1617 to the detriment of the Catholic Church were to be abolished.[2] The guarantee for the execution of the treaty was to be undertaken by the Catholics and the Protestants of the Confederation jointly with the French Crown and the papal nuncio.

The treaty of Madrid was not yet known in Rome when the Bishop of Campagna, Alessandro Scappi,[3] was nominated nuncio for Lucerne and given his Instruction on May 12th, 1621. That document touches chiefly upon the internal ecclesiastical reform and restoration. It was the duty of a good nuncio not only to maintain what had been preserved, but to conquer new ground, and by degrees to make good the losses suffered. For this reason he must have at heart the conversion of heretics, the restoration of property and jurisdiction, episcopal authority, the erection of seminaries, the

---

possono trovar de modi a render sicuri i Valtelini dell'oppressione de Grisoni nella religione e nel governare, ha operati efficacissimi offitii col Re cattolico acciò che voglia accommodare quelle cose e ritornar la Valle alla primiera libertà, ma non se ne è ancora havuta risposta che si spera tuttavia sia ragionevole." *Barb.* 5232, Vatican Library.

[1] See ROTT, *Représent. dipl.*, III., 407.

[2] See SIRI, V., 300 *seq.*; ABSCHIED, V., 2, 2034.

[3] See his credentials of May 5, 1621, in the *Quellen zur schweiz. Gesch.*, XXI., 503.

provision of a remedy for the shortage of priests, the prohibition of heretical books, the convocation of synods, the visitation of parishes and the reform of monasteries and convents. A general line of conduct is indicated in the warning that he should take no part in the domestic differences of the Cantons, nor show himself more favourable to the French than to the Spaniards. The rest of the Instruction deals with the Grisons and the Valtellina. The situation at the moment was thus described : The French, who would not allow the alliance between the Venetians and the Grisons, also refused to tolerate that Spain should assume a dominant rôle and, by occupying the Valtellina, should make it impossible for them to go to the assistance of their allies. Venice also was herself entirely cut off from the Grisons, for whose friendship she had been so anxious. Both, therefore, would be looking for help from heretical princes, and if none other was available, even from the Turks themselves. Among the means which might lead to an agreement, the suggestion recently made by the Spanish ambassador at Genoa, Juan Vives, is mentioned, namely, to hand over the fortified places of the Valtellina to the Pope as to a neutral Power. Although recognizing that a proposal of this kind showed great faith in the Holy See, and whilst admitting the advantages which might accrue to the Catholic cause, several objections are enumerated which made the proposition impossible in practice. The Instruction goes on to say that the Pope would be content with any solution which would satisfy the parties concerned and which would guarantee both the interests of the Church and the preservation of peace. The first and foremost task of the nuncio was to prevent the outbreak of a war between France and Spain.[1]

How keen this wish of the Pope was is shown by the

[1] " *Instruttione a Mgr. vescovo di Campagna, destinato da N.S.re suo nuntio ordinario alli Suizzeri delle sette cantoni," dated May 12, 1621, according to *Inf. polit.*, VII., 262 *seq.*, published in *Archiv für schweiz. Gesch.*, VI., 281 *seq.*, partly in translation and partly in extracts. A better copy is in *Barb.* 5445, Vatican Library, and another in *Cod. Casanat.*, X., V., 14, no. 6, and *Cod.* F. 3, F. 96 of the Library at Salzburg.

Instructions[1] sent to the nuncios in Madrid, Paris and Brussels, as well as by the circumstance that Gregory XV. was inclined to overlook the fact that the Treaty of Madrid safeguarded Catholic interests only very imperfectly, for by its terms only those religious innovations were to be abolished which had been introduced after the beginning of 1617.[2] Though his Holiness, so Cardinal Ludovisi informed the Spanish nuncio, would have desired better terms, he did not condemn the treaty. In this most confidential letter the proposal of Juan Vives was qualified by Ludovisi as a manœuvre on the part of Feria, the purpose of which was to delay indefinitely the execution of the Treaty. The nuncio was invited to do all he could to persuade the King to countermand Feria's proposal.[3] The Pope, so Ludovisi assures the Spanish nuncio once more on July 16th, was assuredly anxious to help the Valtellina Catholics, but he was unwilling to make common cause with those who, on the plea of religion, sought to wreck the Treaty of Madrid.[4]

Whilst Gregory XV. energetically opposed the war policy of that intriguer, the Duke of Feria, he took a step which, if it succeeded, would distract attention from the Valtellina, benefit the Catholic cause, and forward peace in Italy in so far as it would have occupied on the other side of the Alps the Duke of Savoy, who still burnt with a desire to conquer Monferrat.[5] At the beginning of May, 1621, Louis XIII. had put himself at the head of an army and marched into Poitou for the purpose of repressing the Huguenots. The

---

[1] See besides the Instruction to the Brussels nuncio, May 1, 1621, in CAUCHIE-MAERE, *Instructions*, 128 *seq.*; that for the Archbishop of Thebes, nuncio extraordinary, October 17, 1621, in *Archiv für schweiz. Gesch.*, XII. (1858), 185 *seq.*

[2] *Cf.* the letter of the Bishop of Chur to Bellarmine, July 20, 1621, in the *Röm. Quartalschr.*, XV., 329 *seq.*

[3] " *Agucchi a nome del card. Ludovisi al Nuntio di Spagna," July 16, 1621, in *Cod.* 33 D. 23, Corsini Library, Rome.

[4] See the *Aggiunta alla lettera di 16 Luglio 1621* and the note of August 15 and 20, 1621, *ibid.*

[5] See ROTT, *Représent. dipl.*, III., 449.

Calvinist preachers had done their best to force the King to take up arms.[1] A conference at La Rochelle formally organized a rising in which, however, only the Dukes of Rohan and Soubise joined from among the great nobles of the realm. The rapid successes of Louis XIII. against the Huguenots, in the early stages of the campaign, seemed to suggest that the moment had come to make a fresh attempt to overthrow the old metropolis of Calvinism.[2] It is not possible to ascertain with complete certainty whether the idea of an attack on Geneva originated in Turin or in Rome. The readiness with which Duke Charles Emmanuel of Savoy fell in with the plan led many contemporaries to conclude that he was its real instigator.[3] Gregory XV. and his enterprising Secretary of State were keen supporters of the scheme, since Geneva was not only the seed-bed of Calvinist preachers, but by offering shelter to Italian apostates, it constituted a constant danger.[4] Seeing that secrecy was of paramount importance, the Pope entrusted the negotiations in Turin and Paris to a simple Barnabite, Fr. Tobias Corona. Corona's Instruction, dated July 18th, 1621,[5] emphasizes the advantages

[1] See HANOTAUX, in *Rev. des Deux Mondes*, 1902, VII., 501. Cf. RANKE, *Französ. Gesch.*, II., 253 ; *Rev. des quest. hist.*, XXXII., 143.

[2] For the attempt of 1602 see our account, Vol. XXIII, 242 *seq.* In the late summer of 1602, some secular and regular priests from the district of Geneva presented a memorandum to the Holy See : " *Mezzi per potere con destrezza restituire in Geneva l'essercitio della s. fede cattolica (Cod. 33 B. 7, p. 264 *seq.*, of the Corsini Library, Rome). It claimed for the Catholics resident in Geneva the same religious freedom as the Huguenots of France enjoyed ; France was to procure this by her prestige ; *cf.* LÄMMER, *Zur Kirchengesch.*, 175.

[3] See *Instruttione a Msgr. Campeggi, vesc. di Cesena, per la Nuntiatura di Torino (1624 ?), Cod. X., V., 14 of the Casanatense Library, Rome.

[4] The Instruction for Card. A. Medici had already insisted on this point (*cf.* our account, Vol. XXXIII, 142 *seq.*).

[5] " *Instruttione al padre Don Tobia Corona de chierici regolari mandato da papa Gregorio XV. al Re di Francia, e prima

of the moment, for the Huguenots could not possibly defend themselves in France and at the same time go to the help of Geneva; meanwhile the German Protestants and the Dutch were fully occupied with their own affairs; so were the Swiss and the Grisons on account of the complications in the Valtellina. The heretics of Geneva had nothing to hope for from England; Berne alone might possibly help them; but what could one Canton do for another member of the Confederation when its own population was not of a warlike disposition, and one that only took up arms in an emergency. It might be a hundred years before such a favourable opportunity recurred: for all these reasons the Pope urged rapid action. Unfortunately he could not grant the Savoyards any considerable financial help. If demands were made in this direction, Corona was told to explain how heavily taxed the papal exchequer was by the assistance it gave to the League and to the Emperor; that the Poles were also pressing for money for their war against the Turks; and that Avignon had to be made safe against the Huguenots. None the less, Corona was to say that the Pope would not be miserly towards the Duke, as far as his greatly diminished resources allowed.[1]

The centre of gravity of Corona's mission lay in Paris.

al duca di Savoia per l'impresa della città di Ginevra"; in many MSS.; thus at BOLOGNA, University Library, 473 (595), *Miscell.*, D.; FLORENCE, State Archives, *Carte Strozz.*, 312; FRANKFURT A/M., City Library, MS. *Glauburg*, T 36 and 39, no. 1; LEMBERG, Bibl. Ossoniana, *Cod.* 1257; NAPLES, National Library, *Cod.* XI., G. 31; PARIS, National Library, *MS. ital.*, no. 541 *Suppl.* and Bibl. des Arsenals, *Cod.* 8546; ROME, *Cod. Corsini*, n. 491; SALZBURG, Library, *Cod.* V. 3, G. 120; TURIN, State Archives (Ville de Genève Cath., I. 19). Only the MSS., in Geneva and Frankfurt bear the date of July 16, all the others have July 18. In *Barb.* 5469 the date is lacking. RANKE (*Päpste*, III., 125), who used the Glauburg MS. 39, added on his own authority the date 1622, which is certainly untenable. BURCKHARDT quoted an extract in the *Archiv für schweiz Gesch.*, VI., 292 *seq.*

[1] Cardinal Ludovisi wrote in the same strain to the Duke himself; see *Quellen zur schweiz. Gesch.*, XXI., 627 *seq.*

There he was to address himself, not only to the King and the Queen, but also to the King's favourite, the Duke of Luynes, to the King's confessor, Arnoux, and to Cardinal de Retz and the nuncio.[1] To Louis XIII. Corona was to point out that if the King were to protect Geneva he would fall under the suspicion that his proceedings against the Huguenots in France were merely inspired by political interests. The main argument of the Instruction was that the King should be made to see that the interests of the State and the monarchy demanded the destruction of Geneva. But for Geneva the King would not now be entangled in a civil war, nor would republican tendencies be disseminated all over France. The men who held such views were to be found even at Court and in the royal cabinet. The situation could not be worse than it was at the moment. Such were the power and the wide ramifications of the republican party that it could drive the King from his own palace. The fall of Geneva, which was the Huguenots' Rome, would be a mortal blow to that party. The Instruction foresees all the objections which would be raised, if not by the King, then by his ministers. It emphasizes that Geneva would only be a very small gain for Savoy. As for the passage of the Swiss, that could no longer present any difficulty since the King was in possession of Bresse. France had nothing to lose or to gain; but, if Geneva was annexed to Savoy, she would deserve well of the Church and of an exiled Bishop, and that without spending any money or taking up arms, provided she remained neutral and at least allowed the enterprise to be carried out.[2] The papal letters of which Corona was the bearer likewise prove that Gregory XV. would have been quite satisfied with such an attitude.[3]

Louis XIII. was not averse to a policy of neutrality, but

---

[1] See the *Briefs, *ibid.*, 505 seq.

[2] See *Instruttione al padre Don Tobia Corona*, City Library, Frankfurt a/M., and State Archives, Florence.

[3] See the Briefs to Louis XIII. July 16, 1621, in the *Quellen zur schweiz. Gesch.*, XXI., 507.

Luynes and the other ministers strongly opposed it.¹ Now, as before, the Paris Cabinet attached the utmost importance to the inviolability of the western gate of Switzerland as it was on the high road between the Confederation and France. Nor did they wish to infringe the treaty with the Protestant Cantons. For these reasons Gregory XV.'s fresh efforts in Paris were in vain.² To avoid offending the Pope, Corona was courteously told that the time for such an undertaking had not yet arrived; if Charles Emmanuel wished to risk a surprise attack, the King of France might give his approval once the deed was done, but he could not take an active part in it and thus betray the confidence of the Genevese.³ But the ambassador of Savoy was plainly told that if his master attacked Geneva he would come up against the armed opposition of France.⁴

If the wreck of his plan against Geneva annoyed Gregory XV., the menacing situation in the Valtellina caused him even greater anxiety.⁵

Even before the conclusion of the Peace of Madrid became known, Cardinal Ludovisi had pointed out that, in his experience, Spanish ministers did not easily give up their plans.⁶ In point of fact it became increasingly evident that the Spaniards were successfully intriguing against the execution of the Madrid Treaty. Feria was indefatigably active in every direction. All the efforts of the nuncio, Scappi, to make the Treaty of Madrid acceptable to the seven Cantons by means of the additions which guaranteed Catholic interests

---

¹ See the *Instruction for Campeggi, quoted above, p. 206, note 3.

² *Cf.* the Briefs of August 28 and 30, 1621, in the *Quellen zur schweiz. Gesch.*, XXI., 518 *seq.*

³ See the *Instruction for Campeggi, above, p. 206, note 3.

⁴ See ROTT, *Représent. diplom.*, III., 451; CARUTTI, *Storia d. dipl. di Savoia*, II., 234.

⁵ He addressed a further appeal to Louis XIII. in a *Brief of October 21, 1621, see *Quellen zur schweiz. Gesch.*, XXI., 524 *seq.*

⁶ *Letter of Agucchi to the Spanish nuncio of May 10, 1621, quoted in ZELLER, *Richelieu*, 35.

in the Grisons and the Valtellina, were in vain, although he had the support of the French ambassador. By its secret intrigues, Spanish diplomacy successfully persuaded the Catholic Cantons to decline the guarantee for the execution of the Treaty, as " a very dangerous matter ".[1] Now Spain had made this acceptance the condition of her own ratification of the Treaty : she was therefore freed from her promise. Gregory did his best to appease the excitement to which this manœuvre gave rise in France ; unfortunately the Venetians worked against him, for they were doing everything in their power to stir up the Paris cabinet against Spain.[2]

In October, 1621, the revolutionary party in the Grisons, in which the agitator George Jenatsch was again prominent, attempted the so-called " march on Worms ". This ill-considered and defiant invasion gave Feria and the Archduke Leopold a much desired pretext to move their troops from the south, north and east. On November 22nd, 1621, Chur, the capital city, was occupied. The Pope's first hopes that the conquerors would show moderation were not fulfilled.[3] The latter had not the slightest intention of forgoing the advantages they had secured. Both Venice and Paris viewed with anxiety the increase of Austro-Spanish power. The Catholic districts, whose ambassadors came to do homage to the new Pope on November 18th, 1621,[4] seemed not unwilling to consider the claims of Archduke Leopold in the Grisons, but they were opposed to the Spanish occupation of the Valtellina.[5] Gregory XV. considered the danger of war to be so great that at the close of the year he commissioned his nuncio in Madrid to declare to the Spanish Government

---

[1] See ABSCHIEDE, V., 2, 211 ; REINHARDT, *Korrespondenz Casali*, 51 seq.

[2] See the *report of PAOLO SAVELLI to the Emperor Ferdinand II, dated Rome, September 18, 1621, State Archives, Vienna.

[3] See the *letter of Agucchi to the Spanish nuncio, November 26, 1621, in *Cod.* 33 D. 23, Corsini Library, Rome.

[4] See *Quellen zur schweiz. Gesch.*, XXI., 630 seq. ; cf. REINHARDT, *Korrespondenz Casali*, 79.

[5] See REINHARDT, 87.

that if war actually broke out, the Pope would bear in mind that he was not only the universal father of Christendom but also an Italian temporal ruler.[1]

The need to carry out the threat never arose, inasmuch as a completely new situation was created for the Pope when Feria, in agreement with Archduke Leopold, succeeded in mid-January, 1622, in compelling the Grisons to accept the so-called Articles of Milan. In accordance with these the Grisons were compelled to renounce their claims to the Valtellina and to Bormio and to keep their passes open ; in return they received back Chiavenna, and Spain guaranteed to them an annuity of 25,000 crowns. The Protestants of the Valtellina were to leave the country within two months. The valley of Münster, the Lower Engadine, Davos and Prättigau fell to Austria. A number of ordinances safeguarded the interests of the Bishop of Chur and the Catholic Church.[2] Rome was under no delusions as to the significance of the treaty against which France had lodged a protest [3]; on the other hand it was impossible to oppose it because, as Cardinal Ludovisi explained to Corsini, the Paris nuncio, it was their duty to prefer the interests of religion to those of politics.[4] The Pope, so Ludovisi wrote to the French nuncio on February 10th, 1622, pursued a twofold aim in the whole business, viz. the preservation of the Catholic religion and the maintenance of peace. With regard to the first point, the Milan Articles were adequate and could be sanctioned by the Holy See ; with regard to the second, everything depended on whether the Articles threatened the peace.[5] The Bishop of Chur, the nuncio and the Pope himself, insisted that the

[1] See the *letter of Agucchi to the Spanish nuncio, December 31, *loc. cit.*

[2] See ABSCHIEDE, V., 2, 2035 *seq.* ; ROTT, *Représent. dipl.*, III., 500 *seq.*

[3] See ROTT, III., 503 *seq.*

[4] See the *letter of Agucchi to Corsini, January 24, 1622, in *Cod.* X., VI., 16, Casanatense Library, Rome.

[5] See the French translation of Agucchi's letter of February 10, 1622, in ZELLER, *Richelieu*, 47 *seq.*

government of Archduke Leopold should make use of the right of reformation in the newly acquired territories and restore religious uniformity.[1] In consequence, Protestant services were forbidden in the Lower Engadine and in Prättigau, whilst the churches that had been confiscated and desecrated were restored. Capuchins were called in to instruct the people and Gregory XV. granted them very extensive faculties.[2] Among them Father Fidelis of Sigmaringen particularly distinguished himself.[3] Born in 1578,[4] he began by practising the law at Ensisheim, in Alsace; in 1611 he entered the monastery of the Capuchins at Altdorf and became a preacher and confessor, first at Rheinfelden, then at Freiburg in the Üchtland and after 1621 at Feldkirch. As a genuine follower of S. Francis, he won universal esteem by his strict life and his self-sacrificing conduct during various epidemics; by his fervent preaching he brought many Calvinists back to the Church but he was opposed to the use of force in order to effect conversion. At Zizers he obtained the conversion of Count Rudolf Andreas Salis and other Protestants, and he met with similar success at Maienfeld and Malans.[5]

In the Prättigau, however, the success of Father Fidelis was but slender, for there a fanatical population offered a determined resistance to the Catholic restoration. On April 24th, 1622, an insurrection broke out in which bloody revenge was taken for the excesses of the Austrian mercenaries. Within a few hours the peasants of Schiers, Grüsch and Seewis slew 350 persons with their iron-weighted clubs. The defenceless Fidelis of Sigmaringen, who had only just escaped being

[1] See *Bull. Capuc.*, II., 352; ROCCO DA CESINALE, II., 77. Even the Protestant pastor, D. A. LUDWIG ("Der Versuch der Gegenreformation im Unterengadin und im Prättigau Anno 1621/2", in the *Jahresbericht der hist.-antiquarischen Gesellschaft von Graubünden*, Coire, 1906, 143) grants that Archduke Leopold only used his right.

[2] See v. SCALA, *Fidelis von Sigmaringen*, 96.

[3] *Cf.* the authentic account of P. ALEXIUS, in *Anal. Capuc.*, XIV., and the fine monograph by P. SCALA.

[4] See PAULUS in *Katholik*, 1896, I., 286 seq.

[5] See v. SCALA, 111 seq.

shot in the pulpit, was attacked and murdered by a band of Calvinist soldiers on the road from Seewis to Grüsch.[1] Only a few days earlier nuncio Scappi, in the name of Propaganda and in conjunction with the Provincial Chapter of the Capuchins, had appointed him Prefect of the mission in the Grisons,[2] whose proto-martyr he now became.

The success of the Prättigau insurrection was short-lived. Instead of confining themselves to defence the Grisons took the offensive, sacked the villages along the road to Feldkirch and pressed on towards Montafon. The Austrian offensive, which began in August, put an end to these raids and led to the complete subjugation of the Grisons, where the Capuchins now resumed their missionary activities. On September 30th, 1622, the men of the Grisons were compelled to accept the Capitulation of Lindau, which laid on them almost the same conditions as the Milan Articles.[3]

This increase of Austro-Spanish influence in the Rhetian Alps to which Gregory XV., though he maintained his neutrality, attached the greatest importance because of the advantages [4] that would accrue from it to the Catholic restoration,[5] caused France to throw off the restraint which had been

[1] *Ibid.*, 145 seq.; *cf.* MAYER, II., 231. Fidelis of Sigmaringen, the proto-martyr of the Capuchin Order and of Propaganda, was canonized by Benedict XIV. in 1746. His body was translated to the cathedral of Chur, his head was placed in a special chapel of the Capuchin church at Feldkirch; in the convent there, where he had been Guardian shortly before his death, his cell has been preserved.

[2] The *letters of the Provincial and the nuncio, April 21, 1622, in *Annal. prov. Helvet.*, *1613-1633*, are in the Archives of the Capuchin convent of Wesemlin, near Lucerne; trans. by SCALA, 120 *seq.*

[3] See ROBBI, *Urkunden des Staatsarchivs des Kantons Graubünden* (*Jahresber. der Hist.-antiquarischen Gesellschaft Graubünden*, 1914); DIERAUER, II., 482 *seq.* For the activities of the Capuchins see MAYER, II., 232 *seq.*

[4] *Cf.* Savelli's report, September 17, 1622, in SCHNITZER, *Zur Politik des Heiligen Stuhles*, 167.

[5] *Cf.* Agucchi's letter, August 9, 1622, in ZELLER, *Richelieu*,

forced upon her mainly by the war against the Huguenots. On 18th October, Louis XIII. signed a treaty of peace with them at Montpellier, so as to enable him to take up with greater energy the question of the Valtellina.[1] The plan for a coalition between France, Venice and Savoy now took concrete shape. In view of the seriousness of the situation the Paris nuncio, Corsini, suggested that the object of the conflict should be handed over to the Duke of Lorraine on condition that the garrisons were composed of Catholic troops. Spain let it be known that no objections would be raised to Swiss Catholics or even to papal soldiers.[2]

From this it was only one step to the old proposal now raised anew by Spain (in December, 1622), viz. that the Valtellina should be temporarily handed over to the care of the Holy See, and that it should be occupied by papal troops until Gregory XV. could arrive at a final solution of the problem.[3] The Pope, who knew only too well what a thankless task it is to act as intermediary between two rivals, had until then shrunk from such a plan.[4] Now that the situation was changed, he considered that he could no longer refuse the burden since the peace of the Catholic world was at stake.[5] If he still hesitated, he had good reasons—for he wished to make sure that France would be satisfied with this solution.[6] With a view to promoting the plan, Cardinal Ludovisi informed Paris, through the nuncio Corsini, that the new director of Spanish policy, the Duke Olivares, who had come to power

142 seq. The resolution of Propaganda to send two missionaries to the Valtellina, is mentioned in *Avviso, October 19, 1622, *Urb*. 1092, Vatican Library.

[1] See Corsini's report, November 23, 1622, in ZELLER, *Luynes*, 140.

[2] See *Agucchi's letter to Corsini, dated Rome, October 24, 1622, *Cod*. D. V., 31, of the Casanatense Library, Rome.

[3] See ZELLER, *Richelieu*, 183; AREZIO, *Politica*, 16.

[4] *Cf.* SIRI, V., 477.

[5] *Cf.* the postscript to the Instruction of the nuncio extraordinary, the Archbishop of Thebes, in *Archiv für schweiz. Gesch.*, XII. (1858), 194.

[6] See ZELLER, *Richelieu*, 183 seq.

after the death of Baldassare de Zúñiga, would not put up any longer with Feria's tergiversations, that, on the contrary, he was determined to see this interminable conflict settled once for all.[1] The French ambassador in Madrid reported to the same effect. The Paris cabinet now declared itself ready to give serious consideration to the proposal, but insisted, notwithstanding Corsini's objections, on first informing its allies, especially the Venetians. Louis XIII. formally declared to the nuncio that he was agreeable to the Pope's arbitration and that he would send Sillery, his ambassador in Rome, the necessary authority for further negotiations. But should the Spaniards refuse a compromise, war was inevitable.[2] How little Paris trusted the good faith of the Spaniards was shown by the concentration of troops in Dauphiné and the continued negotiations for a league with those Italian States that were independent of Spain. On February 7th, 1623, an offensive and defensive alliance between France and the old enemies of Spain, Savoy and Venice, was concluded; it is known by the name of the League of Lyons and its object was to drive the Spaniards out of the Valtellina. Each of the signatories bound himself

[1] " La morte di Baldassare Zunica," it is stated in the *letter of November 22, 1622 (*Cod.* X., VI., 16, of the Casanatense Library, Rome) " se ben per altro sarà facilmente il pregiuditio alla Monarchia Spagnuola, quanto alle cose della Valtellina non apporterà se non giovamento per finirle. Perchè egli era lungo e tenace e troppo rispettuoso, conosceva che sarebbe stato mestieri levare il Duca di Feria da Milano per assettar questo negotio, o di moderare la sua autorità, ma per non disgustare et innimicarsi li suoi parenti e partiali, lasciava correre ; il conte d'Olivares, che ha la somma de'negotii et è succeduto nel luogo di detto D.n Baldassare, et ha di più tutto il favor del Re, è huomo libero e risoluto, che non havrà tanto rispetto, e s'è dichiarato con i nostri, che la vuol finire, non parendoli bene di tener più lungamente Sua Maestà intrigata in questo negotio, onde se si verrà ad accordo alcuno, si potrà havere assai maggior speranza, che esso lo farà eseguire, e questo è appunto importante, che dovrebbe far maggiormente inclinare i Francesi ad accomodarsi."

[2] See ZELLER, *Richelieu*, 184.

to raise an army. At the same time negotiations were begun with the Dutch States General; it was even proposed to secure the services of the condottiere Count Mansfeld, with the object of conquering Spanish Franche-Comté![1]

Faced with these threats, Spain, which had made fresh difficulties, now resolved to yield. On February 14th, 1623, a convention was signed between Olivares in the name of Philip IV., and the nuncio, Innocent de' Massimi, as representing Gregory XV., by the terms of which the fortresses of the Valtellina and the county of Chiavenna were, for the time being, to be handed over to the Pope, whose troops would occupy them until a final agreement was reached between France and Spain.[2]

Thereupon Gregory XV. took prompt action. As early as February 23rd, he thanked Philip IV. in a flattering letter in Italian, with an autograph postscript, and informed him that he had commissioned his brother, the Duke of Fiano, General of the Church, to lead the papal troops into the Valtellina. In a Brief of February 24th, he once more thanked Philip IV. and begged him to see to it that his orders should be promptly carried out, for the " sons of darkness " who sought to create dissensions among princes were not asleep.[3]

At first the Paris cabinet viewed these measures with marked coldness: hence the nuncio Corsini was repeatedly instructed to urge France by every means in his power to give her assent.[4] The Republic of St. Mark showed open hostility; in Paris it opposed the Pope's intervention, whilst at Rome its ambassador indulged in violent language against the

[1] See SIRI, V., 448 seq.; ABSCHIEDE, V., 2, 2106 seq.; ZWIEDINECK-SÜDENHORST, Politik Venedigs, I., 241 seq.; ZELLER, Richelieu, 187 seq.; ROTT, Représent. dipl., III., 592 seq.

[2] See LÜNIG, Cod. dipl. ital., IV., 317; SIRI, V., 459 seq.; ZELLER, Richelieu, 190; ROTT, III., 601 seq.

[3] Both letters in the Quellen zur Schweiz. Gesch., XXI., 531 seq., 534 seq. Cf. ROTT, III., 607, and AREZIO, Politica, 18. See also Agucchi's *letter to Corsini, March 13, 1623, Casanatense Library, Rome, loc. cit.

[4] See ZELLER, Richelieu, 250.

clergy[1] and practically insulted Cardinal Ludovisi.[2] Savoy also was opposed to the plan [3] and in the meantime the allies could not agree amongst themselves. Louis XIII.'s chancellor, Nicolas Brulart de Sillery, shrank from war with Spain, and the French ambassador in Rome withdrew his opposition.[4] Thus Gregory XV. began to hope for a happy end to the struggle between France and Spain, and for a complete Catholic restoration in the Valtellina. On April 5th, 1623, Orazio Ludovisi, escorted by a brilliant retinue, set out for Civitavecchia where two days later he took boat for Genoa.[5] After celebrating Easter at Milan he was to join the troops which were being assembled in the district round Ferrara.[6] His intention was to return to Rome as soon as the Valtellina

[1] See Agucchi's *letter to Corsini, March 20, 1623. Casanatense Library, Rome, *loc. cit.* *Cf.* ZWIEDINECK-SÜDENHORST, *loc. cit.*, II., 111.

[2] See SIRI, V., 468.

[3] *Cf.* AREZIO, *Politica,* 22 *seq.*

[4] See ZELLER, *Richelieu,* 251.

[5] See the *letter from Agucchi, on behalf of Ludovisi, to Corsini, April 14, 1623, Casanatense Library, Rome, *loc. cit.*, and the *Brief addressed to Feria, April 3, 1623, in the *Quellen zur Schweiz. Gesch.*, XXI., 535 *seq.* A *Brief addressed to Card. Medici, also of April 3, 1623, with regard to Ludovisi's mission, is in *Arm.*, XLV., 21, Papal Secret Archives. The *Istruzione al sig. duca di Fiano destinato a pigliare il deposito a nome della Sede Ap. delli forti della Valtellina,* dated Rome, April 5, 1623, is in *Cod.*, X., IV., 38, p. 39 *seq.*, of the Casanatense Library, Rome. Other copies are in *Cod.* 470, p. 375 *seq.* of the Corsini Library, Rome; in the Library at Parma; in *Cod. Marucell.*, C. 29, Florence; *Cod.* 1257 of the Ossoliniana Library, Lemberg and in the Library at Ferrara, but in this MS. the date is incorrect. The Instruction is printed after a MS. of the State Library, Vienna, in *Archiv für schweiz. Gesch.*, XII. (1858), 221 *seq.* For Orazio Ludovisi's journey from Rome to Milan, see *Cod.* E. 83 of the Boncompagni Archives, Rome. According to Giunti there were, in Ludovisi's train " molti baroni e altre persone gravi et avedute " *Vita del card. Ludovisi,* Corsini Library, Rome.

[6] *Cf.* *Avviso di Roma,* April 1, 1623, *Urb.* 1093, Vatican Library, Rome.

fortresses should have been handed over. The Marchese Ridolfi had been appointed to take his place ; but in view of the fact that the latter was suspected of being a Hispanophil, his place was taken by the Marchese Del Bagno out of consideration for the French.[1]

The assent of France, awaited with so much anxiety in Rome, had been given by mid-April, notwithstanding Venice's effort to prevent it,[2] on condition that the papal verdict should be pronounced before July 31st. The news reached Rome at the beginning of May. Feria's obstinate opposition, however, had still to be overcome. Since that wily personage could not act openly against his orders from Madrid, he had recourse to various manœuvres, though without success. Vienna and Savoy also ended their opposition.[3]

Towards the end of May, Orazio Ludovisi entered the Valtellina at the head of the papal troops. With a view to removing all grounds for mistrust the Pope had seen to it that the troops consisted exclusively of men from the papal States.[4] At the beginning of June Ludovisi occupied the forts of Morbegno, Tirano, Bormio, Torre di Bagni, Chiappin, Platemala and Sondrio.[5] Chiavenna and Riva, which did not belong to the Valtellina, were retained by the Spaniards. This drew a protest from the French ambassador in view of the strategic importance of these places. Cardinal Ludovisi tried in vain to pacify him.[6] Paris also resented the fact that

[1] See ZELLER, *Richelieu*, 250.

[2] See R. ZENO in BAROZZI-BERCHET, *Italia*, I., 189. *Cf.* ZWIEDINECK-SÜDENHORST, II., 11 seq.

[3] See ROTT, *Représent. dipl.*, III., 613 ; AREZIO, *Politica*, 38 seq. The *Brief of May 9, 1623, in the *Quellen zur Schweiz. Gesch.*, XXI., 526 seq., shows with what diplomatic skill Gregory XV. handled Feria.

[4] See Agucchi's *letter to Corsini, April 12, 1623, Casanatense Library, Rome, *loc. cit.*

[5] See SIRI, V., 506 ; ROTT, III. 615 ; AREZIO, *Politica*, 43 seq. ; numerous *letters from Card. Ludovisi to O. Ludovisi, Duke of Fiano ; a *letter of the latter concerning the Valtellina of 1623, are in *Cod.* E. 83, of the Boncompagni Archives, Rome.

[6] See ZELLER, *Richelieu*, 254.

the cost of the occupation of the forts, which proved far in excess of estimates, so that the Pope could not bear it alone, was largely met by Spain. Gregory XV., in order to eliminate every cause of jealousy, suggested that the expenses should be equally divided between Spain and France.[1] The dispute was eventually settled by Spain agreeing to maintain secrecy about the fact that she was providing the money.[2]

With regard to a definitive settlement of the Valtellina question, the Pope had for a long time maintained the principle that in no case were the Valtellina Catholics to become the subjects of Protestant overlords, whereas the French ambassador insisted that, on the basis of the Treaty of Madrid the sovereignty of the Grisons should be restored. On this point there arose some very lively discussions. When Sillery referred to France's old relations with the Grisons, and declared that Louis XIII. must take thought for his reputation, Ludovisi answered that the Pope was under far greater obligations to protect a Catholic people. To do so was a duty not only of honour, but of conscience.[3] This attitude Gregory XV. maintained up to the last. There were only two alternatives, Ludovisi explained: either all the Grisons should become Catholic, which humanly speaking, could hardly be expected, or the Valtellina would constitute itself into a fourth Federation which would be affiliated to the other three Rhetian Federations on equal terms.[4] This,

[1] See the *letter of Agucchi to Corsini, June 23, 1623. It is stated here: " La spesa è molto maggiore di quel che da principio si credette; poichè importerà il primo anno a almeno trecento mila scudi andandoci di paghe et utensile, scudi venti mila il mese senza le spese ordinarie, non possiamo in maniera nessuna sostenerla " (Casanatense Library, Rome, *loc. cit.*) *Cf.* AREZIO, *Politica,* 25, 41 *seq.,* 44, 46.

[2] See the *Relatione d. Nunziat. di Francia fatta da Msgr. arcivescovo di Tarso* (O. Corsini) of October 27, 1623, Casanatense Library, Rome, X., V., 15.

[3] See *Agucchi's letter to Corsini of May 21, 1623, Casanatense Library, Rome, *loc. cit.*, partly translated by ZELLER, *Richelieu,* 55 *seq.*

[4] See *Agucchi's letter of May 24, 1623, *loc. cit.*

however, did not solve the question of the mountain passes : Cardinal Ludovisi, in opposition to the claims of the French, intended to decide it in favour of Spain.[1] In so doing Ludovisi was not actuated, as has been suspected,[2] by the hope of realizing certain family ambitions with the help of Spain : the Cardinal simply argued that in the interests of the Catholic restoration in Germany, military communications between Spain and Austria should not be wholly cut off. For that reason the pass over the Worms Joch and the Valtellina should remain open to the Spaniards, to enable them to throw troops into Germany, though not that they should send armed forces into Italy.[3] Agreement on this point was not yet reached when Gregory XV.'s death supervened. Though the dispute was not finally settled, the Pope could die with the conviction that he had done his best to preserve the peace between France and Spain and to ensure the safety of the Catholics of the Valtellina, in the consciousness also that his appointment as arbitrator had enhanced the prestige of the Holy See.[4]

(2.)

It was necessary to prevent war between Spain and France, because its outbreak would have imperilled the work of ecclesiastical restoration begun in France under Paul V. and which Gregory XV. had greatly at heart. The first duty of the new French nuncio, Ottavio Corsini, as indicated in his

[1] See ZELLER, *Richelieu*, 256.
[2] *Ibid.*, 262.
[3] RANKE (*Päpste*, II.⁶, 330) rightly emphasizes this, quoting Article 9 of the draft of the Convention.
[4] BROSCH (I., 379) is of opinion that " the Ludovisi had utilized the papal military forces to attain distinctly ecclesiastical ends. Thanks to these measures, Gregory XV. appeared in the rôle of confidant of all the Catholic Powers and as the longed-for keeper of the pledge for the possession of which the nations quarrelled. It was an undoubted success which enhanced the prestige of the Church and its Head."

Instruction of April 4th, 1621,[1] was the amelioration of ecclesiastical discipline, a matter of the greatest importance if France was to recover complete unity of faith. The means to that end are discussed in detail.

Since ecclesiastical discipline depends primarily on the worthiness of the Bishops, the nuncio's first care was to induce the King to nominate only good pastors for the flock. Those whose faith was under suspicion, or who required dispensations, as well as men whose scholarship or moral conduct was unsatisfactory, or who had indulged in simoniacal practices must be rigorously banned. As soon as a see became vacant, the nuncio must make inquiries about the candidates and prevent the grave abuse by which stewards were appointed for a vacant see the revenues of which were granted to lay persons and even to women and children. This abuse must be abolished also where monastic houses were concerned.[2] To this abuse, as well as to the infringement of ecclesiastical jurisdiction, to appeals *ab abusu* and similar actions, the misfortunes of France must be ascribed.

Good Bishops, the Instruction proceeds, would appoint good parish priests and would reform the clergy. The nuncio should press the Bishops in this sense and above all else urge them to give their clergy a sound training. He must also insist on the ordinaries visiting their dioceses and on their forwarding the work of the reform of the clergy by their personal good example. The duty of residence is particularly inculcated.

[1] See *Nunziat. di Francia*, Papal Secret Archives, LVII.; also in the State Library, Vienna (on which is based the printed version in *Archiv für Schweiz. Gesch.*, XII. (1858), 194 seq.; in *Cod.* 38, A. 4, of the Corsini Library, Rome, and in *Barb.* 4931, p. 1 seq.; Vatican Library. Here and in the following *Cod.* 18 and 19, *Lettere di Msgr. O. Corsini Nunzio in Francia, 1621/3. Cf.* the reports of Corsini below, p. 224, note 2. The *Lettere di Msgr. Corsini al Nunzio di Venezia 1621/3*, in *Ottob.* 3219, Vatican Library. A collection of letters from Corsini to several persons in Rome, 1621–31 (two vols.) is indicated in Catalogue 7 of the Munich Antiquary, Jacques Rosenthal, under no. 1089.

[2] *Cf.* four these bases our account, Vol. XXIII., 150.

The Instruction lays great stress on the reform of the regular clergy in France which, by its opposition to the representatives of the Holy See, and even to their own superiors, had incurred grave guilt, especially since it sought the support of the government and Parliament for its irregularities. This resistance had frustrated the visitation of the Dominicans of Paris by Cardinal Agostino Galamina as well as another attempt by the General of the Celestines. The spirit of insubordination had affected even the Capuchins who refused to obey both their superiors and the papal legate. The expedient devised under Paul V., by which the King appointed a Congregation without right of appeal, had been rejected by that Pope, for thereby superiors would have been deprived of their rights and any appeal to the Holy See would have been precluded.

The Instruction bestows the highest praise upon the French Jesuits whose discipline outshone that of all other Orders and who displayed the utmost zeal on behalf of the Catholic religion. They could be of the greatest assistance to the nuncio seeing they were held in great esteem and laboured with extraordinary fervour. Let the nuncio support their efforts and cultivate good relations with the King's confessor, Fr. Arnoux. But he must not allow himself to get completely under the influence of the Jesuits, lest he should give rise to jealousies. Corsini was also directed to restrain the Jesuits from raising dangerous controversies in the present situation concerning papal authority and the Bull *in Coena Domini*, for such disputes might harm both the Holy See and the Society itself. For this reason no Jesuit was to publish anything on this matter before it had been examined in Rome and declared opportune.

Great caution is recommended to the nuncio in respect to the Sorbonne, which he should try to win over to the Holy See by treating its members with friendliness and respect. It should be his particular care to prevent relations between the Sorbonne and the Jesuits from becoming even more strained than they were. The Instruction touches more than once on the need of supervising literary publications. The

King must be urged to supress harmful books. But good books also, which were foolish enough to provoke disputes and quarrels, must not be allowed to appear; especially should all writings intended as replies to the Calvinists be carefully censored. The Concordat must be conscientiously observed.

One long-standing and ardent desire of the Holy See concerned the recognition of the reform decrees of the Council of Trent, which had always met with opposition on the part of the Gallican officials.[1] The decrees had indeed been received at the last assembly of the States General but their execution had been committed to the Bishops at their diocesan synods. Accordingly the nuncio was to get in touch with Cardinal Rochefoucauld and with Richelieu, Bishop of Luçon. If he succeeded in satisfactorily settling this matter, on which ecclesiastical discipline depended, he would give boundless joy to the Pope. With regard to the elimination of Calvinism from France, the Instruction places great hope in King Louis XIII., who was then on the point of taking up arms against the Huguenots, in answer to the provocations of their preachers. In conclusion the Instruction stresses the fact that as Head of the Church, the Pope had the care of all the nations, but that it was natural that he should especially love and honour those princes and peoples who gave proof of a genuinely Catholic spirit. That was why he cherished a paternal affection for Louis XIII. His one wish was that the whole kingdom should share the King's disposition and that the portion of the realm still given over to Calvinism, namely one-fifteenth of the whole, should not be lost.[2]

[1] *Cf.* our account, Vol. XXIII., 151, 154, 166 *seq.*
[2] " La S.S. è tutta piena d'una voglia ardente tanto di mostrarsi apparentemente di essere in fatti vero padre et pastore commune, senza che nè i prencipi nè i popoli habbiano da discernere in S.B. distinzione d'affetto inclinato più ad una nazione che ad un'altra, e più partiale di quel prencipe chè di questo. Conosce nondimeno S.S. di essere tenuta a corrispondere alla virtù e religione e pietà di ciascuno, secondo ch'ella è maggiore o minore, e per questa cagione è obbligata ad amare, siccome ama con singolare tenerezza la Maestà del Re, e li suoi più congiunti, e

When, in May, 1621, Louis XIII. took up arms against the Huguenot rebels, Gregory XV. supported him actively by word and deed.[1] We still possess a number of letters from the Pope to the King on the course of the war.[2] The fortunes of the

---

vorrebbe che tutta la Francia fosse imitatrice vera della N.S., acciochè nella diletione non havesse a separare mai per brevissimo intervallo il rè dal regno, ritiene intanto S.S. nella mente li christianissimi e non meno antichissimi meriti di quella corona e natione con la Sede Apostolica, e ne gode nel Signore, ma sospira dall'altro lato quella primiera e costante fede e divotione, e non brama in una cosa più, che di vedere tutti i populi ritornati alla l'figliale obbedienza di S.S., acciochè una quindecima parte dell' anime francesi, che si porta opinione essere occupate dalla peste et heresia, non si perda, e non s'offendi la gloria di quella natione, che vincitrice dell'altre pare che venga poi preda in si sconcia maniera delle proprie sensualità e passioni." Papal Secret Archives, loc. cit.

[1] Cf. Bull., XII., 572 seq., 579 seq., 580 seq., 583 seq. The *Instruttione a Msgr. arcivescovo di Seleucia, Msgr. Donazetti, auditore di Rota, destinato vicelegato in Avignone, April 13, 1621 (Casanatense Library, Rome, X., V., 14; Cod. XI., G. 35 of the National Library, Naples, and Cod. 1257 of the Ossoliniana Library, Lemberg) points out the importance of Avignon as a bulwark against the Huguenots.

[2] Cf. the *Briefs to Louis XIII., June 12, 1621 (Brief of praise); September 4, 1621 (he is to set out against the Prince of Orange); to Henricus Borbonius, princ. de Condé, January 22, 1622 (praise); to Louis XIII., May 21, 1622 (congratulations on a naval victory which he ascribes to the intercession of St. Ignatius); XLV., 22 and 24, Papal Secret Archives. Cf. also the reports of Corsini, in *Registro delle lettere scritte da Msgr. O. Corsini nella nunziat. di Francia 1621-3, Cod. 990 seqq., of the Corsini Library, Rome, and the *Registro di lettere di M. Agucchi scritte per il card. Ludovisi in risposta a Msgr. Corsini nuntio in Francia, Cod. X., VI., 16-17, of the Casanatense Library, Rome, used by ZELLER, Le connétable de Luynes, in which there are also extracts from Corsini's Relatione (p. 1 seq., 286 seq.). This report, dated October 27, 1623, is in Barb. 5891, pp. 488-513, Vatican Library, and in the Casanatense Library, Rome. Cf. above, p. 219, note 2.

conflict were varied and none too brilliant.¹ It came to an end in October, 1622, with the peace concluded at Montpellier, by the terms of which the Edict of Nantes remained in force, though all political meetings were forbidden and the only places of refuge conceded to the Huguenots were Montauban and La Rochelle. Henceforth the power of these heretics began to wane; time came when nobles and commoners, learned and unlearned, returned to the ancient Church.² This step was taken, even before the end of the war, by one of France's most famous captains, viz. Marshal the Duke de Lesdiguières, Lieutenant of Dauphiné, who had always shown great kindness to Catholics and who had congratulated Gregory XV. on his elevation to the Chair of St. Peter. In July, 1622, he made his profession of the Catholic faith in the church of St. Andrew of Grenoble, in presence of the Bishop of the diocese and the Bishop of Embrun. His brother-in-law went to Rome to carry the happy information to Gregory XV. who, on one occasion, whilst acting as legate in France,³ had expressed to Lesdiguières his hopes for his conversion. In his answer to Lesdiguières' letter, the Pope declared that the Catholic religion in France had gained less by the conquest of enemy cities and the occupation of hostile fortresses, than by the high-minded action of so famous a captain which was equivalent to the courage of a whole army.⁴ The Pope's joy was further increased when Louis XIII. made Lesdiguières Connétable of France.⁵ In the previous year a well known Calvinist preacher, Bocquet, had made his profession of faith in the hands of the Capuchin Athanasius Molé, in Paris. Bocquet had a printed circular sent to all the Calvinist

---

¹ *Cf.* DE MEAUX, *La Réforme*, II., 179 *seq.*; -ZELLER, *Le connétable de Luynes*, 63 *seq.*, 85 *seq.*

² *Cf.* RANKE, *Päpste*, II., 311.

³ *Cf.* our account, Vol. XXV., 422.

⁴ The Brief to Lesdiguières is of December 3, 1622 (XLV., 224, Papal Secret Archives) and is printed in the rare work, *Recueil des briefs envoyez par N. St. Père le pape Grégoire XV. à Monseigneur et dame la connéstable des Lesdiguières*, Paris, 1623.

⁵ *Cf.* BENTIVOGLIO, *Memorie*, 312.

preachers in which he explained his reasons for this step.¹ The same Capuchin also brought back to the Church Louise Eugénie de Fontaine who subsequently became Superioress of the first convent of the Visitation in Paris and whose virtues called forth the admiration of St. Vincent de Paul.²

How keenly anxious Gregory XV. was for the publication and execution of the decrees of the Council of Trent in France, may be gathered from the letter which he addressed to Louis XIII. on March 22nd, 1622. Once more the Pope insists that Calvinism must be fought not by force of arms alone but by the reform of the Catholic clergy. The best means for the renewal of the ancient Church was to give practical effect to the Tridentine reforms.³ The Pope also wrote in a similar strain to Henry of Bourbon, to Cardinal Rochefoucauld, Bishop of Metz and to Richelieu, Bishop of Luçon.⁴ The papal Brief was accompanied by a strong covering letter from Cardinal Ludovisi to Louis XIII. The King, we read, might win for himself the title of Restorer of the Christian religion and ecclesiastical discipline, were he to satisfy the Pope's desire with regard to the Tridentine decrees. If he did that he would at the same time confer an immense benefit on his people.⁵ The fact that the French King encouraged the clergy to hold diocesan and provincial synods inspired the hope in Rome that the execution of the decrees of the Council might be obtained in this way.⁶ In a Brief to Cardinal Sourdis,

---

[1] See RÄSS, *Konvertiten*, V., 74 *seq.*, and DUFAYARD, *Lesdiguières*, Paris, 1892.

[2] See RÄSS, V., 172 *seq.*

[3] See the long *letter of March 22, 1622. *Arm.*, XLV., 24, Papal Secret Archives.

[4] These *Briefs in *Arm.*, XLV., 24, *ibia*.

[5] See AGUCCHI, *Registro di Lettere*, in *Cod.* 33 D. 23, Corsini Library, Rome.

[6] See *Lettere di Agucchi scritte per il card. Ludovisio a Msgr. Corsini*, Nunt. in Francia, *Cod.* X., VI., 16, Casanatense Library, Rome.

September 16th, 1622, the Pope returned to this matter.[1] However, all Corsini's exertions were in vain.[2]

By a Bull of October 20th, 1622, the Pope granted Louis XIII.'s wish that the diocese of Paris, which up to that time had been included in the ecclesiastical province of Sens, should be raised to the dignity of a metropolitan Church with Chartres, Meaux and Orléans as suffragan sees.[3] Likewise at the request of the King of France, Gregory XV., by a Brief of April 8th, 1622, empowered Cardinal Rochefoucauld to undertake the reform of the old Orders in France.[4] Among these the Benedictines under Paul V. had already formed themselves into a Congregation named after St. Maurus, the disciple of St. Benedict.[5] A Bull of Gregory XV., May 17th, 1621, confirmed this Congregation, granted to it the privileges of the Cassinese Congregation and named Cardinal Retz its Protector.[6]

In the Spanish Netherlands also the Pope did his utmost to encourage the Catholic reform which was making rapid progress. Besides his anxiety that the door should be closed to religious innovations in those parts, he had greatly at heart the strict execution of the Tridentine decrees and the maintenance of papal jurisdiction. The new nuncio to Brussels, Giovan Francesco Guido del Bagno, Archbishop of Patras, was given the most detailed instructions on these points.[7]

---

[1] See the *Brief to Card. Franc. de Sourdis, September 17, 1622, *Arm.*, XLV., 24, Papal Secret Archives.

[2] See MARTIN, *Gallicanisme*, 392.

[3] *Bull.*, XII., 750 seq. A memory of Paris's dependence on Sens is still preserved in the sadly decayed Hôtel de Sens, not far from the Quai des Célestins and opposite the Île St. Louis.

[4] See PICOT, I., 166, 177; CARDELLA, VI., 138. *Cf.* the biographies of *Rochefoucauld* by P. ROUVIER (Paris, 1645), and P. DE LA MORINIÈRE (Paris, 1646).

[5] *Cf.* our account, Vol. XXVI., 51 seq.

[6] See *Bull.*, XII., 533 seq.; *Freib. Kirchenlexikon*, VIII.[2], 1060.

[7] See CAUCHIE-MAERE, 124 seq., 128 seq.

(3)

Gregory XV. had always been a warm friend of the House of Habsburg[1]; he fully realized how important it was to make good use of the great change which had occurred in favour of the Emperor and the Catholic Church through the suppression of the revolution in Austria.[2] He considered it a sacred duty to restore the ancient Church in the Emperor's domains, especially in Bohemia, to help the Emperor in every way to crush his enemies finally, and by preventing a Protestant majority in the College of Electors, to lessen the danger of a Protestant Emperor. Of the Catholic sentiments of Ferdinand II. he thought so highly that he repeatedly spoke of him as a pillar of the Church in the Empire.[3] Hence he was prepared for any sacrifice which circumstances might require. He would not consider the view of some excessively cautious counsellors who thought that they should wait for further developments; on the contrary, he was of opinion that the victory in Bohemia should be followed up and exploited in a military sense; that the rebellion against the Empire and the Church must be repressed both quickly and completely[4]; and that pecuniary assistance should be granted at once.[5] Gregory's youthful Secretary of State, Cardinal Ludovisi, was wholly at one with the Pope on this question.[6]

As early as February 25th, 1621, a Brief was sent to Ferdinand II. in which the Pope stated that he was quite willing to continue the subsidies already granted by his

---

[1] Cf. the *biography of Carlo Madruzzo in Cod. Mazzetti, 60, of the Communal Library, Trient.

[2] Cf. the *letter to the Spanish nuncio and the King of Spain, June 24, 1621, Cod. 33, D. 23 Corsini Library, Rome.

[3] See ACCARISIUS, *Vita Gregorii XV., lib. III., c. 5, Boncompagni Archives, Rome.

[4] Cf. the *Brief to Wolfgang Wilhelm von Neuburg, March 6, 1621 (State Archives, Munich), translated in the Darmstädter Allg. Kirchenzeitung, 1868, no. 37.

[5] See *ACCARISIUS, loc. cit.

[6] Cf. GIUNTI, *Vita del card. Ludovisi, Corsini Library, Rome.

predecessor.¹ On the same day letters were sent to all the more important Catholic princes of Germany, urgently pressing them to support the cause of the Emperor and the Catholic religion.² At the beginning of March, 1621, Gregory XV. exhorted the Archbishop of Cologne and the Count Palatine, Wolfgang Wilhelm of Neuburg, to fight the rebels with the greatest energy.³ Soon after by means of laudatory Briefs, he also encouraged the members of the League in their efforts to withstand the enemy.⁴ The nuncio, Carlo Carafa, who was dispatched to the Emperor on April 14th, 1621,⁵ was charged

¹ Original in the State Archives, Vienna, *Hofkorresp.*, 11.
² See the *Brief to the Archbishop of Mayence, February 25, 1621, *Epist. Arm.*, XLV., 23, Papal Secret Archives.
³ The *Brief to the Archbishop of Cologne, is dated March 5, that to Neuburg, March 6, 1621. *Ibid.*
⁴ See the *Briefs to the Archbishop of Mayence, April 10, and June 21, 1621, *ibid.*
⁵ An *Avviso of April 14, 1621, *Urb.* 1088, Vatican Library, mentions the departure of Carafa. Misled by RANKE's statement (III.⁶, 133*), everybody has hitherto assumed that Carafa first betook himself to Prague, in May, 1621, and then continued to Vienna. As against that assumption, KOLLMANN (*Acta*, I., 63 seq.) first showed irrefutably from Carafa's letters and other evidence, that the latter first went to Vienna—as was to be expected—and that he did not reach Prague until 1623. The correspondence of Carafa's nunciature, unfortunately only partially preserved, has been well described by PIEPER in *Hist. Jahrbuch*, II., 388 seq. KOLLMANN's *Acta* show important additions. He published two important *Relations* of Carafa's concerning Bohemia, e.g. 1º the *Relatio Bohemica* (*Acta*, I., 93 seq.) which was sent to Propaganda from Vienna on October 8, 1622, and 2º the *Ragguaglio dello stato di religione di Boemia et sue provintie* (ibid., 350 seq.) sent in September, 1623, to Cardinal Barberini, wrongly ascribed by RANKE (III., 133*) to 1624. With this report he sent Cardinal Barberini the *Relatione dello stato presente della Germania (Miscell. Arm.*, III., Cod. 72, pp. 1-84, Papal Secret Archives). This was first shown by PIEPER (*loc. cit.*, 399) ; it was dated October 21, 1623. Besides these documents there was also a *Breve compendio della corte Cesarea* of the same date, which has not been found until now. PIEPER, however, succeeded in finding (*loc. cit.*, 401)

with the direct mission [1] to exhort Ferdinand II. not to lose the *Relatione della riforma del regno di Boemia*, drawn up by Carafa and dated September 25, 1624. Carafa's concluding report, *Relatione dello stato dell'Impero e della Germania*, was published by I. G. Müller, in the *Archiv für österr. Gesch.*, XXIII., 101 *seq*. PIEPER showed that this exists in two versions; the first was sent off in March, 1628, the second enlarged version, at the end of 1628 or the beginning of 1629; this is the one edited by Müller. They agree on all essential points. (PIEPER gives the differences, 411 *seq*.) Finally, there are Carafa's *Commentaria de Germania sacra restaurata*, with an appendix: *Decreta, etc*. Aversae, 1630, Coloniae, 1639, Francofurti, 1641, Viennae, 1748, and 1769. In both these editions the second part, from 1630–35, is lacking. The latter part, first published in the Frankfurt edition of 1641, was transcribed by BURGOS, *De Bello Suecio Commentarii* (published 1633), who utilized the journal of THOMAS CARVE (published 1639) which describes almost exclusively the events of the war. This part, which bears traces of sentiments favourable to the Protestants, was certainly not written by Carafa, for the first part, up to 1628, shows a strong Catholic bias, treats exclusively of the Catholic restoration, and is one of the most important sources for the history of that movement. Even if it was intended for the general public, so that the faults of the Catholics are not mentioned, there is no sign of intentional misrepresentation of facts in their favour; see ANTHENY, *Der päpstliche Nuntius Carafa*, Berlin, 1869 (Program of the Gymnasium zum Grauen Kloster), who arrives at the conclusion (p. 14) that this part is very valuable " because it comes from a man who wrote as an eye-witness, bases himself on trustworthy reports and official documents ". It is regrettable that the *Commentaria* do not always place the decrees chronologically; thus, *e.g.*, the withdrawal of the chalice from the laity is first mentioned in 1623 (p. 186), although it was ordered as early as 1621 and 1622.

[1] The *Instruction, of April 12, 1621, partially quoted by RANKE from a MS. not specified (III.⁶, 119 *seq*.), was used by LÄMMER (*Zur Kirchengeschichte*, 128, and *Melet.*, 462) from the copy in *Cod.* 473, p. 293 *seq.* of the Corsini Library, Rome, and by ANTHENY (*loc. cit.*, 14 *seq*.) from the *Inf. polit.*, XI., p. 259 *seq.* of the State Library, Berlin, who transcribes some passages. Other copies are to be found in the National Library, Paris (*MS. ital.* 10,065, n. 1), in *Cod.* XI., G. 31 of the National Library,

one minute in following up his great victory as rapidly as possible, for in a single hour it had turned aside the most terrible danger and justly raised the most sanguine hopes.[1] Prompt action was essential. Here we have a manifest allusion to the vacillating imperial General Buquoy, of whom even Maximilian was wont to say that the Spanish slowness infected his body.[2] Hence Carafa was to warn the Emperor and his counsellors not to endanger the whole situation by further delay, for relapses are generally worse than the first attack of a disease.[3]

Carafa's Instruction unfolded a full and detailed statement of the measures to be adopted in the political as well as in the religious sphere. Since the Protestants were resolved to bring about the downfall of the House of Austria and the destruction of the Catholic religion in the Empire, means must be taken to ensure that the imperial dignity would remain always in Catholic hands and to preserve and extend the ancient faith in Germany. For this reason, Carafa was to press for the transfer of the Electorate, rendered vacant in consequence of the Palatine, Frederick V., having been put under the ban of Empire, to Duke Maximilian of Bavaria, a staunch Catholic. In this way a Catholic majority in the College of Electors would be assured. At the same time the nuncio was to insist energetically on the

Naples, and in *Cod.* 1257 of the Ossoliniana Library, Lemberg. The best text is in *Barb.* 5232, pp. 1-43. It forms the basis of KOLLMANN's (*Acta*, I., 56 to 62) statements, but he only reproduced in their entirety the passages referring to Bohemia and the person of the nuncio. Carafa's credentials for Eggenberg are dated April 16, 1621 ; the original is in the Herberstein Archives, Eggenberg.

[1] " Dico celeste vittoria che mai si riportasse, poichè da un sommo pericolo si trasportano in poco d'hora le cose in somma speranza di felicità." *Barb.* 5232, Vatican Library.

[2] See HURTER, VIII., 661.

[3] " V.S. perciò solleciterà e stringerà opportunamente Cesare e suoi ministri a non perder il tempo, a non isdegnare con la lentezza l'istessa fortuna, acciò che non si torni a mettere tutto l'Imperio in pericolo, perchè le seconde cadute degli infermi sogliono essere peggiori dei primi mali." *Ibid.*

prosecution of the war against the Protestant rebels. With regard to ecclesiastical conditions in Germany, the Cologne nuncio, Antonio Albergati, had presented to the new Pope a detailed memorandum about the prevailing abuses and their remedies. His conclusion was that the most effective means of all would be the publication and execution of the reform decrees of Trent.[1] This excellent memorandum had a good deal to do with that part of Carafa's Instruction which concerned the state of religion in Germany. Four causes, we read, were responsible for the unhappy ecclesiastical condition of Germany and had probably led to the great apostasy.[2] These were, the bad episcopal elections made by the Canons, the election capitulations, the utterly irresponsible fashion in which Chapters made appointments to the various posts of which they were the patrons, and finally the fact that the Tridentine reforms were not carried out. Accordingly Carafa's first care must be to see to it that good appointments were made whenever an episcopal see became vacant in the Empire, and if unsuitable men were chosen, he was to press the Emperor to refuse the " regalia ". Concerning the bishoprics in the Emperor's hereditary territories and in Hungary, where the Emperor had the right of nomination, the Pope expressed the hope that before all else the abuse of leaving posts unoccupied with a view to applying their revenues to other purposes, would cease. Ecclesiastical jurisdiction must be restored; in this respect not only the Emperor, but the Bishops and the Chapters, had grievously offended in the past. Even more important than this or any other thing was the acceptance and execution of the Tridentine reform decrees which are here styled, as in Albergati's memorandum, the chief remedies for all the ills of the Church in Germany.[3] This must be Carafa's

[1] Concerning this *Memorandum (Vatican Library) see App. no. III.

[2] " *Lo stato degli ecclesiastici è di pessima conditione et forse da mali costumi loro nacquero et crebbero l'heresie." *Barb.* 5232, Vatican Library.

[3] " *Ma il più giovevole rimedio a tutti i mali delle cose ecclesiastiche di Germania sarebbe l'accettatione del concilio di Trento

aim; the reform must be gradually enforced, beginning with the territories of the Emperor, and through the action of the more zealous among the Bishops.

As regards his personal conduct, the nuncio is exhorted to maintain strict discipline in his suite, to accept no gifts,[1] and in his whole behaviour to adapt himself as far as possible to German customs, however different these may be from those of Italy. Since the Germans were not very fond of foreigners, especially of Italians, he should meet them with that charity which does not distinguish between Greeks and Barbarians, and however strange many of their customs may seem to him, let him refrain from any expressions of annoyance and still more from all sarcasm. He should take pains to acquaint himself with the political and religious conditions of Germany and with its history. The more affable the Emperor showed himself, the more should Carafa try to win his confidence and attract to himself the Emperor's favourites, especially Count Eggenberg. He should also make contact with the Emperor's confessor, the Jesuit Becanus, and with the other Jesuits, whilst always combining caution with confidence. Further he was recommended to confer with the ambassadors of the Catholic Powers and to ascertain the aims of the Protestant princes.[2] To the Protestants he must show no hatred, only compassion: he must not repel them, but seek to win them.

The Instruction discusses in great detail the Catholic restoration which had been happily begun, more especially in Austria and in Moravia. In Silesia the Elector of Saxony went at least so far as to refuse to tolerate Calvinism. In Hungary, where the peril was greatest, Protestants must not be granted any more

---

che quei vescovi non hanno mai ricevuto o messo in opera nelle loro diocesi." *Ibid.*

[1] "*Benchè a quello siano i Germani inclinatissimi, ma si odiano sommamente in altri i proprii difetti." *Ibid.*

[2] *Nevertheless the nuncio should find out the true source of information and not allow himself to be deceived, " perchè i Tedeschi sono facili a prestare fede alle novelle et a ridirle." *Barb.* 5232, Vatican Library.

concessions [1]; for the rest he must insist that the Emperor should only appoint Catholics to the higher offices of the State. There fellows a detailed discussion of the means by which the Catholic restoration may be brought about, especially in Bohemia, where it was not enough to apply the axiom: *cujus regio, ejus religio*, but every means of persuasion and instruction, teaching and education should likewise be adopted.

The author of the Instruction sets great hopes on the pious and victorious Ferdinand II. His predecessors had been too ready to give in to the Protestants, to the detriment both of the Pope's authority and their own.[2] The present Emperor could be depended upon to support the efforts of the Holy See. How far-reaching these were appears from the fact that Carafa was specifically commanded to press the Emperor for the restoration of all confiscated ecclesiastical property wherever the reconquest of Protestant districts rendered such recovery possible. This question had already been raised under Paul V. but had been shelved as premature.[3]

[1] " *Rimane a dire alcuna cosa d'Ungheria, provincia forse peggioramente ridotta di quante da qual lato ne siano, poichè la rebellione et l'heresia, Maumettana tirannide fanno a gara per isvellerare quelle poche reliquie della religione cattolica, anzi dell'humanità et fede che ne petti humani erano rimaste. . . . Si teme che S.M.^{tà} non sia per essere costretta a concedere loro la confessione Augustana." He must never allow this and in case of need " dissimulare ". *Ibid.*

[2] " *Ritenendo per loro una maestà più apparente che vera." *Ibid.*

[3] " *Mi rimane nell'ultimo di questo capo di commettere a V.S. d'ordine di N.S. che secondo che si andrano acquistando de paesi tenuti avanti dagli heretici et migliorando negli accordi le conditioni degli ecclesiastici, egli faccia grandissima istanza a S.M. di recuperare beni ecclesiastici occupati da loro et di renderli alle chiese et ai veri padroni. Questo offitio si fe per ordine di P. Paulo quando il marchese di Spinola s'impossessò del Palatinato et l'Imp.^{re} rispose che non era tempo de trattarne. Ma hora che le cose si sono maggiormente assicurate, V.S. tornerà a pregarne efficacemente S.M.^{tà} et le rappresenterà il gran merito che haverà con Dio benedetto e con la Chiesa cattolica se sotto il felice imperio

In the Instruction for Carafa reference is also made to the request already presented by the imperial ambassador, Savelli, for the change of the monthly 20,000 florins into the same number of scudi which would mean an increase of more than double that amount. The concession of a further contribution of 200,000 scudi to be made in one payment was not possible owing to the lack of means; on the other hand the Pope was quite ready to increase his monthly subsidy, but he expressed a wish that the portion of the subsidy exceeding the sums already granted should be used for enlisting pontifical soldiers who would be incorporated in the imperial army under the command of Pietro Aldobrandini. Ferdinand's ambassador, Savelli, was of the opinion that his master would rather have the money than the soldiers. But Gregory XV. attached great importance to the idea that the papal colours should be unfurled in the battle for the Catholic cause. After long negotiations, Savelli, supported by the Spanish ambassador, was able to obtain a subsidy of 20,000 scudi which was to be at the Emperor's free disposal.[1]

di S.M. quasi iure postliminii ella potrà ritornare all'antichissimo possesso de suoi beni, ne V.S. n'abbandonarà l'impresa senza ottenere l'intento e basta fin qui del terzo capo." *Ibid.*

[1] See SCHNITZER, *Zur Politik*, 162, who quotes Savelli's report of September 17, 1622 (State Archives, Vienna). According to the Avviso of May 1, 1621, Pietro Aldobrandini was already at that time preparing for his campaign in Germany. He was also charged with the administration of the subsidies. At the same time the Duke of Zagarolo enlisted five thousand soldiers for the Emperor. According to the Avviso of May 22, 1621, Aldobrandini set out on that day (*Urb.* 1089, Vatican Library). In the Rospigliosi Archives, Rome, I found (1) *Instruttione a Pietro Aldobrandini, luogotenente generale di N.S. per la levata da farsi d'un regimento che N.S. da per aiuto all'Imperatore Ferdinando*; (2) *Instruttione a Matteo Pini, deputato pagatore et collaterale delle genti che si devono mandare in Germania a nome di S.S.^{tà} per servitio dell'Imperatore*, both dated Rome, June 1, 1621. This Instruction is also in *Barb.* 5187, Vatican Library, and in *Cod.* 473 (595) *Miscell. D.* of the University Library, Bologna and in *Cod.* XI., G. 33 of the National Library, Naples.

The notable increase of the subsidy granted to Ferdinand II. roused the jealousy of the representatives in Rome of the League and of Bavaria. There were sharp encounters between them and the Spanish ambassador. The latter maintained that the League should not further importune the Pope; in the preceding year it had received from Italy the sum of 875,000 florins by way of papal subsidies and tithes, and the tenth granted to it in Germany had brought in more than two millions.[1] These statements were considerably exaggerated.[2] Gregory XV. appointed a commission of Cardinals to examine the amount that should be granted to the League. It so happened that on April 21st, 1621, news reached Rome that the Protestant Union had been dissolved, the commission, therefore, declared that further support of the League was unnecessary and recommended a negative reply to its demand.[3] The Pope, nevertheless, decided to yield to the League's request, and in September, 1621, three notes of exchange to the value of 60,000 florins, taken from the Italian tenth, were sent to Augsburg for the benefit of the League; the rest was to follow later.[4] " You serve the Lord of hosts who is mighty in battle," Gregory XV. wrote on September 15th, 1621, to Duke Maximilian of Bavaria, " you shall not have sought the Pope's help in vain." [5]

In the sequel also the Pope did everything in his power to support both the Emperor and the League. The French nuncio, Corsini, was repeatedly instructed to urge Louis XIII. to

[1] See GINDELY, *Dreissigjähriger Krieg*, IV., 350.

[2] The papal subsidy, according to Götz (*Forsch. zur Gesch. Bayerns*, XII., 115) amounted to 368,389 florins in 1621.

[3] See GINDELY, *loc. cit.*, 351.

[4] *Cf.* SCHNITZER, *Zur Politik*, 163. The *Avviso of February 26, 1622, reports a papal edict, in consequence of which priests were to pay the tenth imposed by Paul V., for the Catholic League in Germany; if they paid half of it at once, the remainder would be remitted. *Urb.* 1091, Vatican Library.

[5] The *Brief of September 15, 1621, is in *Arm.*, XLV., 22, Papal Secret Archives. *Ibid.*, a *laudatory Brief to Maximilian, July 17, 1621. *Cf.* SCHNITZER, *Zur Politik*, 163, and *Darmstädert Allg. Kirchenzeitung*, 1868, no. 37.

renounce the anti-Habsburg policy of his father.[1] The representative of the Holy See in Madrid was asked to support the Pope's efforts to raise money for the war in Germany from the Spanish clergy, " the richest clergy in the world ".[2] On his part Gregory XV., convinced that so favourable an opportunity would hardly recur,[3] did his utmost to satisfy the continually renewed requests of the League and the Emperor for further subsidies. Thus, in February, 1622, he agreed that the impending canonizations of Blessed Isidore, Ignatius of Loyola, Francis Xavier, Philip Neri, and Teresa of Jesus, should take place, not singly, as was customary, but simultaneously, and that the money thus saved—it was a considerable sum—should be divided between the League and the Emperor.[4] Not content with this the members of the League, in the same month, once more pressed the Pope for an extraordinary subsidy; they based their request on the expenditure in connexion with the conflict against the adventurers Ernest of Mansfeld and Christian of Brunswick, who had taken the field in support of the deposed Winter King Frederick.[5] The cruelties practised by their wild mercenaries against the Catholics—their looting of the churches, perpetrating the most horrible sacrileges, driving away priests and outraging nuns—filled Gregory XV. with nameless horror.[6] Hence he was more disposed than ever to continue his extraordinary assistance and, if possible, to increase it. The Cardinals were repeatedly called in to discuss in what manner the necessary means might be procured. " One thing only," the Pope wrote

[1] *Cf.* particularly, *Agucchi's letter to Corsini, August 10 and 23, 1621, *Cod.* X., VI., 16, Casanatense Library, Rome.

[2] See the *letter of Agucchi to the Spanish nuncio, September 8, 1621, *loc. cit.* *Cf.* the *Briefs to the Spanish Bishops and Abbots, September 4, 1621, *Arm.*, XLV., 22, Papal Secret Archives.

[3] " *Se si perde questa occasione, Dio sa se tornerà mai più." Letter to Corsini, August 10, 1621, *loc. cit.*

[4] See SCHNITZER, *Zur Politik*, 163.

[5] *Ibid.*

[6] *Cf.* K. A. MENZEL, VII., 78 *seq.*, 80 *seq.*; KLOPP, II., 111 *seq.*, 151 *seq.*

to the Emperor Ferdinand, on January 6th, 1622, " we deplore, and that is that we cannot do as much as we would wish in favour of the Catholic cause in Germany. Nevertheless we shall do our utmost so that the Church may never have reason to regret our government, and that Your Majesty may never be disappointed in the hopes you have placed in the Apostolic See."[1] Gregory XV. rejoiced exceedingly when the course of events in the field showed that the great sacrifices he had made had not been in vain. He followed with admiration the organization of the defence on the Catholic side, especially the victorious advance of Maximilian against the Upper Palatinate which bordered on Bohemia and which, like the Lower Palatinate, West of the Rhine, was one of Frederick's hereditary States. In a Brief to the Duke of Bavaria, dated October 4th, 1621, the Pope expresses his gratitude to God for having raised up such a Prince during his pontificate.[2] There was an explosion of joy when news reached Rome that on September 6th, 1621, Maximilian had taken the town of Cham which constitutes the key to the southern part of the Upper Palatinate. Cardinal Ludovisi and the Pope himself warmly congratulated Maximilian. Gregory XV. wrote to the Duke on October 16th, 1621, that he expected still greater things of him, that is, that he would not rest until the Winter King had been completely beaten and all the remnants of the conflagration caused by him had been put out.[3] The Pope also congratulated the Emperor, urging him at the same time to deprive Frederick V. of the dignity of an Elector.[4] The letters which Maximilian directed to the Pope and to Cardinal

---

[1] The original of the *Brief is in the State Archives, Vienna; in part in SCHNITZER, *Zur Politik*, 164.

[2] See *Arm., XLV., 22, Papal Secret Archives.

[3] *Ibid.*, and *Darmstädter Allg. Kirchenzeitung*, 1868, no. 37, giving the Brief in German.

[4] *Brief to Ferdinand II., October 16, 1621, *Arm.*, XLV., 22, *loc. cit.* It states that " the enemies mocked our trust in God, atque alii Italiae toti vastitatem ac Vaticano ipsi saevitium moliri dicebantur. Sed non oblitus est nostri Deus. . . . The victory must be exploited for the Faith and the Empire."

Ludovisi on November 3rd about his successes in the Upper Palatinate, were answered on November 12th with the warmest congratulations and good wishes. On November 20th Ludovisi reported that he had given the Pope an account of Maximilian's military prowess and of his pursuit of Mansfeld.[1]

In consequence of Mansfeld having escaped with his army to the Rhine Palatinate, that territory now became the chief theatre of the war. As early as December 3rd, 1621, the Pope was able to express to the Duke of Bavaria how greatly he rejoiced at the successes which his troops had obtained there. He warned him at the same time not to allow his victorious advance to be interrupted by negotiations of any kind, lest a final triumph over the heretics, whom he had thus far so successfully opposed, should escape him : " Go boldly forward, beloved son, for the almighty God of vengeance has chosen you to be the instrument of His wrath against His enemies " we read in this fiery epistle.[2]

With Bohemia in the hands of the Emperor, and the Upper Palatinate in those of the Duke of Bavaria, there was, at the end of 1621, only one large territory, the Rhine Palatinate, in which the Emperor's enemies still maintained themselves. Gregory XV. judged that it was of the utmost importance that there also the enemy should be utterly crushed, and with this in view he wrote on December 25th to the Emperor and to the Ecclesiastical Electors, begging them on no account to enter into any kind of negotiations : the conflict must be fought out and Frederick V. deprived of his status as an Elector.[3]

In the new year the position threatened for a moment to

---

[1] See the letter in the *Darmstädter Allg. Kirchenzeitung*, 1868, 324 *seq.*

[2] See *Darmstädter Allg. Kirchenzeitung*, 1868, no. 37 (a German translation of the letter which had already been published in the Latin original in 1856, in the *Serapeum*, p. 197 *seq.*). Similar letters of the same date—December 3, 1621—whereby the three Rhenish Electors were urged to support Maximilian, are in *Arm.*, XLV., 22, Papal Secret Archives.

[3] *Ibid.* The letter to Maximilian is in *Serapeum*, 1859, 198 *seq.*

veer round in favour of the Winter King when three captains took the field on his behalf, though it is true enough that they meant to fight not so much for the Palatine as for their own interests. Duke Christian of Braunschweig-Wolfenbüttel, administrator of the diocese of Halberstadt, whom the Emperor had refused to confirm in that position, had invaded Westphalia towards the end of 1621. In the beginning of the new year, breathing terrible threats, he invaded the diocese of Paderborn which was completely stripped of troops.[1] His mercenaries ravaged the land with fire and sword and perpetrated the most abominable outrages. In Paderborn itself they sacked all the churches and convents as well as the houses of the Catholic burghers. Christian had the silver shrine of S. Liborius, the Patron of the Diocese, melted and minted into coins bearing the legend: " Gottes Freund, der Pfaffen Feind ": " The friend of God, the enemy of priestlings ".[2] The Duke of Halberstadt, by robbery and extortion, soon scraped together enough money to enable him to raise his army to 11,000 men. The Count of Mansfeld, with an even greater force, invaded and ravaged the territories of the Bishops of Speier and Strassburg. At the end of April, 1622, he entered into an alliance with the Margrave George Frederick of Baden-Durlach and together they conceived great plans: viz. the defeat of the Duke of Bavaria, the confiscation of ecclesiastical property and the execution of the Bishops of Mayence, Würzburg and Speier![3]

On February 12th, 1622, Gregory XV., in a letter to the Catholic princes, expressed his deep sorrow at the dangerous turn things were taking in Germany.[4] On the same day he

---

[1] Cf. *Archiv des Hist. Vereins für Niedersachsen*, 1845, 18.

[2] See OPEL, *Der niedersächsische Krieg*, I., 322 seq.; WESKAMP, *Herzog Christian von Braunschweig und die Stifte Münster und Paderborn*, Paderborn, 1884, 79 seq.; DUHR, II., 1, 398 seq.

[3] See GINDELY, *Dreissigjähriger Krieg*, IV., 329.

[4] Cf. especially the *Brief of February 12, 1622, to the Archbishop of Mayence on the " calamitates Germaniae ", *Arm.*, XLV., 22, Papal Secret Archives.

exhorted the Archbishop of Mayence to constancy.[1] To the administrator of the diocese of Strassburg, to the Archduke Leopold, and to the Emperor, he promised a money subsidy for the month of May.[2]

During the year 1622 the Pope granted to Ferdinand II., in addition to the monthly sum of 20,000 florins which were to be turned into scudi, money for the maintenance of 2,000 foot soldiers and 500 cavalry, for which 30,000 florins had to be allowed, so that the monthly subsidy came to more than 50,000 florins. The League received the tenth which amounted yearly to 120,000 crowns, perhaps even more.[3]

The Pope also had repeatedly recourse to prayer. This was done with special solemnity when the Carmelite, Dominic of Jesus Mary, who had taken so prominent a part in the victory of Prague, brought to Rome, at the beginning of 1622, the statue of Our Lady which the Calvinists had mutilated and which had been carried at the head of the army at the battle of Weissenberg.[4] On Sunday, May 8th, the "Madonna della Vittoria", as she was now called, was carried in solemn procession, in which were also seen the forty-five standards captured in the great victory of November 8th, 1620, from St. Mary Major to the church of the Carmelites of S. Paolo, near the Fontana de' Termini. In the sanctuary Gregory XV. awaited the arrival of the sacred image which was encased in a precious shrine and placed above the high altar.[5] When

[1] "Noli timere," he says in this second *Brief of February 12, 1622, *ibid*.

[2] The *Brief to Archduke Leopold is dated May 4, *that to Ferdinand II., May 5, 1622. *Arm.*, XLV., 24, *loc. cit.*

[3] See Götz, *Briefe und Akten*, II., 1, 85.

[4] See *Avviso January 1, 1622, *Urb.* 1091, Vatican Library. From Savelli's report to Ferdinand II., January 8, 1622, it appears that P. Domenico at that time discussed with the Pope the solemn function as well as the place where the image should be preserved. February 19, 1622, *Savelli reports that the statue would be kept in the Carmelite Church near Monte Cavallo, in S. Maria della Vittoria : State Archives, Vienna, *Fasc.* 45.

[5] See besides the *report of P. Alaleone (*Barb.* 2818) and the *Avviso of May 11, 1622 (*Urb.* 1091, Vatican Library) the rare

the church was reconstructed by Carlo Maderno, on a magnificent scale, it was richly adorned with marble and gold and was given the name of " S. Maria della Vittoria ". The statue of Our Lady, before which the Pope celebrated Mass on May 12th,[1] soon became an object of great veneration. It was destroyed by fire in 1833 and a copy had to take its place. A recent fresco by Luigi Serra in the apse of the choir shows the entry of the victorious troops into Prague, with Fr. Dominic in their midst.[2]

Gregory XV., as he wrote on June 11th, 1622, to the Elector of Cologne and the Duke of Bavaria, would gladly have bestowed upon the Catholic League still greater financial assistance had his means allowed it.[3]

Meanwhile, a decision had been obtained on the field of battle. On May 6th, 1622, Tilly won a brilliant victory over the Margrave of Baden, at Wimpfen, north-west of Heilbronn on the Neckar, and on June 20th he inflicted a sharp defeat on the Duke of Brunswick at Höchst on the Main. The Emperor's opponents were completely dispirited, so much so that the Margrave of Baden disbanded what remained of his army, whilst the Winter King Frederick dismissed Halberstadt and Mansfeld. Meanwhile Tilly had turned his attention to the

letter *Relatione della processione e feste fatte in Roma per la vittoria avuta contra gl'heretici e ribelli della Boemia nel collocare l'imagine della Madonna della Vittoria nella Chiesa di S. Paolo a Monte Cavallo alli 8 Maggio 1622, Roma, per il Mascardi 1622, and the acts in MARCELLINO DI S. BERESA, Guida di S. Maria della Vittoria alle Terme, Roma, 1915, 111 seqq., 116 seqq.

[1] See the *report of P. ALALEONE, loc. cit. and the *Avviso of May 14, 1622, Vatican Library. Cf. also ACCARISIUS, *Vita Gregorii XV., liv. III., ch. 6, Boncompagni Archives, Rome.

[2] The standards were damaged by the fire; part of them, through King Louis I., came into the Munich Arsenal. The flags still preserved in the Church, about a dozen, are only in part those of the battle of Prague; the others are Turkish flags; see MARCELLINO DI S. TERESA, 15 seq.; ibid., for the four pictures preserved in S. Maria della Vittoria, which represent the phases of the fight.

[3] See *Arm., XLV., 24, Papal Secret Archives.

THE PALATINE LIBRARY. 243

Rhine Palatinate, where three important fortresses, Heidelberg, Mannheim and Frankenthal still defied him. Heidelberg capitulated on September 19, Mannheim at the beginning of November. Part of the war booty at Heidelberg was the famous State Library, or, as we should say to-day, " The Library of the Palatine State." During the whole of the preceding year the fate of that most celebrated collection, known as *Bibliotheca Palatina*,[1] had occupied the attention of the Holy See, which has always been concerned in the preservation of literary and artistic treasures. This is proved by a Brief of Gregory XV., dated December 18th, 1621, in which he requests the Archbishop of Mayence to protect this Library if Heidelberg should be besieged.[2] The Cologne nuncio, Pietro Francesco Montorio, had given the Emperor to understand that the Holy See was very anxious to obtain this precious collection,[3] which included many pieces from Lorch and other suppressed monasteries.[4] The Capuchin Giacinto da Casale supported the nuncio's request.[5] At that time the Pope's monthly subsidy amounted to as much as 20,000 florins.[6] On September 24, 1622, Maximilian informed the Pope that the Library would be presented to the Holy See. Thus, when Gregory XV. wrote on October 15th to congratulate the Emperor on the conquest of the capital of the Palatinate, he was able to add the expression of his gratitude for the splendid enrichment of the Vatican Library which Ferdinand's letter promised. " The Lord has commanded," he wrote to Maximilian of Bavaria " and His enemies were scattered. With these words do we desire to

---

[1] *Cf.* STEVENSON, *Codices MS. Palat. Graeci Bibl. Vatic.*, Romae, 1885, xxiii. *seq.*, where the bibliography is given.

[2] See the *Brief of December 18, 1621, *Arm.*, XLV., 22, Papal Secret Archives.

[3] See the *report of Montorio in RANKE, *Päpste*, III., 139. *Cf.* HEBEISEN, 101.

[4] *Cf.* STEVENSON, *loc. cit.*, xxviii. *seq.* For the Lorsch MSS. see FALK in Suppl. 26 of the *Zentralblatt für Bibliothekswesen*, 1902, 55 *seq.*; *cf.*, *ibid.*, Suppl. no. VI, 676 *seq.*

[5] See ROCCO DA CESINALE, II., 504.

[6] *Cf.* HEBEISEN, 101.

greet you, after the fall of Heidelberg, for your victories have restored security to the Catholic faith and have subjected fresh territories to the rule of the Holy Roman Empire. These events are not only a glory for the Bavarian name but a subject of rejoicing for the whole world. When we received your letter announcing the happy issue so long awaited, we raised our hands to heaven to give thanks to the Lord of hosts and from this our throne—the nearest to that of heaven—we imparted a most loving blessing to you and your victorious army. But words fail us to describe the pleasure you have caused us with your gift so acceptable to the Holy Roman Church and so glorious for the Bavarian name, which you, the most devout of victorious captains, have resolved to offer to the Prince of Apostles and to us, as a memorial, so to speak, of the downfall of heresy and one which will contribute to the strengthening of the true Catholic faith as well as to your own glory. Who can fail to see that by realizing your anxious desire to remove the *Bibliotheca Palatina* from those territories and to unite its wonderful treasures with those of the Vatican, you wrest from the impious hands of the heretics—those fathers of lies and followers or erroneous doctrines—the two-edged sword which they brandish unceasingly for the destruction of that truth by which men are saved. Henceforth it will be said of you that you have erected a fresh bulwark of Christian wisdom in this august metropolis to which the eyes of the whole world are ever raised and which contains ' a thousand bucklers, all the armour of valiant men ' (Canticle, IV., 4). The weapons which there (at Heidelberg) were used by the impious heretics to attack religion, will be used here for the defence of the Holy Catholic faith, and it will be due to you that the heralds of the saving truth shall henceforth be able to obtain here the armour of light whose splendour will be still further enhanced when by its means the devil's own falsehoods shall have been destroyed."[1]

The Brief announced that Leone Allacci, a Doctor of Theology and Scriptor at the Vatican Library, was being sent to

[1] See THEINER, *Schenkung der Heidelberger Bibliothek durch Maximilian I. an Papst Gregor XV.*, München, 1844, 49 seq.

Germany.[1] This learned Greek of Chios was instructed to obtain from Maxmilian the necessary authority to take over the Library in its entirety, and to transfer it, in the first instance, to Munich, for which purpose he was to ask for an escort of Bavarian soldiers. From this document also, which provides for every contingency, we gather what value Rome set on the acquisition of the Library.[2]

In all this Gregory XV. and Cardinal Ludovisi were not actuated, as has been suggested,[3] by vain glory or by that passion for manuscripts which one might have expected during the era of the renaissance. On the contrary, the interests of

[1] For L. Allacci, *cf.* the *Vita of Steph. Gradius*, in *Mai, Bibl. nova patr.*, VI., 2, 5 *seq.*; HERGENRÖTHER, in *Freib. Kirchenlex.*, I.[2], 546; *Giorn. stor. di Liguria*, 1901, 161 *seqq.*; MARKOVIĆ, *Slavi e Papi*, 290 *seq.*; C. MAZZI, *L'Allacci*, Bologna, 1893. A *Tractatus de gratia iuxta mentem s. Thomae a Leone Allatio*, probably autograph, is in *Barb.* 928, Vatican Library. For Allacci's correspondence see C. MAZZI on the *Riv. d. bibl.*, III. (1889), 103 *seqq.*

[2] The *Instruttione al Dottor Leone Allaccio per andar in Germania per la libreria del Palatino*, dated Rome, October 22, 1622, drawn up by order of Cardinal Ludovisi, was so long only known in such a garbled Latin version that WILKEN (*Gesch. der Bildung, Beraubung und Vernichtung der alten Heidelberger Bibliothek*, Heidelberg, 1817, 235) doubted its genuineness. Later he published the original text according to a Viennese MSS. in the *Archiv für Philologie und Pädagogik von Seebode*, Jahn und Klotz, V. (1837), 5 *seq.*; it was printed again by THEINER, *Schenkung*, 57 *seq.* In Italy the Instruction has been published three times, first in the *Bibliofilo*, VI. (1885) of Bologna, then by C. MAZZI, in *Propugnatore*, V. (1892), 375 *seqq.*, and in the periodical *La Bibliofilia*, II., (1900). THEINER (55 *seq.*) and MAZZI (*loc. cit.*, 355 *seq.*) also print a second instruction for Allacci, written by Sc. COBELLUZIO, the Librarian of the Vatican.

[3] Thus I. WILLE, in the *Neue Heidelberger Jahrbücher*, XIV., (1906), 224. Against Wille's conclusion is the fact that Maximilian did not wish the library to be united with the Vatican, but to be set up as a separate *Biblioteca Gregoriana*. (See HEBEISEN, 101 *seq.*). But Gregory did not consent to this.

religion were the predominant motive in this as in all else that the Holy See undertook at the time of the Catholic counter-reformation,[1] just as it was the decisive factor in Maximilian's acquiescence in the Pope's wishes. To this was added the motive of gratitude for the money subsidies received from Rome, as well as the hope of the Pope's support for his aspirations to the dignity of an Elector. Maximilian was well aware of the Pope's chief concern. Once the material defeat, by force of arms, of the head of the German Calvinists and their auxiliaries was an accomplished fact, it would be necessary to wrest from their hands a dangerous spiritual armoury in the shape of the priceless, world-famed Library of Heidelberg, and by transferring it to Rome to utilize this arsenal of knowledge, which had hitherto supplied weapons against the papacy, for diametrically opposite purposes.[2]

Leone Allacci, who left Rome on October 28th, 1622, carried out his mission with as much zeal as discretion.[3] At Munich he received every assistance from Maximilian. The Duke advised him to hasten the transport of the Library lest the negotiations between the Emperor and the Prince Palatine, with a view to their reconciliation, which had begun through the mediation of the regent of the Netherlands, should

---

[1] " *Io rendo gratie a V.A. della benigna intentione data ai nostri nuntii di Colonia e di Fiandra della Biblioteca Palatina, perchè essendo tanto segnalata questa Vaticana, et havendo giovato tanto con la copia de'fedeli manoscritti alla correttione dei buoni autori, massimamente sacri ed ecclesiastici, quanto più ella si va accrescendo, maggior servitio di Dio e della Chiesa santa può seguire. Onde Sua Santità ha dovuto desiderarla," wrote Cardinal Ludovisi from Frascati on October 8, 1622, to Maximilian I. In like manner on October 23, 1623, to Tilly. *Cod.* X., V., 31, Casanatense Library, Rome.

[2] See the essays, " Zur Geschichte der Heidelberger, Biblioteca Palatina' " in the *Allg. Zeitung*, 1876, Suppl. no. 30 and [MAAS] " Die Instruktion für die Verbringung der Palatina, nach Rom," *ibid.*, 1901, Beil. no. 96.

[3] *Cf.* C. MAZZI, in *Propugnatore*, IV. (1891), 263 *seqq.*

deprive the Pope of the precious treasure at the last minute.[1] When Allacci arrived at Heidelberg on December 13th, 1622, notwithstanding the cold, he spared no fatigue in preparing for transport the Palatine Library which was housed in the two upper galleries over the lateral aisles of the church of the Holy Ghost.[2] He also took possession of any manuscripts he could lay hands on. Tilly gave him permission to take some of these from the Palatine's private library in the castle. Through the intervention of the Governor, Allacci also obtained manuscripts from the University library and from that of the *Sapientia* College. In this way he collected 3,542 manuscripts, to which he added some 5,000 printed books.[3]

When at last the necessary wagons and horses had been obtained, Allacci set out on February 4th, 1623, with fifty transport wagons escorted by Bavarian musketeers. The wagons contained 196 chests[4] of books and manuscripts. After many dangers and difficulties of every kind he brought the whole consignment safe and undamaged to Rome viâ Munich.[5]

[1] The *Ex Libris*, which Maximilian had executed by Raphael Sadeler of Munich (d. 1628), for the MSS. and printed books belonging to the Heidelberg collection, was reproduced by COUNT VON LEININGEN-WESTERNBURG, in *Ex-Libris—Zeitschr. für Bücherzeichen*, 1892, 12, and described in detail.

[2] Not in the choir, as Wilken and later writers have asserted; see *Mitteil. des Heidelberger Schlossvereins*, 1868, 6 seq.

[3] *Cf.* ZANGEMEISTER, in the *Westdeutsche Zeitschr.*, XIV., 359 seq. and *Archival. Zeitschr.*, N.F. II. (1891), 315 seq.

[4] *Cf.* STEVENSON, in *Omaggio d. Bibl. Vatic. nel giubileo episc. di Leone XIII.* (Roma), 1893. The cost, according to an account in the State Archives in Rome, amounted to 5,877 scudi.

[5] Allacci has described the whole transport of the library to Rome in a detailed report. It was published by BÄHR in the *Heidelberger Jahrbücher*, 1872, 485 seq., and again by BELTRAMI in the *Riv. Europ. Ann.*, XIII., vol. XXVIII., Florence, 1882, 1 seq. *Cf.* also ALLACCI's letter of February 3, 1623, in *Zentralblatt für Bibliothekswesen*, VIII., 123 seq., and C. MAZZI, *loc. cit.* Gregory XV. was not to have the pleasure of seeing the *Palatina* with his own eyes. His death, on July 8, 1623 — the *Palatina*

Allacci was still in Munich when a fresh Brief was sent to Maximilian on November 19th, 1622, in which the Pope praised the Duke of Bavaria and urged him to continue the war against the enemies of the Emperor and the Church.[1] A papal letter dated December 23rd, 1622, in which Gregory XV. congratulated the Duke of Bavaria on his capture of Mannheim, compares that success to the victory of 1620, at

arrived in Rome at the end of the month—spared him the sorrow of seeing that the *Palatina* was not made to render to science and to the Church the great services which he had looked for when he acquired it. *Cf. Hist.-polit. Blätter*, XIV., 335. The writer of the paper shows (p. 333 *seq.*) that however greatly all Germans must regret the loss of the Library, yet German science has every reason to be glad of its removal—for it would certainly have been destroyed when the French pillaged the Palatinate. On this point all parties are agreed to-day (*cf.* the opinion of HÖFFLER, in *Hist. Jahrb.*, VIII., 43; NEUDEGGER, in the *Archival. Zeitschr.*, N.F., II., 323, and KOCHENDÖRFFER, in the *Berliner Deutsche Literaturzeitung*, 1887, 1363). HÖFFLER also draws attention to the fact that if the library had remained in Munich it would almost certainly have been taken away by the King of Sweden (*cf.* A. HESSEL, *Gesch. der Bibliotheken*, Göttingen, 1925, 74) and the Palatinate would never have seen it again. In 1815, after the fall of Napoleon, Pius VII. restored the whole of the MSS. which had been carried off to Paris and which had belonged to the *Palatina* library, thirty-eight in all. In 1816, at the request of Heidelberg University, he presented to the representative of the Baden Government 842 German MSS., and four Latin ones which also belonged to the *Palatina* ; see *Serapeum*, 1845, 157 *seq*. The scientific use of the parts of the library which remained in Rome was facilitated by Leo XIII. by the publication of model catalogues (*Codic. ms. Palat. Graeci, rec. Stevenson senior*, Romae, 1885; *Codic. ms. Palat. Latini, rec. Stevenson Junior, recogn. De Rossi*, Romae, 1886; *Inventario dei libri stampati Palatino-Vaticani da E. Stevenson giuniore*, 2 vols. Romae, 1876; the latter being the jubilee gift of the Holy See for the jubilee of Heidelberg University).

[1] *Brief of November 19, 1622, *Arm.*, XLV., 24, Papal Secret Archives.

the White Mountains, near Prague.[1] The joy breathed by that letter was well founded. The successes in the Palatinate set a worthy crown upon the year 1622. It had been a particularly lucky year for Pope and Emperor: its beginning had released Ferdinand II. from the burden of war against Bethlen Gábor, who left the rebels of Bohemia and Austria to their fate; by taking Glatz on October 25th, he had extinguished the last flickers of insurrection in the Austrian lands; by the end of the year the champions of the Winter King lay prostrate and his rule had come to an end, even in his hereditary Palatine State.

The time had now come to fulfil the promise of transferring the honour of the Palatine Electorate, a promise which Ferdinand II. had given by word of mouth to the Duke of Bavaria in 1619 in order to obtain the support of the League against the rebels of Bohemia. If the matter had not yet been settled, the fault was not the Emperor's, who would have been glad to honour his pledge, for he was filled with gratitude and admiration for the man who had saved him; there was, however, much opposition to overcome. In the College of Electors, Ferdinand could only be sure of the support of the Elector of Cologne. The Elector of Trèves was undecided; the timid Johann Schweikart of Mayence was opposed to Maximilian's demands; that the Elector of Brandenburg, as a cousin of the banned Winter King, would resist to the end, was but natural. However, even John George of Saxony, though allied with the Emperor, was against transferring the Electorate to a Catholic; moreover he cherished the hope of saving the dignity at least for the brother or the son of Frederick. More embarrassing than all this was the fact that Ferdinand met with opposition even on the part of his other chief ally, the King of Spain. For fear that England might be driven to participate in the war which the Netherlands had resumed, the Madrid cabinet was inclined to purchase peace in Germany by yielding to the demands of London for the restoration of the *status quo*.[2]

[1] *Brief of December 3, 1622, *ibid.*, in German translation in *Darmstädter Allg. Kirchenzeitung*, 1868, no. 37.

[2] See RITTER, III., 172 *seq.*

In a situation so unfavourable to Maximilian's aspirations to the Palatine Electorate, the powerful intervention of the Holy See proved a decisive factor in his favour. Already Paul V., when the news came of the splendid victory near Prague, had expressed the opinion in the hearing of the imperial ambassador, Savelli, that the best fruit of the victory would be the conveyance of the Electorate to Bavaria.[1] This opinion was also that of Gregory XV. and his Secretary of State, Ludovisi.[2] In a Brief of February 25th, 1621, Gregory XV. warmly commended the Emperor for having laid the ban of Empire on the Winter King and deprived him of his honours and possessions.[3] In a letter of March 6th, 1621, Cardinal Ludovisi impressed on Ferdinand II. the necessity of transferring the Electorate to a Catholic prince in place of the man he had been obliged to ban. If he would act thus, in virtue of his imperial authority, he would be conferring an immortal benefit on Christendom.[4]

The point of view which the Holy See adopted in this affair was made abundantly clear in the Instructions of the nuncios accredited to the great Powers in the spring of 1621. The French nuncio, Corsini, was directed to restrain Louis XIII. from favouring the Winter King in any way whatever.[5] Carafa, in Vienna, as also the nuncios in Madrid and Brussels, were exhorted to direct their efforts to the complete discomfiture of the Winter King, and equally to the

---

[1] See HURTER, IX., 157. *Cf.* our account, Vol. XXVI., 372.

[2] GIUNTI (**Vita del card. Ludovisi*, Boncompagni Archives, Rome) seems anxious to ascribe to his hero a larger share in the settlement of the electoral dispute than to the Pope himself.

[3] See SCHNITZER, *Zur Politik*, 165.

[4] " *Immortale sane beneficium a Caes. M.^{te} Vestra accepturus est christianus orbis, si per vestrae auctoritatis decretum ius Caesaris eligendi perduello Palatino ademptum catholicus princep adipiscatur." M. Lud. Ludovisi to the Emperor Ferdinand II., Rome, March 6, 1621, in the State Archives, Vienna, *Hofkorrespondenz*, 11.

[5] See the *Instruction for Corsini in *Nunziat. di Francia*, LVII., Papal Secret Archives.

transference of the Palatine Electorate to a Catholic prince, because thereby the imperial crown would be permanently assured to the Catholics and to the House of Habsburg.[1] The Pope and his Secretary of State did not allow themselves to be exclusively inspired in this affair by their long-standing relations with Bavaria, but chiefly by considerations of a higher order. Apart from the personality of the Palatine Frederick, the Holy See thought it intolerable to allow the continuance of the risk of the candidature not only of the Protestant Elector of Saxony, but of a second Protestant, for the post of Imperial Vicar during a vacancy of the throne.[2] Moreover, by obtaining a fifth vote, a Catholic majority at an imperial election would be assured. Naturally enough the Pope also had at heart the fate of the Catholics of the Palatinate.[3] Since Rome was well aware of the promise made to the Duke of Bavaria, only Maximilian's candidature for the vacant Electorate could be considered How much the Holy See had made his cause its own appears from the Pope's attitude towards Duke Wolfgang William of Neuburg who, as the nearest relative of the House of Simmerisk, also put in a claim to the Electorate and the Palatine territories. Though that prince's services to the Church were highly valued, so much so that Rome would have been willing to help him, yet, as is shown by the Instruction to the nuncio of Brussels, on May 1st, 1621,[4] in this affair there was no question of giving him any support. For the rest, the question of the Palatine territory could only be resolved after that of the Electorate had been decided.

[1] See the *Instruction for the Spanish nuncio, Sangro, in *Cod.* J., III, 80, of the Chigi Library, Rome, and *Cod.* 1257 of the Ossoliniana Library, Lemberg. For Carafa, *cf.* above, p. 229.
[2] *Cf.* CARAFA's *Relatione*, 163.
[3] In the *Instruction for Carafa the latter is told that if the Emperor was compelled to pardon Frederick, he was to see to it that the rights of the Catholics in the Palatinate were safeguarded. *Barb.* 5232, Vatican Library.
[4] See CAUCHIE-MAERE, *Instructions*, 120 *seq.*

On that point Gregory XV. concentrated all his efforts; for its realization all the nuncios were made to work. Carlo Carafa was busy in Vienna. At first the Emperor gave him great hopes though this was hardly in keeping with the fact that Ferdinand II. put off till August 30th the Princes' Diet which had been convoked for June 24th, at Ratisbon. Rome saw quite well that this move was due to consideration for Saxony. On the other hand prompt action was essential for at that very moment the imperial arms were victorious, the Union had been dissolved and there was nothing to fear from the Turks. The Pope, therefore, insisted that Ferdinand should act rapidly and satisfy the Duke of Saxony in some other way.[1] In order to spur on the wavering monarch to a decision, Gregory XV. resolved, in the middle of June, to send an ambassador extraordinary to Vienna. His choice fell on the Capuchin Giacinto da Casale, a man known far and wide as a mission preacher and one who knew the German situation from personal experience and enjoyed the special confidence of Maximilian.[2] The Pope had the highest opinion of the ability and zeal of this Capuchin,[3] whilst he himself had so lofty a conception of his mission that shortly before leaving he wrote to Zúñiga, the leading Statesman of Spain, that he was going to Germany not merely as the Pope's

[1] *Cf.* the *letter to the Spanish nuncio, June 24, 1621, Cod. 33 D. 33 of the Corsini Library, Rome.

[2] The existing information concerning Giacinto's embassy (see HURTER, IX., 158 *seq.*; GINDELY, IV., 381 *seq.*; RITTER, III., 175 *seq.*) has been very greatly supplemented by W. GOETZ in his essay, "Pater Hyacinth" (*Hist. Zeitschr.*, CIX., 106) in which he made use of the monograph by VENANZIO DA LAGO SANTO (187); he is, however, mistaken when he fixes the nomination of Giacinto as nuncio extraordinary for Germany in February, 1621. It took place on June 24, 1621, as is clearly shown by the Briefs of Gregory XV. of which Goetz was ignorant, *Bull. Capuc.*, III., 241 *seq. Cf.* also ROCCO DA CESINALE, II., 581 *seq.* For a picture of Giacinto see FREDEGARD D'ANVERS, *P. Charles d'Arenberg*, Rome, 1919, 178 *seq.*

[3] See the *letter to the Spanish nuncio, June 24, 1622, Corsini Library, Rome.

envoy, but also as a representative of Christ himself.[1] Besides the ordinary credentials Giacinto received from the Pope special letters of recommendation to the Emperor's chief advisers.[2] At the end of June he set out to cross the Alps. The Pope assigned to him three Capuchins, who were to act as secretaries; Giacinto himself chose from among his brethren P. Valeriano Magno to act as reporter for France, P. Diego da Quiroga for Spain, and P. Basilio for Flanders.[3]

The Pope clearly perceived how much depended upon the attitude of Spain; for that reason, and before Giacinto's departure, he addressed a personal letter to Philip IV. In it the Pope says that God almighty had shown His great mercy so clearly by the victories granted to the Emperor that there was cause to fear His wrath if the advantages gained were not properly exploited while the opportunity lasted. He—the Pope—had the affairs of Germany very much at heart. After having supported the Emperor both with money and with prayers, he was now sending him a religious who would urge him to confer the dignity of an Elector on a Catholic prince and to restore the old religion to its former position at least in his own lands. He begged the King of Spain to give his support to these endeavours by himself also pressing Ferdinand to transfer the Electorate promptly, in as much as both the welfare of Christendom and the maintenance of the imperial dignity in the Catholic House of Habsburg depended very much on such action being taken.[4] The Spanish nuncio was commissioned to support the papal letter and to bring pressure to bear especially on Zúñiga.[5] Whilst the result of these steps was being awaited in Rome, an alarming rumour became current in August to the effect that the Emperor was

---

[1] *Letter of June 23, 1621; see VENANZIO DA LAGO SANTO, 187. *Cf.* ROCCO DA CESINALE, II., 555 seqq.

[2] See *Arm., XLV., 23, Papal Secret Archives. *Cf.* ROCCO DA CESINALE, II., 260 seqq.

[3] See VENANZIO DA LAGO SANTO, *loc. cit.*

[4] See *Gregory XV.'s letter to Philip IV., June 24, 1621, in *Cod.* 33 D. 23, Corsini Library, Rome.

[5] See Agucchi's *letter, June 24, 1621, *ibid.*

inclined to consent to the rehabilitation of the Elector Palatine, and that at the request of Lord Digby, English ambassador extraordinary, a demand prompted by Philip IV. to whom, in return, James I. had promised his neutrality during the war with the Dutch. From the representations which the Spanish nuncio was at once instructed to make, it is easy to see what great importance Rome attached to this matter. The opportunity of crushing the Elector was on no account to be missed, for with him the head of Calvinism would fall. The Palatine is here described as the greatest enemy of the Church. A man who had tried to rob the Emperor of a kingdom, and who had planned to attack the Spanish possessions in Italy, was deserving of imprisonment and execution rather than rehabilitation.[1] Excitement in Rome grew still further when reliable reports came from Germany to the effect that the Spanish ambassador in Vienna, Count Oñate, was making common cause with the English ambassador, Digby, and was working for the cession of the Lower Palatinate to Spain.[2] Giacinto reported that the way in which Oñate and the imperial ministers treated Bavaria was enough to destroy the Emperor and the Spaniards, if Maximilian were not such a good Christian.[3]

Giacinto's negotiations were supported by the nuncio Carafa. The latter succeeded in convincing the Emperor that it was his duty to transfer the Electorate from the Calvinist and rebel Frederick to the Catholic Duke of Bavaria. The progress which Maximilian was making in his campaign for the subjection of the Upper Palatinate came opportunely to support Giacinto's efforts, for it increased the Emperor's long-felt desire to exchange Upper Austria, which was pledged to Maximilian, for the Upper Palatinate.[4] However the consent of the Duke of Bavaria could only be obtained by fulfilling the promise concerning the Electorate. In order to avoid any protests on the part of Spain and Saxony, recourse was

[1] See Agucchi's *letter, August 13, 1621, *ibid.*
[2] See Agucchi's *letter, September 8, 1621, *ibid.*
[3] See ROCCO DA CESINALE, II., 558.
[4] See *RITTER, III., 176.

had to the expedient of keeping the investiture a secret for the time being. On September 22nd, 1621, the Emperor signed the document which conveyed the hereditary possessions of the Elector Palatine to Maximilian and to his brothers, the prince Elector of Cologne and Duke Albert, and to all their heirs. Thus the decisive step was taken.[1] Giacinto had the happiness of personally handing the important document to Maximilian.[2] Now that so considerable a step towards the final goal had been taken, Giacinto was more determined than ever to make every effort to overcome the resistance of Spain and the ecclesiastical Electors. He began by visiting the Elector of Mayence, Johann Schweikart and after conferring with Maximilian, he resolved to go to Spain as well.[3]

Gregory XV., on hearing of the secret transfer of the Electorate, had at once made strong representations to Philip IV. in favour of Maximilian,[4] hence he considered

---

[1] See ARETIN, I., 174.

[2] See GINDELY, *Dreissigjähriger Krieg*, IV., 382. *Cf.* W. GOETZ, *loc. cit.*, 107, and the *letter, unknown to Goetz, of Giacinto in ROCCO DA CESINALE, II., 561 seqq., 563.

[3] *Cf.* W. GOETZ, *loc. cit.* Gregory XV. wrote on September 15, 1621, to the ecclesiastical Electors about the transfer of the Electorate (see GINDELY, IV., 381); by *Briefs of September 18, 1621, he recommended Giacinto also to the Bishops of Speier and Würzburg. *Arm.*, XLV., 22, Papal Secret Archives.

[4] On October 6, 1621, the Pope *wrote in his own hand to the Spanish King (copy in *Cod.* 33 D. 23, Corsini Library, Rome; *cf. ibid.*, the *letter to the Spanish nuncio of October 6, 1621, on the occasion of Philip IV.'s succession to the throne). The nuncio extraordinary for Spain, Msgr. Aquaviva, Titular Archbishop of Thebes, sent to Madrid on October 16, 1621, was to discuss not only the support of the Emperor by Spain in the matter of the Valtinella but also to broach the question of the Electorate. See *Instruttione a Msgr. arcivescovo di Tebe nuntio straord. alla M.^{ta} Catt.*, dated Rome, October 16 (four parts), *Varia polit.*, 117, and *Pio*, 222, Papal Secret Archives; copies in *Cod.* 38 A. 10, p. 221 seq., of the Corsini Library, Rome, and in the Rospigliosi Archives, Rome. *Cf.* MACSWINEY DE MASHANAGLASS, *Le Portugal et le Saint-Siège*, II., Paris, 1899, 26 seq.

Giacinto's journey unnecessary, but eventually he approved his decision, since in so important a matter it was impossible to do too much.[1] Briefs for the King of Spain, for Zúñiga and other important personages were at once written and dispatched to the Capuchin (October 15th, 1621).[2] Furthermore Cardinal Ludovisi, on his part, wrote letters of recommendation to Philip IV. and to Zúñiga as well as to the Fiscal of the Spanish nuncio who was to take charge of Giacinto's correspondence with Rome.[3] On October 21st Philip IV. received a fresh reminder of the necessity of breaking the Elector Palatine ; this document sounds Maximilian's merits with the utmost enthusiasm.[4]

The Emperor Ferdinand also lent support to Giacinto's mission by personal letters to the Spanish King and to Zúñiga. In these he points out that not only the duty of gratitude towards Maximilian, but political prudence also rendered it advisable to make it impossible for the banned Elector to do any more mischief ; in any case he would always have been an irreconcilable enemy. In order that the letters might reach their address safely, the Vienna nuncio, Carafa, undertook to forward them to his colleague in Brussels who would then see that they were dispatched to Spain.[5] This very precaution led to disappointment, for the letters fell into the hands of Mansfeld's soldiers. At the beginning of 1622 the Elector Palatine had them printed and published by Louis Camerarius under the title of " Spanish Chancellery ".[6] In this way the Palatine party hoped to get in a counter blow to the " Secret Chancellery " of the Prince of Anhalt captured after the battle

---

[1] See the *letter to Giacinto da Casale, October 15, 1621, Cod. 33 D. 23, Corsini Library, Rome.

[2] Cf. *Arm., XLV., 22, Papal Secret Archives.

[3] See the *letters of Agucchi written in Ludovisi's name, to Philip IV., to Zúñiga and the Fiscal of the Spanish nuncio, October 15, 1621, Corsini Library, Rome, loc. cit.

[4] *Arm., XLV., 22, Papal Secret Archives.

[5] See GINDELY, Dreissigjähriger Krieg, IV., 400.

[6] Cf. CARAFA, Relatione, 341 ; KOSER, Der Kanzleienstreit, Halle, 1874, 25 seq.

of Prague and published by Maximilian in 1621, in which the plans of the Calvinists for a rising against the Emperor and the German Catholics were laid bare. Though the Emperor was greatly embarrassed by the publication of these letters, a written copy of which had been communicated to the Duke of Saxony as early as February,[1] the psychological result could not be identical in the two cases because, though the captured letters brought to light certain political secrets, these were not concerned with disorder and revolution planned in the course of several years of lies and deception, treachery and felony.[2] None the less, the publication of the letters could not but be painful both to Carafa and to the Pope, for among the captured documents there were some in which the nuncio complained of the indecision of the Court of Vienna and of the great influence of Spain, whilst a letter of Cardinal Ludovisi to Carafa complained that the Spanish ambassador in Vienna, Count Oñate, wanted to tyrannize over everybody at Court and expected that his advice should be regarded on all occasions as oracular, notwithstanding the fact that his answers were always so equivocal and deceptive that it was impossible to know what he really thought.[3]

Whilst Giacinto was on his way to Spain, Gregory XV. took further steps. On December 25th, 1621, he implored the Emperor in two most pressing letters, to grant the honour of the Electorate to a Catholic Duke, and not to listen to those who advised the restoration of the Palatine. So much money, so much Catholic blood has been sacrificed in order to protect the Commonweal from ruthless treachery! Shall we allow the prize of victory to slip from our hands now that the bandit captain has crept away to his den? Surely such a peace would be the bitterest of disappointments for the Catholic Church. If people such as these were spared, they would return to the attack against the Emperor at the very first opportunity; we must not rest until they have been rendered harmless for

---

[1] See RITTER, III., 177.
[2] See KOPP, *Dreissigjähr. Krieg*, II., 139. *Cf.* RIEZLER, V., 227 seq.
[3] See CANCELLARIA HISPANICA, Freistadii, 1622, no. 12, 24, 25.

good.[1] Cardinal Ludovisi also supported the Pope's representations with an emphatic letter to the Emperor.[2] Further Briefs to this purpose were dispatched on December 20th to the ecclesiastical Electors.[3] In the audiences which Cardinal von Zollern and the ambassador Savelli had with the Pope at the beginning of 1622, the latter urged with the utmost energy the speedy transfer of the Electorate. Every delay, he said, was most dangerous and both his conscience and his office would allow him no peace until the affair was settled.[4] In January, 1622, the Auditor of the Rota, Verospi, was sent to Vienna as nuncio extraordinary for the Emperor's wedding.[5] Verospi, whose zeal and knowledge of German affairs Gregory esteemed highly[6], was to insist energetically both on the liberation of Cardinal Klesl [7] and on the solemn transfer of the Electoral dignity to Maximilian without further delay. It was important to counter the intrigues of the Spanish ambassador, Oñate, who displayed such skill in discovering ever fresh means by which to delay a decision that Maximilian complained bitterly about it.[8]

[1] Both *Briefs to the Emperor are in the State Archives, Vienna. Part of one Brief is in SCHNITZER, 165.

[2] "*Qui diuturna bellorum formidine suspensi et crudelitate defessi sumus, pacem timemus. Accepimus agi de Palatino in pristinam dignitatem restituendo : dici vix potest, quam id invitis auribus Roma audiverit." Ludovisi to Ferdinand II., Rome, December 25, 1621. State Archives, Vienna.

[3] These *Briefs are in *Arm.*, XLV., 22, Papal Secret Archives.

[4] See HURTER, IX., 159.

[5] Cf. *Instruttione a Msgr. Verospi, auditore di Rota, nuntio straord. in Germania, January 13, 1622, Cod. 38 A. 9, p. 75 of the Corsini Library Rome.

[6] He is called in *Agucchi's letter to the Spanish nuncio, December 12, 1621, " Persona efficace et ardente e pratica di quei paesi." Corsini Library, Rome, loc. cit.

[7] Cf. above, p. 92 seq.

[8] *Il duca di Baviera si duole sino al cielo e Dio sa che farà. Il conte d'Ognate procede peggio che mai e governa quelle cose al suo modo." Agucchi to the Spanish nuncio, December 21, 1621, Corsini Library, Rome, loc. cit.

At the same time Gregory XV. got the Spanish nuncio to act. For a long time, Cardinal Ludovisi wrote to him, the Pope had been expecting a definite answer from Madrid concerning the transfer of the Electorate. However the fear of dilatoriness in the matter, which he felt from the first, was being increasingly justified. It would seem that jealousy of Bavaria pushed everything else into the background and that the intention was to prevent the transfer of the Electorate, not, indeed, openly, but in a roundabout way. Let the nuncio speak plainly, for the interests of the Catholic religion were at stake.[1]

When Giacinto arrived in Madrid, on December 16th, 1621, he soon perceived that Rome's pessimism was not excessive. His description of the Spanish Court is most incisive: "The King is a child, his counsellors are well disposed, but they act like guardians who are for ever trying to get the best conditions for their wards." At first Olivares felt offended because they had sent him a simple Capuchin. But Giacinto was resolved to make every effort to break the resistance of the Spanish cabinet. His view of the matter is seen in a letter of February 7th, 1622, in which he recommends that prayers should be offered " so that the divine goodness may look upon us as Christ looked upon St. Peter, for it is a matter of bringing many millions of souls under the obedience of his supreme keys and of confirming the Catholic religion and the shaken Empire throughout the North ".[2] Giacinto, who had " gone through purgatory " at Aranjuez,[3] insisted *opportune, importune*, as the imperial ambassador Khevenhiller wrote,[4] but though he stayed on up to the beginning of summer, he failed to obtain a definite promise.

Verospi also encountered great difficulties in Vienna, for Ferdinand would make no decisive step without the consent of Spain. Cardinal Ludovisi complained bitterly of the

---

[1] See *Agucchi's letter to the Spanish nuncio, December 18, 1621, Corsini Library, Rome.

[2] See ROCCO DA CESINALE, II., 567, 570.

[3] *Annales Ferdinandei*, IX., 177 seq.

[4] See W. GOETZ, *loc. cit.*, 108.

" natural indecision, not to say the weakness " of the Emperor.¹ The final reply given to Verospi on April 7th was that His Majesty, in agreement with Maximilian, would not miss any opportunity to grant the investiture to the latter as soon as it could be done without danger.² The successes of Tilly in the Palatinate gave Gregory XV. a fresh opportunity sternly to admonish the Spanish cabinet to cease its resistance. Three vast armies, viz. those of the Margrave of Baden, of Halberstadt and Mansfeld, 50,000 men in all, had been destroyed in a month. In this the Pope saw a clear hint of Providence that the decision must not be sought by negotiations, but by arms. This view was further confirmed by the fact that the patrons of the Palatine were no longer relying upon military, but upon diplomatic means. For this reason the Pope's most ardent desire was that the Electorate should be transferred to the Duke of Bavaria. From such a step the Catholic religion, the Emperor and the House of Austria would derive great advantages, whereas the restoration of the rebel would bring nothing but ruin and destruction. An opportunity like the present, the like of which had been hoped for in vain during a century, must not be allowed to slip by without something being done for the advantage of the Catholic religion.³

Notwithstanding their eloquence, these representations remained without success in Madrid. In Vienna, on the other hand, there occurred a turn for the better. According to the report of the indefatigable nuncio, Carlo Carafa, the incident of the secret letters which had been captured and published, was largely responsible for the change. At first Ferdinand had been so frightened that even Carafa feared he would withdraw from the whole affair in order to avoid worse complications. Soon, however, he took an entirely different view. Since all the world knew of his intentions Ferdinand felt

[1] See *Agucchi's letter to the French nuncio Corsini, March 11, 1622, *Cod.* X., VI., 16 of the Casanatense Library, Rome.

[2] See GINDELY, *Dreissigjähr. Krieg*, IV., 387.

[3] *Agucchi al Nuntio di Spagna, vescovo di Bertinoro* (the copy has *Benevento*), dated August 20, 1622, *Cod.* 33, D. 23. Corsini Library, Rome.

determined to carry them through. Thus the publication of those letters led to a speedier solution of the problem: so different, the nuncio wrote, are the ways of God from the ways of men![1]

A notable symptom of a more resolute policy was a circular of June 17th, 1621, calling a convention to be held at Ratisbon, which was to be not merely a gathering of the Electors but an Imperial Diet. On September 3rd the Pope appointed the Cologne nuncio as his representative at the gathering.[2] The preliminary discussions proved rather difficult so that the Diet had to be deferred to October 1st.[3] The Elector of Mayence, Johann Schweikart, showed decided opposition and his objections were numerous. His health as well as lack of money, he declared, would not allow him to journey to Ratisbon; besides the question of the transfer of the Palatine Electorate was not yet ripe. The consent of Saxony and Spain were lacking. England was adopting a threatening attitude and there was reason to fear that a new war would break out in Germany, in which the Catholics, and especially the ecclesiastical princes, would fare very badly. All this would be avoided if the Electorate were bestowed not on the Duke of Bavaria, who was already powerful enough, but on the Count of Neuburg who had a better claim to it. Gregory XV. had charged the nuncio of Cologne, Pietro Francesco Montorio, to induce the Elector of Mayence to withdraw his opposition. He also sent Giacinto da Casale to assist him; the latter was also to influence in the same sense the Elector of Trèves and the Archbishop of Salzburg.[4] However, even before the arrival of the zealous Capuchin, the nuncio of Cologne had succeeded

---

[1] See CARAFA, *Relatione*, 342.
[2] *Brief to Ferdinand II., September 3, 1622, *Arm.*, XLV., 24.
[3] See GINDELY, *Dreissigjähr. Krieg*, IV., 423.
[4] The *Briefs to the Electors of Mayence and Trèves and to the Archbishop of Salzburg of September 10, 1622, refer to this mission (*Arm.*, XLV., 24, Papal Secret Archives). They were not known to W. GOETZ, who only mentions the activities of GIACINTO in the autumn of 1622 at Neuburg and Munich.

in inducing Schweikart to yield, after negotiations at Aschaffenburg lasting five days.[1]

However, at this very moment, after the death of Zúñiga, a complete reversal of opinion took place in Madrid, to the disadvantage of Maximilian. Olivares, who now took charge of foreign affairs, stood for an Anglophile policy, consequently also for the restoration of the Palatinate to the heir of the Elector.[2] Furthermore, at the end of October, the Elector of Saxony took back his promise to come to Ratisbon in person, as a protest against certain measures taken by Ferdinand against the Lutheran preachers in Prague.[3] He contented himself with sending a representative, as did the Elector of Brandenburg. Of the other Protestant princes only the Margrave Louis of Hesse put in an appearance at Ratisbon, where the Emperor made his entry on November 23rd. From December onwards Giacinto da Casale, together with the Bavarian representative, worked strenuously for an early settlement of the question of the Electorate.[4]

Gregory XV. awaited the issue with keen anxiety. In order to bring pressure to bear on the hesitating Emperor, he reduced the monthly allowance of 50,000 florins, which he had hitherto granted to him, to 20,000. The full sum was not to be disbursed until the Duke of Bavaria was invested with the Palatinate, for if that event did not take place Ferdinand II. would not require assistance.[5]

On receiving reassuring news of the Emperor's intentions, the Pope expressed his joy to him in enthusiastic terms. He would intone a song of praise to God, the Lord of hosts, and the Roman Church would clothe herself with the garments

---

[1] See Montorio's report in RANKE, III., 138*; the source, which is not given, is *Cod.* 6329, p. 236 *seq.* of the State Library, Vienna.

[2] See GINDELY, *Dreissigjähr. Krieg*, IV., 413 *seq.*

[3] See RITTER, III., 183.

[4] See W. GOETZ, *loc. cit.*, 111 *seq. Cf.* also Eggenberg's letter in ROCCO DA CESINALE, II., 377.

[5] *Cf.* GINDELY, IV., 572 *seq.*; GOETZ, *Briefe und Akten*, II., 1 (1911), 85.

of rejoicing when the Emperor, amidst the world's applause, should take the Electorate from the treacherous Palatine and bestow it upon a Catholic. In a second letter of December 10th, the Pope assures him that he can scarcely bear the anxiety of waiting.[1] On December 22nd he admonishes the Emperor to bring the affair to a happy conclusion without further delay.[2] On the same day Briefs were sent to Eggenberg, to the Emperor's confessor Becanus, to the Electors of Cologne and Mayence, to the Archbishop of Salzburg, to the Bishop of Würtzburg and to Wolfgang Wilhelm of Neuburg. The Spanish ambassador, Oñate, was likewise requested not to oppose any longer the transfer of the Electorate.[3] Although the latter appeal fell on deaf ears, Maximilian at length saw his wishes fulfilled. However, in view of the opposition of the Protestant States as well as that of Spain, he had to be content with receiving the Electorate for his own person alone and for his own lifetime. The ceremony took place on February 25th, 1623, with the usual pomp, in a solemn assembly of princes. The Spanish ambassador absented himself from the ceremony whilst the envoys of Brandenburg and Saxony entered formal protests.[4]

Maximilian owed the fulfilment of his dearest wish to the Pope more than to anyone else. Of this he was so persuaded himself that in his letter of thanks he stated that Gregory had not merely furthered the transfer of the Electorate but that he had directly brought it about.[5] In front of the Bishop's palace at Ratisbon a courier was waiting who, as soon as the

[1] The *Briefs of November 12 and December 10, 1622 (State Archives, Vienna) are in part in SCHNITZER, *Zur Politik*, 166.

[2] *Arm.*, XLV., 24, Papal Secret Archives.

[3] All these *Briefs of December 22, 1622, are in *Arm.*, XLV., 24, *loc. cit.* The Elector of Mainz's reply in GOETZ, *Briefe und Akten*, II., 1, 1 note 1.

[4] See GINDELY, IV., 447 seq.; RIEZLER, V., 236 seq.; GOETZ, *Briefe und Akten*, II., 1, 45; *ibid.*, 81 seq., for the " obligation " of Ferdinand to Maximilian, February 24, 1623. See also AREZIO, *L'azione diplomatica*, 23.

[5] *Cf.* KHEVENHILLER, X., 72; AREZIO, *loc. cit.*

investiture had taken place, jumped into the saddle to carry the good news to Rome.

The courier reached the Eternal City on March 5th, 1623 ; on the following day the Pope convened a Consistory in which Maximilian's letter was read. Thus the Cardinals learnt that the College of Electors of Empire had now acquired a Catholic member instead of a Calvinist one.[1] Afterwards Gregory XV. betook himself with all the Cardinals to St. Peter's, there to thank the Lord God of hosts.[2] Salvoes of cannon from the Castle of S. Angelo proclaimed to the Romans an event which was justly considered one of the greatest triumphs of the Catholic cause in Germany and one that could not fail to have far-reaching consequences for the good of the ancient Church

[1] See *Acta consist., Barb. 2926, Vatican Library.

[2] Besides the *report of Cardinal Hohenzollern, Rome, March 18, 1623 (State Archives, Vienna), see also the *account of P. ALALEONE, 1623, 6 Martii ꞉ Papa post consistorium descendit ad S. Petrum (Te Deum) pro gratiarum actione propter electionem ducis Bavariae. In s. Angelo exoneratae bombardae, cardinales fecerunt luminaria (Diarium, Barb. 2818, p. 42, Vatican Library, Ibid., on May 2 : Audientia publica oratoris ducis Bavariae. The ambassador was Wilhelm Freiherr von Fugger, who, together with Maximilian's agent G. B. Crivelli and Cardinal von Zollern, discussed with the Pope the question of papal subsidies. As Ferdinand II. also addressed the Pope in a letter of June 6, 1623, requesting assistance, Maximilian feared for his subsidies. The negotiations had not been concluded when Gregory XV. died : see GOETZ, Briefe und Akten, II., I., 288. OPEL (Niedersäch. Krieg, I., 382) affirms, without indicating his authority, that Wilhelm Freiherr von Fugger sought the papal confirmation of the Electoral dignity for Maximilian in Rome. This is untenable. As RIEZLER shows (V., 238) in the Munich State Archives there is neither papal confirmation nor a request of Maximilian for one. When Riezler says (loc. cit.) that a papal official had advised Maximilian to make a request for the papal confirmation of his dignity, and quotes in support the document : Consilium Gregorio XV. P.M. exhibitum per Mich. Lonigum, he must have overlooked the fact that this work was produced by a Calvinist, J. G. Vossius, and was placed on the Index in 1624 ; see REUSCH, II., 114.

in the Empire.¹ In the evening the Cardinals' houses were illuminated. In course of the following days the papal Chancellery drafted various letters of congratulation. On March 11th Briefs were dispatched to Maximilian, to the Emperor and to Eggenberg. In all of them stress was laid on the significance of the transfer of the Electorate for the Catholic cause: the Emperor had thereby raised an imperishable monument to his name.² On March 18th the Pope wrote to the Elector of Mayence: " At the Diet of Ratisbon the crown of wickedness has been cast down and the mourning of religion has been changed into joy." ³ The letter of congratulation to the Duke of Bavaria was even more enthusiastic ⁴ : " The Lord has grasped His sceptre and the nations who had put their trust in lies and in crime now rage in vain. At last the Catholic religion triumphs by the elevation of your Highness, so greatly desired by the faithful, for you now become a bulwark of the faith and the joy of the whole Church. It is a truly glorious thing to cast out the robbers of the Roman Empire from dominions and dignities which did not belong to them and to earn so great a glory by defending the Catholic religion and defeating the heretics. But the splendour of your good fortune lies in this that both Pope and Emperor consider it to be a triumph for Christ Himself and a joy for Heaven. Now, at last, the Daughter of Sion may shake the dust from her head and put on the garments of rejoicing, for by your attaining to the privilege and honour of electing the

---

[1] *Cf.* the letter of Ludovisi in AREZIO, *L'azione dipl.*, 58.

[2] *Arm.*, XLV., 21, Papal Secret Archives. The original of the Brief to Eggenberg is in the Herberstein Archives, Eggenberg.

[3] *Cecidit corona impietatis et in gaudium versa est religionis tristitia in conventu Ratisbon.*

[4] The Latin text of the letter to Maximilian is in part in ADLZREITER, *Annal.*, III., 114; a German translation in *Darmstädter Allg. Kirchenzeitung*, 1868, 332 *seq.* In his *Brief of April 1, 1622, Gregory XV. again expresses his joy to the Emperor and to the Elector of Cologne (*Arm.*, XLV., 21, Papal Secret Archives). SAVELLI forwarded the Brief with his own *letter of April 6, 1623, State Archives, Vienna.

Emperor, every hope of getting hold of the Roman Empire has been taken from the heretics. Your last letter has given us immense consolation; it is one worthy to be preserved in the chronicles of eternity. As we read it we seemed to taste a heavenly manna and our heart was overwhelmed as with a torrent of joy. In this our delight, we desired our venerable brethren, the Cardinals of the Holy Roman Church, to participate. As your letter was read in the Consistory they listened with the greatest joy to the report of your nomination to the Electorate as well as to the expressions of Bavarian piety. Afterwards, convinced that every victory is a favour of the almighty Lord of hosts, we went in solemn procession to the basilica of the Prince of the Apostles, there to return thanks for so great a triumph for the Church militant. And while hymns of praise to the divine goodness were rising from the sanctuary, the people who crowded the church in dense masses praised the victories and the virtues by which the Duke of Bavaria has shed such lustre upon the Catholic Church. That which we were wont to implore of heaven, of the Father of mercies, for the welfare of those provinces, we now earnestly beg for the dignity and life of your Highness. May the heretics realize that their impious power and their faithless weapons are useless. Now that they have been cast down by so obvious a judgment, their courage will fail them, whilst their awful fate will deter the adventurers of other nations and of future generations from similar criminal undertakings. And if the prince of darkness, spurred by the humiliation he has suffered, should conjure fresh legions out of the hiding places of the rebellious North, in an effort to wrest your dignity from you, you need have no fear : ' Egypt is man and not God : and their horses flesh, and not spirit.'[1] But our help and salvation is God, mighty in battle, whose wrath no man can stand, whom all the hosts of heaven serve. For the rest, this matter which we had so much at heart, will always be the object of our solicitude now that it has been happily realized, that is, your advancement by the pious Emperor and the exaltation of your Highness. But all this you will hear in greater detail

---

[1] Isaias, XXIII., 1 *seqq*.

from our Venerable Brother, Charles, Bishop of Aversa, our nuncio, who brings you our papal congratulations and the assurance of the Holy See's protection on which you may always rely with confidence. We impart to your Highness our Apostolic Blessing, O most beloved son, and we embrace with affection the new Elector of the Holy Roman Empire and the old champion of the Catholic religion." Rome, March 11th, 1623.

(4)

Gregory XV. had taken a leading part in the transfer of the Palatine Electorate to Maximilian. In like manner he also played a great rôle in the reorganization of religious conditions in Bohemia which was set on foot after the defeat of the rebels of that country.[1] The principles which guided the Holy See

[1] The earlier accounts of PESCHEK (*Gesch. der Gegenreformation in Böhmen*, 2 vols., 1843), HURTER (IX., 211 seqq.), and REUSS, (*Destruction du Protestantisme en Bohême*, 1868), are completed by Gindely's work, with which compare HUBER's review in the *Mitteil. des Österr. Hist. Instit.*, XV., 693 seq., and that of HIRN, in *Hist. Jahrbuch*, XVI., 604 seq. BILEK's *Geschichte der katholischen Reformation* (*Reformace katolická*, Prague, 1892) is worthless (*cf.* J. SVOBODA, in *Sbornik hist. Kronžku*, 1893, 98 seq.; HELFERT, in *Wiener Vaterland*, 1893, no. 224); also BILEK's *Jesuitengeschichte* (*Dějiny řádu Tovaryšstva Ježišova*), Prague, 1896 (*cf.* J. HODR, *Tomáše V. Bilka Dějiny řádu Tivaryšstva Ježišova* [*Th. Bileks Geschichte des Jesuitenordens*], Brnč, 1897, and B. SPÁCIL, *Jesuité*, Prazě, 1923). Contrary to the statement of Gindely, that Catholicism in Bohemia represents an exotic growth, it must be remembered that both Lutheran and Calvinist Protestantism are in their origin as little Czech as is the heresy of Huss. Utraquism alone was an indigenous growth, which by that time had become so reduced that it could hardly be regarded as a decisive factor in the Church life of Bohemia. Since many Utraquists had passed over to Lutheranism, SEIFERT thinks (*Hochland*, XVIII., 2 (1921), 150), that " they would have delivered up their people to the Germanizing movement, had it not been for the battle of the White Mountain." On the other hand HELFERT (*Wiener Vaterland*, 1893, no. 224) points out that the defeat of the imperial

from the first are clearly stated in the Instruction, dated April 12th, 1621, for the new nuncio at the imperial Court, Carlo Carafa.[1] There we read that the Emperor could not better manifest his gratitude to God for his victory than by restoring religious conditions as they formerly obtained in the kingdom of Bohemia. He now had the power to do so : let him use it for the glory of Him who had granted it. Since the Bohemians, because of their former and present rebellion, must be kept well in hand, force will have to be used to recall them from their erroneous beliefs. The Emperor was no longer bound by the rights and privileges of Bohemia which he had confirmed at his election, because of the rising, and because the people had not observed the clause which forbade them to tolerate heresies ; in particular the " Letter of Majesty ", which had been extorted from Rudolph II. in 1609, and which, in actual fact, was the first cause of the rebellion of 1618, was no longer binding. Lutherans, Piccards, Baptists and Calvinists must be cast out whilst the Hussites should be reconciled to the Catholic Church. The concession of the chalice which former Popes had granted in order to avoid greater evils, must be withdrawn because it had been used as a cloak for every kind of sect. The Catholic religion must be restored in all its purity. To this end the following means are suggested : the foundation of a Catholic University in Prague, the reinstatement of Catholic priests and schoolmasters, the prohibition of heretical books and the dissemination of good ones, especially the Catholic catechism, help for Catholic booksellers and printers together with the suppression of heretical ones, support for the Jesuit missions and those of other Orders, episcopal visitations for the reform of the secular and regular clergy, the erection of Colleges to remedy the lack of priests, the restitution of confiscated Church property, the revenues

army would have caused the flooding of the land with Calvinist, i.e. foreign elements, and in the course of a few decades would have turned it into a German country. The same would therefore have happened as actually came to pass through the process of the Catholic restoration.

[1] See KOLLMANN, *Acta*, I, 59 *seq.*

of which should be used for the support of the Colleges and the converts.

Carafa devoted all his strength to the duties here outlined. For a proper estimate of his achievement it must be borne in mind that in no part of the Austrian territories had apostasy from the Church been more wide-spread than in Bohemia.

The report to Propaganda by the Jesuit Lamormaini, in the autumn of 1621, allows us a glimpse into the conditions then obtaining in that country.[1] At the very outset, Lamormaini gives it as his opinion that the greatest misfortune for Bohemia was the fact that the Academy founded by Charles IV. had now been in the hands of the Hussites for 200 years. From that centre they had constantly sent out preachers and propagandists of the Hussite impiety into every town and village of Bohemia, and any vacancy that occurred was immediately filled. As a rule these people married rich widows, became notaries, councillors, burgomasters or parish priests, whilst they had always done their best to prevent Catholics from settling in the towns. During the last forty years the University, which had been more than half Lutheran for a long time, had shown a marked inclination towards Calvinism, until it ended by adopting it completely, thus becoming the home and fountain of all heresies and rebellions. The plans for the last insurrection had been drawn up and sanctioned there. The Rector of the Academy, Jessenius, who in company with several others had recently paid with his life for his share in the rebellion, had been secretly dispatched by the rebels to the Hungarian Diet at Pressburg, in order to prevent Ferdinand from being accepted as King of Hungary. Connected with the Caroline Academy was the so-called " Lower Consistory ", a refuge and sanctuary for priests of loose conduct who had thrown off the yoke of their ecclesiastical superiors. Its members were all heretical preachers and it arrogated to itself the right of nominating such preachers to ecclesiastical benefices and of installing them.

[1] First published by LÄMMER (*Melet.*, 458 *seq.*) then by GRISAR (*Zeitschr. für kath. Theol.*, X., 727 *seq.*) and by JEŽEK (*Sbornik hist. Kronžu*, 1899) and lastly by KOLLMANN (*Acta*, I., 17 *seq.*).

An " Ecclesiastical Estate of Empire " had ceased to exist in Bohemia from the time of the tyrant Ziska, and the possessions of priests and Bishops had been confiscated by the laity. There were even civil laws forbidding ecclesiastics of the kingdom to hold real property. A Bishop had neither seat nor vote in the Diet. The Emperors had indeed recently restored the dignity of an Archbishop (1561), but that did not carry the privilege of a seat in the Parliament. The other bishoprics and prelatures were destroyed and up till now their revenues had been devoured by the laity. The monasteries and their many beautiful churches had been destroyed by that same robber (Ziska) and presented a pitiable appearance. True, in Prague the greater number of the churches had been in part restored, with the help of some religiously-minded kings and nobles. For the rest all parish churches in the towns of the district around Prague, and in every other Bohemian town, with the exception of Budweis, Pilsen, Brüx and a few others, had been confiscated by the heretics and remained in their hands.

Of the parishes belonging to the territories of Catholic noblemen, and in the towns and villages where the parochial office was still in the hands of Catholic priests (over a hundred in Bohemia alone and as many or even more in Moravia and Silesia), were deprived of priests and pastors of souls, because the parish priests had either died or had been killed in successive risings, whilst some had fled or had gone over to heresy. As for the men who previous to the insurrection were being trained for the priesthood in the Colleges of the Society of Jesus, they had either adopted another career or had migrated elsewhere. To this must be added that owing to the fact that all tithes have been seized by the laity, the priests' incomes had become so small that they could only support themselves by tilling and cultivating the land like peasants. The right of patronage was mostly in the hands of the heretics, and if a Catholic landowner sold his property to a heretic, the right to nominate the parish priest also passed to him. In this way it had come to pass that even in places where Catholic priests had maintained themselves, preachers of the purchaser's persuasion had gradually substituted themselves in their place. The disastrous practice by which on the death of the parish priest the patrons claim all his property, to the detriment of his successor, had become almost universal.

"Such are the conditions in Bohemia as regards the ecclesiastical state" says Lamormaini, and the Jesuit's account was confirmed by Carafa in a memorandum addressed to Propaganda, dated October 8th, 1622.[1] In Moravia and Silesia and in the Upper and Lower Lusatia, the position was the same, according to Lamormaini, with the exception that in Moravia and Silesia the ecclesiastical state enjoyed the respect due to it and the Bishops had a seat and a vote in the Diet. In Moravia the Society of Jesus had a College at Olmütz and at Brünn, whereas in Silesia and Lusatia all the schools were heretical with the exception of Neisse.

As to civil conditions, Lamormaini's report continues, printers of every sect were to be found in Prague and they printed books as they pleased. They also imported books of every kind from abroad. Moreover the sons both of nobles and others, went abroad in order to frequent Lutheran and Calvinist Universities, just as it suited either themselves or their guardians. In addition to all this, the greater number of officials, whether of a higher, lower or middle rank, were as a rule heretics, even those of the Council which decided on the bestowal of benefices or of what remained of the Church's property. Almost all the lawers were heretics.

Another great abuse in Bohemia was that the sons of subjects might not apply themselves to study nor enter an Order or the ecclesiastical state without the permission of their feudal lord. No less deplorable was yet another abuse, namely, that as soon as students had received a measure of education, they were immediately withdrawn by their lords who made them their stewards, secretaries, administrators and so forth. Thus it happened but rarely that one or other of the subjects, even of a Catholic feudal lord, became capable of assuming any of the more important offices of the kingdom, and scarcely any pursued their studies long enough to enable them to attain

[1] See *Relatio Bohemica* in KOLLMANN, I., 103 seq.

a Doctor's degree. Hence it was that so few Catholics sat in the law courts.

In many towns of Bohemia the artisans had agreed not to allow Catholic craftsmen to join their guilds. In others no Catholic could obtain the right of citizenship or membership of the local council.

As a rule, when the guardians and next-of-kin of orphans were heretics, they took care that their wards got no opportunity for learning the Catholic faith: on the contrary, they saw to it that they were brought up in the hatred of everything Catholic.

Lamormaini expressed the hope that the Emperor would remedy these sad conditions, seeing that he had asked for the advice of the Catholic lords of Bohemia. The latter had recommended as the most effective remedies, in the first instance, the suppression of the schools of heretics and their displacement by Catholic schools; secondly, the erection of two new dioceses which would be supported out of the revenues of such property as had been confiscated. Furthermore the Emperor should restore the dignity and immunity of the ecclesiastical state and repeal the laws which limited or took away from ecclesiastics and the Church in general the right to acquire property. Finally two Colleges should be opened, one for the sons of the nobility and one for those of the middle classes; the latter were to be allowed complete liberty in the choice of a profession. Since many nobles and other distinguished families had come down in the world, it was to be hoped that the opportunity offered by these Colleges would lead back to the Catholic faith a number of men who later on would do the State useful service in divers positions. These schools should be supported out of confiscated property. In addition to this Martinitz and Slawata requested the Pope, through Lamormaini, for a special subsidy in aid of the formation of priests for Bohemia, Moravia, Silesia and Lusatia. They expressed the hope that the Pope would exhort the Emperor to endow the seminaries and to take the Catholic restoration in hand. Since the Catholics placed the greatest hope in the Emperor's zeal and the heretics, conscious of their previous misdeeds, trembled not only for their possessions but for their very lives, the above-named Counts were of opinion that action should not be gradual or dilatory but prompt, lest the Catholics should be disappointed and the heretics should take fresh courage, with the result that the restoration of the Catholic faith would become more difficult.

Suggestions as to how the Catholic religion might be restored in Bohemia, such as those submitted to Propaganda by Lamormaini, were also offered by other counsellors to the Emperor, as, for instance, a memorandum by an anonymous Jesuit which, however, adds nothing to Lamormaini's advice.[1] However, the author expressly recommends the erection of new dioceses in Bohemia and of more Jesuit Colleges ; Abbots should be made to see to it that their monks acquired learning. A meeting of theologians convoked by the Archbishop on August 2nd, stated these various desiderata in great detail ; they demanded that in future the Catholic religion alone should be tolerated, and that all influential positions should be given to Catholics ; the chalice for the laity was to be abolished.[2]

The Archbishop of Prague, Lohelius, was anxious that immediately after the battle of Prague Ferdinand II. should take advantage of the impression created by his victory and strike the iron whilst it was hot,[3] but the imperial advisers held opposite views. They were of opinion that until Bohemia was completely pacified and the Emperor's enemies entirely crushed, it was best not to attempt the restoration of the ecclesiastical situation.[4] But even they indicated rules which could be put into execution in the future. With regard to non-Catholics they were of opinion that prompt action should be taken against the communities of " Fratelli " (Bohemians) and the Calvinists who had no rights in the country ; but it was necessary to give further consideration to the measures to be adopted against the Lutherans and the

[1] See Kröss, *Geschichte*, II., 1, 152 seqq., and *Hist Jahrbuch*, XXXIV. (1913), 1 seqq., 257 seqq.

[2] Kröss, II., 1, 158 seq.

[3] See *ibid.*, 151 seqq., cf. 149 ; Gindely, *Gegenreformation*, 94.

[4] Carafa, *Comment.*, 107.

Utraquists.[1] Even the Emperor's confessor was against treating all non-Catholics alike; all rebels were, indeed, heretics, but not all heretics were rebels; many among them had taken up arms on behalf of the Emperor.[2]

The whole affair depended on the Lieutenant of Bohemia, Charles von Liechtenstein, rather than on the councillors and even the Emperor's instructions. Liechtenstein was in favour of proceeding very gradually. He had given express permission to the preachers of the Augsburg Confession, shortly after the battle of Prague, to remain in the country and to continue their preachment. On the same occasion he withdrew the permission to practise their religion[3] from the followers of Calvin whose privileges had been forfeited in consequence of the insurrection, though he refrained from further measures against them. Thereafter the Calvinist preachers pretended to profess the teachings of Luther and dressed up their sermons accordingly,[4] they even remained in possession of churches to which Catholics had a rightful claim[5]; thus when the parish of Kuttenberg fell vacant, Liechtenstein allowed the townspeople freely to choose a preacher provided that he did not belong to the prohibited Bohemian Confession.[6]

Not until May, 1621, did Liechtenstein, in conjunction with the Archbishop, evict the Utraquist preachers from three churches in Prague in order to give them to Catholic priests. Shortly before that he had sent for the Calvinist preachers when he put the question to them whether they were prepared to embrace Catholicism and to be ordained priests by the Archbishop. After that many Protestant preachers preferred to leave Bohemia.[7]

But decisive measures were not taken until the end of

[1] Kröss, II., 1, 147 *seq.*
[2] Kröss, *Geschichte*, II., 1, 148.
[3] Carafa, *Comment.*, 107.
[4] *Ibid.*
[5] *e.g.* the church of St. Nicholas (property of the Dean of Karlstein). Gindely, *Gegenreformation*, 88.
[6] Gindely, 91; Kröss, 150.
[7] Gindely, 93-5; Kröss, 156.

May, after the arrival in Vienna of the new papal nuncio, Carlo Carafa.[1] He was instructed, in addition to the transfer of the Palatine Electorate to Bavaria, also to promote the ecclesiastical restoration of Bohemia in every way. This was a policy which was at variance with the opinions current in leading circles in Vienna, but it was wholly in keeping with the energetic character of the nuncio and his employers in Rome. In his reports, Carafa severely blames the Viennese councillors for their inability to overcome their slowness even when " the question was to act rather than to deliberate ". In his opinion the Bohemian insurrection would have been easily quelled had it been treated from the beginning with greater boldness and determination.[2] The measures hitherto taken with a view to the ecclesiastical transformation of Bohemia Carafa describes as irresolute and half-hearted. Unshakably convinced as he was of the truth of the Catholic religion, beside which no other religion can have any rights, he regarded the Catholic reformation of Bohemia—whose decline, as well as that of Germany was due to heresy—not merely as a piece of sound statecraft, but as a boon for the nation as well as a duty towards God to whom the Emperor owed special gratitude for his wonderful victory. Imbued with these sentiments, Carafa was determined to take the cause of the Catholic reformation energetically in hand. From the first he was unwearied in his efforts to acquaint himself with existing conditions, and with this end in view he sought information in every quarter. For the conditions in Bohemia his informant was an excellent priest, Canon Platais of Plattenstein.[3] Carafa's reports to Rome show the width of his investigations. He collected an enormous quantity of information about persons, about religious and civil conditions and their historical development, as well as on Germany's relations with the other European Powers. He was often better informed than the Emperor himself. He followed with the closest attention the

[1] See *Relatio Bohemica*, in KOLLMANN, I., 110.
[2] See CARAFA, *Relatione*, ed. Müller, 147.
[3] For Platais von Plattenstein, see KOLLMANN, *Acta*, I., 54, note 6.

course of events lest any opportunity should escape him of furthering his plans. Since there was question of the Kingdom of God, he thought it was not right to make excessive human prudence the sole criterion of what was to be done. "It is our business to do our duty and to leave the rest to the divine goodness."[1] "Earthly considerations," he once said to Liechtenstein, "must not be allowed to stand in the way of God's glory. Hence if we do our duty in the service of God, we may rest assured that the divine Majesty will not allow us to fall into danger on account of that."[2]

Before all else Carafa sought to obtain from the Emperor the banishment of the Calvinist and other sectarian preachers. Soon after the battle of the White Mountain, Ferdinand II. had taken advice on this point with some theologians, especially with certain Jesuits.[3] In some cases he had ordered the restoration of confiscated Church property[4] and within the space of a few months he had contributed 100,000 florins towards the support of reinstated Catholic priests.[5] On March 30th, 1621, at the request of Liechtenstein, he decreed the banishment of preachers "who professed Calvinism or any other teaching not previously tolerated".[6] Notwithstanding the unfavourable circumstances of the times, Ferdinand was determined to take further steps. The numerous battles with Mansfeld, Jägerndorf, and the troops of the Winter King, "which had been fought at the expense of the Emperor, had occasioned plenty of expenses, burdens and dangers, but the Emperor disregarded it all." Carafa, as he himself reports, spurred on the Emperor's zeal.[7] "Thus," the nuncio writes, "at my request the Emperor published a decree on June 3rd, 1621, against all preachers, professors and

---

[1] See *Relatione*, ed. Müller, 243.

[2] Letter of Carafa, September 17, 1622, in the *Zeitschr. für kath. Theol.*, X. (1886), 736.

[3] *Cf.* Kröss, in *Hist. Jahrb.*, XXXIV., 25 *seq.*

[4] Carafa, *Comment.*, 108. *Cf. ibid.*, App. 71-4.

[5] Carafa, 112.

[6] *Ibid.*, Appendix 74.

[7] Carafa, *Comment.*, 117.

schoolmasters who had disseminated the errors of Calvin within the Empire, in Prague and out of it, or any other sectarian teachings forbidden by law, as well as against all those who had encouraged high treason from the professorial chair, who had asserted that it was illegal to recognize the Emperor in Bohemia, those who had crowned Frederick or who, in contravention of their oath of allegiance, had been present at the meetings held in the Caroline College. Those who fell under this sentence were to be granted only a short respite in which to leave the country; they were to be threatened with heavy penalties should they remain, and it was to be explained to them that these penalties were not inflicted because of their religious beliefs, but for high treason."[1]

If this edict had been published, all the preachers would have had to leave the country, " for not one of them had refrained from censorious or insulting discourses ".[2] Liechtenstein, however, did not at once publish the imperial decree. The reasons he alleged were that banishment would be useless seeing that the heretical landowners still possessed the right of patronage, hence they would promptly induct fresh preachers. Moreover, the times were still too unfavourable and no preacher would avow himself a Calvinist.[3] Though the Emperor issued repeated orders, months went by and nothing was done to expel the preachers. Carafa, however, never ceased to urge the Emperor, especially after hostilities in Bohemia had almost come to an end and the Silesians had abandoned the Margrave of Jägerndorf. In view of the politicians' supreme argument, namely that in the event of a popular rising they were not sufficiently armed, Carafa urged that a garrison should be sent to Prague, and this was done.[4]

---

[1] *Ibid.*, 117 *seq.*, and App. 75 *seq.*, where the decree is printed. *Cf.* D'ELVERT, in the documents of the hist.-statistic section of the *Mährisch-schlesische-Gesellschaft*, XVI., 73 *seq.*

[2] CARAFA, *Comment.*, 118.

[3] CARAFA, *Relatione*, 240–41; *Comment.*, 124, 134; GINDELY, *Gegenreformation*, 99–103.

[4] CARAFA, *Relatione*, 241; *Comment.*, 135; GINDELY, 108.

On December 13th, when all external danger had disappeared, an edict of expulsion was published at Prague and the other royal cities; however, it was not to have the character of a religious persecution, but that of a political measure. All those preachers who on May 29th, 1618, had read from the pulpit the document justifying the Protestant Diet of that date, or who had promoted the election of the Palatine and taken part in his coronation, or who had helped to support and widen the "accursed confederation", were to leave the city of Prague within three days and the country within eight days, for being disturbers of the public peace and contemners of His Majesty.[1] About thirty preachers of Prague obeyed the command; six were converted to Catholicism.[2] But a number of preachers of the Lutheran Confession remained in hiding in the country and continued to preach. Contrary to the Emperor's intention and the tenor of the edict, at Prague two preachers of German nationality and belonging to the Bohemian Confession were not notified of the decree of banishment. Consideration for the Saxon Elector was probably the explanation of such restraint. In other cities the decree was even less thoroughly carried out, partly because there were not enough Catholic priests to fill the parishes.[3]

Until such time as he should succeed in obtaining the banishment of the preachers, Carafa had recourse to other means to forward the restoration of the old religion. Shortly after the execution of the most notable instigators of an insurrection which had brought all the horrors of war upon a flourishing kingdom,[4] "whilst the burden of guilt still weighed upon almost the whole of Bohemia and none could feel sure of their lives, the Emperor, on Carafa's advice, let it be known

[1] See LUNDORP, *Acta publ.*, II., 555.
[2] *Cf.* KOLLMANN, I., 117.
[3] See HUBER, V., 212 *seq.*
[4] This is the opinion of K. A. MENZEL (VII., 42). As a further punishment for the revolution, an enormous confiscation of property was also carried out; for this see GINDELY, IV., 70 *seq.*; *Jahrb. für Gesch. des Protestantismus in Österr.*, VII., 174 *seq.*; HUBER, V., 200 *seq.*

that he would be ready to grant a pardon, provided that the greater part of the country were willing to make itself worthy thereof." The words are a pretty clear hint as to what it was the Emperor wanted. " Under the pressure of fear," Carafa reports, "many hastened to be instructed in the Catholic religion, and since little by little God purified their disposition, they embraced the Catholic faith." [1]

In view of the fact that the Archbishop of Prague "though full of apostolic zeal, was a very old and sickly man, who for lack of means and physical exhaustion, the result of the sufferings he had endured, was unable to do as much as he would have wished," Carafa urged the Emperor and his councillors to assist that prelate and to send energetic priests to help him. Thereupon various Orders and the Canons of the Cathedral received grants for the erection of seminaries; soon students, religious and priests flocked from all parts.[2]

Carafa did not rest until he had attained his goal. In his efforts to get the Lutheran preachers driven from Prague, he had a hard struggle with the " politicians ", who stood for the view that the Lutherans were not included in the decree of banishment since they were neither Calvinists nor subjects of the Empire, and their guilt had not been proved. When Carafa furnished evidence that they too were guilty of insurrection, the " politicians " replied that in any case it was necessary to tolerate them so as not to irritate the Duke of Saxony and the other Lutheran princes who, so far, had supported the Empire or at least had remained neutral. Consequently at a meeting held at Vienna, in the palace of the Archduke Liechtenstein, then Governor of Prague, at the beginning of 1622, notwithstanding the clear and irrefragable arguments to the contrary brought forward by von Platais and the Premonstratensian Abbot Questenberg, it was decided to tolerate the Lutherans until Easter of the following year, 1623. On the expiration of that time-limit Carafa renewed his request to the Emperor ; however, he failed in his

[1] See CARAFA, *Comment.*, 121 seq.

[2] *Ibid.*, 123 seq. *Cf. Relatio Bohemica*, in KOLLMANN, I., III seq.

efforts in view of the Hungarian Diet which was about to meet.¹ As soon as the Diet was over, Carafa turned anew to the Emperor: it was not a question merely of the two preachers, but of the free dissemination of the Catholic religion, for as long as these men continued to preach, the teachers of the Augsburg Confession would also spread their heretical tenets in the other towns and on the estates of the nobles.² Carafa was able to supply evidence of the increasing boldness of the two preachers who publicly uttered insults and calumnies against Catholics and attempted to seduce the people by offering them Communion with the chalice. "Who," he asked, "was to prevent the Emperor from applying the right of reformation in his own house and in his hereditary States when Catholic worship was not tolerated in any part of Saxony." ³ The consequence of Carafa's representation was that at last, on October 24th, 1622, Ferdinand II. commanded the Governor of Bohemia, Liechtenstein, to order the expulsion of the Lutheran preachers, beginning with those in Prague, and to close the two churches which they had built there in virtue of the "Letter of Majesty". The same edict of expulsion was to be proclaimed in all the royal cities. The intervention of the Duke of Saxony on behalf of the exiles was in vain; Carafa successfully countered all his efforts. In the same way the attempts of some princes of Empire, among whom there were a few timorous Catholics, to induce the Emperor at the Diet of Ratisbon to change his mind, also failed. With regard to the reform in Bohemia, Ferdinand declared that it was no concern of the Diet; every Prince, whether an Elector or one of lower rank, had the right of reform in his hereditary States; hence there was no reason to suspect the Emperor's loyalty to his pledged word seeing that he had given repeated assurances—and he now renewed them—that he had maintained

---

[1] See CARAFA, *Relatio Bohemica, loc. cit.*, 119 seq.; *Relatione*, ed. Müller, 241 seq.

[2] See CARAFA, *Comment.*, 155.

[3] See CARAFA, *Relatione*, 242 seq.; cf. CARAFA, *Comment.*, 160.

all the articles of the religious peace in the Empire, and that he did not wish to infringe anyone's rights.[1]

Among the measures taken at Carafa's instigation with a view to the restoration of the Catholic religion in Bohemia, not the least important was the abolition of the vernacular in the Liturgy and the prohibition of the chalice to the laity (Communion under both kinds), a privilege which Pius IV. had conceded to Bohemia on certain conditions which had not been kept. Carafa ordered the removal of the chalices placed over the churches as emblems of the Hussite heresy, especially the huge chalice over the porch of the church of Teyn at Prague.[2] At his instance the Emperor commanded the anniversary of the death of Huss, which had been observed as a Saint's day, to be struck out of the Calendar; hence on July 6th, 1622, all the churches in Prague remained closed.[3] In Moravia, where Carafa's energy made itself strongly felt,[4] the same procedure as in Bohemia was adopted: the first step was the expulsion of the Anabaptists, soon to be followed by that of the Lutheran preachers from Iglau. Here also there was no sign of any determined opposition on the part of the Protestants.[5]

One of the greatest difficulties which Carafa repeatedly deplores in his reports,[6] was the lack of suitable Catholic priests; their ranks had been so thinned during the years in which Protestantism was triumphant in Bohemia, that in many places there remained none at all. The Archbishop of

---

[1] See CARAFA's *Ragguaglio*, in KOLLMANN, I., 351 seq. Cf. GINDELY, IV., 547, 550 seq., 556 seq.; RITTER, III., 183.

[2] See CARAFA's *Relatio Bohemica* in KOLLMANN, I., 124 seq., 127 seq.; *Relatione*, ed. Müller, 250 seq. Cf. GINDELY, *Gegenreformation*, 93 seq., 107, 197. See also SCHMIDL, III., 316 seq., 323.

[3] See CARAFA's *Relatio Bohemica*, loc. cit., 132 seq.; *Relatione*, ed. Müller, 251 seq.

[4] See KOLLMANN, I., 85, 87 seq., 181, 246 seq.

[5] The results were great (6,000); see KOLLMANN, I., 332. Cf. GINDELY, IV., 564-6.

[6] See KOLLMANN, I., 135.

Prague and Carafa did everything in their power to remedy the evil. From the point of view of the language, Croat and Slavonic priests could have been pressed into service, but none were forthcoming because a like scarcity of clergy obtained in those parts. Hence Carafa, with the warm support of Propaganda, began by calling for the help of some Polish Franciscans from Gnesen, and later on for that of some Augustinians and Discalced Carmelites.[1] He also saw to the restoration of the old monasteries and the preaching of missions by Capuchins and Jesuits.[2] He likewise suggested the erection of new dioceses. He laid stress on the fact that, on account of the geographic position of Bohemia, no effort should be spared, for the hope of reconquering the whole of the North for the Church depended upon success in Bohemia.[3]

The Jesuits rendered extraordinarily valuable services to the Catholic restoration of Bohemia. Immediately after the battle of Prague they returned to that city; elsewhere also they had gradually taken possession of their old residences and in the course of 1622 they were back at their usual tasks.[4] In their own church at Prague they preached in Bohemian, German and Italian; they also preached in four other churches of Prague, whilst the scholastics of the Order taught the catechism in six churches.[5] In the following year they undertook to serve three more churches in Prague. The fears of the pessimists that their preaching would be poorly attended, were not fulfilled.[6] Pilgrimages were resumed. Every year the feast of Corpus Christi and in 1622 the celebration of the canonization of St. Ignatius and St. Francis Xavier were attended by vast multitudes.[7] From other towns also we have

---

[1] See *ibid.*, 93 *seq.*, 161 *seq.*, 224 *seq.*, 228, 346; CARAFA, *Relatione*, 253. *Cf.* the letter of CARAFA to Propaganda, July 30, 1622, in KOLLMANN, I., 53 *seq.*, and their answer, *ibid.*, 65 *seq.*

[2] See KOLLMANN, I., 151 *seq.*, 161 *seq.*, 224 *seq.*, 228, 346.

[3] *Ibid.*, 155.

[4] KRÖSS, *Geschichte*, II., 1, 19 *seqq.*

[5] SCHMIDL, III., 327 *seq.*

[6] KRÖSS, *loc. cit.*, 163 *seq.*, 169.

[7] *Ibid.*, 168 *seq.*

reports of the great activity of the Jesuits.[1] Contrary to their usual practice, they undertook parochial work, and that even before their General had informed them of the express wish of Propaganda on this point. Furthermore they founded fifteen missions in Bohemia and Moravia in order to repair the ravages of war.[2] From the College of Prague they worked in the towns of Tabor and Pisek, Wodnian, Roth-Aujezd and in the territories of the Premonstratensian monastery of Zion near Prague.[3] Zdenko von Kolowrat called them to Wittingau and in Komotau Count Martinitz gave them the church attached to the almshouses after the Protestant preachers had been expelled.[4] Krumau and Neuhaus, where the Jesuits had been working for some time, became completely Catholic in the year 1622. " During these last days," so we read in the diary of the Jesuit Rector, Chanowski, of Krumau, on March 9th and 13th, 1622, " with the conversion of those who had held out till the end, all the heads of families have become Catholics without exception. Only a few preferred to seek new homes rather than give up their heretical tenets." [5] In Prague, in the years 1622 and 1623, there were 648 conversions of Protestants, among them eleven nobles and three professors of the University.[6] The Jesuit's greatest success was obtained in Neuhaus, in the territory of Count Wilhelm Slawata where, in a short time, they registered 2,000 conversions.[7]

In other places the Jesuits met with serious obstacles. At Rzeczich nobody would at first give them hospitality, nor would anyone speak to them or greet them.[8] In Komotau there were only some twenty conversions to Catholicism because the Protestants still set their hopes on Mansfeld.[9]

---

[1] SCHMIDL, III., 397 seq.
[2] CORDARA, I., 358.
[3] SCHMIDL, III., 320; KRÖSS, 178 seq.
[4] SCHMIDL, III., 329.
[5] Ibid., cf. 407; KRÖSS, 171.
[6] SCHMIDL, III., 327, 404.
[7] Ibid., 336 seq.
[8] Ibid., 336.
[9] Ibid., 329; KRÖSS, 171 seq.

To this must be added the profound ignorance of the populace in religious matters in many places. In Chlumetz the population had retired into the woods during the Bohemian insurrection. They had lived there for four years without any spiritual ministrations and had run wild so that they were "only distinguished from the beasts by their outward appearance." In Serowitz many were found who could not recite the Lord's Prayer and who imagined that all was well, so long as they partook of Communion with the chalice.[1]

In order to stimulate the memory of the unlearned, the Jesuits, in view of the Bohemian's fondness for music, turned the Catechism into verse and set it to tunes so that it could be sung by the children.[2] Other measures were likewise adopted. The Jesuits of Prague spent a large sum of money which had been given to them on the publication and dissemination of 6,000 copies of a book dealing with religious subjects.[3] A legacy left to them by the Bishop of Olmütz, John Grodecius, was spent in the same way.[4] The Jesuit Chanowski did not hesitate, notwithstanding his noble extraction, to walk through the streets with a little bell, calling the children together for Christian instruction, so that one of his relatives began to have misgivings about his sanity.[5]

Besides bringing the people back to the ancient faith, the Jesuit missionaries also had at heart their moral training. It was always a source of particular happiness to them when they succeeded in effecting the removal of deep-rooted enmities. At Olmütz, in 1622, they succeeded in restoring peace in twenty-two families by reconciling husbands and wives. In Krumau, in the same year, one of the councillors was so touched by their preaching that he sought out his

---

[1] SCHMIDL, III., 336 *seq.* On the successful missions on their own estates, see KRÖSS, 179 *seqq.*

[2] SCHMIDL, III., 336.

[3] *Ibid.*, 330.

[4] *Ibid.*, 406.

[5] *Ibid.*, 333 *seq.*

enemy and with tears in his eyes begged forgiveness for the wrong he had done to him.¹

The Jesuits devoted themselves especially to works of charity. In consequence of the savagery of the populace, capital punishment was of frequent occurrence. A Jesuit in Olmütz gave spiritual help in their last moments to forty-one men condemned to death. The simple people were filled with admiration and confidence when they saw one of the Fathers ministering for a long time to a prisoner in whose semi-mortified body worms were beginning to form and to whom the gaolers attended only with a cloth before their nostrils on account of the stench. In Gitschin the non-Catholics were greatly impressed by the fact that the Fathers took the greatest interest in the fate of some soldiers condemned to death. Their own preachers, who considered such services beneath their dignity, had not accustomed them to such examples.²

In Bohemia, as everywhere else, the Jesuits gave special attention to education.³ In this respect it was of the utmost importance that at the beginning of 1623 the University of Prague was handed over to the Fathers and that in conjunction with their own Institute of philosophy and theology it became a new University (Carolo-Ferdinandea), the Rector of which was always to be the Superior of the Jesuit College for the time being.⁴ In November, 1622, the University of Vienna was in

---

¹ *Ibid.*, 348 ; *cf.* 408.

² SCHMIDL, III., 401 *seq.*

³ *Cf.* J. VÁVRA's essay on the beginnings of the Catholic reform in Bohemia in *Sbornik hist. Kronžku*, 1893, III., 3 *seq.*

⁴ KRÖSS, *loc. cit.*, 105 *seqq.* *Cf.* GINDELY, IV., 547 *seq.* ; *Gegenreformation*, 147 *seq.* ; HUBER, V., 213 *seq.* ; *Hist.-polit. Blätter*, CXVII., 541 *seq.* The Rector, the Dean and the President of the Colleges of the University had been compelled by command of Liechtenstein to resign as early as April 22, 1622 ; see KOLLMANN, *Acta*, I., 41 *seq.* *Cf.* also K. SPIEGEL, in *Mitteil. des Vereins für Gesch. der Deutschen in Böhmen*, LXII. (1924), 11 *seq.*, where there is an account of the lengthy and wearisome difficulties, especially with the Archbishop of Prague, which arose from this provision which the General of the Jesuits opposed. (See *Anal. Boll.*, XLIV., 230).

part entrusted to the Jesuits to whom were assigned the majority as well as the most important chairs in the Faculty of philosophy and theology. For the rest Lower Austria, notwithstanding the fact that the majority of the States had taken part in the insurrection against the Emperor, was treated far more leniently than Bohemia, though Protestant worship was forbidden in the towns and in several places, especially in Vienna, Protestants were banished.[1]

Gregory XV., whom Carafa kept most accurately informed, followed the development of things in Bohemia with the greatest attention. On November 5th, 1622, he wrote to Ferdinand II. concerning the Catholic restoration in Bohemia, more particularly about the restoration of the property belonging to the archdiocese of Prague.[2] In a Brief of December 10th, 1622, he discussed the important question of erecting new dioceses.[3] Gregory XV. did not live to see the further development of the Catholic restoration in Bohemia and Austria, nor the full exploitation of the victories of Maximilian and Tilly in 1621 and 1622. In that respect also he only saw the beginnings. In the Upper Palatinate, immediately after the conquest of that old hereditary territory of Frederick V., Maximilian took the necessary steps for the restoration of the Catholic faith. In 1621 he began the work of conversion by calling in Jesuits, Capuchins and Franciscans, for he hoped at first to attain his end by means of peaceful instruction. Out of consideration for Saxony he refrained, for a time, from adopting forcible methods: Lutheran and Calvinist preachers were allowed to remain at their posts, and even the Calvinist church council of Amberg was not touched.[4] On the other hand in the Palatinate of the right bank of the Rhine

---

[1] See KINK, I., 1, 353 seq.; HUBER, V., 240 seq.

[2] *Arm., XLV., 24, Papal Secret Archives.

[3] Ibid.

[4] Cf. besides the earlier literature on the subject quoted by RIEZLER (V., 320), the work, based on research in the archives of M. HÖGL: *Die Bekehrung der Oberpfalz durch Kurfürst Maximilian I.*, vol. 1: *Gegenreformation*, Regensburg, 1903. See also DUHR, II., 2, 341 seq.

he proceeded more sternly. In February, 1623, the Calvinist preachers were exiled from Heidelberg, and later on from all other places. Jesuits were also called in to bring back the inhabitants to the ancient Church.[1] Rome's anxiety for a full exploitation of the successes of the war for the benefit of the Palatinate appears from the fact that a special Congregation was constituted to deal with the religious affairs of the Lower and Upper Palatinate and the restitution of ecclesiastical possessions there.[2] Margrave William of Baden-Baden, previous to his confirmation by the Emperor in his possessions, had promised Carafa to restore Catholicism in his territories.[3] Gregory XV. heard with great joy, in May, 1623, that the Margrave was about to carry out his promise.[4]

Whilst the Catholic restoration was thus progressing in West and South Germany, the nomination of Cardinal Eitel Frederick Hohenzollern to the see of Osnabrück,[5] in April 1623, opened a possibility of the recovery of this diocese with its 300 parishes which had had only Protestant Bishops for almost three generations. Eitel Frederick, who had resided in Rome since 1621, was, according to Carafa, as able as he was well disposed,[6] hence the greatest hopes might well be entertained for the future.

Many memoranda testify to the fresh impulse which recent events had given to the Catholic restoration; memoranda

---

[1] See KLOPP, II., 215; DUHR, II., 2, 327.

[2] See WEECH, in the *Zeitschr. für die Gesch. des Oberrheins*, N.F., X., 632 seq.

[3] See CARAFA, *Germania rest.*, 129.

[4] *Brief of May 27, 1623, *Epist. in Arm.*, XLV., 21, Papal Secret Archives.

[5] *Cf.* RUNGE, in *Mitteil. des Vereins für die Gesch. von Osnabrück*, XXIV.

[6] CARAFA, *Germania sacra*, 222. *Cf.* for the Cardinal, our notes, Vol. XXV., 339, n. 4. Already in the Instruction for the Brussels nuncio of May 1, 1621, he was directed to see to it, together with the Cologne nuncio, that Osnabrück was not given to a Protestant Bishop; see CAUCHIE-MAERE, *Instructions*, 124.

which offered suggestions and counsels for the re-establishment and the diffusion of the ancient faith in Germany [1] and both Propaganda and the Pope paid the greatest attention to them. On June 17th, 1623, Cardinal Ludovisi wrote that the Pope was prepared to do anything to remedy all spiritual needs, especially in Bohemia.[2] However the days of Gregory XV. were drawing to an end.

Weakly and sickly men are often very long-lived. This phenomenon looked like being verified once more, notwithstanding all the gloomy prophecies to the contrary, in the case of the Ludovisi Pope. At the beginning of 1623 he suffered a fresh attack of gout, though this did not prevent him from attending to business.[3] On February 7th, Gregory XV. had sufficiently recovered to grant audiences and to take walks in the garden in the best of spirits.[4] In March also the Pope's health left nothing to be desired : he was able to attend all ecclesiastical functions.[5] At the end of the month he caught a chill which confined him to his bed for almost four weeks.[6] He was unable to preside at the meetings of Propaganda until April 25th.[7] The Venetian ambassador having spread some very unfavourable reports concerning Gregory's health, the Pope, at the beginning of May, ostentatiously went on foot past the Palace of St. Mark, where the ambassador resided,

---

[1] Here belong, besides the memorandum concerning the conquest of Heidelberg in DÖLLINGER-REUSCH, *Moralstreitigkeiten*, I., 662 *seq.*, II., 390 *seq.*, the memorials published by KOLLMANN (I., 191 *seq.*, 199 *seq.*, 202 *seq.*).

[2] *Cf.* KOLLMANN, I., 339.

[3] See the *Avvisi of February 1 and 4, 1623, *Urb.* 1093 A., Vatican Library.

[4] See *Avviso of February 7, 1623, *ibid.*

[5] See *Avviso of March 11, 1623, *ibid.*

[6] See the *Avvisi of March 29 and April 22, 1623, *ibid.* *Cf.* the *report of P. Savelli to Ferdinand II., dated Rome, April 15, 1623, State Archives, Vienna, and the letter of the Medici envoy of April 23, 1623, in GROTTANELLI, *Ducato di Castro*, 33.

[7] *Avviso of April 26, 1623, *loc. cit.*

DEATH OF GREGORY XV.

on his way to the Quirinal.[1] On the following Sunday he visited the Villa Ludovisi.[2]

Audiences were once more granted [3] and the Pope appeared at all functions. On Ascension day, May 25th, he was present at the function in St. Peter's. On his return to the Quirinal he stopped at the Chiesa Nuova to perform his devotions at the tomb of St. Philip Neri whose feast occurred on the following day.[4] In June also the Pope was so well that Antonio Possevino remarked on 24th June that whereas formerly Gregory's pontificate had been reckoned to last months, it was now expected to last years.[5] However not long after the Pope had to take to his bed : for a time he continued to give audiences and to attend to current business,[6] but his illness—gravel—[7] combined with a violent fever, grew worse so rapidly that the sick man himself gave up all hope of recovery. He rejected the suggestion of Cardinals Ludovisi, Sauli, Bandini and Capponi, that he should hold a Consistory for the nomination of Cardinals ; henceforth all his thoughts were turned towards eternity for which he prepared by the frequent reception of the Sacraments of Penance and Holy Communion.[8] He died on the evening of July 8th, at the age of 70. His body was removed from the Quirinal to the Vatican and exposed in

---

[1] *Avviso of May 6, 1623, *ibid*.

[2] *Avviso of May 10, 1623, *ibid*.

[3] *Cf.* the *report in the *Rev. hist.*, LXXV., 31.

[4] See *Avviso of May 27, 1623, *loc. cit.*

[5] " *Il Papa sta bene et dove prima gl'era limitata la vita a mesi, se li conta ad anni." Letter of A. Possevino, Rome, June 24, 1623, Gonzaga Archives, Mantua.

[6] *Avviso of July 1, 1623, *loc. cit.*

[7] See the *report in PETRUCELLI, III., 46. *Cf.* also GUALINO, *La litiosi di Pio V.*, Rome, 1925, 28. For Gregory XV.'s physicians, Vincenzo Alsario Croce, and Giov. Marira Castellani, see RENAZZI, II., 92 *seqq.*, and the MS. addition in the copy in the Casanatense Library, Rome.

[8] See the *letter of Vincenzo Agnelli Soardi, Rome, July 8, 1623, Gonzaga Archives, Mantua ; ACCARISIUS, *Vita Gregorii XV.*, lib. III., ch. 20, Boncompagni Archives, Rome. *Cf.* CIACONIUS, IV., 470, and GROTANELLI, 34.

St. Peter's in the Chapel of St. Gregory.[1] He was temporarily buried in St. Peter's. On June 13th, 1634, the mortal remains were provisionally translated to the church of the Annunziata of the Roman College,[2] where they remained until the completion of the church of S. Iganzio. In this magnificent church, erected by Cardinal Ludovisi, at the end of the right transept may be seen the tomb of Gregory XV., the splendour of whose marbles surpasses even the work of Bernini. The monument was planned and in great part executed by Le Gros, at the end of the seventeenth century. In a niche above the sarcophagus and under a richly decorated baldachino stands the statue of the seated Pope. He is represented in full pontificals. On either side angels floating upon the folds of curtains wrought in dark marble proclaim on their trumpets the greatness of the deceased. The centre is occupied by the small sarcophagus surrounded by the figures of two Virtues, and below appears the medallion portrait of the Cardinal Secretary of State, Ludovisi, for he too has here found his last resting place.[3]

The Popes have always found it difficult to satisfy the Romans. When a pontificate lasted as long as that of Paul V., they were anxious for a change; but if a Pope's government was of short duration they were, as a rule, equally discontented. On this occasion it was the eminent position of Cardinal Ludovisi which caused so much resentment that many completely forgot the services of Gregory XV. to the City of Rome,[4] such as his care for the poor and the sick to whom he made over the palace of the Lateran,[5] the measures he

---

[1] See GATTICUS, I., 458; *Avviso of July 12, 1623, loc. cit.; the *report of P. Savelli to Ferdinand II., of July 8, 1623, State Archives, Vienna.

[2] See *Avviso of June 17, 1623, in POLLAK-FREY, 151.

[3] Cf. FERRARI, La tomba, 165 seq.; SMOUSE, in the Gaz. d. Beaux-Arts, 4, series X. (1913), 202 seq.; for Monot's angels see BRINCKMANN, Barockskulptur, 269, 274 seq.

[4] See opinion in Gigli's Diario, printed in FRASCHETTI, 31.

[5] See ORBAAN, Documenti, 210.

took for the importation of cheaper provisions,[1] the installation of a water supply for the Borgo,[2] and the restoration of the city walls.[3] On account of the shortness of his pontificate and his constant preoccupation with the troublous events of Germany, the Pope could do but little for the arts. However in that sphere Cardinal Ludovisi kept his own with as much éclat as Scipio Borghese under Paul V. Among the painters Gregory XV. gave preference to his compatriots of Bologna.[4] He carried out some repairs to the Lateran [5] and in St. Peter's he decorated the Choir Chapel.[6] The garden of the Quirinal was adorned by him with two fountains.[7] For the promotion of learned studies the acquisition of the Library of Heidelberg was an event of the first order ; other purchases also were made for the Vatican.[8] The city benefited by the blessings of

---

[1] *Cf.* ACCARISIUS, *Vita Gregorii XV., lib. III., ch. 19, Boncompagni Archives, Rome. See also *Avviso of October 20, 1621, *Urb.* 1090, Vatican Library.

[2] See CIACONIUS, IV., 470 ; FORCELLA, XIII., 109 ; GUIDO FONTANE, 28, 37 ; *cf.* also A. BETOCCHI, *Le acque e gli acquedotti di Roma*, Rome, 1879, 27.

[3] See NIBBY, *Mura*, 316, 337 ; FORCELLA, XIII., 8 ; *Inventario*, I., 95, 344.

[4] See PASSERI, 20 *seqq.*, 475. According to BAGLIONE, Giovanni Fiamingo died of disappointment that he had not been made *sopraintendente* of St. Peter's.

[5] See CIACONIUS, IV., 470.

[6] See FORCELLA, VI., 141. *Cf.* BONANNI, *Numismata templi Vatic.*, 95, and *Bull.*, XII., 586 *seqq.*

[7] The Fontana della Pioggia and the Fontana Rustica. In front of the latter, which has waterducts that still play, there is a mosaic laid in the floor with the arms of Gregory XV. and the inscription : *Gregorius XV. P.M. A° II°*.

[8] See CARINI, 80 *seqq.* Gregory XV. showed his interest in letters by taking part in the sessions of his nephew's Academy ; see TIRABOSCHI, VIII. (ediz. di Napoli), 19. *Cf.* BORZELLI, *Marino*, 166. CIACONIUS, IV., 471, gives an index of the works dedicated to Gregory XV. See also SIL. BRANCHI, *Rime per la Sta di Gregorio XV.*, Bologna, 1621, and NIC. VILLANIUS, *De laudibus Gregorii XV.*, Viterbii, 1621. One work dedicated to

peace at a time when Germany and France were filled with the alarms of war.¹ Gregory's further plans for the embellishment of Rome were frustrated by his death.²

Gregory XV.'s activity was wholly concentrated on the interests of the Church. His great services in this sphere were summed up in the funeral oration spoken at his Requiem by the Jesuit Famiano Strada, a famous Latinist and author of the classical history of the insurrection in the Netherlands.³ Gregory's government did not last beyond two years and five months, but in that short space of time so many important events occurred that the funeral inscription composed by the Jesuit John Baptist Ursi [4] could truthfully boast that every month of his pontificate was equal to a lustrum. Elected three months after the battle of the White Mountain, Gregory XV. was privileged to witness the great revolution in favour of the

---

Gregory XV. is still unprinted : MAGNUS PERNEUS, *De efficacia divinae gratiae ex electione Gregorii XV.* (818 pages !), Vatican Library. *Cf.* above, p. 40, note 3.

[1] A. POSSEVINO *reports on May 22, 1621 : " La città è cresciuta fino alla somma di 135 000 habitatori " (Gonzaga Archives, Mantua). This statement is incorrect ; according to the statistics of CERASOLI (*Studi e documenti*, XII., 175), Rome in 1621 had 118,356 inhabitants ; in 1623, 111,727.

[2] For Gregory XV.'s building plans (*cf.* SCHREIBER, 3, note 2) see in Appendix no. VII., the *Report of A. POSSEVINO of August 14, 1621, Gonzaga Archives, Mantua. The same writer also reports on July 22, 1621 (*ibid.*) concerning Cardinal Montalto : " Con elemosine grandi proseguisce la fabrica della chiesa de padri Theatini (*S. Andrea della Valle*), quale fa gran progressi et sarà assai bella, benchè non sia per arrivare una gran lunga quella de padri Giesuiti, se bene le capelle de Theatini sono infinitamente più belle et preciose che quelli dei Giesuiti. . . . Le due chiese che si sono cominciate in Roma in honore di S. Carlo, l'ho trovato nel medesimo stato che erano tre anni sono quando fui a Roma."

[3] The *Oratio* of STRADA, printed at Rome, 1623 ; see SOMMERVOGEL, VII., 1607. *Cf.* *Avviso of July 19, 1623, *Urb.* 1093*a*, Vatican Library.

[4] See CIACONIUS, IV., 470.

Catholic cause. The proud structure of Protestant solidarity had crumbled like a house of cards at a puff of wind. The obstinacy of the Elector Palatine and the selfishness of his allies quickly led to the complete downfall of Frederick as well as that of Calvinism.[1] Gregory XV., supported by his excellent Secretary of State, Ludovisi, did all he could to exploit so favourable a position to the advantage of the Catholic Church. Whereas division and uncertainty gained the upper hand among the Protestants, the Catholics were very fortunate in that the Holy See pursued a well-considered, firm and homogeneous policy. The magnificent triumphs of the Catholic restoration under Gregory XV. grew out of this force of unity as opposed to dissension, and from the Pontiff's energetic intervention wherever religious interests touched on political ones. That historic movement, under the impulse of an action that was both far-seeing and far-reaching, was now nearing its climax.

Never, perhaps, has so short a pontificate left such deep marks in history. The government of Adrian VI., notwithstanding its brief duration, was an important one, but whilst the last of the German Popes was destined to meet with nothing but disappointments, almost uninterrupted success fell to Gregory XV.'s lot. Adrian's attempts at reform failed because he lacked adequate means for carrying them through[2]; Gregory XV. found these ready to his hand and in great abundance; his merit is, however, that he knew how to use them and that in the person of his nephew and Secretary of State, he chose the right man to help him for, trained as he had been in the same strictly religious school of the Jesuits, the Cardinal worked in fullest harmony with his uncle for one and the same object, namely the exaltation and extension of the Church.

For other reasons also the co-operation of Cardinal Ludovisi with Gregory XV. was fraught with important consequences. In the last years of the aged Paul V., the policy of the Holy See had been excessively cautious not to say vacillating. In

[1] *Cf.* OPEL, I., 590 *seq.*
[2] *Cf.* our notes, Vol. IX., 2, 123 *seq.*

view of the age and poor health of Gregory XV. it was to be feared that a similar policy of reserve would be continued. But this was countered by the Pope's keenness, whilst the physical energy that the Pontiff lacked was amply supplied by Ludovisi who put into his uncle's policy the fire and assurance of youth. Thus guided by a frail old man, the papacy developed an energy and power of action which aroused astonishment. Its most significant activity was its strong intervention in German affairs where the favourable situation was exploited with unsurpassed ardour for the furtherance of the Catholic restoration. The results achieved in this respect in Bohemia through the decisive influence of the nuncio Carafa are so important that by themselves alone they would perpetuate the memory of Gregory XV. This is equally true of his reform of papal elections; but Gregory XV.'s peculiar and outstanding achievement was the formation of Propaganda. This creation, which had already been planned by his cousin of the same name, Gregory XIII., is like a shining beacon pointing to a field in which the Church was to display her beneficent activity for centuries to come.

Roman breadth of vision, sagacity and circumspection shine forth in this world-embracing creation which was destined to be of the highest importance not for the missions alone but also for philology and ethnology, appear likewise in the Instructions to Gregory XV.'s nuncios which were first drafted by Ludovisi and received their final shape at the skilled hands of Agucchi. The precision and smoothness of the language and the aptness with which thought is expressed in these documents, are best realized when they are compared with documents from other chancelleries of that period, especially those of Germany! It is not surprising that these Italian State documents were quickly disseminated in numerous transcripts and became justly famous.[1] They

[1] In Rome, the Barberini Library is especially rich in Instructions by Gregory XV., see *Cod.*, 5188, 5203, 5528, 5586, 5587, 5958-63. Other copies are in the Altieri Library (2 vols.), Casanatense Library (X., V., 14 and 16), Chigi (J., III., 80), Corsini (38, A. 9, 10, 11), and naturally numerous copies in the

are models both as regards form and contents and evince matchless skill in the art of handling men and of taking into account every imaginable possibility. By their severely objective sober tone they constitute a marked contrast as well as a complement to the pompous, fiery Latin Briefs of Gregory XV. composed by the Florentine Giovanni Ciampoli.[1] The emphatic language, the dramatic swing, the expressions which frequently verge on the extravagant betray the poet. These new forms of speech affect the man of to-day in the same odd way as does the exaggerated emotionalism of the contemporary baroque art. The former, like the latter, were meant to give expression to the enhanced religious feeling of the period of the Catholic restoration by the greatest possible display of splendour and fiery pathos. The religious fire which glows here corresponds to the flaming enthusiasm

---

Vaticana (especially *Ottob.* 1103 and 2725) and in the Papal Secret Archives (*Arm.*, II., *Cod.* 117, and *Nunziat. di Francia*). Outside Rome, I have noted Arezzo, Library of the Fraternità di S. Maria, *Cod.* 190 (from the Fossombroni Library) ; Bologna, University Library, *Cod.* 78 ; Ferrara, Library (Collez. Riminaldi, T 4) ; Florence, State Archives (*Carte Strozz.*, 160) ; Genoa, Civic Library, D. 3, 8, 16 ; Naples, National Library, XI., G. 31, 33, 35 ; XII., B. 14 ; *Bibl. d. stor. patria*, XI., G. 10, XI., F. 10 ; Perugia, Communal Library, E. 17 ; Rovigo, Libr. of the Acad. dei Concordi, 8, 5, 25. Copies are also found at the State Libraries, Berlin (*Inf. polit.*), Paris (see Marsand's catalogue) and Vienna (see *Tabulæ codic.*) ; the Municipal Library, Frankfurt a.M., and the Library of Studies at Salzburg (V. 3, G. 102, 127). Even in Poland there are copies ; see *Cat. codic. Bibl. Ossoliniens*, III., 436 seq. Some copies make it quite clear that the form is due to Aguccini, *e.g. Barb.* 5188, *Ottob.* 1103. The letters to the nuncios were also frequently copied.

[1] For G. Ciampoli see Bentivoglio, *Memorie*, 115 seq.; Belloni, *Seicento*, 51 seq., 55 seq., 474. For the life of Ciampoli see *Cod.* K. II. 44, p. 95, and K., IV., 20, p. 32 seq. of the Library at Siena ; and *Cod. Nelli*, 145, p. 107 seqq. of the National Library at Florence. The *Poesie sacre* of Ciampoli appeared at Bologna, 1648 ; his *Lettere* have been frequently printed (Florence, 1650, Venice, 1657, Macerata, 1666).

of the great Saints of that age of Catholic restoration, of whom the outstanding ones, such as Ignatius of Loyola, Francis Xavier, Philip Neri and Teresa of Jesus, were raised to the altars by Gregory XV. To what extent this fire inflamed the whole Catholic world, filling it anew with the medieval pilgrims' enthusiasm for the Eternal City, has found poetical expression in the verses with which the youthful scion of an ancient Polish noble family, the Jesuit Matthew Casimir Sarbiewski, greeted the seat of the papacy when, soon after Gregory XV.'s death, he was summoned to Rome :—

. . . Salve pulcherrima mundi
   Roma, Palatinis ardua Roma iugis.
Pulchraque tergemini salve domus hospita mundi :
   Divinae salve religionis honos,
Quae mare, quae terras et utroque rubentia sole
   De Capitolino vertice regna vides.
Hinc Quirinales, rerum fastigia, clivi,
   Hinc Vaticanae regia tecta domus.
His Pater attonitum speculatus ab arcibus orbem
   Regna cui flexo procubuere genu,
Cui polus et late liquidi patet aetheris aula,
   Et reserat famulas ad pia iussa fores,
O quanta rerum se maiestate coronat !
   Quantaque vicinis invidet aula polis !
Ille tamen, qui se mirantibus invehit astris,
   Et cava non humilis nubila tronat apex ;
O quantum spatiis indulget, et aëra quantum
   Occupat, et brutam vertice spernit humum !
Scilicet ampla patet Laurentis regia Petri,
   Constantine, tua regia coepta manu.
Hanc circum tot iam lassantur saecula molem,
   Et senium mundi grande fatigat opus.
Interitus abiisse suo tot vidit in ortu,
   Regnaque dum pereunt, nascitur una domus.[1]

[1] *Sarbievii Iter Romanum*, V., 221 *seqq.*, translated by DIEL, in *Stimmen aus Maria Laach*, IV. (1873), 347.

APPENDIX

OF

UNPUBLISHED DOCUMENTS

AND

EXTRACTS FROM ARCHIVES

APPENDIX

PRELIMINARY NOTICE.

THE following documents are intended to confirm and complete the text of my book; it has formed no part of my plan to provide a true and full collection of documents. In every case the place where the document was found is given with the greatest possible exactitude. From considerations of space I have had to be sparing in the matter of explanatory notes. As far as the text is concerned, I have, as a rule, preserved intact the wording of the documents or letters, which for the most part I have had before me in the original; there is no need for me to justify the changes I have made in the matter of capital letters and punctuation. Where I have ventured on alteration, I have always noted the fact, though small mistakes and obvious copyist's errors have not been specially noted. The additions which I have made are enclosed in square brackets, while unintelligible or doubtful passages are marked by a note of interrogation or by the word *sic*. Those passages which I have purposely omitted, either when copying the documents or in preparing them for the press, and which were not essential or were unnecessary to my purpose, are marked by dots (.....).

The extracts from the *Avvisi* which are so rich in information, as well as those from the *Epistolae Urbani VIII.*, have been made by my friend Professor Schmidlin, and those from the Vienna Archives by my pupil Dr. Gutmensch, whilst for the copy of the two documents from the Paris Archives I am indebted to my esteemed colleague J. Doulcet, French ambassador to the Holy See, who died in March, 1928. A great deal of material from the works of Nicoletti and other material which had been prepared under the supervision of the prematurely deceased Professor A. Pieper was put at my disposal by his executor, Professor Lux. To all these I offer the expression of my sincere gratitude for their assistance in collecting documentary material which is more abundant for the Barberini Pope than for most Pontiffs.

I. On the Policy of Urban VIII. during
the Thirty Years' War.

(A criticism of Siri, of the final narratives of Angelo and Alvise Contarini, Ranke, Gregorovius and Schnitzer.)

The meagre treatment by RANKE (in his *Päpste*, II., 351 *seq.*, and 367 *seq.*) of the policy of Urban VIII. during the years 1628-1635, was supplemented in 1879 by the monograph of Gregorovius, the tendency and content of which are indicated by the title : " Urban VIII. in opposition to Spain and the Emperor. An episode of the Thirty Years' War."

A source of the first importance and one easily accessible both to Ranke and Gregorovius, was the correspondence between the Papal State Secretariate and the nuncios at Vienna, Madrid and Paris,[1] which is found almost in its entirety in the work of Nicoletti. Although Ranke recognized the value of this correspondence,[2] and asserts that he had carefully studied it for the section dealing with the policy of Urban VIII., as also in other parts of his work, he chiefly relies on the last reports of the Venetian ambassadors, that is, on those of Angelo Contarini for 1629, and those of Alvise

[1] *Cf.* Vol. XXIX, Appendix 26.
[2] See *Päpste*, III, 158 *seqq*. An important fault in Schnitzer's meritorious work : *Zur Politik des Heiligen Stuhles usw.*, is that, notwithstanding repeated long stays in the Holy City, he was so taken up with the documents on the Peace of Westphalia (152) that he had no time to examine the first-class sources for the previous period. His only quotation of a Roman document (250) is taken from LÄMMER, *Analecta*, 38. Schnitzer's (152) remarks on the value of the nunciature reports and the instructions of the Secretariate of State, are only partly correct. PIEPER aptly remarks (*Papst Urbans Verhältnis zum Kaiser, zu Spanien und Frankreich im Mantuaner Erbfolgestreit* : *Wissensch. Beilage der* "*Germania*", 1899, no. 37) : " In the dispatches of the nuncios we see their activities at the various Courts, in the answers from Rome they are told what attitude they are to take on the questions under consideration, and information is also supplied on the transactions of the Imperial, Spanish, French, and other ambassadors in Rome. Any misrepresentation of facts on one side or the other would have been discovered at once, for alongside of this correspondence there was that of the respective Governments with their agents in Rome. The ambassador in Rome informed his Government of his dealings with the Pope whilst the latter informed him of the conduct of the papal nuncio. The historian will control facts by means of this correspondence, as did the Powers of those days.

Contarini for 1635. Since Ranke wrote, opinion on the Venetian reports has undergone a change ; weighty critics have remarked that they are a source to be used only with great caution. A. PIEPER gives a striking example to this effect in *Hist. Polit. Blätter*, XCIV. (1884) 492. EHSES, in his essay, *Urban VIII. und Gustav Adolf* (*Hist. Jahrb.*, XVI., 336) rightly points out that these reports should not be ranked as first-class sources, as Ranke has done, all the more so as, owing to the continued strained relations between Venice and Urban VIII., the reports of the representatives of the City of the Lagoons could not be free from partisanship.

Gregorovius uses even more doubtful authorities, and he, as well as Ranke, neglects the sources of great importance made accessible through Nicoletti. The proof of this has been furnished by PIEPER in his *Beiträge zur Geschichte des Dreissigjährigen Krieges* (*Hist. Polit. Blätter*, XCIV., 471-492). In a sequence of striking proofs he shows that Gregorovius made of Urban's policy a " perfect caricature ", so much so that this " needs an entirely new treatment based on authentic sources ". In the light of the examples adduced by Pieper, a critical student will hesitate to rely either on the reports of the agents of the Duke of Modena, largely coloured by passion and interest and frequently getting their facts at second and third hand, or on the quite untrustworthy Theodor Ameyden.[1] Apart from such unreliable sources, Gregorovius loses himself in suppositions, which " proceed as much from ignorance of Catholic affairs as from the most exaggerated mistrust of contemporary reports ". The examples quoted by Pieper are reinforced by a very apt one mentioned by Ehses, on the attitude of Urban VIII. at the death of Gustavus Adolphus. None the less many historians still regard Gregorovius and Ranke as reliable authorities in determining the position of Urban VIII. in the Thirty Years' War. Nationality makes no difference here : German [2] as well as distinguished French writers [3] blindly follow the aforesaid. The only

[1] *Cf.* Vol. XXIX, Appendix 25.
[2] Thus, quite recently, L. OLSCHKI, *Galilei und seine Zeit*, Halle, 1927, 297 seq.
[3] CHARVÉRIAT, *Politique d'Urbain VIII. pendant la guerre de 30 ans*, in *Mém. de l'Acad. des sciences de Lyon*, XXII. (1882), DE MEAUX, in the 2nd vol. of his *La Réforme* (1889), and even FAGNIEZ in his otherwise valuable monograph *of Fr. Joseph* (1894).

Italian dissentient voice, ADEMOLLO, writing in the *Rassegna Settimanale*, 1879, no. 104 (December 21st), p. 470 *seq*. has remained unnoticed. The opinion of BILDTS, in *Dagens Nyhetter*, 1923, February 18th, on the "uncritical and fantastic" work of Gregorovius, is known to very few scholars. It is therefore not superfluous to insist once more on the critical exposition by Pieper and Ehses, and to substantiate it in some instances.

The key to an understanding of Urban VIII.'s attitude in the period 1630 to 1632, lies in his relation to the Emperor and to Spain during the struggle for the Mantuan succession. Ranke bases his account of Urban's attitude towards this imbroglio on two dispatches of the French ambassador, Béthune, of September 23rd and October 8th, 1628, quoted by SIRI in his *Memorie*, VI., 478. (RANKE, *Päpste*, II., 356 *seqq*.) These two extracts make it appear that Urban summoned the French to Italy, " addressing most urgent appeals to Paris, begging the King to send an army into the field even before the fall of La Rochelle, for his intervention in the Mantuan trouble would be as pleasing to God as the siege of that bulwark of the Huguenots ; if the King were but to appear at Lyons and declare himself for the freedom of Italy, he, the Pope, would not hesitate to put an army in the field and add it to that of the King." This narrative is in direct opposition to the actual conduct of Urban VIII. as shown not only by the correspondence published by Nicoletti between the French nuncio Bagno and the Papal Secretariat of State, but also by the numerous other dispatches of Béthune. With regard to Béthune's specific messages of September and October, 1628, and comparing them with his other reports, it seems very improbable that the Pope, whom Béthune had frequently, but vainly, implored to take hostile action, should now suddenly have changed his obstinate refusals into " urgent appeals ". If we study the originals of Béthune's reports in the Archives of the Ministry for Foreign Affairs in Paris, we see with amazement that they differ entirely from Siri's quotations from them. In both dispatches, the dates of which are also incorrectly given by Siri (the first is of September 25th, not the 23rd, the second is dated October 7th, not October 8th), there is not a word of the Pope having addressed an urgent appeal to France asking that the King should put an army in the field even before the fall of La Rochelle. On the contrary, the appeal and request for intervention in Italy proceeded from the French ambassador. The latter succeeded, in an audience of October 6th, in obtaining from the Pope a promise of armed help, a promise qualified by the condition that the Spaniards should first be requested to desist from their purpose. In the course of the conversation it became quite clear that Urban refused even then to intervene at once, though the Spaniards had grievously provoked him, and that he was very pleased at the successful continuance of the French attack on La Rochelle. Béthune does not hide from himself the fact that the fulfilment of the Papal promise cannot be expected before the fall of that fortress. (See the passage Vol. XXVIII, 221.)

Siri has also distorted documentary evidence in other places: Fagniez (i., 206) shows that the report of Spada and Nari of January 31st, 1625, has been trimmed and altered by Siri (v. 766). Ranke himself, later on, came to see the unreliability of Siri (see *Französische Geschichte*, V., 211), but could not make up his mind to alter his account of the matter in the new edition of his *Päpste*.

In the case of Gregorovius also, blind trust in Siri has proved fatal. He repeats several times that Urban VIII. called Louis XIII. to Italy, after which he adorns his tale in such a way (p. 10, *seq.*) that Pieper, (*loc. cit.*, 477) rightly remarks : " As many untruths and false insinuations as there are assertions ! " As a basis for his estimate of Urban VIII.'s attitude during the Thirty Years' War, Gregorovius repeatedly (pp. 8 and 40) quotes certain remarks to the Imperial ambassador Savelli, in which the Pope is made to say that there was no question of a religious war, that Gustavus Adolphus was merely combating the excessive power of Austria. Here again Siri is the first authority on which Gregorovius relies. (*Memorie* VII, 481 *seq.*) As against this statement, Pieper has shown (p. 473) that Siri's assertion, given without reference to any source (*loc. cit.*), is at variance with every authentic account of that audience. Pieper's presumption that Siri has followed here, as in other places, the *Avvisi*,[1] an unreliable source, full of the *dicerie* so much beloved in gossiping Rome, is as right as his further observation (362), that Siri's *Memorie* should only be

[1] This defect of Gregorovius' monograph has already been pointed out by ADEMOLLO in the *Rassegna settimanale* of Dec. 28, 1879 (see above).

used with the greatest caution, not only because of the unreliability of his sources, but in view also of the manner in which he uses them. Until now, too little attention has been paid not only to the fact that Siri's *Memorie* constitute a collection for which the Government of Louis XIV. placed at his disposal a quantity of important diplomatic reports—a very large quantity for those times—but that the selection and use thereof was conditioned by the fact that the compiler was in the pay of a man who stood in sharp conflict with the Apostolic See, namely the " Roi Soleil ". As a matter of fact, even before Pieper, others had already pointed out the partisan spirit and untrustworthiness of Siri, who had given proof of his violent opposition to Urban VIII. in the first volume of his *Mercurio*.[1] These writers are: TIRABOSCHI (VIII., 303), AFFÒ (*Scritt. Parmig.* V., 208 *seq.*), RONCHINI (in *Atti e Mem. d. Deputaz. di stor. patr. p. le prov. Mod. e Parm.*, V., Modena, 1870, 381 *seq.*), also WACHLER (in his *Gesch. der hist. Wissensch.*, i., 483), REUMONT (II., 164, *cf.* V., 141), and GOLL (in *Mitteil. der Gött. Gesellsch. d. Wissensch.*, 1872, 379 *seq.*, 384). Such a writer's statements about Urban VIII. deserve no credence unless they are substantiated by other and unexceptionable sources. The judgment of Wachler cannot be impugned when he says that in the work of Siri, " the dross must be separated from the gold ", and " the inevitable individualism of the times, personal relationships, one-sidedness of outlook and appreciation, must be distinguished from facts and documents ". In another place Wachler rightly qualifies (485) Siri's works as a " storehouse containing heterogeneous contents that require careful sorting ". Similar criticisms have been recently expressed by BELLONI (*Seicento*, 389), and ADEMOLLO, (*Independenza*, 58). As a critic of the duties of a Pope, Siri carries even less weight, for he himself gravely neglected his duties as a member of the Benedictine Order.[2] BÜHRING, too, in his monograph, *Venedig, Gustav Adolf und Rohan* (Halle, 1885), justly criticises Siri. He describes the battles of Vallegio in May, 1630, according to contemporary reports, and adds (p. 6) : " Siri's anecdotal narrative must be discounted." In the appendix he thus sums up his opinion : " The value of Siri's Memoirs would be far greater if the author had not attempted to enhance the interest of his official

[1] *Cf.* AFFÒ V., 208 *seq.*
[2] *Cf. ibid.*, 223.

APPENDIX.

sources by adding private gossip, which often proves to be untrustworthy, even when he claims to have heard the words from the lips of the person concerned." (280).

It is remarkable that SCHNITZER, in his essay, *Zur Politik des Heiligen Stuhles in der ersten Hälfte des Dreissigjährigen Krieges*, which is valuable because based on documents in the Vienna and Munich State Archives, keeps to the story (p. 228) with which Siri (VII., 484) prefaces his untenable version of the audience of Savelli—for which no authority is given—and this notwithstanding the fact that Schnitzer was acquainted with the conclusions of Pieper and Bühring. He must have been induced to do so because Ranke, though he does not quote Siri, had not been able to omit so racy a tale (*Päpste*, II., 369). In passing I may remark that the Berlin historian puts the complaint against Urban into the mouth of " the members of the Curia and the inhabitants of Rome ". This is in direct contradiction to Siri, who says expressly that the complaints were raised by the Austrians, for the inhabitants of Rome were at that time wholly on the side of Urban, and even directly urged him not to touch the treasure in S. Angelo though pressed by the representatives of the Habsburgs.[1]

Schnitzer's confidence in Siri is also seen in his vain attempt to save his version of the audience of Savelli at the end of February, 1632, though it is in contradiction with all authentic sources.[2] In these circumstances it is not surprising that Schnitzer refers indeed to Siri and Gregorovius in connexion with the important Consistory of March 8th, 1632, in which Borgia made his protest, and completely ignores the authentic account in the Consistorial Acts printed in Lämmer.[3] Siri describes the Consistory as if he had been present, but gives no authorities for his account.[4] It is clearly influenced by the Roman *dicerie*. The extent of Siri's hatred for Urban VIII. may be gauged by the fact that he goes so far as to assert that the Pope had not spared one drop out of the ocean of his wealth (" una sola stilla ") for the hard-pressed Emperor (VII., 488). The truth is that in the years 1632-4 alone Urban VIII. contributed about two million francs out of his private means,

---

[1] *Cf.* Vol. XXVIII., 301 *seq.*
[2] *Cf.* Vol. XXVIII., 286.
[3] *Zur Politik*, 231.
[4] Opinion of HÄBERLIN (XXVI., 536).

the greater part of which went to the Emperor. (*Cf.* PIEPER, *loc, cit.*, xviv, 480).[1]

What is to be thought of the credibility of Angelo and Alvise Contarini, the Venetian ambassadors' final report ?

The answer to this question is the more important as the estimate of Urban's character and of his policy during the Thirty Years' War by RANKE (*Päpste*, II., 351 *seq.*, 368 *seqq.*) rests almost entirely on the reports of these two ambassadors, which Gregorovius also quotes for choice (20, 23, 70, 228, 229). Neither of these historians investigated their credibility. On the contrary, Ranke unreservedly admires the account of Alvise, (III., 149 *seqq.*) and Gregorovius also accepts all the opinions of Alvise without question. Pieper, however, (*loc. cit.*, 491 *seq.*) writes that great caution is necessary in accepting the facts related in the final reports of the Venetian ambassadors, and still greater discretion in accepting their opinions. In proof, he dwells on the totally opposite estimates of Cardinal Francesco Barberini by Angelo Contarini and by his successor, Giovanni Pesaro, because the former met with opposition from the Cardinal and the latter found him favourable to Venice. If personal interest played such a part in judging Cardinal Barberini, how much more would it have influenced the opinion of the writer on a Pope who was repeatedly in disagreement with Venice on matters both political and ecclesiastical !

Angelo Contarini's embassy fell into the period of the Mantuan war of succession. One of the chief duties which his Government laid on him was to induce the Pope to enter the anti-Spanish league which was being formed, and to support Nevers by arms. Contarini did his utmost in this respect, but all his efforts were in vain. His disappointment at his failure strongly influenced his opinion of Urban VIII. This bitterness was so great as to make him lose sight of the duty of mediating for peace which arose for Urban VIII. out of his position whenever Catholic Powers were in conflict. In his desire to fulfil this duty, Urban avoided the partisan measures advocated by Venice, an attitude which also partly resulted from the fact of the exposed position of the Papal States. Angelo Contarini

---

[1] *Siri* is probably responsible for the satires on the war of Castro which FRATI discusses in *Arch. stor. ital.* 5, *Series* XXXVII., 389 *seq.*

only saw excuses in these reasons. The real reason why Urban VIII. would not " entrar nel ballo ", so he states, (p. 283) was first, his innate timidity, on account of which he lacked resolution for " azioni generose " and inclined to look only to his own advantage and tranquillity. To this was added his unwillingness to expend money, and lastly, the counsels of his brother, Carlo who, remembering the fate of the Carafa, did not wish to embroil himself with Spain. In vain, Contarini complains, had he frequently represented to Carlo and Francesco Barberini that this was no precedent. In his next remarks Contarini so openly vents his wrath at his failure to induce Urban VIII. to relinquish his neutrality in the Mantuan affair that no one can call his an unbiased account. Contarini even allows himself to assert that the only object of the Curia was to secure its own advantage, the enjoyment of luxury and the amenities of life, an end easier to attain during an apparent peace than in a peace grounded on " virtù, generosità ", and " sentimento del pubblico bene " (286). Such a picture might have fitted the Court of Alexander VI. ; it is at the very least a signal anachronism when applied to that of Urban VIII.

The real motives of the Curia are clearly seen in numerous authentic documents, in the letters of Cardinal Spada and in the Instructions to the French nuncio Bagno of April 2nd, 1629. These[1] cannot have remained hidden from Contarini, but in his vexation at his failure, he entirely passed them by. Again and again this disappointment appears in his dispatches ; for example, when he describes how, after the Emperor's interference in Italy, the Pope would still not be persuaded to make war, but continued indefatigably to make offers of peace (287 *seqq.*). This pacifying activity of Urban VIII. is incontestable ; it makes it very unlikely that Urban should have said in Angelo Contarini's presence that the " *poca religione* nello stesso Imperatore " compelled him, " di non aver disgusto dei progressi torbidi in Germania, anzi di *desiderarli* per contrapeso di tante temerità che in Italia sotto titolo ingiusto s'andavan esercitando." (291.) Urban VIII. certainly did not speak of the Emperor's " poca religione ", for he knew and appreciated Ferdinand II.'s pious dispositions and always distinguished between the

[1] *Cf.* XXVIII, 210, 231.

personal temper of the Emperor and that of his ministers. The true explanation of Contarini's story may be that Urban VIII. regarded the events in Germany as a punishment for the Emperor's action in Italy.

Even more passionate than Angelo Contarini's reports are those of Alvise Contarini in the course of the year 1635. This is not to be wondered at, for the relations between Venice and the Holy See had meanwhile become much worse and the Relation was penned while the quarrel about the inscription in the Sala Regia was enraging the Venetians.[1] Diplomatic relations had actually been interrupted: from September, 1631, the Venetian Embassy in Rome remained unoccupied for nine months. Not until Alvise Contarini was nominated in April, 1632, were diplomatic relations resumed, but during his period of office, which lasted until 1635, disputes continued both on political and ecclesiastical matters. Contarini reports very fully on this in the last part of his Relation. It cannot be a matter of astonishment that he takes exclusively the point of view of his Government. How one-sided this was is made plain when we hear the other side.[2] But how about the other portions of his Relation? In these the religious and secular policy of the Pope, the personality of Urban VIII., that of his nephews, and his relations with the different States of Europe, are considered. The many valuable indications found here, and the clever handling of the subject, have induced Ranke and Gregorovius to base their account on this information. As against this we must protest that Alvise Contarini's statements have no critical value unless they furnish proof of their reliability. Is this ambassador a really unprejudiced observer? Is all his information supported by facts? Our doubts are raised by his passionate, hateful, and partisan judgment of Roman affairs. He opens with a gloomy picture of the Curia. The only deity worshipped in Rome is self-interest (353); the whole endeavour of the " preti " is set on combining spiritual and worldly affairs (354). The stricter co-ordination of ecclesiastical affairs, consequent upon the Catholic counter-reformation, does not appear as what it was: that is, a legitimate development of the monarchic character of Church government due to the changed

[1] *Cf.* XXIX.
[2] *Cf* XXIX.

conditions of the times, but is represented as a tyrannic rule (355 *seq.*). Contarini exaggerates so manifestly that he asserts that formerly consistories were held almost daily ! His further statement is equally untrue (356), viz. that before the time of Urban VIII. disputes on ecclesiastical jurisdiction had been rare. In order to provide his gloomy picture with a suitable background, Contarini recalls the saintly Popes of earlier times. This, as well as his complaints of the " temporalizzata spiritualità " (356), remind us of the tricks which the enemies of the Papacy invariably employ. To prove how greatly the former reverence for the Popes had diminished in his time, Contarini refers to the lampoons and the public protests of the Spaniards against Urban VIII., as if such attacks had not been just as frequent in former days. Stranger still is the remark that all this had been borne in Rome " con troppa viltà ", and the attackers had been rewarded instead of receiving punishment ! (356) The attitude of Urban VIII. towards Cardinal Borgia shows [1] what is to be thought of these accusations. Contarini concludes : " Le antiche forze della chiesa nella dependenza, nell'amore e devotione dei principi consistevano, ma hoggidì, che questi non hanno di Padre commune altro che il nome, grandemente diminuite et indebolite rimangono (356)." In reality Urban VIII. in the Valtellina affair, in the dispute over the Mantuan war of succession, and in all subsequent difficulties, had done his best honestly to fulfil his duty as " padre commune " [2]; but it was just this which was regarded with suspicion in Venice, for there they wished to see the Pope become a party man and take part in the war against the Spaniards.[3] Contarini's complaint that the Pope inflicted the punishment of excommunication too easily is equally groundless, for Urban VIII. had refused to pronounce it against Louis XIII. when urged thereto by Spada.[4] Contarini gives himself away altogether when he unctuously laments the circumstance that the Popes were disinclined to call the " venerable Councils ", which " used to stand up so beneficially against heresy " (357), as if he did not know that the Venetian Government, in spite of Urban's

[1] *Cf.* XXVIII., 285 *seqq.*
[2] *Cf.* XXVIII., 216.
[3] *Cf.* XXVIII., 212 *seqq.*, 229 *seqq.*
[4] *Cf.* XXVIII., 71.

great displeasure and in opposition to the Councils, kept up close intercourse with heretics of every kind and allowed them greater freedom in Venice than they enjoyed under any other Catholic Government. As an introduction to the discussion of the affairs of the Papal States, Contarini enunciates the principle that the Church may not be defended like a fortress.[1] This remark is in keeping with the sense of irritation which appears elsewhere in the Relation (*cf.* especially 362) on account of the fact that Urban VIII. was anxious to strengthen the military defences of the States of the Church. Contarini's principle was forgotten in Venice when they urged the Pope to arm, in the hope of inducing him to take part in the war against the Spaniards.[2]

Contarini justly censures Urban VIII.'s nepotism, but he goes beyond all bounds when he asserts that the Pope only thought of enriching his nephews and did not trouble about anything else ! (369). It is a manifest untruth when Contarini repeatedly affirms that Urban had consciously nurtured hostility between the Catholic Powers (367 and 368). In point of fact the ambassador becomes more and more passionate in the course of his report. He does not hesitate to describe the Cardinals without distinction as common hypocrites (374). We are involuntarily reminded of Sarpi when we read such accusations. In other ways also Contarini shows himself an apt pupil of Sarpi, whose ideas had always strongly influenced the ambassadors of Venice,[3] as when he accuses conscientious and loyal Catholics of playing the part of domestic enemies within the State (365), and advises his Government to confiscate the property of the Jesuits in order to deprive them of every hope of ever returning into Venetian territory (395). In some places Contarini's passion goes so far as to lead him into misrepresenting facts and making false assertions. I quote one instance at haphazard which strikingly illustrates how little Alvise Contarini can be considered a trustworthy authority once his passionate dislike for Urban VIII. is roused. In proof of the Pope's bias in favour of France, Contarini

---

[1] Ecclesia Dei non est defendenda more castrorum (357). This is a saying of S. Thomas of Canterbury (*Rom. Breviary*, December 29).

[2] *Cf.* XXVIII., 211 *seqq.*

[3] See D'Ancona, *Varietà stor.*, I. Series, Milano, 1883, I, 108 *seq.*

gives it as a fact that Urban VIII. approved, even if he did not advise, Richelieu's treaty of peace with Protestant England in 1629 : " I speak of this with good reason," Contarini boldly declares, " for I have been present at all the negotiations ; the Pope's nuncios have always favoured Richelieu's undertakings by supporting him during periods of internal difficulties, and in his efforts to draw Bavaria and the League into an alliance with France. They refrained from comment on his alliances with Holland and the German Protestants ; one might almost say that they approved of them. Other Popes might have been troubled in conscience by such circumstances ; the nuncios of Urban VIII. won for themselves high recognition and personal advantages " (377).

Contarini's assertions are so categorical that they are bound to lead the reader into thinking that Urban VIII. was in secret collusion with France. Now, it was precisely Contarini's predecessor, Giovanni Pesaro, who clearly showed that Urban VIII.'s friendship for France never went so far as to induce him to abandon his reserve and neutrality (*Relazione*, 337). If Contarini's account is tested by comparison with authentic documents, the untrustworthiness of his assertions becomes manifest. Let us examine only one of the more important points, viz. the attitude of Urban VIII. towards Richelieu's treaty with England. Documents which have recently become known prove beyond a doubt that Urban VIII., so far from approving such a peace, opposed it from the beginning and repeatedly protested against it. Even when, after the death of Buckingham and the fall of La Rochelle, the Pope foresaw that he could not prevent the negotiations, orders were issued to the nuncio in Paris to inform Richelieu that he could not inflict a greater sorrow upon the Holy Father than if he concluded a peace treaty with a heretic.[1]

Contarini also sins against the truth by the manner in which he represents the promotion of the Franco-Bavarian relations through the papal nuncios, for here one important circumstance should not have been passed over in silence, namely that Urban VIII. was influenced in this matter by his desire to prevent Richelieu from allying himself with the German Protestants.[2] Contarini kept this motive secret because it

[1] See KIEWNING, I, 299 A 2 ; *cf.* 246 A. 2.
[2] *Cf.* XXVIII., 234.

would have confuted his assertion that the Pope was indifferent to alliances with Protestant Powers. Contarini knew very well how Urban VIII. viewed the situation. When he discussed it with the Pope, at the end of July, 1632, the latter insisted that religion, in so far as he was concerned, must be the first consideration, but even from a purely political point of view he considered the victory of the Emperor less dangerous than that of the Swedish King, because Ferdinand II. could always be kept in check through Bavaria and the League.[1] Contarini's further statement that the nuncios had passed over in silence France's alliance with the Protestants is also untrue, for they repeatedly protested against it.[2]

It is just this account of Contarini's, which teems with untruths and is written with such passion, that Ranke has used as altogether trustworthy in proof of his assertions that " if not direct, then indirect alliances were in force between the Holy See and those Protestant Powers which were pressing forward once more in a victorious struggle " (*Päpste*, II., 368). He is so completely persuaded of Contarini's reliability that, in order to prove the partisanship of Nicoletti, who speaks of " the bitter agony of heart of Urban VIII. at the peace treaty between England and France ", he adduces Contarini as a striking witness to the contrary, when he writes : " We see from Alvise Contarini, who assisted in person at all the negotiations, that the Pope had even advised those negotiations and that treaty " (*Päpste*, III., 158).

Just as accurate research in the archives has disposed of this statement of Contarini, so do the documents in the Papal Secret Archives prove the untenableness of Ranke's account of Urban VIII.'s policy during the Thirty Years' War, especially that of his statement that the Pope " had in effect done much to ruin the plans of the Catholics " (*Päpste*, II., 372). ANTON GINDELY, who devoted his whole life to research in the archives on the subject of the Thirty Years' War, and who, through the liberality of Leo XIII. and

---

[1] See BÜHRING, 265. To Contarini's reply that a victory of the Emperor would have lasting consequences, that of Gustavus Adolphus, who had no male heir, merely temporary ones, the comment was : " ragione che non le (Urban VIII.) despiaque." See BÜHRING, 254.

[2] *Cf.* XXVIII., 210, 258, 273, 278.

Cardinal Hergenröther, had access to the Papal Secret Archives, was the first to realize this fact. In his essay, *Wallenstein in der Beleuchtung des Vatikanischen Archives* (*Beilage zur Münchener Allg. Zeitung*, 1882, Nr. 103), Gindely writes, " Since the attitude of Pope Urban VIII. in the course of the Thirty Years' War is of outstanding importance, and since he is considered to have been an opponent of the Habsburgs and a friend of the Bourbons, proofs of which are to be found in plenty in other archives, it was a matter of great interest to the present writer to be able to ascertain on the spot, viz. in the Vatican Archives, how far the rumour of this hostility was based on truth, how far the Pope allowed himself to be influenced by it in his foreign relations, and whether the counter-reformation in Bohemia and Austria, which had been initiated by his predecessors, was in any way affected by this policy. All these questions received exhaustive and, in part, wholly unexpected answers. I confess that until now I had believed and was persuaded of the truth of all the accusations against the Pope, and that I was convinced of his having been in close alliance with the French and hostile to the Habsburgs. I now found, as a matter of fact, that he opposed the growth of the Spanish power in Italy, a circumstance which cannot be brought as a charge against him, either as Pope or as an Italian. Nor was his alliance with France so close as the sources in the archives at Vienna and Simancas had led me to believe, as if he had desired a partial victory for the Protestants, to the end that the Habsburgs might suffer some injury. He was never hostile towards the Emperor, even though he disapproved of his action in the Mantuan dispute and consequently strongly favoured French aspirations. When the fortune of war turned against the Emperor in Germany, he was anxious to settle the dispute between the Habsburgs and the Bourbons and in 1630–34 he demanded of the former no more than the surrender to the latter of Pinerolo and Moienvicq; consequently neither the Spanish Netherlands nor Alsace were to change masters. The result of my investigations surprised me, for in accordance with the information in Simancas, I was fully convinced that the Pope wanted to hand over Alsace to the French and only opposed the Prague peace negotiations on that account and subsequently disapproved that treaty. He was not ignorant, of course, of the fact that already in 1634 the French had turned covetous eyes towards Alsace."

Unfortunately a verdict like this, by an authority on the story of the Thirty Years' War, has not received the attention it deserves, as was the case with the researches of Pieper and Ehses. Nearly all historians, even Catholic ones, have maintained to this day the views advocated by Ranke and further stressed by Gregorovius.[1] A complete change of opinion on Urban VIII., whose life could only with difficulty be told with equity and impartiality owing to the lack of authentic documents,[2] has recently been brought about by two non-German historians. These scholars studied the attitude of Urban VIII. during the Thirty Years' War, not on the basis of such partisan reporters as were the Venetian ambassadors, but in the light of extensive research in the archives; their investigations led them to quite different conclusions. Whilst ROMOLO QUAZZA, the indefatigable explorer of the Gonzaga Archives, discussed in two volumes the question of the Valtellina which was the prelude of the Mantuan War of Succession and that war itself, AUGUSTE LEMAN, the distinguished editor of the Instructions to the French and Flemish nuncios, in a volume of 600 pages dealt with the policy of the Barberini Pope towards France and the Habsburgs in the years 1631-5. Both these publications have largely contributed towards clearing up one of the most difficult questions of Modern History. The point of view they represent has been widely adopted even in Germany.

So important a student as GUSTAV WOLF devotes a cordial review to Leman's work in the *Zeitschrift für Kirchengeschichte*, XLIV. (1925), 139 *seq.* In it he sacrifices entirely the chief source of Ranke's and Gregorovius' account—the Venetian reports—on the just ground that " Venice was at that time in sharp opposition to the Curia, a circumstance which naturally reacted on diplomatic relations and coloured the embassy reports. Moreover the Venetians viewed the papal policy with Italian eyes, that is, they troubled less about German affairs and great international questions than about the effect of the latter upon conditions in the Apennine Peninsula ".

PAOLO NEGRI, who died prematurely in 1926, had planned

[1] *Cf. Hist. Jahrb.*, XLI. (1921), 328.
[2] M. OTT in *The Catholic Encyclopedia*, XV, 220.

some important additions to Leman's work. Though he does not agree entirely with the French scholar he nevertheless pays a warm tribute to his merit and rejects the opinion of Ranke and the even more unjust one of Gregorovius. Negri justly complains that the French historian took no account of Italian politics. In his essay *Urbano VIII. e l'Italia* in *Nuova Riv. Stor.*, VI. (1922), 168-90, he has thrown much light on it, and in general he has done much for the understanding of the general policy of Urban VIII. Unfortunately, he never published the detailed account he had planned.[1] With regard to Negri's view of Urban VIII.'s Italian feelings, BORNATE, in the *Riv. stor. Ital.* XLII., N.S. III., 1-2, page 162 *seq.* has justly remarked : " Il Negri vorrebbe vedere, almeno in Urbano VIII. un Papa italiano, il più italiano di quanti sedettero nella cattedra di S. Pietro dopo Alessandro VI. . . . Allo stato degli atti mi pare che questo titolo di italianità non possa competere ad Urbano VIII. più che a Giulio II. od a Clemente VII."

Quazza adds to this judgment (II., 362) : " Urbano aveva certamente compreso, come del resto tutti i governi italiani, che sarebbe stato necessario, per la quiete d'Italia, che Carlo Emanuele e il Nevers si accordassero direttamente per evitare che un intervento della Francia e della Spagna provocasse un conflitto più vasto. Alle parole che egli diceva all'ambasciatore sabaudo Ludovico d'Agliè nel febbraio 1628 : ' Alla gloria del signor duca di Savoia, il quale si può chiamar difensore della libertà d'Italia, comple il terminare da sè solo questa differenza senza intervento di Spagna e di Francia. E quando ciò non si possa senz'opera di mezzano, farlo per la via nostra o d'altro principe che non sia straniero, e che non abbi in mira di fabbricare la sua monarchia sopra le ruine degli altri ' (CANTÙ *op. cit.*, t. V., p. 782, n. 8), non si può attribuire il valore di un grido d'Italianità come oggi la intendiamo noi, ma solo l'espressione di un intimo desiderio di pace e della consapevolezza del pericolo che dall'allargamento del conflitto sarebbe derivato ad ogni singolo stato italiano, compreso lo stato della Chiesa, che per la sua posizione geografica aveva fortemente da temere l'ingrandimento della potenza spagnuola in Italia. Per dare una giusta interpretazione alle

[1] Only a kind of preliminary account has appeared under the title : La guerra per la successione di Mantova e del Monferrato, Prato, 1924.

parole di Urbano non bisogna astrarre dalla considerazione del momento in cui vennero pronunciate ; l'allusione del Papa ad un principe straniero che potesse aver, ' in mira di fabbricare la sua monarchia sopra le ruine degli altri,' non poteva riferirsi che alla Spagna dato che la Francia, impegnata alla Rocchelle, notoriamente, per allora, favoriva gli accordi diretti tra Carlo Emmanuele e il Nevers ; inoltre bisogna tener conto del fatto che nel febbraio del 1628 si riteneva ancora che la prima spinta alla guerra provenisse esclusivamente dal duca di Savoia, e si aspettava, ma non si conosceva con certezza, l'esistenza di un accordo segreto tra lui e la Spagna."

If Quazza, in my opinion also, dwells too much on the position of Urban VIII. as Lord of the States of the Church (II., 359), and forgets that the independence of the Holy See, in the circumstances of the times, was intimately bound up with this position, he is quite right in saying that no anachronistic meaning should be attached to the expression " libertà d'Italia " used by the Pope and by other contemporaries ; it meant no more than that " il desiderio d'ogni singolo stato d'essere immune da pericoli immediati, di non essere soffocato da potenti vicini ". Thus Urban VIII. understood it ; hence his opposition to the further spread of Spanish power in Italy and his desire to use France as some sort of counterweight. For all that he had no wish to exchange dependence on Spain for dependence on France (II., 359-62) ; what he wanted was to remain independent so as to be able, as the common father of Christendom, to restore and maintain the unity of the Catholic world which was indispensable in view of the power of the Protestants and the Turks. The Machiavellian policy of Richelieu cut across these intentions for it pursued merely national aims in opposition to supernational Catholic policy.

II. THE PAPABILI BEFORE THE OPENING OF THE CONCLAVE OF 1621.[1]

" Di soggetti che sono più in predicamento del Papato degl'altri, sono gli seguenti :

Sauli portato da Montalto, gradito da Spagnoli, dal Granduca voluto, ma escluso da Aldobrandino, non accetto a Borghesi nè alli Francesi n'alli Venetiani.

Monti portato dal Granduca, da Montalto non escluso nè

[1] See above, pp. 32, 33.

da Aldobrandino nè da Borghese, ma dubbio de' Spagnoli et Francesi.

Giustiniani portato da Montalto aiutato da qualche Spagnolo, non escluso da Aldobrandino nè da Borghese, ma dubbio de' Spagnoli et Francesi.

Bandino portato da Aldobrandino nel primo loco, amato dal Granduca, stimato da Montalto et da spirituali, ma escluso in primo capite da Borghese et Savelli.

Ginnasio portato da Aldobrandino in secondo loco, grato a Spagnoli et non ingrato a Borghese, ma non accett'a Montalto nè a Giustiniani nè a Farnese nè a malcontenti et spirituali.

Carafa portato da Borghese come sua creatura, non discar'al collegio, ma rifiutato da Spagnoli.

Ludovisio portato da Borghese nel secondo loco, voluto da Montalto, non rifiutato da Aldobrandino nè contrariato da Spagnoli nè da Fiorentini nè da spirituali. Nè può haver contrario se non il collegio vecchio. Tonti et forse gli Francesi non v'anderanno prontamente.

Araceli [1] portato da Francesi et da spirituali, non escluso da Aldobrandino.

Aquino portato da Borghese nel terzo loco,[2] da Montalto amato, ma scorge che gli Spagnoli non lo vorranno.

Campori portato da Borghese nel primo loco, aiutato da Este et da altri, dubbio fra Spagnoli che l'escluseron da Novara, poco grato agli spirituali et al collegio, et Orsino gli prattica contra.

S. Susanna [3] stimato giovine, voluto da spirituali, ma v'anderanno lento."

Copy: *Cod.* Ib 55, pp. 304-5 of Servite Library, Innsbruck.

III. PROGRAMME FOR THE REFORM OF THE CHURCH IN GERMANY PRESENTED TO GREGORY XV. BY THE NUNCIO OF COLOGNE, ANT. ALBERGATI.[4]

In *Barb.* 2338 and 2430 (Vat. Lib.), we find: *De Germaniae infirmitate (1621) ac medela considerationes viginti, S.D.N.

---

[1] Galamina.
[2] This statement by the usually so well informed author proved to be erroneous; see p. 30.   [3] Cobelluzio.
[4] *Cf.* above, p. 232. Albergati was nuncio until April 26, 1621 (*cf.* Biaudet, 249); he was succeeded by P. Fr. Montorio, August 4, 1621; on the latter, see Mergentheim, II, 153, 202 *seq.* The Instruction for Albergati's successor Msgr. Monorio, vesc. di Nicastro, of April, 1621, in *Barb.*, 5528, Vat. Lib.

Gregorio XV. Antonius episcopus Vigiliarum (Bisceglia). Ant. Albergati, nuncio in Cologne 1610-1621, had been requested already by Paul V. to draw up a report on the condition of the Church in Germany. He wrote it after the battle of the White Mountain, basing it on his long diplomatic experience. He begins by describing the causes of the evil; viz.

(1) Gravamina Sedi Apost. in religionis negotio ab Imperatoribus illata (since the days of Charles V. they have been far too yielding to the Protestants).

(2) Gravamina Sedi Apost. ab ecclesiasticis praelatis illata.

(3) Gravamina Sedi Apost. a capitulis illata.

(4) Defectus Regularium (abuses in the noble abbeys, especially those of women; Monast. Benedictin. Syburgense nobilium: Prior respondit se numquam vidisse S. Benedicti regulam. " When at Heisterbach I exhorted them to observe the decrees of Trent, responderunt se numquam vidisse decreta Conc. Trid." The wealthy noble abbey of Kappenberg refused to reform itself. Ita religiones introductae ad Sed. Apost. defendendam et cath. Religionem propugnandam contra illam pugnant vel saltem inutiles ad propagandam redduntur). The Holy See must apply a reform, as had been the intention of Gregory XIII., Clement VIII. and Paul V.

(5) Gravamina ad politiam spectantia.

(6) De causis gravaminum.

By way of remedies Albergati suggest the following:—

(1) Unio Sedis Apost. cum Imperatore ac consiliorum communicatio.

(2) Concilii Trid. publicatio et observatio in omnibus locis catholicis in Germania. Ex illo pendet salus Germaniae. Advantage is often taken of the Council against the Pope; some refuse to accept the disciplinary decrees. The Pope and the Emperor should jointly publish the decrees of the Council and enforce their observance by Bishops and clergy.

(3) Reform by the holding of Provincial Councils which was the best way to carry into effect the decrees of the Council.

(4) Erectio novorum episcopatuum. The dioceses were too large; those Bishops who were also temporal lords carried out their ecclesiastical duties only through a vicarius in spirit. (for the most part vilis conditionis and without authority, the Chapters arrogating all power to themselves). Hence the vicarius is practically powerless and the flock is at the mercy of the wolves. This caused the apostasy of Bohemia, Moravia,

Silesia and Austria where there are not enough Bishops, the loss also of the free towns of Nuremberg, Ulm, Lübeck, Frankfort and Hamburg which had no Bishops. Those Belgian towns which had Bishops remained faithful. Proposals for new dioceses and their endowment. The Emperor must erect at least three new dioceses in Bohemia and two in Silesia and Moravia respectively. In Lusatia as well as in Neuburg the territorial lord might very well establish a diocese. At Cologne, Mayence, Trèves and Münster, which were too extensive, new dioceses were wanted; the thing was not easy but the Emperor and the Pope could enforce it.

Albergati makes the following suggestions for the reform in the Empire :—

(1) Cancellation and prohibition of all separate alliances which were injurious to the Empire.

(2) Prohibition to have troops without the Emperor's permission.

(3) A real observance of the religious peace, hence exclusion of the Calvinists.

(4) Reform of the tribunal of the Camera.

(5) Visitation of that tribunal in accordance with the prescriptions of the Constitution.

(6) Restitution of the dioceses and of ecclesiastical property (Ut detentores moderni archiepiscoporum, epicopatuum et praelaturarum Imperii ac omnium bonorum ecclesiasticorum contra jura et constitutiones pacis religionis ac post transactionem Passaviensem occupatorum eosdem et eadem plene restituant nec in ullis actionibus Imperii pro statibus et ordinibus Imperii habeantur).

(7) The gravamina religionis should be decided at the Diet in accordance with the Constitution.

(8) The decisions of the majority to be laws of Empire.

(9) The Emperor should have part of his army in readiness with a view to keeping the rebels in check.

In conclusion Albergati remarks that, however difficult all this may appear, there was no reason to despair, neither should they hope for the salvation of Germany solely by force of arms or exclusively by prayer : Cum nec solum armis agendum sit nec sine nostris conatibus soli orationi res sit committenda, alia remedia erunt quaerenda, ut duobus illis extremis evitatis securius procedatur.

IV. Giunti's Life of Cardinal Ludovisi.

It is due to the extraordinarily influential position of the Cardinal nephew, Ludovico Ludovisi, that the latter's biography by Lucantonio Giunti of Urbino [1] is more informing and important for the pontificate of Gregory XV. than the work which Ant. Accarisi devoted to that Pope. In its pages a trusted servant of many years' standing paints a glowing picture of the life and achievements of his employer, and though it is written in the manner of an official panegyric, it nevertheless contains much useful and credible information [2] which one looks for in vain elsewhere. The author wrote after the death, on November 18th, 1632, of Ludovisi whose secretary he had been for many years and whose papers he was able to use; he also gives a detailed account of the last years of the Cardinal. The execution of the work betrays a good deal of inexperience [3]; the whole thing is a collection of materials more than anything else. It is not surprising if Giunti does not distinguish between what was done by the nephew and what proceeded from the Pope alone. This is all the more regrettable as in view of his intimacy with Ludovisi he would have been in a position to give us information on this point as no one else could have done. Since Cardinal Ludovisi had so marked a share in all that Gregory XV. undertook, his biography cannot but be a valuable source of information for the pontificate of the Ludovisi Pope. A number of important statements by Giunti have already been made use of in our narrative,[4] but several lengthy passages which I have likewise used deserve to be reproduced textually.

[1] *Vita e fatti di Ludovico cardinal Ludovisi d. S. R. C. vicecancallario, nepote di Papa Gregorio XV., scritta da Luca Antonio Giunti suo servitore da Urbino.

[2] Opinion of RANKE, *Päpste*, III⁶, 118. Ranke, who also gives a short extract, used *Cod.* 39, D. 8 of the Corsini Library, Rome. Other copies of the *Vita* I found in *Vat.* 11733, p. 1 seqq. of the Vatican Library and in *Cod.* B. 8, of the Boncompagni Archives, Rome.

[3] Giunto himself was aware of his lack of the requisite literary ability, hence he insists that all he intends is to give a *semplice sbozzo*. Later on he says: " Reputo convenevole di notificare a chiunque leggerà questi mal composti fogli, che se in essi manca ogni circostanza che possa rendergli grati alle loro orecchie, non manca di verità che li reppresenta pura et senza accrescimento."

[4] *Cf.* p. 54 *seq.*, 59 *seq.*, 71.

1. Instructions for the Nuncios.

"Quanto fossero prudenti, pii et importanti i ricordi e l'instruttioni che dal cardinal Ludovisi furono dati ai Nuntii, spedite in diverse parti ; testimonianza ne può rendere chi l'ha vedute, e quantunque fossero distese da Monsignor Agucchio prelato Bolognese di sublimissime parti secretario di stato del Papa, non di meno il cardinale fece in esse particolar fatica nell'annotazione de' capi, de' motivi del senso di Sua Beatitudine, de' ripieghi e consigli suggeriti col suo proprio avedimento e sapere.

Et acciò che non restino le predette istruzioni e le materie contenute in esse del tutto ignote in questi fogli, si annoteranno quì sotto i Nuntii e ministri, a quali furono date et i negotii, et affari importanti, i quali furono trasmessi, i Nuntii straordinari in particolare..."

2. Nomination of Cardinals.

"Hebbe il cardinal Ludovisi nel pontificato del zio una somma applicatione a tutte quelle cose che potevano riuscir di profitto alla Chiesa universale, di riputazione e gloria alla Sede Apostolica, al Pontificio Solio et a lui medesimo. Onde si conformò egli intieramente al genio di Sua Beatitudine nelle promozioni de' cardinali senza riguardo de' suoi interessi col pretendere d'inalzar quelli a così eccelso grado, che o per dependenza di servitù, di patria o d'amicizia potessero essergli in maniera soggetti che di loro potesse disporne ne' conclavi et havere sopra di loro dominio, ma hebbe solamente mira a prelati qualificati per nascita, bonta e dottrina..."

3. Ecclesiastical Dignities and Benefices of Cardinal Ludovisi.

"Oltre l'arcivescovato di Bologna di sopra narrato hebbe il cardinal Ludovisi gli infrascritti officii, dignità, abbadie et entrate ecclesiastiche :

Il camerlengato di santa Chiesa per morte del cardinal Pietro Aldobrandino, il quale carico esercitò con molta accuratezza, e non solamente tenne con ogni puntualità, ma s'ebbe la giurisdizione nel tempo e l'esercitò di più per lo spazio di due anni incirca.

La Cancelleria Apostolica fu nel 1623 conferita nella sua persona, vacata per morte del cardinal Alessandro Montalto nepote di Papa Sisto V., e nel possesso di tali dignità abbracciò tutti i pesi arbitrarii d'elemosine e li faceva detto cardinale tanto nella parrocchia quanto fuori.

Il titolo di S. Lorenzo in Damaso con la Cancellaria sempre unito e il governo di quella chiesa con la collazione di quei canonicati e beneficii s'appoggia al cardinal Vicecancelliere. Onde il cardinal Ludovisi lasciando il titolo di S. Maria Traspontina, fece ottione in concistoro del predetto di S. Lorenzo in Damaso, di cui prese solennemente il possesso, facendo nell'istesso tempo distribuire grossa somma di denari per l'elemosina ai poveri della parrocchia et a loro che si trovarono presenti.

La sommisteria delle lettere apostoliche conseguì il cardinal Ludovisi con la Cancellaria, alla quale per il più và unita, et è di buona rendita.

La prefettura de' Brevi del Papa gli fu conferita per morte del suddetto cardinal Pietro Aldobrandino di gloriosa memoria, la quale rende d'entrata sopra mille scudi.

L'abbadie quì sotto nominate furono da Papa Gregorio conferite in persona del cardinale per morte del cardinal Pietro Aldobrandino, del cardinal Montalto e d'altri cardinali e prelati:

L'abbadia delle Tre Fontane, sotto la cui giurisdizione temporale e spirituale sono i castelli di S. Oreste, Ponzano, Monteroso col monte Soratte; la terra di Orbetello e l'isola del Giglio solamente in spirituale.

L'abbadia di S. Maria di Fossa Nuova di Piperno, sotto la cui giurisdizione temporale e spirituale è la terra di Palazzo Adriano detta la Baronia di Sicilia in quell'isola di Sicilia.

L'abbadia di S. Maria della Ferrata in Regno.[1]

L'abbadia di S. Maria delle Grotte di Vetulano in Regno.

L'abbadia di S. Maria di Real Valle in Regno.

L'abbadia di S. Andrea di Brindisi.

L'abbadia di S. Maria di Corano in Calabria.

L'abbadia di S. Maria di Galeata, sotto la cui giurisdizione è detta Terra, Civitella, Pondo S. Sofia et altre terre del Gran Duca.

L'abbadia di S. Silvestro di Nonantola, sotto la cui giurisdizione spirituale è l'istessa terra di Nonantola ... molte altre terre e benefici curati e semplici, la collazione de' quali appartiene al commendatario.

---

[1] Naples.

L'abbadia di S. Pietro d'Assisi.
L'abbadia di S. Eufemia di Padova.
L'abbadia dei SS. Gervasio e Protasio di Brescia.
L'abbadia di Dionigi di Milano.
L'abbadia di S. Celso di Milano.
L'abbadia di Gratasolio di Milano.
L'abbadia di S. Maria in Regola e S. Matteo d'Imola.
L'abbadia di S. Lorenzo in Campo nello stato d'Urbino.
L'abbadia di S. Maria di Castiglion di Parma.
L'abbadia dell'Assunta di Morola e della SS. Trinità di Campagnola di Reggio.
Il priorato di S. Martino in Campo di Parigi.
Il priorato di Corinaldo dello stato d'Urbino.
La prepositura di Cresenzago di Milano.
Il priorato di Camaldoli di Bologna."

4. Cardinal Ludovisi's Charities.

"Alle zitelle sperse di Roma nove doti l'anno, di cento scudi l'una.

Ai Padri di S. Isidoro per il vitto e vestito di sei giovani ibernesi scudi cinquanta il mese	sc.	600
Alle monache di S. Urbano sc. 30 al mese	sc.	360
Alla parrocchia di S. Lorenzo in Damaso scudi cento il mese, che distribuiva la Congregazione del soccorso	sc.	1 200
All'istessa parochia il Natale, la Pasqua di Resurrezione e S. Lorenzo scudi cento	sc.	300
Alla detta parochia libre cento di pane ogni giorno che sono decine 300 il mese e l'anno decine 3 600, che ridotte a decine 47 per rubbio sono decine 80, quali valutate a giulii 75 il rubbio fanno	sc.	680
Alla detta parochia medicinali per i poveri tutto l'anno in circa	sc.	800
Alla detta parochia per il medico	sc.	60
A S. Lorenzo in Damaso per le 40 ore il Giovedì Grasso un anno per l'altro	sc.	100
Alla Compagnia del SS. Sacramento di S. Lorenzo in Damaso doti a tre zitelle e vesti	sc.	100
Alla Compagnia della Concettione della Beat^{ma} Vergine in S. Lorenzo doti a tre zitelle e vesti	sc.	900

Alle messe di S. Lorenzo in Damaso vino fogliette

sei il giorno, et alla communione in giorno di festa incirca barili venti l'anno, che a giuli 25 per barile fanno sc. 50

Al capitolo e canonici di S. Lorenzo in Damaso si paga l'anno sc. 432 per li cantori e musica di S. Lorenzo. Li cantori del Palazzo importano sc. 350 incirca l'anno, e la musica ch'è aggiunta da scudi sette al mese incirca, che si può calcolare per limosina essendo valutata sc. 80

Alla Compagnia de' Bolognesi di Roma doti trè l'anno alle zitelle e vesti sc. 90

A Teatini di S. Andrea della Valle scudi dieci al mese sc. 120
A Barnabiti di S. Carlo a Catinari sc. 120
A Frati Scalzi della Scala come sopra sc. 120
A Frati Scalzi di S. Paolo a Termini sc. 120
A Padri di S. Lorenzo in Lucina come sopra sc. 120
Alla Compagnia della Pietà de' carcerati sc. 120
Alle zitelle sperse ogni anno oltre le doti e fabriche sc. 300
Alle zitelle di S. Catarina de' Funari sc. 25 al mese sc. 300
Alle medesime pranso per la festa parato per la chiesa ed altro sc. 50
Ai poveri di litterato sc. 12 al mese sc. 144
Ai padri Giesuiti della casa professa scudi venti al mese sc. 240
Alle Capuccine a Montecavallo sc. 8 al mese sc. 96
Alle monache convertite sc. 5 al mese sc. 60
Ai frati d'Aracoeli come sopra sc. 60
Ai Padri riformati di S. Nicolò di Tolentino sc. 60
Ai frati di S. Andrea delle Fratte sc. 60
Ai frati Fate bene fratelli sc. 60
Alla casa di penitenza in Trastevere sc. 60
All'ospedale di S. Giacomo degl'incurabili sc. 60
Ai frati di S. Potentiana sc. 60
Alle monache di S. Maria Maddalena sc. 60
Alle monache di Casa Pia sc. 60
Alle monache scalze di S. Egidio sc. 60
All'ospedale della Consolatione sc. 60
All'ospedale de' pazzarelli sc. 36
Alle monache di S. Marta sc. 60

APPENDIX. 325

[Agli] Eremiti di S. Maria dei serviti	sc.	60
Ai preti delle Scuole Pie	sc.	60
Ai Catecumeni	sc.	60
Ai poveri di S. Vitale	sc.	60
All'ospedale della SS. Trinità di Ponte Sisto	sc.	60
Ai frati Ibernesi di S. Isidoro	sc.	60
Alla Congreg. de' convertiti alla fede	sc.	72
Ai frati de' SS. Apostoli	sc.	24
Ai frati di S. Pietro [in] Montorio	sc.	24
Ai frati di S. Bartolomeo all'Isola	sc.	24
Ai padri di S. Agata della Dottrina Christiana	sc.	24
Alla Congreg. della Dottrina Christiana	sc.	24
Ai frati di S. Onofrio	sc.	24
Ai preti di S. Maria in Portico	sc.	24
Ai frati di SS. Cosma e Damiano	sc.	24
Ai frati di S. Bernardo a' Termini	sc.	24
Ai frati della Madonna de' miracoli	sc.	36
Ai padri ministri degl'infermi	sc.	36
Alle povere donne Inglesi	sc.	36
Alla Compagnia de' SS. Apostoli di Roma ogni anno scudi duemila	sc.	2 000
Ai padri Capuccini carne, polli et ova per l'infermeria, carta da scrivere, vino et altro, si calcola scudi cento l'anno	sc.	100
Limosine a minuto 50 sc. il mese	sc.	600
All'abbadia delle Tre Fontane il giorno della consecratione della chiesa rubbia otto di pagnottelle, barili 10 di vino, pranzo per i frati, candele et altro incirca scudi cento l'anno	sc.	100
Ai predicatori di S. Lorenzo in Damaso la Quaresima, a fisso di tutto l'anno	sc.	150
Ai predicatori che predicano all'Isola del Giglio soggetto alle Tre Fontane	sc.	10
Alle monache di S. Oreste per limosina di droghe per la loro spezieria	sc.	20
Diverse elemosine straordinarie si possono calcolare circa	sc.	300
Alla fabrica della chiesa de' PP. dell'Oratorio a Casale Monferrato ad istanza del P. F. Giacinto sc. 500 ogni anno	sc.	500
Alla fabrica della chiesa di S. Ludovico in Valtellina ogni anno	sc.	300

Alla fabrica della metropolitana di Bologna et ai
luoghi pii e poveri di quella città ogni anno   sc.   12 000
Alla fabrica di S. Ignatiio haveva fatto assegna-
mento di 6000 scudi l'anno   sc.   6 000
Tutte le suddette elemosine ascendono alla somma
di scudi trentaduemila ottocento ottantadue

$$\text{Totale } 32\,882\text{ "}$$

V. Jacopo Accarisi's Biography of Gregory XV.[1]

One looks in vain for a printed biography of Gregory XV. whose pontificate, notwithstanding its shortness, was a very successful one from more than one point of view. The Vita Gregorii XV. by A. Ciccarelli [2] is so bare that it does not deserve attention. The biographical sketch by Theodore Ameyden also is almost worthless, for that writer is unreliable in every one of his works.[3] In view of the fact that Giunti's manuscript life of the papal nephew and Secretary of State, Cardinal Ludovico Ludovisi, though full of valuable information, is more concerned with the latter than with the Pope,[4] a still unpublished biography of Gregory XV. based on contemporary information and documentary sources acquires exceptional importance. I had the good fortune to discover the original MS.[5] of this work which has not as yet been exploited by historians, in Cod. B. 7 of the Boncompagni Archives in Rome. The title is: Vita Gregorii XV. P.O.M. auctore Jacobo Accarisio Bononiensi, episcopo Vestano ac sanctae universalisque Rom. Inquisitionis theologo qualificatore, ad Ill. et ex. Nicolaum Ludovisium Piombini ac Venusti Principem, sanctorum pontificum Gregorii XV. ac

---

[1] Above p. 42.

[2] Printed in the later editions of PLATINA's *Vitae Pontificum*, in the Cologne edition of 1626, pp. 530-36.

[3] ZELLER (*Richelieu*, 301 seq.) gives a quotation from this wretched piece of work preserved in Cod. E. III, 12, of the Casanatense Lib. in Rome, but he is quite mistaken as to its value. The *Vita Gregorii XV* of Ameyden is as worthless as his Lives of Urban VIII and Innocent X; see CIAMPI, *Innocenzo X*, 63; Pieper in *Hist.-polit. Blättern*, XCIV, 489 seq. Cf. of Appendix.

[4] Cf. No. IV of App.

[5] That it is an original appears plainly from the numerous corrections in the MS.

Innocentii X. nepotem.[1] There is a copy in the Vat. Lib. *Cod. Ottob.*, 923.

The author, Jacopo Accarisi, was a countryman of the Pope's.[2] Born at Bologna in 1599, Accarisi read philosophy and theology at the University of his native town. He took his doctorate in 1620 and taught logic for the space of one year. For another four years he taught rhetoric at the Academy of Mantua and acted as secretary to the Duke.[3] He then went to Rome where he became secretary for Latin letters to Cardinal Guido Bentivoglio and *qualificatore* of the Roman Inquisition. In 1636 he began a course of lectures on philosophy at the Sapienza. On October 17th, 1644, he became Bishop of Viesti and there he died on October 9, 1654.

Many discourses and writings of Accarisi have appeared in print; they were selected by Allatius (*Apes Urb.*, 137 f. and Fantuzzi, *Scritt. Bolognesi*, I., 31–2) [cf. *Catalogo d. Bibl. Chigiana*, Roma, 1764, 2]. Two of these works deserve mention because they treat of Gregory XV.: (1) In funere anniversario Gregorii XV. Oratio habita Romae in templo s. Joannis Evangelistae, dum sodalitas Bononiensium iusta faceret XVI. Calendas Augusti, 1629, Romae, s.a.; (2) Vindicationes tum nonnullarum Gregorii XV. constitutionum, tum quorumdam Alphonsi Ciaconii ac Ioannis Baptistae Adriani locorum in describendis summorum pontificum sanctaeque Romanae Ecclesiae cardinalium vitis ac rebus gestis, Iacobi Accarisii Bononiensis S.R. universalisque Inquisitionis theologi qualificatoris anno 1641.[4] Fantuzzi (loc. cit. 32) also gives a list of Accarisi's unpublished works in which he mentions the *Cod. Ottob.*, 923, but without any hint as to the contents: probably he did not examine it personally.

We get some information on the origin of Accarisi's Life of Gregory XV. in a copy of a letter of Cardinal Niccolò Albergati-Ludovisi,[5] dated Rome, April 23rd, 1650, and addressed to Accarisi, from which we learn that Niccolò Ludovisi did not

---

[1] On Niccolò see p. 67, 68.

[2] For what follows *cf.* besides MORONI, XLIX, 51, and C. 95, especially FANTUZZI, *Scritt. Bolognesi*, I., 30 seq.

[3] See *Il Bibliofilo*, XI., Brescia, 1890, 74.

[4] Accarisi mentions this work in the *Vita Gregorii XV.*, lib. III., c. 17.

[5] On this nephew of Cardinal Ludovico Ludovisi who became a Cardinal in 1645, see MORONI, XL., 110.

want the Life of his uncle to appear in print. Accordingly, Accarisi's work, like A. Nicoletti's [1] biography of Urban VIII., was only intended for the family circle. The biography originated, as we learn from the dedication to Niccolò Ludovisi, on the occasion of the latter's marriage to Costanza Pamfili under Innocent X., during the war of the Venetians against the Turks.[2] He remarks that the Prince had given him access to private documents to enable him to write his history of Gregory XV.

Though the origin and the dedication of the biography suggest that its purpose was the glorification of the Ludovisi Pope, the work is nevertheless based on varied and valuable manuscript material. The sources quoted by the author are very abundant for the period. He repeatedly refers to documents on the Secret Papal Archives, for instance, Lib. I., c. 5, 8, 9 ; Lib. II., c. 3, 11 ; Lib. III., c. 4, 10 ; and also quotes pieces from the Archives of the Capitol (Lib. I., c. 1), the Roman College (I., c. 2), the family Archives of the Peretti (I., c. 5), the Aldobrandini (nunc apud Borghesios, I., c. 6 ; cf. c. 5, 7, 11), the Farnese (II., c. 4), and Savelli (III., c. 10). Besides the Briefs of Gregory XV. (III., c. 4), though he uses them only sparingly, Accarisi also made use of a Diarium Gregorii XV. (III., c. 1) ; of Agucchi's letters (II., c. 11 ; III., c, 5. 10),[3] the letters of Cardinal Cobelluzio (II., c. 2) and a MS Compendium Vitae Clementis VIII.[4] As a member of the Rota he also made use of diaries belonging to that body (II., c. 9). As regards the recantation of De Dominis he quotes (III., c. 12) the evidence of people who had been concerned with the matter ; he does the same with regard to the foundation of Propaganda (III., c. 15).

The Vita, in excellent Latin, is in three books. The two first relate the antecedents of Gregory XV. up to his election as Pope, the first book being divided into ten, the second into fourteen chapters. The pontificate of Gregory XV. is told in Book III., in twenty-one chapters.

The Pope's life before his election is told with far greater detail than his pontificate. It constitutes the chief value

---

[1] Vol. XXIX, app. 26.
[2] Cf. ZINKEISEN, IV., 756 seq.
[3] On these letters see XXIX, 177.
[4] It is remarkable that Accarisi does not seem to have known the MS. work of Giunti on Cardinal Ludovisi.

of the work for it is everywhere based on good sources and nowhere do we get so much information. But the story of the pontificate suffers from this circumstance. Accarisi's statements are nearly always accurate but they are too general: for the most part he does no more than give a general view of events. He refrains from all flattery and exaggeration; with regard to Ludovico Ludovisi's elevation to the cardinalate, he remarks (III., c. 2) that one might question the wisdom of the immediate elevation to the Sacred College of a nephew, but the choice did not appear blameworthy since it had fallen on an excellent man.

Whilst in his biography of the Cardinal, Giunti puts the latter too much in the foreground, to the disadvantage of the Pope, Accarisi, with a greater sense of proportion, never fails to do full justice to the merits of Gregory XV. whilst not forgetting those of the Secretary of State.

VI. Antonio Possevino to the Duke of Mantua.[1]

Rome, July 16th, 1621.

. . . Tutta Roma è piena di Pasquinate sopra Papa et parenti, sono però porcherie et indegne d'esser lette, et come penso, fatte da persone idioti et inconsiderate. Il contenuto è che questo Papa sia l'imagine di Gregorio XIV., di cui fu scritto:

Vir simplex, fortasse bonus, sed praesul ineptus;
Videt, agit, peragit plurima, pauca, nihil.

Certo, Sig., che s'intende essere il Papa christianissimo et di ottima mente, anco per detto di chi ha occasione di non se ne laudare. . . .

Orig.: Gonzaga Archives, Mantua.

VII. Antonio Possevino to the Duke of Mantua.[2]

Rome, August 14, 1621.

. . . Il papa havendo compro un palazzo qual era del card.le Ginnasio attende ad allargarsi et ad aprire strade, con pensiero di farvi una bella piazza avanti, con spianare una isola de case che li sta sulla porta. . . . Fui l'altro giorno in Tivoli per vedere quel giardino Estense; assicuro V. A. che

[1] See p. 72.
[2] See pp. 62, 291.

se un principe grande lo vedesse, mai li verria voglia di farne a casa sua, cognoscendo non poter giongere a questa bellezza. È inestimabile la vaghezza, il sito, la copia et secreti dell'acque, la grandezza, la bontà dell'aere, et in somma bisogna che il paradiso sia molto bello, se vuole superare questo luogo. Io ho visti giardini in Fiorenza, Roma, Francia, Fiandra, Napoli et mille altri luoghi, nè mai ho trovata cosa che si possa paragonare con questo. Vi sono boschi, vigne, frutti, prati, grotte, monti, valli, fiumi, fonti, parco, peschiere. case nobili, statue etc. . . .

Orig.: Gonzaga Archives, Mantua.

INDEX OF NAMES IN VOL. XXVII.

ABBOTT, Archbishop of Canterbury, 195.
Accarisius (biographer of Gregory XV.), 88.
Adrian XI., Pope, 3, 85, 293.
Agucchi, John Baptist (nuncio in Venice), 70 seq., 132, 294.
Albergati (collector of Portugal), 144 seq.
Albergati, Antonio, 68, 86, 106, 232.
Albergati-Ludovisi, Lavinia (mother of Cardinal L. Ludovisi), 51, 65, 68.
Albert, Archduke (primate of Spain and cardinal), 44.
Albert of Wittelsbach, 8.
Albert of Lauingen, St., 122.
Albuquerque, Duke of, 34, 36, 100, 113 seq.
Aldobrandini, Giovanni Giorgio, 54.
Aldobrandini, Ippolito, Cardinal, 43, 88.
Aldobrandini, Pietro, Cardinal, 10, 30 seq., 33-48, 54, 88, 235.
Alexander VI., Pope, 11, 109.
Alexander of Rhodes, 149.
Alphonsus of the Cross, Augustinian, 151.
Algardi Alessandro, 58, 62.
Allacci Leone, 244-6 seqq.
Altemps, Duke of, 57.
Andover, Lord, 193.
Andrade, Antonio d', 150.
Andrade, Louis d', 149.
Anne, wife of Louis XIII., 198.
Anthelius, Zacharias, 154.
Aquino, Cardinal, 30 seqq., 38.
Arnoux, J., S. J., 222.
Aston, 142.

BABINGTON, Anthony, 158.
Baden-Durlach, Margrave of, 17, 242, 260, 287.
Bagno, Guido del, Nuncio, 153, 155, 227.
Bandini, Cardinal, 31 seq., 69, 92, 105, 132, 156, 169.
Barberini, Antonio, Cardinal, 31 seq., 44, 132, 156.
Barberini, Maffeo, Cardinal V., Urban VIII., Pope.
Baronius, Cardinal, Cæsar, 12, 91.
Basilio, Father, Capuchin, 253.
Bassompierre, Ambassador, 198, 203.
Becanus, S. J., 233, 263.
Bellarmine, Cardinal Robert, 12, 31 seq., 36, 38, 91, 110.
Benedict XIV., 213.
Bennett (English priest), 156 seq.
Bentivoglio, Cardinal Guido, 31, 71, 119, 156.
Bernini, Lorenzo (sculptor and architect), 1, 13, 49, 62, 92.
Bérulle, Cardinal, 12.
Bethlen, Gabór, 249.
Bevilacqua, Boniface, Cardinal, 31, 34, 36, 68.
Bianchini, Camilla (mother of Gregory XV.), 42.
Birkhead, Archpriest, 156.
Bishop, William (Titular Bishop of Chalcedon), 157.
Blackwell, Archpriest, 156.
Bocquet (Calvinist convert), 225.
Bolanos, Luis de, Franciscan, 150.
Bolivar, Gregory of (Franciscan Observant), 152.
Bologna, Giovanni da (sculptor), 62.
Boncompagni, Francesco, Cardinal, 87.

Boncompagni, Ugo V., Gregory XIII.
Bonsi, Cardinal, 35.
Borghese, Cardinal Scipione, 30-41, 54, 62, 113.
Borgia, Valentino, Duke, 29.
Borgia, Cardinal Gaspare, 30 seq., 105, 129, 132.
Borromeo, Cardinal Carlo, St., 69.
Borromeo, Federico, Cardinal, 21, 32, 91, 110, 114.
Brendel, Daniel, 8.
Brézé, Marquis de, 26.
Bristol, Earl of, V., Digby.
Brouwer, Jacob de, 153.
Brulart de Sillery, Nicolas, 68, 217, 219.
Buckingham, George Villiers, Duke of, 169, 176-180, 183 seq., 186, 192.
Buquoy, General, 231.
Buzoni, S. J., 149.

CAETANI, Cardinal Antonio, 86 seq.
Calasanza, Joseph of, 195.
Camerarius, Louis, 256.
Campori, Cardinal, 30-40, 119.
Canisius, Peter, St., 11.
Capponi, Cardinal, 31-40, 57.
Carafa, Cardinal, 2, 3, 31, 32.
Carafa, Carlo, Nuncio, 93, 125, 197, 229-235, 250, 252, 260, 268, 275-282, 286, 287, 294.
Charles Emmanuel I. (Duke of Savoy), 46, 205 seq., 209.
Charles (bishop of Aversa), 267.
Charles I. (Prince of Wales), 163, 172-196.
Charles IV. (King of Bohemia), 269.
Charles, Louis (son of Frederick V., Elector), 174.
Casale, Giacinto da, Capuchin, 95, 99, 243, 252-9, 261.
Cecchini, Cardinal, 47 seq.
Cennini, Cardinal, 30, 200 seq.
Centini, Cardinal, 31 seq., 105.
Cervini, Cardinal, 3.

Cesi, Cardinal, 31.
Cesi, John Frederick (Duke of Acquasparta), 60.
Chanowski, Albert (S.J.), 283 seq.
Chantal, J. F. de, St., 12.
Christian (Duke of Braunschweig-Wolfenbüttel, 240.
Christian, William (Duke of Brunswick), 17, 237, 242.
Christian IV. of Denmark, 19.
Ciampoli, Giovanni, 295.
Claver, Peter, St., 151.
Clement VIII., Pope, 9 seqq., 29, 32, 41, 43 seq., 54, 67 seq., 87 seq., 105, 107 seqq., 125, 131.
Clement XII., Pope, 61.
Cobelluzio, Cardinal, 30 seqq., 92, 105, 132.
Cœuvres V., d'Estrées.
Cohelli, Giacomo, 34.
Coke, Edward, 162, 164, 166.
Coloma, Spanish ambassador, 194.
Colonna, Family of, 56.
Colonna, Pier Francesco, 55.
Condé, Henry II., Duke of Bourbon, 226.
Contarini, Pietro, Ambassador, 95.
Corona, Tobias, Barnabite, 206-9.
Corsini, Ottavio, Nuncio in Paris, 157 seq., 202, 211, 214 seqq., 220, 222, 227, 236, 250.
Cortona, Pietro da, 13.
Cottington, English ambassador, 173, 184, 187 seq., 191 seq., 195.
Crescenzi, Cardinal, 31 seq., 35.
Croft, William, 192.
Cueva, Alfonso della, Cardinal, 90.

DANTE, Poet, 63.
Darcy, Francis, 162.
Del Bagno, Marchese, 218.
Delfino, Cardinal, 31, 37.
Dernbach, Balthasar von, 8.

INDEX OF NAMES. 333

Deti, Cardinal, 31.
Digby, Earl of Bristol, 167–170, 178.
Digges, M.P., 162.
Dietrichstein, Cardinal, 32.
Domenichino, Painter, 13, 47, 58, 71.
Dominic of Jesus and Mary, 130, 134, 241 seq.
Dominis, Marcantonio de, 102, 106 seq.
Doria, Cardinal, 32.

ECHTER, Julius von, Bishop of Würzburg, 8.
Eggenberg, Count, 233, 263, 265.
Eleanore of Mantua, 93.
Elias II., Patriarch of Mosul, 114.
Elizabeth, Queen of England, 5, 157, 164.
Elizabeth, Archduchess, daughter of Maximilian, 172.
Este, Cardinal, 31 seq., 34 seqq., 39 seq.
Estrées, Marquis Cœuvres, 30, 37.

FARNESE, Alessandro, Cardinal, 127.
Farnese, Odoardo, Cardinal, 31, 34 seq., 37, 39, 45, 127, 132.
Farnese Ranuccio, Duke, 45.
Farrar, English priest, 157.
Feria, Duke of, 205, 209–211, 215, 218.
Fidelis of Sigmaringen, St., 138, 212.
Frederick V., 15, 17, 19, 231, 237–242, 251, 277, 286.
Frederick, Elector Palatine, 159 seqq., 243.
Ferdinand II., Emperor, 16 seq., 23, 25, 89, 93 seq., 230, 234–241, 243, 249–252, 259 seqq., 269, 273, 276, 280.

Ferdinand, Prince, 177, 228.
Filonardi, Cardinal, 31, 35.
Floyd, Catholic lawyer, 161 seqq.
Fontaine, Eugénie de, 226.
Fuente, Diego de la, O. P., 167, 181.
Fürstenburg, Theodor von, 8.

GAGE, George, 167, 169, 175, 181, 184, 191.
Galamina, Cardinal, 30 seqq., 95, 222.
Galli, Cardinal, 57.
Garnet, Henry, S. J., 162.
Gessi, Cardinal, 101.
Gesualdo, Cardinal, 66 seq.
Gesualdo, Isabella, 66 seq.
Gherardi, Cardinal, 31.
Giberti, 2.
Giles, Edward, 162.
Ginnasio, Cardinal, 30 seqq.
George Frederick, Margrave of Baden-Durlach, 17, 240.
George William of Ansbach Brandenburg, 249 seq.
Gondomar, see Sarmiento.
Gonzaga, Aloneius, St., 93.
Gozzadini, Cardinal, 88.
Gravita, Pietro, S.J., 65.
Green, Thomas, O.S.B., 156.
Giunti, Lucantonio, Biographer, 53, 71.
Giustiniani, Cardinal, 32, 34, 38, 114.
Gregory XIII., Pope, 6 seqq., 12, 41, 43, 128–131, 294.
Gregory XIV., Pope, 43.
Gregory XV., Pope, 12, 16 seqq., 41 seqq., 52, 55–8, 65, 67 seq., 71–81, 84 seq., 87 seqq., 95, 100–119, 122–8, 131–4, 141, 144–150, 155–8, 167 seq., 181, 188, 196–220, 224–9, 235–245, 248, 250, 252, 255–265, 267, 286–296.
Grodecius, Bishop of Olmütz, 284.
Guercino, painter, 58.
Guevara, Mgr., 52.

INDEX OF NAMES.

HABSBURG, Family, 8, 44, 177.
Harrison, Archpriest, 156.
Henry IV. (Navarre), 9, 15, 44, 155, 177.
Henry VIII. (England), 181.
Henry of Bourbon, Bishop of Metz, 226.
Hesse, Louis of, Margrave, 242.
Hohenzollern, Cardinal, 95, 132, 153, 258, 287.
Horace, poet, 63.
Huss, John, 281.

IGNATIUS, Loyola, S.J., 2, 13, 120, 296.
Ingoli, Francesco, 132, 135, 152.
Innocent IX., 109.
Inojosa, Ambassador, 194.
Isabel, Clare Eugenie, Infanta, 182.
Isidor, St., 120 seq.

JÄGERNDORF, George, Margrave, 276 seq.
James I. (England), 157, 159 seqq., 163-170, 173-182, 185-8, 191-6.
Jansenius, Nicholas, 153.
Jenatsch, George, 210.
Jerome, St., 42.
Jessenius, Rector, 269.
John George of Saxony, 249.
Julius II., Pope, 109.
Julius III., Pope, 109.

KHEVENHÜLLER, Ambassador, 177, 191, 259.
Klesl, Cardinal, 92-6, 258.
Kolowrat, Zdenka, 283.

LAMORMAINI, William, S.J., 269, 271 seq.
Lante, Cardinal, 31.
Leni, Cardinal, 31.
Leonardi, Giovanni, 125.
Leo XI., Pope, 109.
Leopold, Archduke, 93, 99, 210 seqq., 241.
Lerma, Cardinal, 95 seqq.
Lesdiguières, Duke of, 225.

Liechtenstein, Charles von, 269 seqq.
Lohelius, John, Archbishop of Prague, 273.
Ludovisi, Alessandro, Cardinal, 16, 30, 31-3, 38-41, V., Gregory XV., Pope.
Ludovisi, Ippolita, d., 65-7.
Ludovisi Ludovico, Cardinal, 47, 51, 57, 60-2, 64, 68-81, 95-9, 106, 110, 113 seq., 119, 121, 127 seq., 131-3, 135, 155, 178, 182 seq., 201, 205, 209, 211, 214, 217-220, 226, 228, 238, 239, 245, 250, 258 seq., 288-291, 293 seq.
Ludovisi, Niccolò, 65 seqq.
Ludovisi, Orazio, Duke of Fiano, 51, 65-8, 216 seqq.
Ludovisi, Pompeo, Count, 42.
Louis XIII. (France), 16, 20, 90, 198, 205 seq., 208, 214-227, 236, 256.
Luynes, Duke of, 209.

MADERNA, Carlo, Architect, 57, 242.
Madruzzo, Cardinal, 30-3, 36, 38, 105.
Magalotti, Cardinal, 65.
Magno, Valeriano, Capuchin, 253.
Malaspina, Nuncio, 11.
Mansfeld, General, 17, 19, 237, 239-242, 260, 276, 283.
Marcellus II., Pope, 3.
Margaret, Archduchess and Carmelite, 172, 178.
Maria, Infante of Spain, 168, 170, 172 seq., 182, 185, 187, 193, 196.
Mariana, Father, S.J., 146.
Martinitz, Count, 283.
Massimi, Innocenzo de, 100, 180, 188, 216.
Maximilian I., Duke of Bavaria, 15, 17 seq., 119, 231, 236, 238 seq., 243-6, 248, 250-8, 260, 262-5, 267-286.

INDEX OF NAMES.

Maximilian II., Emperor, 172.
Matteuci, G., 38.
Matthews, John, 157.
Matthias, Emperor, 15, 95, 216.
Mazarin, Giulio, 27.
Medici, Cardinal, 31 seqq., 37, 39.
Medici, Marie de, 15.
Menelaus, Greek sculptor, 61.
Michelangelo, 62.
Millini, Cardinal, 30 seqq., 105, 112 seq., 116, 132, 157.
Minutoli Giacomo, S.J., 53.
Molé, Athanasius, Capuchin, 225.
Monopoli, Cardinal, 130.
Montalto, Cardinal, 31, 34, 37, 48, 127.
Monte, Cardinal, 32, 34, 39, 57.
Montorio, Nuncio, 243, 261.
More, George, 162.
Muti, Cardinal, 31.
Murillo, 171.

NARNI, Girolamo da, 128, 130.
Neri, Philip, St., 13, 120, 296.
Nobili, Robert de, S.J., 148.
Nogaret, Cardinal, 105.

OLDECOP, John, 1.
Olivares, Spanish minister, 170, 173 seq., 176–180, 183–6, 189, 191 seq., 196.
Oñate, 214, 216, 258, 259, 262, 263.
Orsini, Cardinal, 31-6, 38, 40, 91.
Orsini, Giovanni Antonio, 57.

PACHECO, Cardinal, 105.
Paul III., Pope, 1, 3, 4.
Paul IV., Pope, 3 seqq., 11 seq., 69, 109.
Paul V., Pope, 12, 14 seq., 29, 41, 45 seq., 68, 87–93, 98, 101, 103, 106, 108, 112, 130, 155 seq., 196, 220, 232, 234, 250, 293.
Pasquale, Scipio, 69.
Pastrana, Duke of, 180.

Pedrosa, Preacher, 187.
Perrot, 160, 163.
Peter, Alcántara, St., 122.
Phelps, 161, 163.
Philip II., King of Spain, 4, 44, 129.
Philip III., King of Spain, 46, 90, 95, 110, 167, 171, 174, 200, 202.
Philip IV., King of Spain, 22, 25 seq., 36, 96 seq., 100, 108, 167 seq., 172, 174 seqq., 181, 183, 185 seqq., 193, 196, 203, 216.
Pico, Alfonso, Ambassador, 112.
Pignatelli, Cardinal, 36.
Pio, Cardinal, 31, 34, 36, 40.
Pius IV., Pope, 4, 109 seq., 281.
Pius V., Pope, 4 seqq., 11, 29, 42, 54, 97, 107, 109, 129, 167.
Pius X., Pope, 119.
Platais, Canon von, 275, 279, 280.
Poggio, Sabastian, 65.
Porta, Gulielmo della, 1.
Porter, Endymion, 173, 175.
Possevino, Antonio, Ambassador, 54, 72 seq., 125, 289.
Preston, Thomas, O.S.B., 156.
Priuli, Cardinal, 31, 37.
Pym, John, 164.

QUESTENBERG, Premonstratensian, Abbot, 279.
Quiroga, Cardinal, 44.
Quiroga, Diego da, 253.

RAPHAEL, 62.
Rangel, O.P., 146, 149.
Rangoni, Nuncio, 90.
Reni, Guido, 13, 58.
Retz, Cardinal, 227.
Ricci, Matteo, S.J., 11.
Richelieu, Armand, Cardinal, 18 seqq., 90, 223, 226.
Ridolfi, Marchese, 218.
Rivarola, Cardinal, 31, 34.
Rochefoucauld, Cardinal, 223, 226 seq.
Rudolph II., Emperor, 15, 268.

INDEX OF NAMES.

Rodolfo, Cardinal, 89.
Roe, 125.
Rohan, Duke of, 206.
Roma, Cardinal, 31 seq.
Rubens, 13.

SACRATI, Cardinal, 87, 132.
Sales, Francis, St., 11 seqq.
Salis, Count Rudolf Andreas, 212.
Sandro, Alessandro, Patriarch of Alexandria, 98 seqq.
Sandys, 162.
Sangro, Alex. de, 201 seq.
Sannesio, Cardinal, 31.
Santinellus, 144.
Santori, Cardinal, 129, 130, 133.
Sarmiento, Count Gondomar, 159 seq., 165 seq., 169 seq., 172 seq., 176.
Sarpi, Paolo, Servite, 101 seqq.
Sarbiewski, Matt. Casimir, S.J., 296.
Sassoferrato, painter, 13.
Sauli, Cardinal, 32, 39, 132 seq., 135, 289.
Savage, Walter, 172.
Savelli, Cardinal, 31, 36, 95.
Savelli, Ambassador, Paolo, 235, 250, 258.
Savoy, Maurice of, Cardinal, 91.
Scaglia, Cardinal, 31, 105.
Scappi, Alessandro, Nuncio, 203, 209, 213.
Schacht, Henry, S.J., 154.
Schweikart, Johann, 249, 261 seq.
Serra, Cardinal, 31, 34.
Serra, Luigi, painter, 242.
Seymour, Francis, 162.
Sforza, Cardinal, 31, 36.
Sigismund III., 90.
Sillery V., Brulart.
Simeon, Patriarch, 144.
Sixtus V., 8 seqq., 27, 29, 32 seq., 41, 43.
Slawata, Count Wilhelm, 283.
Socinius, Emp. of Ethiopia, 46.
Sourdis, Cardinal, 31 seq., 226.
Speciani, Caesare, 30.
Spinelli, Cardinal, 130.

Stephanos, Sculptor, 61.
Stali, Sculptor, 62.
Strada, Famiano, S.J., 292.

TASSO, Torquato, poet, 12.
Tassi, Agostino, painter, 58.
Teresa of Jesus, 13, 120.
Tilly, General, 17, 19, 242, 247, 286.
Thomas of Jesus, Carmelite, 130 seqq., 296.
Tonti, Cardinal, 31 seq., 35.
Torres, Cardinal, 90.
Truchsess, Gebhard, Archbishop of Cologne, 8.

UBALDINI, Cardinal, 31 seq., 34 seqq.
Urban VIII., Pope, 1, 18, 20 seqq., 24-8, 88.
Ursi, John Baptist, S.J., 292.
Ursinus, George, 154.
Uzeda, Duke of, 95, 200.

VALARESSO, Ambassador, 167.
Valiero, Cardinal, 31, 37, 132.
Van Dyck, 13.
Vanmala, 182.
Velasquez, painter, 171.
Verallo, Cardinal, 31, 105.
Verospi, Cardinal, 93 seq., 258, 260.
Vincent de Paul, St., 28.
Virgil, 63.
Visconti, Cardinal, 130.
Vitelleschi, M., S.J., 123.
Vives, Juan, 204 seq.
Vives, John Baptist, Spanish bishop, 123.

WALLENSTEIN, 19.
Ward, English preacher, 161.
Williams, Minister of James I., 167, 193 seq.
Winckelmann, 61.
Wittelsbach, Albert of, 8.
Wittelsbach, William of, 8.
Wolfgang, Wilhelm, of Neuburg, Count Palatine, 229, 257, 263.

www.ingramcontent.com/pod-product-compliance
Lightning Source LLC
Chambersburg PA
CBHW032041220426
43664CB00008B/810